Orange County

Picture Research by Robin Mastrogeorge and Diann Marsh

Partners in Progress
by Marie H. Cole, John F. Elliott, and Nancy E. Fister

Sponsored by the Charles W. Bowers Memorial Museum

Windsor Publications, Inc.
Northridge, California

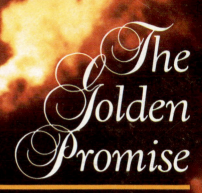

The Golden Promise

AN ILLUSTRATED HISTORY
of
Orange County

Pamela Hallan-Gibson

*To my friend, historian Jim Sleeper, who has opened doors
into Orange County history for all of us to enter.*

Windsor Publications, Inc.—History Books Division

Publisher: John M. Phillips
Editorial Director: Teri Davis Greenberg
Design Director: Alexander E. D'Anca

Staff for *The Golden Promise*

Senior Editor: Susan L. Wells
Assistant Editor: Marilyn Horn
Director, Corporate Biographies: Karen Story
Assistant Director, Corporate Biographies: Phyllis Gray
Editor, Corporate Biographies: Judith Hunter
Editorial Assistants: Kathy M. Brown, Laura Cordova, Marcie Goldstein, Pat Pittman, Sharon Volz
Corporate Biography Layout: Mari Catherine Preimesberger
Sales Representative, Corporate Biographies: Leslie West
Designer: Christina McKibbin

Library of Congress Cataloging-in-Publication Data

Hallan-Gibson, Pamela, 1944-
    The golden promise.

    Bibliographly: p. 424
    Includes index.
    Partial contents: Partners in progress / by Marie H.
Cole, John F. Elliott, and Nancy E. Fister.
    1. Orange County (Calif.)—History. 2. Orange County
(Calif.)—Description and travel. 3. Orange County
(Calif.)—Industries. I. Bowers Museum. II. Title.
F868.06H35 1986   979.4'96   86-7819
ISBN 0-89781-160-7

Page three: *A spectacular sunset glows with golden promise. Photo by Charles Weckler, courtesy, THE IMAGE BANK/ West*

Page seven: *Gulls circle overhead as these beachgoers watch the sun dip below the horizon at Laguna Beach. Photo by Jeff Marks*

Page nine: *The Orange Plaza is seen in this 1920s photograph. The fountain now graces the front of the City Council Chambers on East Chapman. Courtesy, First American Title Insurance Company*

CONTENTS

Preface   6
Acknowledgments   8

PART ONE: THE PROMISE EXPLORED

CHAPTER I: The Mission Period   13
CHAPTER II: Rancho Halcyon Days   29
CHAPTER III: American Conquest and Social Change   45
CHAPTER IV: The Decline of the Old Order   57

PART TWO: THE PROMISE CHALLENGED

CHAPTER V: New Towns, New Promises   75
CHAPTER VI: The Formation of a County   105
CHAPTER VII: The Emergence of a New Century   141
CHAPTER VIII: War, Boom, and Depression   181

PART THREE: THE PROMISE FULFILLED

CHAPTER IX: World War II and the Stirrings of Change   217
CHAPTER X: The 1950s Boom and the Impacts of Growth   235
CHAPTER XI: New Immigrants, New Opportunities   253
CHAPTER XII: Orange County Today   265
CHAPTER XIII: Partners in Progress   305
Bibliography   424
Index   427

PREFACE

As Orange County approaches its centennial many books will be written about its past. Old knowledge will be reexamined and new facts will be revealed. Each publication will make its contribution to the growing library of Orange Countiana and will make us richer in our knowledge about our heritage.

This book has been written especially for and about the people of Orange County. It is about the issues and events that have affected their lives, from the Native Americans who were the first to discover the golden promise, to those who have come in the last quarter of the twentieth century, still seeking it. It is not meant to be a definitive history, but a popular one—a sample, a taste, a broad brush stroke that conveys meaning without definition, that provides form without detail, and makes you want to learn more.

And there is much to learn about Orange County as it moves purposefully into the future. There are archaeological remains to be dug up and analyzed, documents in archives of Spain and Mexico waiting to be translated, and old pictures, letters, and diaries in family cubbyholes that will someday help us understand life as it was for others in an earlier time. And there are historians who will give us new hypotheses peppered with humorous tidbits to keep us from taking ourselves too seriously.

Orange County has grown by spurts and sputters, but throughout its history there has been one unifying theme—the promise of prosperity and well-being to all who settle here. Today Orange County represents the epitome of the Southern California lifestyle, and while the picture may not always be totally accurate, the promise is still alive. *The Golden Promise: An Illustrated History of Orange County* is meant to whet your appetite as the centennial draws near and your own search for the golden promise continues. We hope it will give you new insights and will make you want to learn more about this "most California county."

ACKNOWLEDGMENTS

veryone who writes a book needs a support group. Mine was larger than most and I count myself most fortunate.

First, I would like to thank William Lee and the Board of Directors of the Charles W. Bowers Memorial Museum for their sponsorship of this book, and for believing that Orange County history should be written for a wider audience than scholars and history buffs.

Speaking of scholars and history buffs, I would like to extend sincere thanks to my friend, Don Dobmeier, past chairman of the Orange County Historical Commission, who was my chief proofreader and nitpicker, and who spent countless hours challenging facts, style, commas—anything that needed improvement. Without Don's assistance, this project would not have been possible for me. A thank you also goes to my friend, Loretta Zimmerman, and my husband's family, Bob and Jean Gibson, who all contributed their time to making this book more interesting and readable.

During the research period for this book I visited many libraries in Orange County and always found a warm welcome and enthusiastic assistance for this project. I would like to thank the librarians of Orange County who made my job so much easier, and the San Juan Capistrano Historical Society Board of Directors who allowed me to borrow priceless materials from their Research Library for extended periods of time (without a library card!). I would also like to thank Virginia and T.J. Meadows, Jack and Patty Kubota, and Jim and Yaz Okazaki for lending me their cottage for writing. Thanks also to my fellow employees at the San Juan Capistrano City Hall who provided much-needed moral support, and my husband, Mark, and my children, David and Shelley, who were my biggest boosters throughout this project.

Last, but not least, I would like to thank Rob Selway of the Orange County Historical Commission staff for initially recommending me for this project, the staff at Windsor Publications, especially Senior Editor Susan Wells, for their friendly encouragement, and the other members of the publication team who shared my commitment to make this golden promise a reality.

9

The Promise Explored

P A R T I

The first baptism performed in California took place in Cris-
tianitos Canyon near San Clemente when two Indian chil-
dren who were thought to be dying were baptized by Father
Juan Crespi and Father Francisco Gomez. Every summer the
La Cristianita Pageant commemorates this event. Courtesy,
First American Title Insurance Company

The
Mission
Period

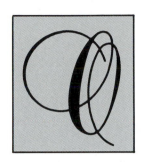

range has been called the "most California county." It is a place where amber hills mold themselves into well-formed ridgelines, where foam-topped seas stretch endlessly into golden sunsets, where people can enjoy a richness of life by simply lifting their faces to the warming sun. Orange County, California, is 782 square miles of homes, businesses, agricultural lands, and national forests tucked between Los Angeles and San Diego counties. More than two million people of all nationalities call Orange County their home—many would not live anywhere else in the world.

Orange County today is the fulfillment of the golden promise that began with the missions, found emphasis during the gold rush, and ever

Among the most popular and widely circulated postcards were those of the Mission San Juan Capistrano, as seen in this 1930s view of the veranda. Out-of-state visitors were drawn to the mission by postcards sent to them by friends, and it was the first "must see" attraction in Orange County. Courtesy, Marsh Collection, Anaheim Historical Society

The carreta was pulled by oxen and was frequently used in
California during the early mission days as the main means of
transporting goods. Courtesy, Marsh Collection, Anaheim
Historical Society

after dangled before the bemused eyes of travelers and would-be settlers. Like the promise of land and religious freedom drew Pilgrims to the New World, Orange County's rich soil, real estate booms, and mild climate have lured settlers to its golden shores. And while these settlers struggled to find the proffered wealth of land and sunshine, they soon learned that the golden promise was in themselves.

Orange County's wealth lies not in its land, agriculture, or industries, but in its people. And this legacy of wealth began a long time ago.

Frustration and weariness met the grim-faced soldiers of the Portolá expedition that set out from the newly founded settlement of San Diego in 1769 in search of Monterey Bay. Their promise of adventure and discovery must have seemed hollow as they hacked their way through cactus and chapparal, fighting insects and summer heat, knowing that behind rocks and distant hills were the ever-watchful eyes of Indians—both friendly and hostile.

The expedition left San Diego on June 14 and made slow progress. Diarist and engineer Miguel Costansó noted that marches weren't long because the expedition was in unfamiliar lands with unknown obstacles and nonexistent trails. Early stops were also necessary so that scouts could be sent out by daylight to see what the next day's terrain would be like and to locate water. There were sick to be tended, stray animals to gather, and soldiers to feed. Much care was taken to use food sparingly, as it was to be a long journey.

The land expedition, led by Gaspar de Portolá, was one of the initial steps in the Spanish government's plan to colonize Alta California. This plan called for establishing a system of missions throughout the territory that would tend to the spiritual and temporal needs of the Indian populations. The head of these missions was Father Junipero Serra, a Franciscan monk from Mallorca, who had

Above: *Juan Rodriguez Cabrillo was a very early explorer of Southern California. He sailed along the coast in 1542, stopping briefly in the area that would become Orange County. Cabrillo's statue can be seen today at the entrance to the Charles W. Bowers Memorial Museum. Courtesy, Charles W. Bowers Memorial Museum*

Facing page: *Two friars made the trek from San Diego to Monterey Bay, searching for future sites for a chain of missions as portrayed in this drawing by Alex Harmer. Courtesy, First American Title Insurance Company*

helped develop the plan for Alta California. Two expeditions would set out from San Diego—one by land and one by sea—both to meet at Monterey Bay to establish the second mission.

The Portolá expedition was accompanied by two priests, Father Juan Crespi and Father Francisco Gómez, whose primary function was to select future mission sites as they traveled. They crossed into what became Orange County on July 22, 1769, where they stopped to baptize two Indian children in Cristianitos Canyon, northeast of San Clemente. The next day the expedition passed near the future site of the mission of San Juan Capistrano. Father Juan Crespi described this place as:

a very pleasant green valley, full of willows, al-

ders, and live oak and other trees not known to us. It has a large arroyo, which at the point where we crossed it, carried a good stream of fresh and good water, which, after running a little way, formed into pools in some large patches of tules. We halted there, calling it the valley of Santa Maria Magdalena.

A more startling entry is that for the date July 28, when the party camped along the banks of the Santa Ana River: "I called this place the Sweet Name of Jesus de los Temblores because we experienced here a terrifying earthquake, which was repeated four times during the day."

The Portolá expedition proceeded northward, making a total of seven campsites in what would become Orange County. After

This Indian maze stone was discovered by J. Joplin in about
1885, and is now on display at the Charles W. Bowers Memorial Museum. Courtesy, Charles W. Bowers Memorial
Museum

two months on the trail the group successfully arrived at their destination—but did not recognize it. They continued onward for another month and finally realized their mistake at San Francisco Bay. By then the promise had faded into a nightmare. Provisions were gone, soldiers were sick, and contact with the sea expedition at Monterey had been missed. The travelers turned back and painfully made their way to San Diego, leaving a legacy of trails, potential mission sites, and knowledge of a land never before seen by Europeans. Perhaps most significantly, they left behind names such as Santa Ana, which was given to the mountains that framed the future county's eastern boundary.

What the Portolá expedition learned was useful six years later in 1775, when Father Serra received permission to establish the seventh mission—San Juan Capistrano. It was to be named for a Franciscan saint, the hero of the 1456 siege of Belgrade, Saint John of Capistrano. "They took possession of the site and made a beginning of the Mission on the 30th of October," wrote Father Francisco Palóu, Serra's friend and biographer.

Fathers Fermín Francisco de Lasuén and Gregório Amúrrio were sent from Monterey to establish the new mission. Father Amúrrio stopped at Mission San Gabriel to pick up supplies while Father Lasuén proceeded to San Diego to do the same. Father Lasuén was the first to arrive at San Juan Capistrano with Lieutenant Francisco Ortega and a group of soldiers. Construction began with the help of friendly Indians and the grudging help of some of the soldiers. They had erected a cross, built a corral for animals, and decided on the site of the church building by the time Father Amúrrio returned with the supplies. But work halted when a messenger arrived with news that some Indians in San Diego had staged an uprising November 6 and had

killed a priest. The soldiers were needed in San Diego and so the padres were urged to leave with them. The church bells, too cumbersome to transport, were hastily buried and the party departed.

The uprising lasted only one day, but its effects were far-reaching. Fearing the instability of the Indian population, Father Serra temporarily stopped the establishment of new missions. One year later, when Serra felt comfortable about the Indians once again, the missionaries returned to San Juan Capistrano. They dug up the bells and hung them for service near the cross they found still standing. Father Serra was present for the official founding ceremony that took place on November 1, 1776, and included the celebration of Mass. Fathers Amúrrio and Pablo Mugártegui, who would remain at the site along with ten soldiers, were present, as well as some friendly natives from the surrounding villages, curious about the strange-looking Europeans and their ceremonies. Given the name "Juaneños" after Juan in San Juan Capistrano, it was they who would become the beneficiaries of the day's proceedings.

Since the primary function of the missions was to save souls, attracting Indians to the establishment was the first goal. This was done by enticing them with food and glass beads and by having Indians from San Gabriel translate the missionaries' description of the benefits to be obtained by becoming a neophyte of the mission. In the words of Father Palóu, the job was not difficult in San Juan: "Unlike the Indians at other missions . . . who would pester the missionaries by begging eatables and other presents, these of San Juan Capistrano pestered the missionaries with petitions for baptism."

Conversion to Christianity was to be voluntary, but once achieved the Indian was bound to the mission forever. His life was controlled by the missionaries, who regulated all aspects of his existence. If he rebelled, he was punished. If he ran away, he was brought back. Serra felt that this degree of control was necessary to fulfill the mission's purpose. For the Indian to survive in a western European culture he needed the discipline and the skills taught in the mission establishment. To learn, he would have to remain—by force, if necessary. He was to be a Christian, a landowner, and a productive member of society. The Spanish crown had given the church the right to control thousands of acres of land to be held in trust for the Indians, who were to be trained and given title to the land within ten years. The process actually took fifty years and the promise tarnished before it was ever fulfilled.

The mission's second goal was the construction of buildings. Father Serra went to San Gabriel to get the workmen and supplies that would be needed in the coming months. The founding document for Mission San Juan Capistrano listed those items as nine milk cows, a breed bull, a yoke of oxen, eight pack mules, three saddle mules, three broken horses, two mares, one colt, a male and female pig, chickens, saddles and bridles, twelve hoes, two axes, six large machetes, six new knives, and a branding iron. Arrangements were also made for articles necessary to establish a church, portraits of saints, and food to get the settlement started, some of which were provided by other missions. Since these items had originally been intended for the 1775 founding, it is not known if the same list was used a year later.

Construction began as soon as the caravan with supplies and workmen arrived. A place of worship, a shelter for the missionaries, and corrals for animals were built first, probably a mile and a half to the east of the current location of the mission, near San Juan Creek.

Above: *This statue of St. Anthony Padua is a prime example of the religious artwork that could be found in the San Juan Capistrano Mission. Courtesy, Charles W. Bowers Memorial Museum*

Facing page, top: *This Matt Brown drawing helps to illustrate the vitality and activity of the San Juan Capistrano community during the turn of the century. Courtesy, Anaheim Public Library*

Facing page, bottom: *This 1900s view of the decaying San Juan Capistrano Mission was taken before it was restored. Courtesy, Anaheim Public Library*

SAN JUAN
CAPISTRANO

MATT BROWN

During the prime of the mission system, local traders often stopped to converse and trade with the missionaries, as depicted in this sketch by C.R. Couch. Courtesy, Anaheim Public Library

On October 4, 1778, the mission was transferred to its current site near the secure water supply of Trabuco Creek. The exact location of the original mission site has long been a mystery, and is still the subject of controversy.

The first building at the new location was the Serra Chapel, built in 1778 on the east side of the quadrangle. The rest of the mission contained a centralized patio supplied with water, surrounded by the priests' quarters, guestrooms, dormitories, cooking areas, and rooms for candlemaking, food storage, shoemakers, carpenters, spinners, weavers, and dressmakers. The mission's neophytes were employed as blacksmiths, tanners, soapmakers, fishermen, brick and tile makers, plasterers, hunters, and agriculturalists. Most of their activities took place on the mission grounds or in nearby locations.

In 1794 two large granaries were built and forty small adobe houses for neophytes and married soldiers. These were located outside the mission grounds, and became the nucleus of the village that grew around the mission. Also outside the quadrangle were the soldiers' barracks, a hospital, and the mission plaza. The most prestigious project of the period, however, was the construction of the Great Stone Church, begun in 1797.

Who designed the church for San Juan Capistrano is unknown, although it is believed that Father Juan Norberto de Santiago and his companion Father Vicente Fustér were the moving forces behind its construction. The fathers deemed it necessary, since there were approximately 1,000 neophytes living at the mission at this time, 700 of whom were adults and required to attend Mass. An ambitious project, the church was to be built in the form of a Latin cross with a baptistry, tower, and vaulted ceiling constructed in a series of domes. It was to be 146 feet long, 27 feet wide, and its belltower was to be 120 feet high. Not having a master mason available to supervise the construction, the missionaries asked Governor José Joaquín Arrillaga to find one for them. He sent Isídro Aguilár from Culiácan, Mexico, to undertake the task.

The job took nine years to finish and many changes were made in the process. Dimensions were altered and the ceiling had seven domes instead of six. Some of the revisions may have resulted from changes in the work force and in supervision. Father Fustér died in 1800, followed by Isídro Aguilár in 1803. Progress continued, and on September 7, 1806, the Great Stone Church was formally dedicated. It was a time to rejoice, particularly for the Indians who had carried out all the work. The fiesta, attended by neophytes from neighboring villages, soldiers in glittering uniforms, and dignitaries from San Diego, Los Angeles, and Santa Barbara, including Governor Arrillaga, went on for three days.

But all the feasting and praying could not foresee the disaster of 1812. That year, while neophytes gathered for morning Mass on December 8, the ground shook, walls trembled, and the masonry domes came crashing to the ground. The belltower swayed and finally toppled, pealing a horrific cacophony while people ran screaming from the falling stones. Forty people died in the earthquake, along with the dream that the Great Stone Church would stand as long as the mission system and its golden promise.

Other calamities beset the San Juan Capistrano Mission—crops failed one year, disease struck the next, drought diminished the water supply, mustard invaded the fields—but the mission survived. Threats of nature were expected and overcome. But challenges that were made by man, such as the raid by the pirate Hippolyte Bouchard, were not so easy to surmount.

Hippolyte Bouchard raided the California

CHINIGCHINICH

The life and culture of Orange County Indians prior to the mission period is described in the essay "Chinigchinich," written by Father Geronimo Boscana, a missionary at San Juan Capistrano from 1814 to 1826. The essay is a part of Alfred Robinson's book, *Life in California,* published in 1846. This book, which gave important insights into the life-styles of the Californios, was the first book published in English by a Californian. While the importance of Robinson's narrative is indisputable, many historians feel that Boscana's essay has the greater value because it provides the only written description of Orange County's pre-mission Indians.

After the establishment of the missions, the Indians of Orange County were divided into two groups: those who lived south of Aliso Creek were called Juaneño after "Juan" in San Juan Capistrano, and those north of the creek were called Gabrieleño after Mission San Gabriel. These designations were for administrative purposes, identifying who was attached to which mission. The tribes themselves had their own names, many of which have been lost.

The Indians of both northern and southern Orange County were of Uto-Aztecan origin, belonging to the Shoshone family and sharing common linguistic roots. Their culture was also similar, and though "Chinigchinich" describes the mission Indians of San Juan Capistrano, much held true for the people who lived to the north.

Boscana found an essentially deistic culture where people worshipped a god called Chinigchinich. In very simple terms, the Indians believed that if they were good, Chinigchinich would reward them, and if they were bad, they would be punished.

Religious ceremonies were held in a temple called a *vanquech,* which was usually built in the center of the community. It was an enclosure four or five yards in circumference and five or six feet high, usually oval in shape, and divided into two rooms. On a dais at one end of the main room was a figure representing Chinigchinich.

The Chinigchinich figure was usually a coyote skin filled with feathers, deer horns, mountain lion claws, hawk beaks, and talons and parts of crows. The figure was partially covered by a skirt of hawk feathers. Arrow shafts protruded from the mouth and the entire figure resembled a fierce, invincible animal.

Few were privileged to see this fearsome effigy. Only the puplem, or council, could gain admittance to the inner temple and then only on special occasions. Some of these occasions were tribal feast days, ceremonies to protect warriors and hunters, and special days set aside for adoration of the god.

The temple, aside from religious ceremonies, also served as a sanctuary. Criminals fleeing pursuers after committing a crime would be safe if they reached the grounds of the *vanquech.* Boscana wrote:

Whatever criminal, guilty of the highest misdemeanor—of homicide, adultery, or theft, escaping from justice, should be enabled to reach its sanctuary, unknown to his accusers, from that moment he would become free and at liberty to go abroad without any fear of molestation, on the part of those aggrieved.

Although the criminal was allowed to go free, the crime would be avenged. In this culture revenge was permitted and vendettas carried from one generation to another. If the person who committed the crime went free, another member of his family would eventually be punished.

Law-abiding Indians obeyed the tribal leader and council. The early Indians of Orange County had a monarchic form of government.

There was one chief whose title was eventually passed to his eldest son. A daughter could succeed her father as chief, but in such situations the nearest male relative held power until her son was old enough to rule.

A succession was the cause of feasting and celebrating, and chiefs of all neighboring villages were invited to participate. The new chief would dress in a skirt of feathers, his upper body painted black. His hair was plaited, tied close to his neck, and wound around his head. Upright feathers comprised his headdress. During the ceremony, the new chief danced before Chinigchinich, followed by a dance including the other chiefs. The celebration took three or four days.

Although obedience and respect were given to the chief and members of the council, people lived much as they pleased. There were no written laws, nor was there formal administration of justice. But there were some rules the Indians had to follow. Only certain people could enter the *vanquech,* hunters could not eat their own kill, fasting was mandatory during the puberty ceremony, and if a person broke a taboo or angered the chief—intentionally or by accident—he could lose his life.

Members of the tribe were informed of a misdeed by the town crier, who went through the village announcing the nature of the crime and the name of the criminal. Sometimes people were asked to kill the criminal. If the offender escaped, the sentence might be carried out on one of his relatives. If the wrong person was executed, or if the relatives felt the execution was not warranted, a vendetta was carried. Sometimes vengeance led to war.

"War was never waged by them for conquest, but for revenge," wrote Boscana, "and in many cases for some affront given to their ancestors which had remained unavenged. Their quarrels and disputes arose from trivial motives, for their wealth was trifling and consisted merely of seeds, skins, or beads which were universally esteemed amongst them as money."

Sometimes wars were waged to avenge the theft of a rabbit or a woman, or because a visiting chief failed to bring a customary present to a ceremony.

When war was considered, it was debated among the entire council. Debate was centered not on the rightness or wrongness of the dispute, but whether or not they thought they could win. When the decision was made, the town crier went through the village calling everyone to prepare for war. The day of the first battle men led the attack and women followed behind, picking up the fallen arrows of the enemy. Victors of the war completely destroyed the opposing village: all the men were killed and the women and children were taken as slaves.

Aside from the perils of war, life could also be perilous for disobedient children. Children who continually misbehaved were put to death and the parents were dishonored. For well-behaved children, life was generally carefree. Boys were taught how to fight, hunt, and construct bows and arrows. Girls were taught housekeeping techniques, and how to gather and prepare edible plants.

At the age of six or seven each child was assigned an animal to be his protector. This was usually done by giving him a hallucinatory drug and encouraging him to describe what he saw. Wrote Boscana, "Soon after taking this preparation they became insensible, and for three days were deprived of any sustenance whatever. During this period they were attended by some old men or women, who were continually exhorting them to be on the alert, not to sleep for fear the coyote, the bear, the crow, or the rattlesnake might come." The first animal seen by the

child was thought to be the one that would keep him from harm.

When a boy reached puberty, another ceremony took place, one more difficult to endure. He was taken to the outer rooms of the *vanquech* to fast for three days. When the fasting was completed, he was branded on the upper arm to make him fierce in battle, and whipped with nettles and covered with ants to make him invincible. If he survived these rites, he would take his place among the men of the tribe.

A girl, when she reached puberty, was placed in a supine position on a bed of heated stones in a shallow pit. Women of the tribe danced around the perimeter, during a similar fasting period, calling to Chinigchinich to make her fertile. Once a girl completed her puberty ceremony she was eligible for marriage.

The main work of the household was done by the woman. Her ability to gather and prepare food was a part of her courtship ritual. Once a man selected a woman to be his bride, and had obtained not only her consent but the consent of her parents, he was expected to move in and to take care of the entire family.

"During the time of their matrimonial promise, his obligations were to supply the house with fuel and game and the girl attended to the domestic affairs, ever rising at the dawn of the day, bathing herself and supplying the house with water," wrote Boscana, "after which she put everything in order, with the utmost precision, and prepared their customary repast." In this manner, both could judge if the other was ready for marriage.

The marriage ceremony included three or four days of feasting. At the culmination, the groom sat on a mat in a shelter built in front of his house and the council escorted the bride to him. As the bride took the final steps toward her husband, the women of the tribe disrobed her and seated her next to her husband. They

were then considered married in the eyes of the tribe.

The announcement of the first pregnancy was also a cause for celebration. The husband was required to adhere to a rigid diet during his wife's confinement, and could not eat fish or meat. Neither could he leave the house or smoke. When the child was born the grandparents selected the child's name.

Not all marriages resulted in children. Homosexual marriages were permitted and some male children were raised from birth to take the place of females. Males raised as females were thought to be better wives because they were stronger and could do more work.

Generally the daily life of the females was stringent, and they were treated much like slaves. The Indians did not plant or cultivate crops, but subsisted on wild seeds and acorns. It was the woman's job to mash and grind them in hollowed rocks and to make them into gruels called atole and pinole. Fruit and herbs were also consumed, and honey collected from beehives. Women gathered wood for fuel and carried water from springs, many of which were great distances from the village. Some of the utensils they used are still found today near streambeds.

Men led a different kind of life, one that included hunting, fishing, and making the tools of war. Occasionally, there was fighting to do, but life was generally peaceful.

There was room for change in the Indians' lifestyle, but many traditions ran too deep to discard. Yet the Orange County Indians' deism and ingrained respect for authority assisted the missionaries in convincing the Indians to adopt a new way of life, one that would for a time totally stamp out their traditions and culture.

This 1938 view of the San Juan Capistrano Mission illustrates its successful restoration, which began in the 1920s. Courtesy, Anaheim Public Library

coast in 1818. The territory he represented (present-day Argentina) was in revolt against Spain, and the Spanish province of California was ripe for plundering. When he reached the coast near Mission San Juan Capistrano, Bouchard sent men ashore under a flag of truce to get supplies. The mission had been forewarned and posted a lookout. Neophytes had fled with their belongings from the chapel; only the mission garrison remained. Santiago Arguello, inflated by his responsibility, answered Bouchard's request for supplies with a note saying they could land if they pleased, but he would only give them a supply of powder and shot. Bouchard, incensed by the reply, landed a party of 140 men and two cannons and marched on the village while its handful of defenders fled.

Peter Corney, commander of Bouchard's second ship, wrote:

We found the town well-stocked with everything but money, and destroyed much wine and spirits and all the public property, set fire to the king's stores, barracks, and governor's house, and about two o'clock we marched back though not in the order that we went, many of the men being intoxicated, and some were so much so that we had to lash them to the field pieces and drag them to the beach, where, about six o'clock we arrived with the loss of six men. Next morning we punished about twenty men for getting drunk.

The six men who were lost apparently were not injured, just too intoxicated to find their way back.

Bouchard set sail, his threat ended. But another man-made situation posed a more serious problem for the mission system: Mexican independence.

The independence movement had begun in 1810. When Mexico finally won its independence in 1821 it created land policies that stifled the growth and prosperity of the Spanish missions while forcing implementation of a basic mission goal—to give land to the Indians. The new government also used the available land to accomplish its own goals, including the opening of new settlements and the promotion of agriculture. The clamor for the confiscation of mission lands, actually owned by the crown, came in 1826. This prompted the Secularization Act of 1833, which took control of the missions, the Indians, and the land away from the Catholic Church and brought the mission era officially to an end.

In practice it had ended earlier. The new Mexican Constitution had emancipated the Indians, freeing them to leave the mission establishments. Many had scattered, some to the hills and their old culture, others to settlements where they were poorly treated. Still others drifted without purpose, victims of the system that had always made decisions for them. A few settled down to farm in government-created pueblos, populated and run by Indians. Most pueblos failed and the Indian was forced to join the work force of the rancho system with little hope of social mobility.

Mission San Juan Capistrano fell into a hopeless decline: walls crumbled, tiled roofs cracked and caved in, the once well-tended patio fell prey to weeds and wandering sheep. Eugene Duflot de Mofras, a visiting French diplomat, described San Juan Capistrano in 1842 as "... an establishment which is in a most ruinous condition, despite the efforts made by its Spanish missionary, Father José María Zalvidea, to arrest the destruction." At the height of its prosperity in 1812, the mission claimed 1,400 residents and produced 500,000 pounds of wheat, 190,000 pounds of barley, 202,000 pounds of corn, 20,600 pounds of beans, and had 14,000 cattle, 16,000 sheep, and 740 horses. When Duflot de Mofras arrived it had 100 Indians, most of whom were old and infirm, 500 cattle, 150 horses, no sheep, and produced only a small amount of grain and wine.

The destruction of the mission system was a manifestation of the new liberalism among native-born Californios. While on the surface the breakup seemed to be anti-clerical, its real purpose was to weaken the church's power in temporal matters and to sever the tie with Spain. It also released thousands of acres of land from mission control—land that became available for private ownership. Secularization, designed to benefit the Indians and make them self-sustaining, instead disintegrated the missions, subjected the Indians to poverty, revolutionized the land system, and made the rancho the dominant economic and social institution in the province.

The golden promise of the mission period had gone unfulfilled. The new era would bring new promises, new problems, and a new social order.

Dependent almost wholly upon the variable rainfall and native grasses, the early cattle industry was subject to great fluctuations between wealth and poverty. In the 1800s the flocks and herds of the Spanish dons roamed over the hills and valleys, but well before the turn of the century much of the grazing land would be replaced by farms and citrus groves. *Courtesy, First American Title Insurance Company*

Rancho

Halcyon

Days

ather Serra had two wishes for the Spanish soldiers who populated Alta California: he wished them to marry and to have land. All the land was owned by the Spanish crown, and most of it was under control of the missions. But a new law established in 1773 by Antonio Maria Bucareli, viceroy of New Spain, permitted presidio commanders to assign lands to colonists under these conditions: at least 2,000 cattle had to be grazed, a house must be built, and the applicant must not interfere with the operation of the neighboring missions or pueblos.

The first land grant in Orange County was assigned in 1784 to a soldier, Manuel Pérez Nieto, and covered all the territory between the

Santa Ana and San Gabriel rivers. Mission San Gabriel complained that the vast grant encroached on areas it needed, so Nieto's grant was reduced. Even so, this smaller tract would eventually be the site of more than fifteen cities.

The second land grant and the first to be granted totally within Orange County was to Juan Pablo Grijalva and his son-in-law, José Antonio Yorba. The grant, which exceeded 62,000 acres, was called Rancho Santiago de Santa Ana, and would one day include Santa Ana, Orange, Tustin, Olive, El Modena, Villa Park, Costa Mesa, and parts of Newport Beach.

Grijalva had retired from military service in 1796. A few years later he applied for grazing rights, as land grants were then called. When Mission San Juan Capistrano voiced no objection he moved stock onto the property. After Grijalva's death in 1806, José Antonio Yorba and Grijalva's grandson, Juan Pablo Peralta, continued to use the land. They formally filed a petition for a grant in 1809 which was confirmed in 1810.

The Yorba-Peralta petition claimed that the land would be worked by Peralta and Yorba's son, José Antonio Yorba II. They continued to raise cattle, horses, and crops, such as grain and fruit, for their own consumption. The Yorba and Peralta households each had a work force of Indians not attached to the missions. The Indians, whose ranks swelled after emancipation from the missions, lived in separate villages and served as cooks, servants, field-workers, and vaqueros. They were given food and left alone.

Land was plentiful and life was full of promise. Unfortunately, the Yorbas, Peraltas, and Nietos had a poor relationship with their neighboring missions. Besides constant squabbles over straying cattle, the missionaries were displeased that Indians were in rancho employ and were sometimes allowed to practice their

Above: *This surveyor's transit was used by early land surveyor Richard Egan in the early 1800s. Courtesy, Charles W. Bowers Memorial Museum*

Facing page: *Abel Stearns, a native of Massachusetts, came to California in 1829 and found wealth and promise in Orange County. Courtesy, First American Title Insurance Company*

old religion. As they quarrelled over changes at home, even more change was on the horizon; the missionaries and rancheros could not gauge the turmoil it would bring.

The changes came with the end of the Mexican Revolution. A series of acts stripped the missions of their land and power and opened new areas for settlement. The new Mexican Republic also boosted the economy by opening trade with foreign ships. Spain had allowed only its own ships to bring supplies to the missions and to colonists. The Spanish ships brought items such as flannels, furs, cotton, silks, hosiery, sugar, rice, bells, and cooking utensils. Hides, tallow, soap, wine, and brandy were traded in exchange. Though there was some illegal trade with foreign ships, the majority of California's wealth lay untapped. Opening the ports to foreigners was a welcome policy not only to the rancheros, of which there were only a few when the policy was adopted, but also to the mission administrators who had warehouses full of goods. Trade with the missions was illustrated by Richard Henry Dana in *Two Years Before The Mast.* Dana, who sailed on the ship *Pilgrim* owned by the Boston trade firm of Bryant, Sturgis, and Company, visited the Orange County coast in 1835, leaving for posterity his impressions of the coast, its villages, and the people he met.

The most welcome policy to the landless was the Secularization Act of 1833. This led to the confiscation of mission properties one year later and opened opportunities for land ownership to anyone who was a Mexican citizen (native or naturalized), a Catholic, and who had good moral character. The procedure for obtaining a grant, made in square leagues (4,438 acres), began when the applicant sent a petition to the governor including a description of the property and a *diseño,* or map, indicating the owners of neighboring lands. The

governor or his aide then sent the petition to the *Ayuntamiento,* the provincial council in the applicant's area, to see if the petition met all legal requirements. Land could not be too near a mission or a pueblo, and must be unclaimed and suitable for grazing. The *Ayuntamiento* also reviewed the personal qualifications of the applicant and determined if he had sufficient stock and the means to raise crops and occupy the land. If the *Ayuntamiento* was favorable to the request, the applicant's petition was approved and copies of his request, his *diseño,* and minutes of the transaction were all put in a file called an *Expediente.* The applicant next contacted his new neighbors to be present when the land was measured and the new boundaries marked. The last act, juridical possession, included a ceremony in which the new owner turned over dirt, broke tree branches, pulled up grass, and threw rocks to indicate possession. This was done in the presence of witnesses and the land was thereafter his.

FRONTIER LAND BARONS

Spanish policies discouraged foreign settlement and foreign trade in Alta California. But with Mexican independence came a new point of view: ports were opened, although trade was still strictly controlled, and Anglos could settle and own land, as long as they became Mexican citizens.

Two men who helped shape the future of Orange County took advantage of both opportunities. One was John Forster, an Englishman; the other Abel Stearns, an American.

Forster, whose name is listed as Foster in early census reports, came to California in 1833 on the ship *Facio*. He was twenty-two years old and employed by his uncle, James Johnson, who was a trader operating out of Guymas, Mexico. Forster returned to Guymas as master of the ship, but chose not to pursue a permanent career as a sea captain. Instead he journeyed overland, back to California. He continued to work for his uncle until 1836 when, compelled by the vast opportunities of the new territory, he became Juan Forster, a Californian.

The following year he married twenty-three-year-old Ysidora Pico, sister of Pío and Andrés Pico. Little did he know that political fortunes awaited him, and that in 1845 Pío would become governor of California.

Forster did not immediately acquire land. From 1840 to 1843 he was a shipping agent at San Pedro and a port captain. But soon he was ready to become a ranchero.

His first acquisition was the purchase of the 46,432-acre Rancho Mission Viejo on April 6, 1845. This ranch was originally granted to José Antonio Estudillo in 1841 under the name Rancho La Paz, but Estudillo failed to satisfy the conditions of ownership required by Mexican law. Rather than have the land revert back to the government, he sold it to Augustín Olvera, who in turn sold it to Forster just two days after his title

was confirmed.

Forster also acquired Mission San Juan Capistrano. He and a partner, James McKinley, purchased the mission at public auction from the Mexican government in 1845 for $710 in gold and hides. Forster later bought out his partner and moved into the mission, occupying the area used as the gift shop today. But he was not through buying land.

That same year he was granted Rancho Potrero Los Piños, a small pasturage near Los Piños Peak, and two other potreros, El Carrizo and La Cienega, just past the Riverside County line. Later he acquired the 9,000-acre Rancho Los Desechos that comprises San Clemente today, and lands in San Diego County. His holdings totalled 200,000 acres.

After Forster moved into the former mission, he became closely identified with San Juan Capistrano. He and his wife raised several children there, but only three lived to adulthood: Marco Antonio, born in 1839, Francisco Pío, born in 1841, and John Fernando, born in 1845.

The Forster family lived in the mission until 1864, and while there gained the reputation of warm, generous hosts. When bandits raided the community, Forster provided sanctuary behind the thick mission walls. When the Americans marched from San Diego to Los Angeles during the Mexican-American War, he provided them with fresh horses and food. At first, however, the Americans were unsure where Forster stood, because of his family ties to the Picos.

In an interview conducted by Thomas Savage in 1878, Forster stated,

Frémont and his whole force (Kit Carson, Alexander Godey, and a Shawnee Indian company) surrounded the mission buildings at San Juan Capistrano, believing I would attempt to escape. He was savage against me until we had an explanation when he

became convinced that I was favorably disposed to the U.S. at the same time that I was trying to save the interests of my relatives, the Pico family.

Forster's main wish was to see California under the control of the United States or any other stable government. California had long been plagued by political unrest that was socially and economically unhealthy for its citizenry.

Affiliation with the United States did not immediately solve California's problems. Lawlessness continued to threaten life and property for years to come; United States land policies threatened the economic system of the southern counties; and although the government was politically stable, it was too far away to provide meaningful direction in the lives of the rancheros. Forster's frustration found its way into many letters to government officials. Writing an equal number of letters was his friend, Abel Stearns, whose life in California was similar to Forster's.

Stearns, a native of Massachusetts, came to California in 1829 from Mexico. A naturalized Mexican citizen, he opened a store in Los Angeles exchanging goods for hides and tallow from nearby ranchos, and purchasing furs from trappers. As his business grew he purchased a larger building in San Pedro, near the center of trading activities, and used it as his office, warehouse, and store. In time he became extremely wealthy.

Stearns' wealth did not make him immune to political pressures. In 1831 he found disfavor with Governor Manuel Victoria, and was asked to leave the country. Fortunately the governor was deposed and Stearns remained. Another governor, Mariano Chico, also ordered Stearns to depart. This time Stearns and a group of other prominent citizens joined together and overthrew Governor Chico.

Stearns survived allegations of

smuggling and bribery, and a physical attack that left his speech impaired and his face disfigured. Despite slurs on his character, discounted by most of his influential friends, and a face that could not be called handsome, Stearns married well. At the age of forty-one he married Arcadia Bandini, the beautiful fourteen-year-old daughter of his best friend, Don Juan Bandini. He set her up in his home, nicknamed "El Palacio" because of its grandeur, but fathered no children.

Reputed by his various biographers as a shrewd businessman, Stearns had little tolerance for Mexican bureaucrats, but was fond of the native Californios. His generosity to his wife, numerous public charities, and many civic enterprises left him highly regarded among his peers. This regard was demonstrated at the polls where Stearns was elected to the Los Angeles City Council and the state assembly.

During the years Stearns amassed thousands of acres of land, beginning with Rancho Los Alamitos that he purchased in 1840 for $6,000. During the United States Land Commission hearings he successfully defended his title. Because of his wealth Stearns was able to loan large amounts of money to his fellow rancheros, who were running up big legal bills. The loans were strictly business and he charged as much as 5 percent per month, compound interest. Some were able to pay, some were not. By 1853 Stearns, like Forster, owned more than 200,000 acres of land.

In addition to Rancho Los Alamitos, Stearns acquired portions of Rancho Santiago de Santa Ana, most of Rancho San Juan Cajón de Santa Ana, Rancho Los Coyotes, and Rancho Las Bolsas. In other counties he purchased Rancho La Laguna (near Elsinore) and part of Rancho San Antonio (southeast of Los Angeles). He also bought Rancho Jurupa (in San Bernardino County) and part

interest in Rancho Temescal (near Riverside).

Improving these properties required funds that he borrowed from, among others, Michael Reese of San Francisco. But the droughts of 1862-1864 put him in a bad financial position and by 1865 all of his land holdings were in jeopardy. He couldn't pay his bills or his taxes, and creditors pounded on his door in greater frequency. But Stearns was not one to give up easily. He had acquired many close friends through the years who were ready to prove their friendship.

Some of them formed a syndicate called the Robinson Trust to acquire and subdivide the remaining properties of Stearns' ranchos. Stearns was made a partner and was able to pay his debts. He also took an active interest in the new company, which had advertised the properties throughout the United States and Europe, and had subdivided nearly 278 square miles of land. But Stearns was too used to having his own way to deal successfully with a number of partners. He continued to make decisions without consulting them, ignored their advice, and angered them

Ranchero John Forster made the San Juan Capistrano Mission his home. Courtesy, Pamela Hallan-Gibson

continually. But despite this internal friction the Robinson Trust was a successful project, coming at a time when California was changing from the home of a few wealthy landholders to a land of diversified farming.

Both Stearns and Forster had seen two Californias. They had entered the territory when land was plentiful and cheap and the right connections—political or familial—put them on the receiving end. They endured political and economic upheavals, hanging on to their land and property when even the fates seemed against them. They fought drought and creditors, and came back to continue their lives as productive members of society. Unfortunately, both died before the new face of the future Orange County was revealed. Stearns died of a sudden illness in 1877 and Forster died five years later. Neither lived to see the new cities that replaced the ranchos that had once made their fortunes.

Above: *Bernardo Yorba was one of the largest land grantees of early Orange County. He was granted the land of Rancho Cañon de Santa Ana, which includes the present-day site of Yorba Linda. Courtesy, Charles W. Bowers Memorial Museum*

Facing page: *This photograph of Bernardo Yorba's adobe, taken around 1905, does not depict it as the lively center of activity it had been from its construction in 1834 until the mid-1880s. The home, which included a chapel, a store, and a barroom, was the hub of activity for miles around. The house was called San Antonio, after Saint Anthony, the saint whose statue stood in its chapel. Courtesy, First American Title Insurance Company*

From 1833 to 1846 more than 700 land grants were made or reconfirmed in California. Twenty of those were all or partly in Orange County.

The first land grant which included territory in what would someday be Orange County was the Nieto tract, which managed to remain intact until 1834, thirty years after Nieto's death. His heirs asked for a partition of the vast estate that was divided into the following ranchos: Las Bolsas, granted to Catarina Ruiz, widow of a Nieto, today a part of Huntington Beach, Westminster, Garden Grove, and Fountain Valley; Los Alamitos, granted to Juan José Nieto, which included Seal Beach and Los Alamitos; Los Coyotes, also granted to Juan José Nieto, which contained Stanton, Cypress, La Palma and Buena Park; Santa Gertrudes, granted to Nieto's widow, Josefa Cota de Nieto, which lay mostly in Los Angeles County, and Los Cerritos, which also lay entirely within Los Angeles County.

Rancho Santiago de Santa Ana, the other early land grant in Orange County, experienced little change although the Yorba family had to reconfirm title to it in 1839. In 1834 Bernardo Yorba, a son of José Antonio Yorba I, was granted Rancho Cañon de Santa that today includes Yorba Linda. His brother, Teodocio, also applied for his own grant. He was given Lomas de Santiago in 1846, which lies between Rancho San Joaquín and the Cleveland National Forest. Two more brothers, Tomás Yorba and José Antonio Yorba II, who stayed on Rancho Santiago de Santa Ana, contested lands granted to neighbor José Sepúlveda. Two separate grants to Sepúlveda from Governor Juan B. Alvarado established Rancho Ciénega de las Ranas in 1837 and La Bolsa de San Joaquín in 1842. Called Rancho San Joaquín, Sepúlveda's eleven square leagues today include Irvine, Corona del Mar, and portions of Newport Beach and Laguna. The grants were disputed because La Bolsa de San Joaquín had belonged to Mission San Juan Capistrano before Sepúlveda began to use it and because the boundaries of Rancho Ciénega de las Ranas encroached on the Santa Ana land. The grants were nonetheless issued, with modifications.

Other grants made in Orange County included Boca de la Playa, granted to Emigdio Vejar in 1846, which included Capistrano Beach and parts of San Clemente; Bolsa Chica, granted to Joaquín Ruiz in 1841, which included Sunset Beach; Cañada de los Alisos, today's El Toro and Lake Forest, granted in 1842 and 1846 to José Serrano; Rancho La Habra, granted in 1839 to Mariano R. Roldan, which included La Habra; and San Juan Cajón de Santa Ana, granted in 1837 to Juan Pacífico Ontiveros. Today this rancho includes the cities of Anaheim, Fullerton, Placentia, and Brea.

In 1846 Augustín Olvera was granted Rancho Mission Viejo, also called La Paz, which he sold the next day to John Forster. Today the community of Mission Viejo occupies this area. Forster received his own grant in 1845, that of Potrero Los Piños, a grazing area in the Cleveland National Forest, and acquired two other *potreros,* El Cariso and La Ciénega. Santiago Arguello was granted Rancho Trabuco in 1841. He later sold to Forster, whose land adjoined it. Another San Juan Capistrano resident, Juan Ávila, was grantee of Rancho Niguel in 1841. Today this ranch encompasses Laguna Niguel and portions of Laguna Hills. The smallest grant was to Santiago Rios, who obtained a seven-acre portion of Capistrano Beach. Two other ranchos had small portions in Orange County: Rancho La Puente and Rincon de la Brea.

Above: *Shortly before its demolition in 1926, Bernardo Yorba's adobe stood in final decline along the Santa Ana River. Courtesy, Anaheim Public Library*

Left: *This section of an early Mexican saddle shows the detailed, hand-tooled craftsmanship of the ranchero era. Courtesy, Charles W. Bowers Memorial Museum*

Facing page: *This portrait of Don José Andrés Sepúlveda astride his mare, the Black Swan, was painted by Henri Joseph Penelon in about 1856. Courtesy, Charles W. Bowers Memorial Museum*

Though land changed hands, life took on a routine that would not be altered until mid-nineteenth century. Rancheros lived in adobe houses; some, like Bernardo Yorba's eighteen-room mansion, were spacious and well-appointed, while others were simple two- or three-room cottages. Most had dirt floors and shuttered windows. Whatever their size or the economic status of their owners, the houses were always filled with family and visitors. The wealthier rancheros had servants who cooked, baked, cleaned, washed, mended, and attended to personal needs. Outside workers tended vineyards and crops of grains, beans, pumpkins, squash, and corn while workmen cared for fruit trees of every variety, and ranch hands—vaqueros, blacksmiths, saddlemakers, tanners, soapmakers—also helped the rancho run smoothly. Tomás Yorba allegedly even had a silversmith, hatmaker, and cigar maker in his employ.

The day often began before sunrise with prayers and a breakfast of beans, tortillas, and (if available) chocolate. Indians did most of the manual labor, while rancheros, who lived like feudal masters, managed their property and accounts, discussed politics, or arranged their daily schedules with friends. Many were expert horsemen, adept as their workers in the daily tasks of running a ranch. A special event was the coming of a trading ship. Cartloads of hides, tallow, horns, wine, soap, and other goods were taken to the ship and traded for chocolate, cigars, lace, rice, and sugar. Other entertainments were fiestas, the yearly rodeos or cattle roundups, runs through the tall mustard, hunting, and bull, bear, and cock fights. Most popular of all was horse racing.

Rancheros loved to gamble on horse races. Wagers were not simple—important races were preceded by a contract drawn by the participants outlining what each was to receive if he won. Many famous races took place in Or-

ange County, but perhaps the most famous was one in 1852 between Sarco, sponsored by Andrés and Pío Pico, and Black Swan, sponsored by José Sepúlveda. It is said that $50,000 in money, cattle, horses, and land was wagered on this race that Black Swan won by seventy-five yards. Sepúlveda eventually bought the horse, only to see it die soon after.

The wealth that permitted some rancheros to engage in gambling, lavish hospitality, and expensive amusements also showed in their dress. In the rancho period women wore long skirts and short-sleeved blouses trimmed in lace. They often wore satin or velvet shoes and *rebosos* (shawls) that could be worn over the shoulders or to cover the head. The high combs and *mantillas* were not stylish in California until the 1840s. Men's styles featured knee britches, embroidered shirts, and flat hats worn with a kerchief underneath. The fa-

mous description of Tomás Yorba by Alfred Robinson, who visited him in 1829, epitomizes what has become the stereotype of the prosperous ranchero:

Upon his head he wore a black silk handkerchief, the four corners of which hung down his neck behind. An embroidered shirt, a cravat of white jaconet tastefully tied, a blue damask vest, short clothes of crimson velvet, a bright green cloth jacket, with large silver buttons, and shoes of embroidered deer skin, comprised his dress. I was afterwards informed . . . that on some occasions, such as some particular feast day or festival, his entire display often exceeded in value a thousand dollars.

While his biographers discount the latter statement it is well known that on one particular feast day he was as extravagant as described. The occasion was his marriage at the age of forty-seven to eighteen-year-old Vicenta Sepúlveda. On that day he spent nearly $1,500 on the fiesta.

Tomás Yorba also spent time engaging in politics, although not on a grand scale. It was a time of political trouble in Alta California, when governors seemed to change as rapidly as the seasons and golden promises seemed as far away as the seat of government in Mexico City. The turmoil started with the appointment of José María Echeandía to the governor's post in 1825. It was during his tenure that the Indians were freed, the lands of the church were confiscated, and rivalries between the northern and southern parts of Alta California emerged. Minor revolts flared up and were quelled and plans for the creation of the Indian pueblo system moved forward.

In 1831 Echeandía was replaced by Manuel Victoria, who disagreed with Echeandía's plans and rescinded them. He also created many enemies—among them such prominent

Above: *Pío Pico was the last Mexican governor of California before American conquest in 1846. Facing the loss of California, Pico wrote: "We find ourselves suddenly threatened by hordes of Yankee immigrants . . . whose progress we cannot arrest." Courtesy, Anaheim Public Library*

Facing page, top: *This is the only known picture of Don Juan Avila's adobe in San Juan Capistrano as it appeared in the 1860s. Avila is standing on the porch with his family in the foreground. Courtesy, Charles W. Bowers Memorial Museum*

Facing page, bottom: *Believed to have been built as an estancia in 1827, the Sievers Adobe, shown here in 1945, is located twelve miles to the east of San Juan Capistano. It received its name from Henry Sievers, a beekeeper, who lived there from 1887 until 1911. Courtesy, First American Title Insurance Company*

This panoramic view of the San Juan Capistrano Mission captures the great amount of reconstruction work accomplished by the Landmarks Club of Los Angeles from 1895 to 1900. In addition to roofing most of the buildings, the club roofed the corridors and reconstructed the wall at the west end of the front wing at center. Courtesy, Conde-Yorba Collection

Californios as José Antonio Carrillo, Pío Pico, Juan Bandini, and Abel Stearns—and fostered a mood of revolt with his autocratic practices, which included arresting "troublemaking" prominent citizens and abolishing the territorial legislature. Victoria did not have enough troops to keep his plans in effect and was forced to retire to Mexico. The Californios took matters into their own hands. In the South, prominent citizens elected Pío Pico governor, but Echeandía objected and was supported by the territorial legislature. Insurgents led by Augustín Zamorano, a former supporter of Victoria, raised an army in the North and moved south. Echeandía raised troops and moved north. They met at the San Gabriel River, but decided not to fight and instead divided the governmental power.

The next elected governor was José Figueroa, who took office in 1833, moved forward with the secularization plans, and tried to unify factions. But he died in 1835 and was replaced by José Castro, and then Nicolás Gutiérrez, followed by Mariano Chico, all in quick succession. Chico was not popular in the South, and when he left for Mexico to raise an army to help reinforce his policies

Gutiérrez was once again left in charge. He, too, had his enemies and had to confront an army led by Castro and Juan Bautista Alvarado. On November 8, 1836, the territorial government elected Alvarado as governor and declared California independent. This move was not generally supported and another confrontation was readied when Mexico appointed Carlos Antonio Carrillo as governor. In 1838 Alvarado and Carrillo clashed in Ventura. Alvarado's forces won and Carrillo retreated to Las Flores, south of San Clemente. Alvarado and Castro gathered their forces at San Juan Capistrano. The two enemy camps met, fired a few cannons, shouted abuses, and Carrillo fled. The independence movement dropped, Alvarado officially became governor in 1838 and was peacefully succeeded by Manuel Micheltorena in 1842.

Micheltorena's term of office was equally odious to the Californios, primarily because of the 300 soldiers he brought with him, men reputed to be convicts released from prisons for military duty. The rumor soon proved to be true. Alvarado was again declared governor in 1844, but it took a successful military action to get Micheltorena and his troops out. Pío Pico became the next governor and remained so until the American conquest.

It was during Pico's term that the mission system was symbolically closed in Orange County with the sale, at public auction, of Mission San Juan Capistrano.

By 1840 it was apparent that the Indian pueblo set up by the Mexican government at San Juan Capistrano had failed. Free from mission control and owners of their own land, Indians were still forced to care for mission property, support the elderly who resided in the mission, and contribute to the support of the program's secular administrator. Those who stayed in the pueblo and tried to farm became discouraged and left. A succession of administrators were appointed to solve the pueblo's problems, but each found the task too difficult. Finally Augustín Janssens, a Belgian, began to make some progress. He sent two respected Indians to Los Angeles to try to bring back those who had left Capistrano; he also set about to repair the town's water system that had not worked for fourteen years and to inventory the pueblo resources. But behind-the-scenes events would eventually make his efforts futile. Individuals who wanted land in San Juan Capistrano pressured the governor to dissolve the Indian pueblo. In May 1841, despite the pleas of Janssens, the resident priest at the mission, and other townspeople, the Indian pueblo was disbanded. The town was chartered as a regular pueblo with land available for anyone who wished to petition for it.

The plans for the town failed as miserably as the Indian pueblo. A series of administrators came and went, discouraged by the vice and crime that flourished there. Few persons who petitioned for land fulfilled the requirements and actually settled on it. Rains and floods took their toll, and even the mission suffered from squatters who made bonfires of mission documents and used the buildings for immoral purposes. In 1845 Mission San Juan Capistrano was a debt-ridden burden to the government. In December, Pío Pico sold it at public auction to his brother-in-law John Forster and trader James McKinley for $710.

The once-proud mission, the symbol of Junipero Serra's golden promise, stood silent, its brown walls slowly melting into the earth and its windows staring blindly into an empty courtyard. It had once housed a thousand souls, and had been the center of political and social strife that rocked its foundations; it would see even more turmoil before the century ended. But it would survive to fulfill another promise—in another time.

Above: *Ysabel Forster, great-granddaughter of Don Juan Forster, sits with Robert Coffey in a tree in front of the San Juan Capistrano Mission in 1911. This tree can be seen ten years earlier on page forty. Courtesy, Marie Patterson Swanson Collection*

Right: *The once stately and vital San Juan Capistrano Mission is shown here in a state of decline and ruin, as tangible evidence of the decaying mission system. Courtesy, Anaheim Public Library*

Above right: *Captain Stanislado Morales, in an old California costume, posed in the central plaza of the mission. Looking at him is Doña Lucrezia Yorba in old Spanish dress, and nearby is Soledad Pryor y Avila de Landell, working at Spanish drawnwork. Courtesy, Conde-Yorba Collection*

Far right: *This photograph at the San Juan Capistrano Mission was taken in about 1905. Seated on the floor is the Indian saint carver, Mesa. In the chair is Don Geronimo Ruiz y' Ibarra. Celestino Martinez is sitting next to him and standing behind is Juan Valles. Courtesy, Conde-Yorba Collection*

This hand-painted map of early Orange County illustrates the number of ranchos and adobes that were once present in this area. Courtesy, Charles W. Bowers Memorial Museum

American Conquest
and
Social Change

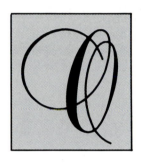

n June 15, 1846, two men in Sonoma raised a crudely made flag depicting a grizzly bear and declared California to be a free and independent country. Though short-lived, the Bear Flag Republic sparked a chain of events that changed not only the ownership of California, but the nature of its promise.

The early 1840s were years of prosperity in Orange County, as well as the rest of Southern California. Cattle prices were stable, natural disasters were not overwhelming, and social patterns were reasonably well regulated. Political unrest, predictable with the seat of government so far away, was ever present, but the future looked bright.

One who did not share this outlook was Governor Pío Pico. Since taking office he had heard rumblings that some rancheros favored annexation to the United States and he could see examples of the growing American influence in the territory. Yet he was afraid to prepare the defense of California for fear that his old rival, General Castro, would take power. The events in Sonoma gave him no choice, for less than a month after the abortive and unsupported attempt to declare independence, the American military invaded California. Commodore John Sloat seized Monterey while Commodore Robert Stockton landed at Los Angeles and John C. Frémont marched north from San Diego. The war between Mexico and the United States had reached California.

With danger apparent, Pico and Castro joined forces and tried to muster an army. But it was too late. Stephen W. Kearny was marching westward with 300 troops, Stockton and Frémont had taken Los Angeles, and the Californios were demoralized. Pico, putting safety before pride, fled.

Of the many skirmishes in the months ahead, the most notable was the Battle of San Pasqual near Escondido. In this battle, the governor's brother, Andrés Pico, and a band of Mexican patriots partially redeemed the Pico name by defeating Kearny, who had sent most of his men back to Santa Fe, New Mexico, when he heard of Stockton's victory. In turn, Stockton's success in Los Angeles was undermined by Captain José María Flores, who led a revolt against the American military commanders in Los Angeles and recaptured the city. Stockton and Kearny joined forces and marched north from San Diego to retake Los Angeles. En route they were given fresh horses by John Forster and were met later by a contingent of pro-American Los Angelinos. A turning point may have occurred while the Stockton-Kearny forces marched through Orange County. Forster, who had accompanied

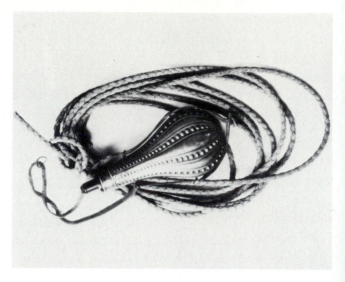

This authentic Mexican lariat and copper powder flask from the mid-1880s was probably used by the rancheros in their daily routines. Courtesy, Charles W. Bowers Memorial Museum

the group, was thrown from his horse near Coyote Creek. On his way to a nearby ranch house for aid he encountered Ramón Carrillo who was leading a group of Mexican forces. Forster, who was Pío Pico's brother-in-law, was not harmed and continued to the nearby house, where he inadvertently learned that an encampment of 600 men was lying in wait for the Americans. Forster returned to camp and told Stockton and Kearny of the ambush. They took another route and avoided a disaster. In January 1847 Flores surrendered Los Angeles to the superior forces of Stockton and Kearny, but it wasn't until 1848 that the Treaty of Guadalupe Hidalgo officially ended the war between Mexico and the United States.

The war itself did not have a significant impact on Orange County, although some hoped that California would be reclaimed by Mexico. Life continued on the ranchos much like it had under Mexican rule with rancheros enjoying their status as leaders of the new social order. They held the land, the cattle, and the benefits of foreign trade. They also held the Indians who comprised most of their work force.

When gold was discovered at Sutter's Mill the Orange County rancheros enjoyed a tremendous increase in the price of beef. Because of the demand for beef in the goldfields, rancheros altered some of their old patterns: instead of slaughtering cattle for hides and tallow, they formed huge cattle drives to the San Francisco area, letting the animals feed along the way. Prices remained inflated through 1856 but dropped thereafter, leaving many of the rancheros with depleted herds, debts from extravagant spending, and a drought to face. They also had debts from another source— one that no one had foreseen, yet affected every landowner—called the Land Act of 1851.

The Treaty of Guadalupe Hidalgo guaranteed Californios' property rights. Yet three years later in faraway Washington, D.C., Congress adopted legislation that challenged every title, forced every landowner to spend huge sums of money in defense of his property, and created economic and social chaos that would take decades to overcome.

Two bills were considered in Congress. The first, submitted by Senator Thomas Hart Benton of Missouri, supported the status quo and left disputes to be settled by local officials; the second, sponsored by John C. Frémont and William M. Gwin, the senators from California, nullified all titles until proven valid. Congress supported the latter and the Land Act was passed, which called for the creation of a three-man commission appointed by the president that would review all land claims in California over a three-year period. Those who failed to submit claims within the first two years would forfeit their land. The decision of the commission and the courts could be appealed by either side. The commission began

hearing cases two months later, but soon found that the time period would not be adequate and extended it to five years. During that time they heard more than 800 cases involving twelve million acres. Three-fourths were upheld.

Preparing a case, gathering the documentation, and traveling to the cosmopolitan city of San Francisco to have it heard was time-consuming and costly. Many of the documents were lost or non-existent; witnesses to events such as the survey or act of juridical possession were often elderly or dead. Orange County rancheros spent years in the courts, but most were successful in defending their titles. One case, that of Juan Pacífico Ontiveros, was particularly poignant.

Ontiveros, grantee of Rancho San Juan Cajón de Santa Ana, had been involved in a boundary dispute with his neighbor, Juan Bautista Leandry of Rancho Los Coyotes, in the early 1840s. During that process he lost some of the papers that proved his ownership of the ranch. When he filed his claim with the Land Commission in 1852 he admitted they were lost, and instead produced witnesses who could swear to his ownership. His claim was denied. Undaunted, Ontiveros hired a new attorney, J.R. Scott, reputed to be the best in this field, and filed an appeal. This time his claim was upheld. The Land Commission appealed the court's decision to the U.S. Supreme Court but the appeal was denied. The year was now 1857. It had taken Ontiveros five years to successfully defend his title. It would take twenty more before bureaucracy released the title and he held the document in his hand.

The cost of defending their land titles forced many rancheros to sell their herds and compromise their land. In addition, they had problems with squatters. Enticed by unscrupulous promoters' glittering promise of free land,

squatters were assured that the land was in limbo and needed the firm hand of a hard-working farmer to put it to good use. Some of the squatters were disillusioned miners who had hoped to make their fortune in the gold-fields, but instead found themselves without property, funds, or self-esteem. They looked covetously upon the thousands of acres of land, occupied only by cattle, and decided to stake out a corner for themselves. In their view there seemed to be so much that wasn't being used.

Despite squatters and debts, a declining economy and an unfamiliar system of government, Orange County remained a cattle frontier until the mid-1860s. Life on the ranchos

Above: *The Trabuco Adobe, located on the mesa above O'Neill Park, is shown here in ruins in the mid-1930s. The name Trabuco was given to this mesa in 1769 when one of Portolá's soldiers lost his blunderbuss, or trabuco, nearby. Courtesy, First American Title Insurance Company*

Left: *The San Antonio Chapel was built on the Yorba Rancho property to fulfill the request Bernardo Yorba made in his will. The remains of an earlier chapel can be seen behind the new one. Courtesy, Charles W. Bowers Memorial Museum*

Facing page, top: *Juan Pacífico Ontiveros, the land grantee of the Rancho San Juan Cajón de Santa Ana, is pictured here with his wife Martina in 1850. Courtesy, Anaheim Public Library*

BANDITS OF THE CALIFORNIA FRONTIER

Lawlessness was a major concern of early Orange County settlers between 1850 and 1870. Bandits attacked people and destroyed property, cattle and horse thieves took entire herds of stock, and bands of renegade Indians terrorized the isolated ranchos and towns.

The situation became so bad in Los Angeles County, of which Orange County was a part, that Stephen C. Foster, district prefect, asked the governor for weapons and ammunition. He planned to distribute the firearms so that citizens could adequately defend themselves. It is not known if his request was honored.

Outlying ranches suffered most from attacks. Sweeping in through unprotected passes were renegade bands of Utes, Mojaves, Paiutes, and mixed bands of Indians, former miners, and vengeful Californios. Most were after cattle and horses, for in the 1850s cattle prices were the highest they had ever been. Rustling reached epidemic proportions, and in 1851 Governor Peter Burnett suggested to the state legislature that rustling be made a capital offense.

Most rancheros had no way to protect their herds that wandered across thousands of unfenced acres. They relied on their *vaqueros* to keep watch, and in rare cases would put particularly prized animals in a walled enclosure near the main ranch buildings. Sometimes this enclosure was surrounded by a deep ditch, similar to a moat; some had sharp horns along the tops of the walls to discourage climbers.

Crime was not confined to rustling. Desperados preyed upon stagecoaches, travelers, caravans, even ranch houses. They robbed banks, stores, and saloons, and committed assault with the slightest provocation. According to newspaper accounts, criminals were so numerous and legal institutions so poorly organized that most crimes went unpunished. When a suspect was caught, citizens took matters into their own hands and strung him up on the spot, asking questions later.

From Monterey to San Diego, bandits terrorized the countryside, singly and in groups. Some of the bandits were the subject of colorful folk tales that found their way into dime novels and eastern magazines. When fact and fiction were confused many bandits were portrayed as "Robin Hoods of the Old West," when in fact they were common murderers and thieves. Part of this confusion stemmed from the background of some of the more notorious Californios. Many were raised in wealthy families and had refined tastes and fine manners. Adding to this picture were interviews with the bandits themselves, usually conducted in jail, in which the bandits were seen as likeable fellows, wronged by society.

One who cultivated such an image was Tiburcio Vasquez.

Vasquez, who led a life of crime for nearly thirty years, was born in Monterey in 1835. He was educated and from a respected family. Of medium height, Vasquez had dark hair, a light complexion, and a dazzling smile. He always took pains with his appearance and became a favorite with the ladies.

In his own words, which appeared in the *Los Angeles Star* on May 16, 1874, Vasquez described his entrance into the world of crime:

My career grew out of the circumstances by which I was surrounded as I grew to manhood. I was in the habit of attending balls and parties given by the native Californians, into which the Americans, then beginning to become numerous, would force themselves and shove the native-born men aside, monopolizing the dances and the women. . .

A spirit of hatred and revenge took possession of me. I had numerous fights in defense of what I believed to be my rights and those of my countrymen. The officers were continually in pursuit of me. . .

I went to my mother and told her I intended to commence a different life. I asked for and obtained her blessing, and at once commenced the career of a robber.

Although the native Californios were treated poorly, particularly in social situations, Vasquez's biographers have a slightly different interpretation of his decision to lead a life of crime. According to Ralph Rambo, in his book *Trailing the California Bandit Tiburcio Vasquez*, the situation that prompted Vasquez to become a bandit occurred at a dance in a Monterey saloon. Vasquez had become friends with Anastacio Garcia, also known as Three-Fingered Jack, a well-known horse thief and robber. One night, when they and a companion went to the dance, Garcia got drunk and caused a disturbance. When the local constable intervened, he was killed by one of the trio. Garcia and Vasquez fled, but the companion, José Higuera, was caught and hanged by a mob.

Vasquez continued his career as a robber under the tutelage of Garcia, and then in the company of such notorious brigands as Juan Soto and Tomás Redondo (alias Procopio). During these years he spent time in prison for various minor crimes. Once he actually acted as the court interpreter during a trial in which he was the accused. Needless to say he was acquitted.

In 1870, after his release from San Quentin for attempted cattle theft, he took up residence in San Juan Bautista. There he moved in with the Abelardo Salazar family and soon was amorously involved with Salazar's wife, whom he would meet secretly on the outskirts of town. Vasquez finally ran off with the young woman and Salazar swore out a warrant for his arrest. Running into him one night in town, Salazar shot Vasquez

This old sycamore tree, located on Junipero Serra Street one mile north of San Juan Capistrano Mission, has the dubious distinction of being the "Bandits' Rendezvous Tree." Courtesy, Pamela Hallan-Gibson

in the side of the neck. Vasquez was able to escape and recover.

The bandit continued his career, marked by his special stamp. When robbing a stage or traveler he would order them to lie flat on the ground while he tied their hands and stole their goods. He would then profusely apologize for the inconvenience and promise to return the funds "with interest" at a later date.

Vasquez, in his interview, admitted to committing many crimes. But he also claimed that he was often a victim of circumstantial evidence, that his associations with various criminals were assumed rather than factual, and that this assumption of guilt had pushed him further into a life of crime.

On May 13, 1874, Vasquez was captured at Rancho La Brea by a posse sent by the Los Angeles County sheriff. He was returned to Santa Clara County for trial and spent several months in jail as a much-interviewed, much-visited celebrity. He was found guilty and was hanged March 19, 1875.

While his exploits in Northern California are better documented, it is well known that he made several forays into the future Orange County. In San Juan Capistrano, on Junipero Serra Road, there is a large sycamore tree called the Bandits' Rendezvous tree. It has long been associated with Vasquez, although his use of that tree to rally his companions is not documented.

Another undocumented but popular story in Orange County concerns a house in San Juan Capistrano that supposedly housed the famous bandit Joaquín Murieta. Although Murieta's exploits did not reach into Orange County there is a persistent story, handed down by the Rios family of San Juan Capistrano, of his friendship with Gregorio Rios. The story goes that whenever Joaquín needed a respite from the posses that constantly hunted him, he would make his way to San Juan Capistrano and quietly enter the Rios Adobe. A secret room in the attic held a candle and a bed for his use. He would leave as quietly as he came, a small pouch of gold coins the only evidence of his occupation.

Other bandits who frequented the territory were not so generous. But some were portrayed as just as romantic. One was Juan Flores.

Flores was reputed to be the scion of a wealthy, respected Santa Barbara family. His good manners and personal magnetism attracted many followers. Horse stealing put him in San Quentin, from which he escaped in 1856. With Pancho Daniel and fifty others whom he gathered he robbed and pillaged his way south. He chose San Juan Capistrano as his base, but in the end it proved an unlucky choice.

Flores' demise started with a visit to the store of Miguel Kraszewski. In a later interview, Kraszewski commented on Flores' politeness and likeable personality. Unfortunately the visit ended with the theft of a pistol, which led to a raid on the town and the killing of another merchant, George Pflugardt.

Juan Forster, who resided in Mission San Juan Capistrano, had gathered a number of townspeople behind the thick walls of the former courtyard. One of these was sent to Los Angeles to inform Sheriff James Barton of the activities in town.

Before the Flores incident ended, the sheriff and several of his men were killed, two posses hunted down the bandits, and many hangings took place. Rumors ran wild in Los Angeles that Flores would attack the town. For a time women and children were actually guarded in the local armory hall. Flores was eventually apprehended and hanged at public execution on February 14, 1857. The incident involving his gang and the aftermath of lynchings left a strain between Anglos and Californios for years to come.

Other bandits such as Manuel Marquez, who struck between San Juan Capistrano and Santa Ana, Jack Powers, known mainly for his exploits in the Santa Barbara area, and Saloman Pico, a black sheep of the famous Pico family, became quite famous in their day.

The acceptance of lawlessness and violence as inevitable was symptomatic of a society undergoing change. But the drought and the growth of outlying settlements eventually discouraged the rustling of cattle and horses. In addition settlers from the "civilized" parts of the country brought more formalized institutions and a respect for law and order.

Crime did not disappear, but the colorful bandits of the California frontier passed on. Some were reborn in the pages of novels that romanticized their lives and exploits, that in reality are best left in the darkened past.

appeared to remain unchanged, as though the rancheros would not let go of a system that had provided security and pleasure. They seemed unwilling to recognize a new social order characterized by the profit motive, interest rates, and saving for the future. They still operated their establishments like small, self-contained communities, providing for scores of dependents and letting tomorrow take care of itself.

In the 1850s Bernardo Yorba's ranch was the social center of the Santa Ana Valley. His fifty-room establishment, including a main house, school, winery, and areas for his skilled craftsmen, also included housing for thirty-two primary workers and more than 100 lesser employees. On nearby Rancho San Joaquín, José Sepúlveda continued to enjoy horse racing, gambling, and elegant clothes. He paid for his lifestyle through a series of mortgages, which he paid just as they were due by borrowing from someone else.

Andrés Pico, owner of Rancho La Habra, was not so lucky. Having too many notes due, he was forced to sell his land to Abel Stearns. A shrewd New Englander, Stearns became one of California's wealthiest merchants and landowners, but eventually also got caught in the credit trap. Natural disasters and declining markets made it increasingly more difficult to stay ahead of one's creditors. By the late 1850s the profit from one steer was only seven or eight dollars as opposed to seventy-five dollars during the height of the gold rush beef boom. Yet rancheros did nothing to improve their stock. They had enough trouble trying to keep what they had out of the hands of rustlers.

Rustling had always been a problem. As early as 1832 William Wolfskill had achieved notoriety by tracking a gang of Indian cattle thieves to Black Star Canyon where they were massacred without mercy. Rustling got worse during the gold rush when cattle prices were high. In 1851 the problem was so bad that the state legislature considered making rustling a capital offense.

But cattle thieves weren't the only criminals to plague Orange County. It was a lawless time when golden dreams seemed far away, particularly for those who had no land and no work. Unsuccessful miners, unemployed remnants of the army, young Californios who hated the land-grabbing Yankees, and Indians with no social standing in American society made up the bandit class that preyed on ranchos, settlements, and unwary travelers. Bandits such as Tiburcio Vasquez, Manuel Marquez, Pancho Daniel, Juan Flores, Jack Powers, and Joaquín Murieta were well-known names in Southern California. For a time the law seemed incapable of controlling the thievery, harassment, and murders that were a part of daily life. One of the most famous incidents in Orange County occurred in San Juan Capistrano in 1857.

Juan Flores, accompanied by members of the Manilas gang, stopped in San Juan Capistrano to visit his girlfriend while en route to Mexico. He had just escaped from San Quentin and needed supplies and ammunition he hoped Chola Martina could provide. He and some of his gang became bold and harassed some shopkeepers before invading the well-stocked store of George Pfluggardt. Firing shots, they hauled merchandise into the street and wouldn't let anyone in or out of town. Some people fled to the mission, the home of John Forster, for protection. Forster remained inside.

At nightfall Flores made his big move. He sent Chola Martina to Pfluggardt's store to redeem a shawl which she had pawned to get the shopkeeper to open his door. When he did, Martina lit a cigarette, the signal for the bandits to rush in. Pfluggardt was killed in the struggle and the bandits fled with the sup-

Above: *The Carpenter Adobe, shown here in 1936, was one of the many isolated adobes populating the hill and canyon regions of the Santa Ana Mountains. It was located in Black Star Canyon, which is to the north of Silverado Canyon. Courtesy, First American Title Insurance Company*

Left: *These spurs belonged to Juan Forster, one of the largest property owners in early Orange County. Courtesy, Charles W. Bowers Memorial Museum*

plies. In the meantime, a messenger had been sent to Los Angeles to get help. Sheriff James Barton, his deputies, and a few other law enforcers set out for San Juan Capistrano the day after the messenger arrived, but were ambushed by Flores near Laguna Canyon. After removing the victims' valuables, the bandits rode off to hide in the Santa Ana Mountains.

Two posses pursued the bandits. When one of their number was caught and turned informer, the gang was tracked down. Flores and two others were caught and taken to the home of Teodocio Yorba, but Flores escaped in the night. The other members of his gang were not so lucky—they were hanged from the nearest tree when news of Flores' escape reached their captors. Flores was recaptured in a few days near Simi Pass and was taken to Los Angeles to stand trial. But the trial never took place. On February 14, 1857, Flores was hanged by vigilantes at a public execution. This account appeared in the *Los Angeles Star*:

The prisoner walked with firmness and seemed as composed as anyone in the crowd. The distance from the jail to the hill on which the scaffold was erected is about a quarter of a mile. The prisoner was dressed in white pants, light vest and black merino sack coat. He was a young man, about twenty-two years of age, and of pleasing countenance. There was nothing in his appearance to indicate the formidable bandit which he had proved himself to be.

Flores turned to the crowd and told them he was ready to die, that he had committed many crimes, and was repentant. The trap door opened but the fall was too short. Flores struggled for a time before his body became lifeless and still.

It would take more settlers, more towns, and better communication before the law

The Don Juan Forster family lived in the San Juan Capistrano Mission for approximately twenty years. Forster purchased the property in 1845 after the mission properties were broken up. His grandson, Don Marcos Enrique Forster, stands in front of the room where he was baptized at the mission in 1865. This photo was taken in 1935, and is part of the Conde-Yorba Collection. Alfonso Yorba, who bicycled from Santa Ana to Capistrano in the 1930s and 1940s, collected old documents, rare books, photographs, and conducted interviews of Capistrano residents. He donated his extensive collection to be enjoyed by the community. Courtesy, Conde-Yorba Collection

could adequately protect society. Settlements were still too isolated and towns too few. In 1851 Los Angeles County was divided into six townships. Two of these were in what would become Orange County: one township was Santa Ana, the other, San Juan Capistrano. Both were judicial townships covering vast areas. The "seats" of the townships were Bernardo Yorba's ranch headquarters and the village of San Juan Capistrano. These sites also had the two townships' only schools. Both had the same teacher in the early years, Thomas J. Scully, who spent three months in one place then rode off to spend three months at the other. Instruction was given in Spanish, which was still the predominant language.

The 1850 Census listed only 3,530 people for Los Angeles County, indicating that except for the more prominent rancheros most of the people were illiterate. Cultural pursuits, practically non-existent, were limited to private homes, the two township centers, and faraway Los Angeles. Though Bernardo Yorba had his own chapel, the main church for the area was still at Mission San Juan Capistrano where the Serra Chapel was in use and a resident priest maintained.

Forster still lived in the mission, but his tenure was coming to an end. During the Land Commission hearings Bishop Joseph Sadoc Alemany petitioned the commission for the return of the missions confiscated by the Mexican government. The commission ruled

in his favor and Mission San Juan Capistrano was returned to the Catholic Church. Forster and his family remained until 1864, one year before the patent, signed by President Abraham Lincoln, finally arrived. He then took his family to Rancho Santa Margarita in San Diego County, which he had acquired from his relatives, the Picos.

Forster, one of the largest property owners in Orange and San Diego counties with more than 200,000 acres, survived the financial pressures incurred by the defense of his land titles. But even he would be strained to the limit by the events of the next decade—events conceived by nature, not man. The decade of the 1860s would culminate with the end of the rancho system and the beginning of a new promise for Orange County.

These tourists are shown in this 1910 photograph enjoying a visit to Mission San Juan Capistrano. Courtesy, Anaheim Public Library

*During the 1860s and 1870s sheep ranches ranged through-
out much of Orange County, including the Bastanchury
Ranch in the La Habra Valley seen in this 1870s photograph.
Large herds of sheep also ranged on the Irvine Ranch to the
south. Courtesy, Anaheim Public Library*

The Decline
of the
Old Order

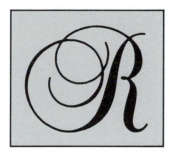

ancheros of the 1850s understood horses, laws of the plains, and family obligations. They knew the current price of cattle, the name of the best saddlemaker, and the dance steps to the *varsuovianna.* They did not know, nor did they care, about American banking policies. Compound interest rates were a mystery and a shock. And when notes came due and could not be paid, they found themselves without land and their creditors without honor.

One who lost his land as a result of his debts was José Serrano of Rancho Cañada de los Alisos. Another was Teodocio Yorba of Rancho Lomas de Santiago, who sold his 47,000-acre ranch to William Wolfskill for $7,000. Yet another was Andrés Pico who sold his portion of Rancho

The Rancho Los Coyotes Adobe, seen here in about 1886, was acquired by Abel Stearns, an early ranchero. Courtesy, Anaheim Public Library

La Habra to Abel Stearns to satisfy a debt. Stearns, who loaned money far and wide, was able to add several ranches to his collection through prudent purchase or by collection of debts. In Orange County alone he acquired Rancho Los Coyotes, Rancho Bolsa Chica, Rancho Los Alamitos, Rancho Las Bolsas, and parts of Rancho Santiago de Santa Ana. He also purchased 30,672 acres of Rancho San Juan Cajón de Santa Ana from Juan Pacífico Ontiveros for $6,000 in the midst of the cattle drought of the 1860s.

Ontiveros was luckier than most because he looked ahead and planned for his future. Perhaps his bad experience in the Land Commission tribunals had made him more cautious; perhaps he merely wanted a change of scene. For whatever reason in 1856 Ontiveros pur-chased a new rancho near San Luis Obispo. He and his sons took 1,200 head of cattle up and began building a home on the property. The following year Ontiveros received a curi-ous request. George Hansen, a surveyor who had helped survey the ranch boundaries dur-ing the title confirmation hearings, asked Ontiveros if he would sell a portion of his Rancho San Juan Cajón de Santa Ana to a group of German immigrants who wished to organize a vineyard colony. Ontiveros consid-ered it, discussed it with his German son-in-law Augustus Langenberger, and agreed. The purchase was made—1,165 acres at two dol-lars per acre. The colony became known as Anaheim.

The idea for the colony originated with two musicians-turned-wine merchants, John Frohling and Charles Kohler. Their business venture had become so profitable that they decided to sponsor a colony to raise grapes so they would have a constant supply. Frohling

and Kohler sent Hansen to San Francisco to locate a group of German immigrants who might be interested in the idea. Since San Francisco was the gathering place for settlers entering California it was not difficult to find interested Germans and the Los Angeles Vineyard Society was soon formed.

The proposal was to purchase the land, lay it out in small farms of twenty acres each, and plant it in vineyards. All the work would be done under one manager who would try to keep costs down. Each of the fifty colonists would pay $1,400, which would include water rights. With the group in agreement, Hansen and Frohling paid for the land, deeded it to the Vineyard Society, and purchased an additional easement to the Santa Ana River for water access. Then Hansen got to work, laying out the community in fifty twenty-acre lots plus fifty home lots and fourteen village lots for public buildings. Hansen hired Indians to clear the land and dig the five-mile ditch to

Above: *In 1850 Petra Ontiveros married Augustus Langenberger, a German immigrant. Seven years later Petra's father, Juan Pacífico Ontiveros, sold to George Hansen the property on which Anaheim was to be founded. By the time the first settlers arrived in 1859, Petra and Augustus Langenberger had founded Anaheim's first store in an adobe building on Center Street, which was later Lincoln Avenue. Courtesy, Anaheim Public Library*

Above left: *Civil engineer and surveyor George Hansen arrived in Los Angeles in 1853. After borrowing $100 to purchase some equipment, Hansen proceeded to survey much of Los Angeles County and the entire townsite of Anaheim. Courtesy, Anaheim Public Library*

Above: *This residence, which belonged to Augustus Langenberger, was located on Sycamore and Lemon streets, and boasted a beautiful and peaceful garden in the settlement of Anaheim. Courtesy, Anaheim Public Library*

Left: *Clementine Zimmerman Schmidt Langenberger was Augustus Langenberger's second wife. Arriving in Anaheim in 1860, she divorced her first husband, Theodore, in 1873 on the grounds of desertion. In 1874 she married Langenberger, who, along with his partner Benjamin Dryfus, owned a thriving dry goods store. Courtesy, Anaheim Public Library*

Facing page, top: *Amelia Hammes Frohling, shown here in 1895, was a member of the first family to arrive in Anaheim in September 1859. She tells in her memoirs of the trip down the coast on the steamer, The Senator, transferring to a smaller steamer in San Pedro Bay, then to a row boat, and finally being carried ashore on the shoulders of an Indian. She became Anaheim's first bride in November 1859, when she married one of Anaheim's founders, John Frohling. Courtesy, Anaheim Public Library*

Facing page, bottom: *Augustus Langenberger's two-story adobe, shown here in this 1858 photograph, served as residence, general store, bank, and headquarters for the Wells Fargo Express Company. Located on Center Street, the adobe was the hub of activity of early Anaheim and was the principal trading center between Mission San Gabriel and Mission San Juan Capistrano. Courtesy, Anaheim Public Library*

Above: *This 1896 photograph of the W.L. Hale home on East Chapman in Fullerton features the Hale family in the foreground and the winery at the far left. Courtesy, Fullerton Public Library*

Facing page: *These three workers shown bottling wine for the Ernest Browning Winery are a prime example of the new colonists in Orange County. Coming from a variety of backgrounds, these colonists learned new skills to help fulfill the needs of their blossoming agricultural society. Courtesy, Anaheim Public Library*

the river. Next, he had vineyards planted with eight acres of every lot planted in mission grapes. He then fenced the entire community with willows. At the end of three years the land was ready for its owners.

The colonists who set out for the new settlement in 1859 to raise grapes were not farmers. They were watchmakers, mechanics, blacksmiths, shoemakers—people from many trades and professions. There was even a poet. They all shared dreams of owning land and being their own masters. The Anaheim colonists were filled with ideals and spurred by a promise—to work hard and make their new life a success.

With that vow, they set out for Anaheim. Upon their arrival they participated in a lottery to see which property would be theirs. Since the lots were valued differently and since each owner had originally put in the same amount of money, each either paid a larger assessment to the company or received money back, depending on the value of the lot. Much trading went on amongst the colo-

nists, with property changing hands when one who drew a lot with a higher assessment could not afford to pay. Lumber was acquired for houses, town lots were sold to merchants like Augustus Langenberger, a school was built, and the remaining assets of the company were deeded to the Anaheim Water Company, which had the same membership. The Vineyard Society was then dissolved and the town officially launched.

Life was not easy for the early settlers. Loneliness and isolation were the most difficult problems to overcome. Yet one could look out in the evening after a hard day's work and see the neat rows of vineyards and know they were a good source of income, that markets were plentiful, and that one's property was appreciating. And some of the problems of the day would not seem as great.

But isolation was not the colonists' only concern. The people of the Anaheim Colony had some serious problems to solve. One was water which, despite the ditch, was a constant worry, and the other was transportation. Products were only profitable if they could be taken to market; though markets were available, getting to them was proving a difficult and costly problem. To solve this dilemma the colonists built their own port and called it Anaheim Landing. The location they selected was Alamitos Bay near Seal Beach. Since it was too shallow to let ships come in, a wharf was built and cargo was taken in and out by means

Pansy Pellegrin, the child in front, is pictured here with her family around 1900. She was a descendant of the Hammes family. After this house burned in 1933, Pellegrin wrote that the house, built in 1859, contained a center hall that ran from front to back, papered walls and balloon ceilings, cornices over the windows, lace curtains in the living and dining rooms, and drapes in the bedrooms. The kitchen was in a separate building in the back. Courtesy, Anaheim Public Library

The Dietrich Strodhoff residence, built in 1863, was located at the corner of Lemon and North streets in Anaheim. Adele Strodhoff, pictured here as a young girl in the foreground, later married Fritz Yungbluth. Courtesy, Anaheim Public Library

of small, shallow-bottomed boats called lighters. In 1864 a group of investors formed the Anaheim Lighter Company which had two boats and a warehouse for goods storage. Trade was maintained with a coastal steamer that stopped at the port until 1867 when floods changed the course of the San Gabriel River that emptied into the bay. The company moved its facilities a mile and a half south, where it remained for many years.

Anaheim was a successful colony that continued to grow. In addition to its original acreage, it acquired 233 acres more toward the end of 1857 and another 1,398 in 1863. That same year Juan Pacífico Ontiveros sold the rest of his land to Abel Stearns, reserving 3,900 acres for his two sons. He then moved permanently to his ranch in the North.

The property assigned to the sons did not remain long in their hands. It was sold im-mediately to their brother-in-law, Augustus Langenberger, who in turn sold it to Daniel Kraemer. Kraemer was an early settler who had come to the area in response to a letter from friends in Anaheim. Deciding to stay, Kraemer brought his family from Illinois to the former Ontiveros adobe in 1867. Others who came in this period included Joseph Pleasants, who worked on the Wolfskill Ranch in 1861 and eventually settled in Santiago Canyon, and Sam Shrewsbury, who built a kiln in Limestone Canyon but eventually switched to honey production near Pleasants'

Looking west down Center Street from the corner of Los Angeles Street, this view of Anaheim in the late 1800s depicts the success of this settlement. The Goodman & Rimpau store is located at the far left across the street from the Langenberger Building and the Planter's Hotel. Courtesy, Anaheim Public Library

property. The early settlers changed more than the vistas and landscape of Orange County—they changed its heart and soul. But it was not easy. In their efforts they encountered death and destruction.

It began with rain.

Rain was usually welcome in semi-arid Orange County, where rancheros dug ditches from nearby rivers to irrigate crops and for household use. But on Christmas Eve in 1861 it began to rain hard and didn't stop for thirty days.

"Never before in the memory of the oldest inhabitant, had there been such floods," wrote historian James Miller Guinn in *Historical and Biographical Record of Southern California*. "The Santa Ana River for a time rivaled the Father of Waters in magnitude. In the town of Anaheim, four miles from the river, the water ran four feet deep and spread in an unbroken sheet to the Coyote Hills, three miles beyond."

There was widespread destruction of life and property. Soil, livestock, and loose belongings were swept away. In Southern California alone more than 200,000 cattle were lost in the floods. When the waters receded and the sun came out everyone rejoiced. But their joy was short-lived. They would not see much rain again for two years. While the floods caused damage, the droughts completed the destruction of an entire social system, one that had lived beyond its years on the glittering promises of self-delusion.

The droughts scorched the land until grass turned brown and the raging rivers of a season before dried into sluggish streams. Cattle, parched beyond endurance, roamed across the hills, their shrunken bodies painful to carry, looking for grass which had long-since shriveled to dust. Those rancheros who could, drove their cattle to better water sources. Others sold their stock at sacrificial prices.

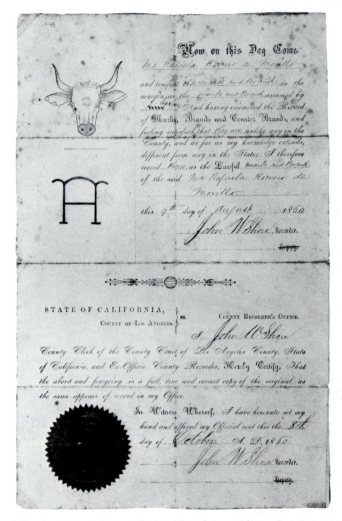

This document registers the brand and ear markings for Maria Rafaela Romero de Morillo in August 1860. When marking cattle, ear markings were as distinctive as brands and each ranch had its own registered pattern of ear clipping. The document reads, "Now on this day come Maria Rafaela Romero de Morillo and tendered the mark and brand in the margin as the mark and brand assumed by her and having examined the record of Marks, Brands and County Brands, and feeling satisfied that they are unlike any in the County and as far as my knowledge extends, different from any in the State; I therefore record them as the lawful mark and brand of the said Maria Rafaela Romero de Morillo." Courtesy, Conde-Yorba Collection

Some had little choice but to either slaughter their cattle or to sit by and helplessly watch them die.

In 1880, Albert Wilson, in Thompson and West's *History of Los Angeles County,* wrote:

Cattle died by the thousands and the plains were strewn with their carcasses. Generally the hides were stripped from them, but in some cases it is said that even the hides were worthless through extreme starvation. In April 1864 50,000 head of cattle were auctioned in Santa Barbara at 37.5 cents each. In view of this fearful loss, it seems almost like mockery to read one year later of grass waist-high throughout the country, and the cattle that should enjoy it, all dead of starvation.

More disasters were yet to come.

Smallpox raged throughout Orange County during the drought years. The death register at Mission San Juan Capistrano listed 129 deaths between November 16 and December 31, 1862—all Indians. Seventy more would die before the end of the epidemic, though some efforts were made to vaccinate any person who wished it. The disease took its toll in the ranchos, but the Anaheim Colony escaped, having a resident physician who saw that vaccinations were administered and precautions taken.

Drought and disease took their tolls and moved on, leaving behind an economy that had come to a standstill. Rancheros had no money and no cattle. They had only the land that was taxed with regularity by the state of California, causing their names to appear frequently on the delinquent tax rolls. Taxation policies had long been an issue with rancheros of Southern California, who felt that they were carrying excessive burdens placed on them by legislators from the North. In 1851 and 1859 they had attempted to divide the

state into two separate entities, but were unsuccessful. Now it was too late. Land began to devaluate and parcels had to be sold. What the Land Act started, the droughts finished. Those who had managed to survive the first could not hang on any longer.

The American Civil War probably did as much to promote Orange County settlement as did the aftermath of the drought. Wounded in spirit and without land, many young men packed up and joined the movement west. They were encouraged by travel guides and promotional campaigns that painted golden promises onto canvasses of cheap land, plentiful water, and a healthful climate. Many hoped to homestead and buy unoccupied land from the government at $1.25 an acre. Yet

Above: *Gabriel Allen was an early settler on the mesa, which later became the area of Costa Mesa. He was once the proud owner of the Estancia Adobe. Courtesy, Costa Mesa Historical Society*

Above left: *The Estancia Adobe of Costa Mesa is shown as it looked in 1969. The adobe was once owned by early settler Diego Sepúlveda and later by Gabriel Allen. Courtesy, Costa Mesa Historical Society*

when they arrived they found the picture marred by what the promoters did not tell them. Water was not plentiful, land titles were so confused that purchasers had to assume that they were clear, transportation systems were totally inadequate to get crops to markets, and money was very tight with interest rates that sometimes were as high as 4 or 5 percent per month.

Nevertheless they came, from the East and from Europe, in increasing numbers after the completion of the transcontinental railroad in 1869. Some still came by ship and by wagon train, using traditional routes. Those who found their way to Orange County usually stopped in Los Angeles, San Bernardino, or San Diego first, then made their way to Anaheim or San Juan Capistrano, the only two settlements just after the Civil War. But change was coming. Old ranchos were purchased and subdivided into tracts suitable for farming. Land prices were rising again. And settlers were encouraged to raise traditional crops such as wheat, barley, corn, and grapes.

Cattle as a major industry was gone, although some efforts to revive it on a smaller scale were successful. The sheep industry was enjoying a boom during this period because of the unavailability of cotton during the Civil War, and had successfully replaced cattle on the open ranges. Prominent sheepmen in Orange County were Jotham and Llewelyn Bixby, Thomas and Benjamin Flint, and James Irvine. In 1866 the Flint-Bixby-Irvine interests bought Rancho Los Cerritos, and parts of Rancho Palos Verdes and Rancho Los Alamitos. They also bought Rancho San Joaquín, Lomas de Santiago, and a part of Rancho Santiago de Santa Ana. José Sepúlveda had sold his ranch, his debts finally catching up with him, for $18,000.

Wool production was profitable because the climate was generally good, food was plentiful, and sheep were not expensive to raise. Extremes such as floods or droughts caused trouble, as did grasshoppers who ate the grass, and predators who ate the sheep. Most flocks were tended by shepherds who usually had about 1,000 sheep to look after; if possible, the animals were corralled at night. According to historian Robert Glass Cleland, it cost about thirty-five cents a year to keep a sheep yielding about six pounds of wool that could bring up to thirty-five cents per pound. Wool was shipped from Anaheim Landing to San Francisco, then on to Eastern markets. Even inferior varieties were marketable, though stockmen like Irvine made an effort to improve the stock by importing purebred Spanish merinos costing as much as $500 each in

the 1860s. Other early sheepmen were William Wolfskill, who purchased Teodocio Yorba's ranch in 1860 and later sold to Flint, Bixby, and Irvine, and Domingo Bastanchury, who leased land in the La Habra Valley from Abel Stearns for ten cents a head per year. More sheepmen would come in the 1870s, and those who were established increased their holdings. But the real wealth was in land. People were beginning to look at their holdings, and those of others, in terms of plat maps to be filed and promises to be made.

Rancho Santiago de Santa Ana, the only Spanish-period land grant to be made entirely within Orange County, was partitioned in 1868. More than 100 people—Yorba and Peralta heirs and persons to whom heirs had sold interests—claimed an undivided interest in the property. The partition took six months and when it ended, those who had received portions of the ranch, in addition to family, included the names of many who would mold the future of Orange County—Frederick Koll, James McFadden, Jacob Ross, Columbus Tustin, the company of Flint, Bixby, and Irvine, Andrew Glassell, and Albert Chapman.

A new era was about to begin.

THE PROMISE CHALLENGED

PART II

Irrigation played an important part in the early development of Orange County. An example of irrigation, shown here in the late 1800s, is the outlet of the Tuffree Reservoir built by the Anaheim Union Water Company. Courtesy, Anaheim Public Library

New Towns, New Promises

ich soil, good climate, and cheap land made Orange County of the 1870s an attractive place for its first promoters. Water was still a problem, but one that could be surmounted with careful planning, airtight agreements, and a little venture capital. New owners of partitioned ranchos strode with confidence through the mustard fields, their surveyors not far behind, marking the spots where the hotel would be, the general store, and the school. They were ambitious and sure, and for some the promise of riches was secondary to the dreams of creating a grand city in the wilderness.

Such a man was William Spurgeon.

Spurgeon was a native of Kentucky who came to California a few years after the gold rush to try his hand at mining. In 1869 he and Ward Bradford purchased a seventy-four-acre tract that was once a part of Rancho Santiago de Santa Ana. They paid eight dollars per acre and thereafter divided their property. Spurgeon received the easterly thirty-three acres and platted a new city that he called Santa Ana. He filed his tract map in December 1870 and began selling lots.

Spurgeon enjoyed great success, selling fifty lots in the first few months, although he gave away several others. He opened a general store and post office at Fourth and Broadway to provide the necessities; he even cut a road through dense fields of shoulder-high wild mustard to the main road so the stagecoach would stop in his new community. While Spurgeon could boast that his town was served by an artesian well, he soon heard complaints that it did not provide enough water for irrigation. To solve that problem the Semi-Tropic Water Company was organized in 1873. Its purpose was to extend to Santa Ana the Chapman Ditch, a canal that had been dug as far as Orange. This accomplished, "Uncle Billy" Spurgeon sat back and watched the seeds of his ambition sprout and grow, confident that Santa Ana's golden promise would be fulfilled.

The next stop on the stage line running between Los Angeles and San Diego was Tustin, founded in 1867. Columbus Tustin and Nelson Stafford purchased 1,300 acres of Rancho Santiago de Santa Ana for $2,000; Tustin took the eastern portion and platted his town. Like Spurgeon, he gave away some of his lots in the beginning to attract buyers. He, too, was successful, particularly after the Chapman Ditch was further extended to his settlement.

The ditch, providing water to many communities on the east side of the Santa Ana River, was originally constructed by Alfred Chapman and Andrew Glassell. They were the founders

Above: *William Spurgeon plotted the city of Santa Ana from part of the tract of the old Rancho Santiago de Santa Ana. Courtesy, Anaheim Public Library*

Facing page: *William Spurgeon built this small redwood board-and-batten store building soon after he laid out the townsite of Santa Ana. It served as the first post office and general store, and was located at Fourth and West (Broadway) streets. Courtesy, History Room, Santa Ana Public Library*

This family stopped to have their portrait taken on an outing to one of Orange County's lovely beaches. Courtesy, Fullerton Public Library

of Richland, which later became Orange. Glassell's brother, William, surveyed the property—a farming community of 600 acres situated around a central townsite of forty acres and served by water from the nearby Santa Ana River.

With the establishment of three farming communities south of the Santa Ana River, the time seemed right to open a seaport to take products out and bring supplies in. The place chosen for this enterprise was San Joaquín Slough, called New Port after 1870, and the persons who decided to undertake the task were Robert and James McFadden.

James McFadden had acquired land as a result of the partition of Rancho Santiago de Santa Ana. In 1868 he sold a portion located

in upper Newport Bay's Gospel Swamp, so named because of a preacher who resided there, and hoped it would develop into a prosperous farming community. He left Orange County for a time, then returned and purchased additional land. In 1873 he applied for a permit from the state for twenty acres of frontage on the bay that for a short time had been used as a port by two early traders, Samuel Dunnells and William Abbott. He then reached an agreement with the owners of Rancho San Joaquin, who had operated a rival wharf dur-

Located near Anaheim, this early pumping station provided much needed water to the nearby settlements. Courtesy, Anaheim Public Library

ing Dunnells and Abbotts' time, and ordered a steam schooner called the *Newport* to serve the wharf. The *Newport* arrived in late 1875 and entered the bay every two weeks for the next three years. By then the McFaddens had established a thriving lumber business at their landing and had enlarged their warehouse and improved their road. Despite disagreements with Rancho San Joaquín, a dangerous shifting sandbar at their harbor's entrance, and rate wars with the railroad, the McFaddens continued to expand their activities and serve Orange County for nearly three decades.

The landing did not just serve farmers from the Santa Ana Valley. It was also available to the farmers of the Stearns Ranchos west of the Santa Ana River whose settlements were beginning to form in the 1870s.

Abel Stearns, owner of more than 177,000 acres in 1868, found himself in danger of losing his holdings. Some of his properties had already been claimed by creditors who loaned him money to see him through the drought, and other loans were now due. To keep himself financially solvent, Stearns agreed to turn over all but a small portion of his property to a syndicate headed by his friend, Alfred Robinson. In return, Stearns received a $50,000 cash advance to pay his debts and $1.50 per acre for every acre sold plus one-eighth of all the profits made in the land sales. The syndicate organized themselves as the Los Angeles and San Bernardino Land Company, but were popularly referred to as the Stearns Ranchos. And though Stearns' deal turned out to be a wise one, he lived only three years after its consummation and never saw the budding communities that would someday grow into important cities.

Among the early settlements on the Stearns Ranchos was Westminster, started in 1870 by Presbyterian minister Lemuel P. Webber. He hoped for settlers who had a strong interest in

Above: *Placed in slated trays, walnuts were dipped in bleach and then laid out to dry in the sun. Courtesy, Charles W. Bowers Memorial Museum*

Facing page, top: *Strawberries were one of the new fruit crops brought into Orange County in the late 1890s. Workers are shown picking strawberries in this expansive field. Courtesy, Anaheim Public Library*

Facing page, bottom: *Apricots were placed in drying racks after being picked in this apricot grove located north of a Santa Fe depot. On the average, workers earned approximately sixty cents per day. Courtesy, Anaheim Public Library*

Orange pickers stop for a break at the Rimpau Grove, which is now the current site of the Anaheim Public Library on West Broadway. Courtesy, Anaheim Public Library

As the center of an active farming community, Santa Ana was one of the major agricultural centers in Orange County. This photo was taken in 1900 in front of the Santa Ana Mercantile Company. Courtesy, History Room, Santa Ana Public Library

religion, education, and temperance. His colony was divided into forty-acre tracts and proved very productive, even after Webber's death in 1874. Land was irrigated by artesian wells, natural underground springs that produced a plentiful supply of water, relieving settlers of one worry that plagued most others.

Another settlement served by artesian wells was Garden Grove, which attracted settlers since 1870 and acquired the trappings of a village after the arrival of Alonzo G. Cook in 1874. Other communities that had similar beginnings were La Habra and Placentia. These cities were also settled early, but they did not have a secure water supply, and so they were developed at a later time. The settlements of Orangethorpe and Fairview (near Anaheim)

were already in existence, as was Savanna (near Buena Park). But these communities disappeared as others took their places.

Most Orange County settlers did not live in established communities. Most bought isolated property planted in barley, wheat, or grapes, or one of the newer crops such as walnuts, oranges, or lemons. Walnuts were introduced into the area in 1870 by Joel Congdon, a settler in San Juan Capistrano; oranges were first

Windmills were not a common sight in Orange County. The Starbuck family is pictured here in the backyard with their treasured windmill and tank house. The house was located on West Commonwealth Avenue, which is now the site of the Fullerton Public Library. Courtesy, Fullerton Public Library

set out by W.N. Hardin of Anaheim in 1870 when he extracted seeds from a barrel of rotting Tahitian oranges and was rewarded by sprouting trees. Richard H. Gilman of Placentia is credited with having the first commercial grove of Valencias, and lemons were first planted by A.D. Bishop. Other crops included raisins (which flourished near Orange), apricots, corn, and experimental crops of cotton, bananas, and tobacco. Orange County's soil would grow just about anything—as long as it had water.

The problems with water seemed endless. There were squabbles over when and how much water was to be used, and by whom. There was the cost and inefficiency of the ditches, the threat of a flood or a drought, and jurisdictional battles between companies. Sometimes battles went on for years, while land dried up as fast as the monetary resources of its owners. A typical example of these fights was the battle over the Santa Ana River which served many settlements and was diverted by many different companies. Two companies that controlled areas on opposite banks were the Anaheim Water Company and the Semi-Tropic Water Company, later called the Santa Ana Valley Irrigation Company. Problems intensified in the 1870s with the formation of the Cajón Water District.

According to historian Virginia Carpenter farmers in the Placentia area were not served by a formal canal, although they had been promised one by the Stearns Ranchos. In 1875 they began work on their own and formed the Cajón Water District the following February. When completed, the ditch they planned was twelve miles long, eleven feet wide at the top (five feet at the bottom), and two feet deep. Built by Chinese laborers from San Francisco, the canal cost $25,000. In 1876 the Stearns Ranchos finally formed its own water company, filed suit against the Cajón, and took the

Above: *W.L. Hale pauses in his buggy in front of the Botsford Ranch. The use of irrigation can be seen in the field. Courtesy, Fullerton Public Library*

Left: *The Zanjero, who regulated the supply of irrigation water running through open ditches, was considered an important person in Anaheim. Rafael Navarro, shown here with his horse, Tom, served in this capacity for several years. A concrete irrigation box, once part of Anaheim's extensive irrigation system, still exists on Sycamore Street in Anaheim. Courtesy, Anaheim Public Library*

canal. Work stopped. By 1877 it still hadn't restarted. Desperate for the water and with their financial resources depleted, the farmers re-formed as the Cajón Irrigation Company and filed suit against the Stearns' water company to regain the canal. At the same time, the Anaheim Water Company and the Semi-Tropic were in court over the same water rights. The major controversy, very simply, was whether the water belonged to the first person to use it, or if everyone along the way had right to what flowed past. The suits were finally settled after many appeals in favor of the latter concept. The Cajón group continued work on their canal, having offered half to the Anaheim Water Company, and finally completed it in 1878. When the two partners squabbled over amounts of water allotted to each, the courts consolidated the two warring entities and several peripheral companies into the Anaheim Union Water Company, thus ending years of fighting.

Left: *Anaheim Union Water Company's flume Number 8 helped to irrigate the dry land of the surrounding communities. Courtesy, Anaheim Public Library*

Below left: *Drilling for water in the 1890s provided the life-giving substance that made the desert bloom. Courtesy, Anaheim Public Library*

Below: *Members of the Anaheim community gathered together in 1894 for a picnic in Santiago Canyon, enjoying a little sport and relaxation. Courtesy, Anaheim Public Library*

Above: *Members of Anaheim's State Guard Company G entertain at an 1885 picnic in Santiago Canyon. Courtesy, Anaheim Public Library*

Facing page: *Sunday school children posed with their teachers in front of the Anaheim First Presbyterian Church in 1893. Courtesy, Anaheim Public Library*

Water wasn't the only worry for early settlers. There were pests, droughts, and financial uncertainty. The recession of 1875 closed many banks, the drought of 1876-1877 was ruinous to the sheep industry, and there was still a lack of markets and poor transportation for farm products. The Southern Pacific Railroad had finally extended its line to the outskirts of Anaheim in 1875, vowing not to enter the town until a fee was paid. The community of Santa Ana paid the necessary fee and obtained a station in 1877 along with Southern Pacific's exorbitant freight charges. The railroad brought more than freight opportunities and potential land purchasers. It also brought communication and made the world a little smaller. By 1880 most settlers had a school, church, and general store within a day's drive. There was usually a post office, a blacksmith, and sometimes even a doctor

Typical of those seen in larger towns, this store offered a variety of goods. Cornstarch, ingredients for baking and candy making, chewing gum—Adams Tutti-Fruiti or Pepsin—candy, several kinds of tobacco, and tonics were among the available items at C.H. Schaefer's candy shop in Anaheim. Courtesy, Anaheim Public Library

Students and teachers posed in front of the Fullerton Elementary and Union High School, formerly the Fullerton Grammar School, in 1897. Courtesy, Fullerton Public Library

Above: *The first schoolbus system in Orange County as established in 1910. This bus is carrying students to Fullerton Union High School. Courtesy, Fullerton Public Library*

Right: *Many churches were built to serve the blossoming communities in Orange County. The First Presbyterian Church of Fullerton was built in 1900 at the corner of Commonwealth and Malden. Courtesy, Fullerton Public Library*

Santa Ana's first stores were made of redwood shipped from
Northern California. Between 1880 and 1890, these wooden
buildings were replaced with brick buildings. S.W. Smith,
right, and his son were in the undertaking business for many
years. The firm eventually became known as Smith and Tuthill Mortuary. Courtesy, History Room, Santa Ana Public
Library

Above: *Jim Gardiner and his companions pose in front of the Eureka Stables, which Gardiner established to serve the livery needs of the Fullerton community. Courtesy, Fullerton Public Library*

Right: *The Fullerton Grammar School was built in 1889 to fill the educational needs of the community. These children posed for an Arbor Day portrait in 1890. Courtesy, Fullerton Public Library*

Facing page: *This view of the interior of the Fullerton Post Office in 1912 shows clerks Henry Dyckman, right, and Charles Clark, left, at work. Courtesy, Fullerton Public Library*

While trailing a fugitive into the Santa Ana Mountains, United States Deputy Marshall Jonathan Dunlap entered a canyon and stumbled upon oxidized silver ore lying on the surface of the ground. He staked out his claim to the Blue Light Mine, which proved to be the richest silver mine in the district. Courtesy, First American Title Insurance Company

nearby. But best of all there were neighbors—people to take with you on a picnic, or to visit after church. Spending the day in the field digging irrigation ditches or standing over a boiling cauldron of laundry didn't seem as bad when there were people with whom you could share your concerns and your news. Orange County, not yet a county in its own right, was beginning to grow up and although the golden promise was still elusive, many believed it was within reach.

For some the promise took a different form, one that was not always understood or tolerated.

The Societas Fraternia, or Placentia Grass Eaters as they were called by their detractors, was an organization founded by George Hinde, who brought his family from England in 1876 and settled in the Placentia area. A spiritualist, he built a fourteen-room mansion that supposedly had rooms without corners in order to discourage evil spirits who might hide in them. Hinde settled down to farming. Two years later he teamed with Dr. Louis Schlesinger, who took over leadership of the vegetarian commune Hinde had founded and called it the Societas Fraternia. Members lived on a diet of uncooked fruits and vegetables, had property in common, and did not believe in marriage. And although they professed to

engage in sexual activities only for the sake of procreation, their reputation spread throughout the territory as a group that practiced free love and other "evils." People's opinions were confirmed in 1879 by the news that the Hinde group had starved a baby to death. Although acquitted, he and his group were viewed with suspicion even after the departure of Schlesinger in 1883. Despite the ostracism he encountered, Hinde continued producing prizewinning loquats, avocados, and persimmons, and introduced the Placentia Perfection, for many years one of the most popular varieties of walnuts.

While the Grass Eaters provided the most titillating gossip, there was much going on in the rest of the county. Coal and then silver were discovered in the Santa Ana Mountains in the late 1870s. The latter created several mines, the most prominent being the Dunlap

The Silverado Blue Light Mine was formed during the coal and silver boom of the late 1870s in the Santa Ana Mountains. Shown here is an entrance to the once flourishing mine. Courtesy, Anaheim Public Library

In 1889 James Irvine, Jr., rode his highwheeler from San Francisco to San Diego, stopping at the Irvine Ranch to look at the huge property he had inherited from his father in 1886. Courtesy, First American Title Insurance Company

Blue Light Mine. It also created the boom town of Silverado, which during its height claimed three hotels, seven saloons, and a tent city rivalling the gold rush days. There was also activity on Rancho San Joaquín, where James Irvine had bought out his partners to become sole owner in 1876. The selling price was reported to be $150,000 and some newspapers of the day, printing details of the sale, advocated the breakup of the ranch that they felt was too large to be under one ownership. There was also activity in Anaheim—there would be more as the new decade of the 1880s progressed.

Anaheim, a flourishing incorporated city by 1880, gained a reputation as a health resort. Several visitors to the colony during the 1870s published accounts of the wonders to be seen in Southern California and wrote glowing accounts of the healthful climate found among the vineyards. The reports persuaded one doctor to build a two-story sanitorium for invalids in the middle of town, but he didn't remain long. Another settler who was attracted by farming opportunities more than the climate, but who also didn't stay long, was the famous Polish actress Madame Helena Modjeska. She, her husband Count Karol Bozenta Chlapowski, their friend Henryk Sienkiewicz who wrote *Quo Vadis,* and several others wanted to start a new life in the "Mother Colony." But their efforts were unsuccessful, mostly because they knew nothing about farming, and they moved on to other pursuits for which they were more suited. Madame Modjeska went back to the stage to earn her living and eventually built a grand home in Santiago Canyon where she lived for many years.

Most people who settled in Anaheim found farming to their liking. In 1879 Benjamin Dreyfus was reputed to be the largest grape grower in the colony. Some historians report that he had 70,000 vines in mission, black

MADAME MODJESKA: QUEEN OF THE THEATER

Cultural opportunities were limited in the newly emerging cities of Orange County. Education was the first priority once subsistence was assured, and what cultural activities there were centered around the nearest school. Music, literature, and art were luxuries unavailable to most rural residents who spent all their time working in the fields or doing endless household chores.

Into this environment in 1876 came Madame Helena Modjeska, one of the most celebrated actresses of the European stage. Modjeska briefly played the role of an Orange County farmer's wife before finding success in the American theater.

Modjeska was born October 12, 1840, in Cracow, Poland, one of twelve children. As an adult, her talent and success grew, and she was placed under life contract to the Imperial Theater of Warsaw. In 1868 she married Count Karol Bozenta Chlapowski and became a wealthy hostess in addition to a national celebrity.

Modjeska loved to surround herself with artists, and she often held soirees in her home. Although she was not a political person, these activities seemed suspicious to the Russians who controlled Poland and were ever alert to insurrection.

The tension caused by this surveillance, overwork from constant road trips, and the emotional trauma of losing both her brother and best friend in the same year, caused Modjeska's physical collapse. When Modjeska's doctor approved an extended sea voyage, her husband decided something more permanent would cure both physical and emotional ills.

Bozenta, as Modjeska's husband was called, was fascinated by the concept of utopian colonies. Since Modjeska's son, Rudolphe, was eager to visit America, it was decided that the group would emigrate to America together and either form or join a colony. Jules Sypniewski and Henryk

Sienkiewicz went ahead to find an appropriate site for the group's great adventure.

The spot they chose was at the new Anaheim Colony, populated by Germans, which they thought well organized, well established, and destined for continued success. After renting a small house Sypniewski returned to Poland to spread the news to the others.

"What wild dreams we dreamt! What visions of freedom, peace, and happiness flitted across our brains!" wrote Modjeska in her autobiography *Memories and Impressions of Helena Modjeska*. "I was to give up the stage and live in the midst of nature, perhaps in a tent! I pictured to myself a life of toil under the blue skies of California, among the hills, riding on horseback with a gun over my shoulder. I imagined all sorts of things except what really was in store for me."

In July 1876 the group set out for their new home. In the group were Modjeska, her husband and son, Jules Sypniewski, his wife and two children, Lucian Paprocki, and Modjeska's maid, Anusia. Their friend Henryk Sienkiewicz, who had remained, would meet them.

They landed in New York where they remained long enough to enjoy the Centennial, then sailed to California via Panama, ending their sea voyage in San Francisco. Wishing to sample the culture of the city, Modjeska and her husband remained behind a few days to attend the theater. The others pushed on to their destination, a small house on West Center Street in Anaheim.

"We found the rented house rather small: two bedrooms, a dining room, a so-called parlor, with a square piano and sofa," wrote Modjeska. "The commonplaceness of it all was painfully discouraging, and the front yard, with its cypresses, shaggy grass, and flowers scattered at random, looked like a poorly kept small graveyard."

Although they expected a totally different lifestyle, the reality of becoming farmers in a community without the refinements of a European capital overwhelmed the band of emigres. Nevertheless, they took up their assigned chores. Modjeska, who had always had servants, became housekeeper and cook, but was soon frustrated by the demands put on her and the limited supply of available goods.

"Quantity was often more appreciated than quality, especially after a day spent in the fields," wrote Modjeska. "Though Anusia and I tried our best, yet it happened sometimes that the chops were too dry, the steak too well cooked, but our men were good-natured and never grumbled. Hunger was a helpmate of mine and I fear, sometimes, my accomplice."

The men had similar problems—only Sypniewski had any agricultural knowledge. Since they were unaccustomed to the grueling farm work, lateness in rising, sore muscles, and back trouble soon developed. After just three days only Bozenta and Rudolphe had not found an excuse to stop working.

Everyone was disillusioned. And everyone was homesick.

Thinking the problems might be with the particular farm they rented, Bozenta purchased another on what is today State College Boulevard. The group moved and started work again, but the situation did not improve. There were still fields to maintain, cows to milk, clothes to wash, crops to harvest, and markets to find. And there was no time for books, plays, or music. Modjeska noticed that her husband was depressed and nervous. She, too, had grown restless:

Everything seemed to be a sad failure. We had several cows, but there was no one to milk them, and we had to buy milk, butter and cream from the neighbors. We had chickens

*but our fine dogs made regular meals
of the eggs. We had a vineyard,
which yielded beautiful muscat
grapes, but there was nobody to buy
them, and often people would come
and fill their wagons with them without more ado; they said that such
was the custom of the country.*

Too disillusioned to care, they let
passersby rob them of their produce
and let cattle eat their barley. What
rabbits they had became diseased.
Their cash was dwindling and their
dream dying.

Bozenta finally admitted failure.
He gave the farm away, sent the
Sypniewskis back to Poland, and said
goodbye to his friend Sienkiewicz who
went off to reside in a city. Bozenta
and Paprocki moved to Santiago
Canyon to stay with their friends,
Mr. and Mrs. J.E. Pleasants.

In January 1877 Modjeska went to
San Francisco. It was a family decision that she would find a tutor,
learn English, and return to the stage.
Rudolphe, who knew some English,
would help her. Modjeska interviewed
many tutors, but finally settled on
Josephine Tuholski. A Polish emigre
who spoke perfect English, Tuholski
agreed to teach Modjeska without
compensation. After six months of
study, she was ready. In June 1877
Modjeska applied for her first job.

Despite her fame in Europe, Modjeska was not well known in America. The manager of the California
Theater in San Francisco did not
want to audition her, particularly
since the owner of the theater company was away.

"Supposing he had before him
only an amateur stage struck society
woman, he tried to get out of this
difficult situation as smoothly as possible," wrote Modjeska of Barton
Hill, the manager.

She was disappointed, but her
friends were incensed. Arguing on
Modjeska's behalf, one of them convinced Hill to reconsider. She was

given a chance and immediately
thereafter, a job.

Modjeska achieved immediate success on the American stage. Known
for her ability to become the characters she portrayed and to make the
audience experience her feelings, she
was acclaimed throughout the United
States. At the height of her success,
Modjeska was on par with Sarah
Bernhardt. She played opposite all
the famous leading men of the time,
including Otis Skinner and Edwin
Booth, and was especially known for
her portrayal of tragic heroines such
as Mary Stewart, Camille, and Lady
MacBeth. She made contracts
through New York agents, had her
own railroad car for traveling, and
moved in the best circles. Her husband traveled with her and took care

*Helena Modjeska came from Poland in
1876 to live in Anaheim, and soon took
the theater by storm. Courtesy, First
American Title Insurance Company*

of all her arrangements.

Despite her unsuccessful experiences in Orange County, Modjeska
always had a soft spot in her heart
for the Santa Ana Mountains. Whenever she completed a tour, she always
found the rest she needed in the
peaceful surroundings of Santiago
Canyon. In 1888 she and her husband purchased the ranch of their
friends, the Pleasants, in Santiago
Canyon. A spring in Harding Canyon was dammed and water piped to
the house. Needing more space to
house the many friends that visited,

Modjeska had a new house built to her specifications, designed by famed New York architect Stanford White. It was built in the same location as the Pleasants' cottage and incorporated the existing house into the new design. When it was completed she called it "Arden" because its surroundings reminded her of the Forest of Arden in Shakespeare's play *As You Like It.*

A warm, generous person, Modjeska made many friends in Orange County. Among them were Mr. and Mrs. James Rice of Tustin, Mr. and Mrs. Joseph Yoch, Dr. J.P. Boyd and Rosa Boyd of Santa Ana, and Judge Richard Egan of San Juan Capistrano. She dubbed the latter the "King of Capistrano," and once painted him a picture of the old mission.

In a letter to Egan from Poland dated August 12, 1887, she wrote, "You are very kind indeed to keep my horrid painting in the frame. If I ever paint any better I shall send you some view of my own country and my new house in Cracow."

Although she made periodic trips back to her homeland, she always returned to California where her health was better. She participated in local activities and supported many local charities. In July 1890 she appeared at the benefit opening of French's Opera House in Santa Ana. She loved parties and once rented a deserted hotel for an entire summer, a remnant of the boom town San Juan by the Sea, so that her friends could visit while she rested at the seashore. Her fondness for the sea prompted her to purchase property and build a home on Bay Island in Newport Beach. She then divided her time between Arden and the Newport home.

In her memoirs she wrote,

When I sit on the porch of my cottage, looking at the purple hills of Santa Ana and the peaks of Sierra Madre or at the blue waters of the bay, I feel calm and contented. The love for my dearest ones fills my heart to its very brim and though my thoughts are often visited with the images of the glorious moments of my stage life, yet no regret, no bitterness disturbs my mind but gratitude for all I received from God and men.

Madame Modjeska's theatrical trunk was filled with memorabilia from her performing years of the late 1800s. Courtesy, Charles W. Bowers Memorial Museum

In 1905 Modjeska gave her last performance at the Metropolitan Opera House in New York. She retired to Orange County and died four years later. Her remains were sent to Cracow.

Although little is remembered of her today, except for a canyon and an occasional street that bear her name, Madame Helena Modjeska had a tremendous impact on her times. For decades her name added luster to the golden promise of Orange County.

Above: *The Dreyfus Winery was established southwest of Anaheim, and is seen here in about 1884. Courtesy, Anaheim Public Library*

Right: *This wine pump was used at the Dreyfus Winery. Courtesy, Anaheim Public Library*

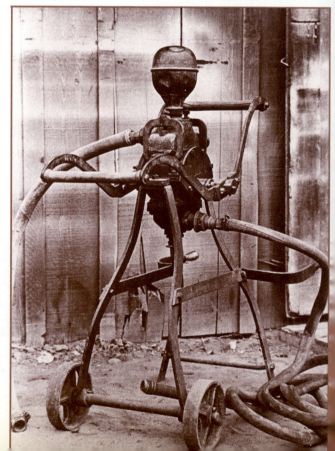

The Koenig Vineyard, located near West Street in Anaheim, was typical of the many small vineyards surrounding the towns of Anaheim and Orange. Anaheim grapes were used mainly for wine, while Orange and McPherson grapes were used for raisins. Courtesy, Anaheim Public Library

malvoise, zinfandel, fontenac, muscat, and riesling grapes. Also a vintner, he produced 87,000 gallons of wine and 15,000 gallons of brandy. Others in the colony were equally successful. Anaheim was, without question, the leading producer of wine and brandy in what was still Los Angeles County. But change was coming.

As early as 1884 there were problems with the vines. Many were dying, yet there seemed no cause. Perhaps it was the winter rains, since the year had been the wettest one on record. Or perhaps it had something to do with the soil. Farmers scratched their heads and continued to do what they had always done, hoping for improvement. But more vines died and nothing seemed to help. By 1885 the disease was rampant in the Anaheim vineyards and was turning up in Orange and even the Santa Ana Mountains. By the end of the year 25,000 acres of vines were dead in Southern California and fifty wineries lay idle. An investigation by the Department of Agriculture found that the disease known everywhere as Pierce's Disease was a virus spread

by leafhoppers. By 1886 farmers gave up hope of reviving their vines. With heavy hearts they went out into the fields and pulled up the stumps they had hand-watered during droughts, had shot stampeding herds of cattle to protect, and had harvested with pride. The Anaheim Colony had lived up to its golden promise. The vines were dead, but they still had the land. And in Southern California at the end of the 1880s land was beginning to appreciate in value.

It was the beginning of the great boom of the 1880s, when land changed hands faster than cards in a poker game and the stakes were just as high. And Orange County would become firmly established as a mecca for farmers who need only plant a seed to reap a golden harvest.

Substantial brick buildings line both sides of the still unpaved Fourth Street in Santa Ana in 1890. The city had become the county seat just ten years earlier. The building on the right was home to the First National Bank. Courtesy, History Room, Santa Ana Public Library

CHAPTER VI

The Formation
of a
County

or richness of soil, for the variety and quality of its productions, this valley is without a rival on the Pacific Coast. The semi-tropic and northern fruits raised here are not surpassed in size and flavor by any portion of Southern California, while our vineyards rival those of France in the variety and excellence of their productions. —Santa Ana Valley Immigration Association, 1885

Orange County was a promoter's paradise in the great boom of the 1880s. It had the beginnings of a strong agricultural economy, more secure supplies of water, and a mild, saleable climate. It also had an active group of supporters who in January 1885 published a promotional brochure which extolled the virtues of the Santa Ana Valley.

"Where so lately the wildflowers bloomed and died and bloomed again in undisturbed luxuriance, tasteful and often elegant homes are springing up, surrounded by orchards and vineyards, which promise rich returns in the future," wrote the promoters. But not wanting to scare away prospective settlers with so much luxuriance, they hastened to add, "Expenses of living can be regulated here as elsewhere, so that persons, by confining themselves to the absolute necessities of life, can live for almost nothing."

While optimistic in the promises it made, the Santa Ana Valley Immigration Association only slightly exaggerated the attractions of their home territory. It was a good time to buy in Southern California. Interest rates were down, land prices were growing steadily, and land was as fertile as promoters claimed. The

Above: *The W.F. Botsford Ranch house, located on what is now East Chapman Avenue in Fullerton, is a prime example of the distinctive homes that were being built at a relatively rapid rate in the late 1880s. Courtesy, Fullerton Public Library*

Facing page, top: *The Almon Goodwin home, the second oldest house in Fullerton, was built in 1882. Courtesy, Fullerton Public Library*

Facing page, bottom: *These workers toil to construct a fill on the W.F. Botsford Ranch. Courtesy, Fullerton Public Library*

grape blight was still thought to be temporary in 1885, and most of the problems involving water rights had been or were in the process of being settled. As the Santa Fe Railroad inched closer to Los Angeles, farmers hoped that competition with the Southern Pacific would bring lower freight rates and greater access to markets.

Travel journals, letters home, and eyewitness accounts of miners returning from the goldfields made California sound attractive to future settlers. Promotional materials were distributed across the United States and Europe, touting the healthful climate and the low cost of living. It was easier to pull up stakes and head for a new place if friends or family were already there. But even if they weren't the promise of rich land and fortunes to be made in two or three years in the warm, dry climate was enough to make a Midwest farmer turn in his snow shovel for a railroad ticket.

Left: *Built in 1882, the Dillin Flour Mill provided the small community of Olive with its principal industry. Wagons full of grain came from Spadra, Wilmington, Pomona, and San Fernando. A disastrous fire struck the mill in 1889 and the great quantities of wheat and corn stored there smouldered for days. Courtesy, Anaheim Public Library*

Below, left: *The promise of fertile land and low interest rates helped to promote farm sales, as this newspaper advertisement illustrates. Courtesy, Fullerton Public Library*

Below: *This Santa Fe station in Anaheim was dedicated in 1941. Courtesy, Anaheim Public Library*

When the Santa Fe Railroad reached Southern California, the Fullerton Train Station, shown here in 1888, was built along the Santa Fe route. Courtesy, Anaheim Public Library

This train engine was called the Cottontail Switch. *It ran on the Santa Ana-Newport Road in 1892. Courtesy, Charles W. Bowers Memorial Museum*

The cost of a ticket for a casual visit, however, was too high until 1885 when the Santa Fe Railroad finally reached Los Angeles and provoked a rate war with the Southern Pacific. It began with the introduction of excursion fares that gradually lowered the rates from the Midwest to the West Coast and sometimes included a reduced price on a lot owned by one of the railroad's land firms. As competition grew, fares got lower and lower. Then, on March 10, 1887, they fell to one dollar—the excursion fare from Kansas City to Los Angeles. Declaring a truce, the rates for both railroads went up but remained relatively low for nearly a year. During that time the floodgates opened and the tide of immigrants swirled into the southland ready to sign on the dotted line.

When the trains pulled into the station at Los Angeles, travelers were accosted by employees of realty syndicates or boards of trade who bombarded them with promotional materials extolling the attractions of the land they had for sale, even before they left their seat. Many offered a free lunch, a band concert, and gifts from area merchants if the visitor would get on the next available train and visit their project site. The Santa Ana Valley promoters circulated their pamphlet in much the same way but cautioned visitors to "look before you buy . . . and give land sellers that meet the train a wide berth," excluding their own, of course. But their methods, once the audience was in hand, were much the same as all the others who hawked land from the railroad platform.

One of the most popular ways to sell sever-

THE IRON HORSE

A passenger train pulls into the Fullerton Train Station in the early 1900s. The Stern & Goodman Warehouse Number 5 can be seen at the right. Courtesy, Anaheim Public Library

1862. The bill provided a 400-foot right-of-way, substantial construction loans, and huge land subsidies amounting to 1,280,000 acres for every 100 miles of track laid. All of thi largesse went to the owners of the Central Pacific and the Union Pacific who were hurrying toward their historic moment near Ogden, Utah.

While the Big Four wanted to build as quickly as possible, reap as many rewards as they could, and then sell the completed railroad to an operator, their plans went awry. There were no buyers, their debts were astronomical, and the incentive to hang on to the railroad were growing. In 1864 the federal government doubled the land grants and other financial incentives to keep the rails moving.

In 1865, before the completion of the transcontinental link, the Big Four chartered the Southern Pacific Railroad to expand their empire within California. For decades, the railroad directors squeezed money out of the rate-paying public to keep their fortunes intact and to pay off their debts. Not only did the new railroad accept federal subsidies, but demanded local ones as well. A community paid a huge price in land and dollars to have the Southern Pacific pass through its town. Most felt it was a waste of money.

In 1900 Frank Norris published *The Octopus*, a fictionalized indictment of the Southern Pacific's method. The book sold 60,000 copies and reflected public sentiment toward the railroad, whose power greatly declined after the reform movement of 1910 and the election of Governor Hiram Johnson.

But in Orange County's early lar

A nineteenth century farmer needed three things to be successful: good soil, cooperative weather, and a nearby railroad.

In the early land booms of the 1870s Orange County promoters could boast of soil and weather better than most places in the state. But it wasn't until December 1877 that the Southern Pacific extended its lines to Santa Ana; when it did, some farmers weren't sure it was a blessing.

The Southern Pacific, directed by Leland Stanford, Collis P. Huntington, Charles Crocker, and Mark Hopkins, was a power to be reckoned with in California. The railroad had money to contribute to political campaigns, which it spread about freely.

In the years of its empire building—1860 to 1900—the Southern Pacific dominated the political and economic development of California. Its influence was also felt in Washington, D.C. From 1885 to 1893 Stanford served in the nation's capital as a California senator. Before that he had a stint as governor.

The "Big Four" formed their partnership on June 28, 1861, as the Central Pacific Railroad. Joining them was a young civil engineer, Theodore Judah, who had expertise in railroad construction, but who died in 1863 before his dreams were realized.

To spur the completion of a transcontinental railroad, Congress enacted the Pacific Railroad bill in

boom years, the Southern Pacific was needed to get crops to market.

Even though the railroad's tactics skirted the edge of legality and its freight rates kept spiralling upward, farmers used it anyway. For many, there was no choice.

According to railroad historians, a common tactic of the Southern Pacific was to raise the freight rates of individual farmers. When a farmer complained that he could no longer pay and would soon go out of business, the railroad would send its auditors to examine the farmer's books. The auditors would determine the highest rate the farmer could afford, without ruining his business. This insured the best rate for the Southern Pacific and the retention of a customer.

Another tactic used by the railroad was to buy out competitors to form a monopoly. In the early 1880s it was estimated that the Central Pacific-Southern Pacific conglomerate owned 85 percent of the state's transportation facilities from rails to shipping. If a competitor wouldn't sell, other methods were employed, such as the formation of dummy companies to disguise the identity of the real buyer. This tactic may have been used on James McFadden, owner of the Santa Ana-Newport Railroad and McFadden's Landing.

The McFadden brothers—James and Robert—built a railroad from Santa Ana to Newport Beach in 1890, bringing rails, ties, and even the engine in by ship. Completed in 1891, it carried freight and passengers six days a week. The trains did not run on Sundays because James McFadden believed in observing the Sabbath. Unfortunately, Sunday was often the only day off for many who might have used the railroad to get to the beach.

The station was located on the wharf and the rails extended out into the pier. The rail line was a community landmark, as well as the largest employer in Orange County. To increase business, in 1897 a spur line was built to the celery fields of Smeltzer.

McFadden knew for the harbor to be really successful, costly improvements were needed that required federal aid. But after six years of deliberation the government selected San Pedro as the site of a publicly-owned, improved, deep water harbor, thus sounding the death knell for expansion in Newport Bay. The decision also dealt the Southern Pacific a blow by overlooking Santa Monica Harbor, which the railroad owned.

Depressed, perhaps, over the loss of federal assistance in improving Newport Bay, McFadden agreed to sell his railroad to a promoter, Colonel William Holabird. He claimed to represent J. Ross Clark and W.A. Clark who wished to extend the Smeltzer line to their sugar factory in Los Alamitos. Two months after the sale, the railroad mysteriously fell into the hands of McFadden's competitors, the Southern Pacific. The new owners opened the railroad on Sundays and increased freight rates. The shipping business to McFadden's Wharf died and three years later the McFaddens sold.

Many believed the Southern Pacific had purposely tricked the McFaddens. One who may have shared this view was James Irvine II, who began shipping his crops to San Diego via the Santa Fe, rather than give his business to the Southern Pacific. His dislike of the Southern Pacific was of long duration and had begun with his father.

James Irvine I had come to California on the same ship as Collis P. Huntington in 1849. According to historians they had a disagreement during that voyage and were unfriendly ever after. Huntington founded his railroad; Irvine founded his ranch. When Irvine bought out his partners in 1876, the Southern Pacific persuaded the federal government to file suit to invalidate his claim to nearly two-thirds of Rancho Lomas de Santiago. The motive: to gain right-of-way through the Irvine Ranch to San Diego, which James Irvine would never grant. Irvine fought the suit for two years. In 1878 his title was upheld and the suit dismissed.

The Southern Pacific extended its line as far as Santa Ana but could go no further. Meanwhile, Santa Fe arrived in Orange County in 1887. Farmers now had a choice and were further delighted when rate wars ensued. Southern Pacific realized it needed to extend its line before Santa Fe usurped the coastal route. It renewed its fight to get right-of-way through Rancho San Joaquín. Even though James Irvine had died in 1886, the trustees continued to refuse its request.

Santa Fe also wanted the route and took the matter to court, suing for right of access through the ranch by means of its subsidiary, the San Bernardino and San Diego Railroad. Fearing a successful outcome, Southern Pacific decided it was time for desperate measures.

On a Saturday afternoon, when courts and government offices were closed, a Southern Pacific crew went to work laying rail line through Tustin and into the Irvine Ranch. A group of ranch hands and neighbors, alerted to the activity, met the crew with loaded shotguns. Bowing to a superior force, the crew departed and did not return.

The Irvine Ranch trustees promptly granted right-of-way through their property to the Santa Fe subsidiary on April 25, 1887, for which the railroad paid $4,500 and guaranteed the ranch access across the tracks.

In an era when the Southern Pacific was all powerful, it lost its fight in Irvine.

al lots at once was the land auction. One of the first land auctions held in Orange County took place in Santa Ana in December 1886. It was so successful that another was held in January under the sponsorship of the Los Angeles and Santa Ana Land Bureau. The January auction drew 486 people who spent $18,000 for ninety-one town lots after being lured to the Santa Ana Valley by the promise of the exhilarating sounds of a brass band, a complimentary hot meal, and a ride in an open carriage in the moonlight. They were under no obligation to buy, but buy they did since the terms were usually one-third down with the balance due in semi-annual installments.

The briskest selling went on in established communities such as Santa Ana, Orange, Tustin, and Anaheim, where progress was visible and on the rise. But there were new towns being platted in between where land was cheaper

and promised gains were greater. Farmers and speculators alike looked at the maps, picked out their lots, and tucked away their deeds.

For some the gamble proved profitable.

Edward and George Amerige joined California's land rush in 1886. They bought 390 acres north of Anaheim for $175 per acre and additional odd properties with the idea of laying out a new town. Needing some financial assistance, the Ameriges formed a partnership with H. Gaylord Wilshire and the Pacific Land and Improvement Company. In 1887 they subdivided the property and began selling lots. The new town was called Fullerton after

This ostrich farm, located in the Fullerton area, was one of the largest in the state. Ostrich farms were successful in Southern California because the cold weather made the birds' plumage thicker. About 100 birds were kept at a time—there was a steady market for their plumage for fancy hats and gown trims. Courtesy, Fullerton Public Library

and Frank Eastman, shown here with Napoleon ... arte, tried to train their ostriches to race and per- ... circus. Capable of speeds up to fifty miles an ... g birds were more successful at racing than as a ... After a year in the circus, Billy gave up and ... act home. Courtesy, Anaheim Public Library

George Fullerton, president of Pacific Land, which was a subsidiary of the Santa Fe Railroad. The map was officially filed August 18, 1887. In just one year all debts on the original land were paid and the Santa Fe company sold its interests to the Fullerton Land and Trust Company of which the Ameriges and Wilshire were principals. The company continued to sell lots and make improvements throughout the next several years.

Another success story was that of Buena Park, founded in 1887 by James A. Whitaker near the Santa Fe Railroad's line from Los Angeles to Orange. A third boom town that managed to survive was Aliso City, today called El Toro, which was platted by the firm of Cook, Gardner, and Victor in 1887 near the end of the boom. Dwight Whiting, who acquired most of the lots, is credited with developing the town. The fourth town to survive the boom was Villa Park, which had its beginnings in earlier subdivisions of land but was officially filed and named in the boom period. The last was Olive Heights, founded in 1887 by Louis Schorn and Thomas Dillon on the San Bernardino-Orange branch of the Santa Fe Railroad (then called California Southern) at Burruel Point. It was the site of one of the area's first industries, a flour mill.

The boom saw a flurry of activity and the growth of many communities. But not all of the boom towns were successful. According to historian Glen Dumke in *The Boom of the Eighties* there were more than 100 towns platted in the greater Los Angeles area between 1884 and 1888. Of these sixty-two failed outright and several others exist today only as parts of other communities. In the Santa Ana Valley there were twelve that did not live up to the sparkling promise of its promoters. McPherson, two miles east of Orange; St. James, near the mouth of the Santa Ana Canyon, south of Olive; Carlton, a mile south of

Above: *One of Santa Ana's most prominent early merchants, D.W. Swanner, sold groceries, provisions, crockery, glassware, and household items in his Fourth Street store. Brooms, a basket of corn, and a washboard and tub can be seen in front of the store windows. Courtesy, History Room, Santa Ana Public Library*

Facing page: *One of Tustin's most elaborate Victorian buildings housed the First National Bank of Tustin. This photo, which pictures E.J. Cranston and William Lineberger, was taken around 1916 and shows little change in the interior of the building from its original 1887 appearance. Courtesy, Tustin Area Historical Society Museum*

Left: *George Amerige is seen riding along Willow Avenue in Fullerton in about 1890. Amerige plotted and sold the lots of land that formed the town of Fullerton. Courtesy, Fullerton Public Library*

Right: *The Amerige brothers were prominent citizens of Fullerton and successful real estate entrepreneurs. Edward is seen here. Courtesy, Fullerton Public Library*

Below: *Annette J. Amerige was married to George Amerige. Courtesy, Fullerton Public Library*

Facing page, top: *George and Annette Amerige pose in front of Fullerton's first building. Built in 1887 by the Amerige brothers, the structure was located on Spadra Street between Commonwealth and Santa Fe. Courtesy, Fullerton Public Library*

Facing page, bottom: *With his office in the distance, George Amerige of Fullerton surveys his land from his buggy in 1887. Courtesy, Fullerton Public Library*

Above: *The year after Fullerton was founded in 1887, these five gentlemen, pictured in front of the Dunbar, Wiggin, and Stevens Real Estate office, appear ready to tour the 3,900-acre site of the new town. Courtesy, First American Title Insurance Company*

Above: *The "father" of Fullerton was George Hubert Fuller-ton. Courtesy, Fullerton Public Library*

Right: *A common form of calling card in the 1880s was the carte-de-visite. This 1887 example carries the portrait of Mr. and Mrs. Albert Burrows of Fullerton. Courtesy, Fullerton Public Library*

Carbon Canyon; Richfield (Atwood) and Yorba, on the north banks of the Santa Ana River; San Juan-by-the-Sea, south of San Juan Capistrano; and Earlham, which would become El Modena, were all early towns, duly platted and recorded, and most with a hotel for prospective buyers. Fairview, near Newport Beach, also had a hot springs, but an earthquake closed the springs and the resort that grew up around it quickly died. Other communities such as Catalina-on-the-Main, Crestline, Fruitland, and Aliso Beach survive today only as names on documents in the Hall of Records, and not as the grand cities their promoters had envisioned.

The boom came quickly and departed just as fast. Paper cities, many without water and some with unscrupulous developers who had no intention of making improvements, faded as fast as the ink on their deeds. Most properties bought by speculators did not involve cash, but promissory notes, with the same lot often changing hands two or three times be-

Farming in Villa Park required the whole family to do its part. Clearing the land and planting new trees, vines, and row crops required patience and hard work. This unidentified family, dressed in its Sunday best, is seen some time around the turn of the century. Courtesy, First American Title Insurance Company

William Starbuck was a prominent Fullerton citizen. He is pictured here in this 1890s family portrait with his wife and his son Raymond. Courtesy, Fullerton Public Library

fore the first payment was due. Sometimes speculators would buy options for a few dollars, standing in line for choice lots that could be resold quickly at a profit if the value went up before any cash had changed hands.

The system created many victims—people who had followed the golden dream to California and had watched it die in the wake of unkept promises. Yet the boom that ended in 1888 brought many benefits: improvements to irrigation and road systems, an increase in population leading to the creation of many new school districts, church congregations, and markets for local products, and the development of a heightened sense of community. The people of Orange County had a new awareness of themselves and of their potential. It was time to loosen the ties from Los Angeles County and stand on their own.

An earlier attempt at county division had been led by Max Von Strobel of Anaheim in 1870. The bill to create the new county of Anaheim had passed the state assembly but died in a senate committee. Attempts were made during the next twenty years to revive the issue, substituting the name Orange for the name of the proposed county. There weren't many productive orange groves in the area at this time, but there were many who had high hopes for the new crop and felt it conveyed the proper picture of what the territory would become. But these efforts were also unsuccessful. In 1889 divisionists in the Santa Ana Valley had a little more political knowledge and decided to try again. This time they lined up their votes early. Fierce opposition was encountered by the parent county of Los Ange-

HOT SPRINGS OF HEALTH

In the 1890s, when doctors were scattered and called only for emergencies and home remedies were used to cure common ailments, many sought relief from discomfort in natural hot springs. At one time, there were three hot springs in Orange County.

The San Juan Hot Springs are located in a rustic canyon twelve miles east of San Juan Capistrano. La Vida Hot Springs are two miles east of what is today Carbon Canyon Regional Park. The third and most interesting of the three, Fairview Hot Springs, was in the heart of what is today Costa Mesa.

Fairview Hot Springs had a good location, all the necessary amenities, and high-powered promoters, yet were never a major success. In time, the springs disappeared altogether, as though they were never meant to be.

The springs took their name from a boom town that grew out of the railroad rate wars of the 1880s. Its promoters filed a tract map on November 10, 1887, and lots were divided and offered for sale. In addition to the usual hotel, store, and residential and farming tracts, the promoters boasted that Fairview would have a 100-foot-wide boulevard running the entire length of the tract and its own railroad originating in Santa Ana. They also touted the hot springs at the southern edge of town, and bragged that there would soon be a top-quality bathhouse.

The promoters generally lived up to their promises and the town flourished. There were a few setbacks—the railroad was not a great success and some of the original settlers found better land elsewhere—but the town continued to prosper until early 1889 when, like in many of the paper cities of Southern California, the real estate bubble burst and its promoters went bankrupt. In addition, a flood washed out a portion of the rail line and there was no money to rebuild it. Businesses declined and other settlers

moved away. But the hot springs remained and in 1891, in an effort to revive interest in the community, the town's hotel was moved directly across the street from the bathhouse. Unfortunately, the move did not attract business and the hotel was put up for sale.

In 1903 the hotel was purchased by W.S. Collins, an early developer of Newport Beach, who launched a publicity campaign to turn the hotel and springs into a health resort. He renovated the old hotel and bathhouse, built new cottages, and added recreational facilities including a warm water swimming pool. The resort was successful for a time, but never lived up to Collins' expectations or the thousands of dollars he invested. The resort changed hands several times, each time falling into more difficult times. In 1918 an earthquake cut off the flow of water to the surface and the Fairview Hot Springs disappeared, as did the town for which it was named.

While the Fairview Hot Springs never reached their potential, the San Juan Hot Springs had great success. "Almost all diseases of a chronic nature are cured by a stay from three to six weeks at this thermal bathing place," wrote Alexander Hamilton Rowan, a physician who doubled as a newspaper columnist for the *Santa Ana Standard* during the 1890s. "Drinking the water, too, will speedily work almost a miracle in rheumatism, skin disease, trembling nerves, uterine troubles of all kinds, indigestion and melancholia."

Rowan was not the only one to write about the San Juan Hot Springs. Several guidebooks of the day also extolled the virtues of the place. Visitors to Southern California were encouraged to stop and test the waters, either internally or externally, depending on one's need.

In *California of the South*, a guidebook published in 1888, the San Juan Hot Springs were described as a

primitive place noted for curing rheumatism and syphilis, particularly by immersing in mud:

Mud-baths are considered very efficacious, and, as there are no permanent buildings, these anxious seekers after health improvise mud bathing-houses of a primitive type. There are over a dozen of these springs spread over an acre of ground, and another hot spring, known as McNight's a half mile away. There are also cold springs near by.

The use of these springs for curative purposes can be traced back to the pre-mission period. Missionaries stationed at San Juan Capistrano wrote of being shown a place of healing by the Indians. The place became so popular that a mission station was set up there.

The springs continued to be popular during the Mexican period, long after the mission system had faded away. The area was used for picnics, dances, and even to do laundry. Some visitors would not venture past the settling pools, thinking the place was haunted by Indian spirits.

The area eventually became part of John Forster's holdings, and was later sold to Richard O'Neill and James Flood in 1882. In 1883 it was leased to Michael Kraszewski who turned the area into a resort.

"There are fine shade trees and a camping ground for all who can get there," wrote Rowan. "There's a good boardinghouse for those who don't want to do their own cooking. Rates are five dollars or six dollars per week. Every person must furnish his own bed and bedding and good tents can be hired on the grounds, cheap."

In 1888 the railroad was completed through San Juan Capistrano. Visitors to the springs could ride the train to San Juan and hire a wagon or a buggy from one dollar to $1.50 to take them out to the resort. Luggage handling was free.

One writer who made frequent visits to the springs was the editor of the *Standard*, Dan Baker of Santa Ana. In one of his columns, appearing in 1890, he wrote that the water of the San Juan Hot Springs could cure violent temper, malignant disposition, fault finding, a desire for blood letting, jealousy, and ". . . all feelings of remorse, a canker that may be lurking in the heart of the fairest flower."

Baker usually visited the springs in the summer. But he made one trip in the fall and was amazed to find a different kind of visitor.

Tents are scattered through the woods and brush, but they are unoccupied except by hordes of cats which seem to multiply and grow and increase like the majority of the Republican returning board. The hungry, half-starved little nuisances make life a burden. They've stolen everything here in the meat line and have now started on my onions.

With business booming in spite of the feline population, Kraszewski expanded the resort, adding a store, dance hall, swimming pool, cabañas, and a hotel. He also built cabins for those who did not want to camp out.

The hot springs were more a place of vacation than recuperation. There were dances, hiking, fishing, hunting, and card playing. Even seances were held by visiting mediums, who tried to rouse the Indian spirits.

The San Juan Hot Springs prospered under several proprietors, weathering storms, fires, and an occasional poor season. But in 1936 the establishment closed, unable to fight bureaucracy and the edicts of the county health department. The coun-

ty wanted improvements made in the interest of public health and safety—improvements the proprietor could not afford. The springs are now part of Caspers Regional Park and have been leased to a private entrepreneur who has piped the water into hot tubs and reopened the springs to the public.

Also open are the springs in Carbon Canyon. The La Vida Hot Springs, located on Carbon Canyon Road two miles east of Carbon Canyon Regional Park, drew visitors from as far away as Los Angeles and San Bernardino counties in its early days. Like those of San Juan, these springs were well known to the Indians and the early Spaniards, and continued to be popular during the Mexican period. No haunted tales of dying Indians kept people away from the healing mud in which they would immerse in hopes of curing their ailments.

In 1893, while attempting to drill an oil well in Carbon Canyon, a workman struck a fissure at 800 feet that produced a flow of warm mineral water. Visitors to the springs now had the choice of soaking in mud or in wooden barrels filled with hot, fresh spring water.

By the 1920s the area had a reputation as a place where aches and pains were soothed in the warm, healing waters. A bathhouse and six tubs were built by William Newton Miller in 1924, who, with his son-in-law, established the La Vida Mineral Springs Corporation. The resort became so popular that a hotel had to be built in 1927. Ever-increasing numbers of visitors came to the springs, particularly after the road was paved.

In 1928 the La Vida Bottle Works Company was organized and pro-

The San Juan Hot Springs has been a popular health spa from early Indian times until the present. This photo was taken in the 1890s when the Hot Springs Hotel was a popular vacation spot for health-seekers. The springs are still providing a mecca for those who find relief in the waters. Courtesy, First American Title Insurance Company

duced a drink called La Vida Lemon and Lime. The mineral water, which had a high soda content, was bottled and sold. During the Prohibition era another beverage was said to have been abundant in the area, but it wasn't produced at the hot springs. Bootleggers used the nearby canyon for illegal beverage handling, but this ended with the repeal of Prohibition.

The springs are still operating with 25,000 gallons of water a day bubbling out of the ground at a temperature of 110 degrees. In 1953 a small outdoor pool was built, and a larger pool was added in 1957. Although the bottling plant and hotel were both destroyed by fires in the 1960s, both were rebuilt and are still in use.

In the 1890s Dan Baker commented that the most common users of hot springs were those with "stiff legs, swollen joints, contracted muscles and, more melancholic of all, those with the tired out look from overwork and study who have aged prematurely."

The visitors to the springs today haven't changed. As Howard Kiesig, current operator of the San Juan Hot Springs recently commented in a *Los Angeles Times* article, "It (the water) won't cure anything more than a warm glass of milk or chicken soup will," and added, "Boy, does the world need more chicken soup."

Above: *A week at the beach has been a popular pastime for Orange Countians from the time the first settlers arrived in 1859. This group, enjoying the sand and sun in front of a Laguna Beach resort hotel, depicts life in that town around the turn of the century. Courtesy, Santa Ana Public Library*

Facing page: *One of the many fine Victorian houses built during the boom of the 1880s was this elaborate Queen Anne home located in Tustin. Built in 1887 by Sherman Stevens, it was designed by well-known Los Angeles architect Costerigan and Merithew. The house was recently restored by Gfeller Development Company. Courtesy, Gfeller Development Company*

Above: *This sidewalk view of the Greater Gem Pharmacy in Fullerton taken in 1892 depicts William Starbuck (far left) and Ed Amerige (far right). Courtesy, Fullerton Public Library*

Left: *The pioneer Ford family stand in front of their Fullerton area home, which is now occupied by the Christian Science Church. Courtesy, Fullerton Public Library*

Facing page, top: *Herbert Alvin Ford was the owner of one of the first stores in Fullerton, which opened in January 1888 selling hardware and groceries. Courtesy, Fullerton Public Library*

Facing page, bottom: *The T.J.F. Boege family proudly stand in front of their Anaheim home in the late 1880s. Courtesy, Anaheim Public Library*

Above: *The first stores in Fullerton were Stern & Goodman and the Fullerton Grocery located on the corner of Spadra Street (now Harbor Boulevard) and Commonwealth Avenue, shown here in 1889. Courtesy, Fullerton Public Library*

Facing page, top: *Many items of luxury or necessity could be found in the newly thriving communities of Orange County. Courtesy, Fullerton Public Library*

Facing page, bottom: *These three men take a break from their day's toil in 1900. Courtesy, Anaheim Public Library*

Downtown Santa Ana in 1888 was a busy commercial center with several well-built brick buildings. The building on the left, the Shaffer-Wakeham Block, was built between 1885-1887 and still exists today. A major remodeling in the 1930s and 1950s altered the front, but the rear and the second floor have seen little change. There are several buildings in downtown Santa Ana dating from the 1880s that are hidden under newer facades. Courtesy, History Room, Santa Ana Public Library

les, but there were many businessmen in Los Angeles who didn't mind losing their southern competitors, and there were also many politicians from San Francisco who were glad to deflate their southern rival by taking away some of its power.

On January 4, 1889, Assemblyman E.E. Edwards introduced a bill to create the County of Orange. The name was thought appropriate since oranges now promised to become a major crop. Assessing the bill's chances and finding lackadaisical support, Edwards called in reinforcements in the form of William Spurgeon and James McFadden. In the words of historian Jim Sleeper, the group "spread the largesse of the Santa Ana Valley where it would argue loudest." The amount spent to convince fellow legislators of the value of creating the new county was reputed to have been $10,000. By the beginning of March both houses had voted in favor and on March 11, 1889, the bill was signed by Governor Robert Waterman, despite opposition by Anaheim, which found that the northwest boundary would be Coyote Creek instead of the San Gabriel River, making their bid for the county seat less feasible.

The fight was far from over.

Strong anti-divisionist sentiments were voiced in Anaheim since it was no longer a prime candidate for the county seat. Rhetoric flew from both supporters and objectors. On the eve of the election a contingent from Santa Ana tried to influence voters in Anaheim by scheduling speeches at a local hall. Nobody came. At sunrise on June 4 the polls opened. Of the 3,009 ballots cast county-wide, 2,509 voted for division and 500 voted against. The new county, heralded by fireworks and lively marches, was officially established.

Los Angeles did not let go of its tax base easily. Lawsuits were filed immediately contesting the legality of the Edwards bill, and the right of the state legislature to appoint an interim commission to set up the new county government. Arguments were given on both sides and the court voted in favor of Orange County. Additional suits were filed contesting other points. The county was again upheld. Meanwhile, the business of forming a new county continued. On July 17 the election to select Orange County's first officers and its official county seat took place. There were three slates of candidates and four towns in contention: Santa Ana, Anaheim, Orange, and Fairview (Costa Mesa). Ballots were cast and Santa Ana won a predictable victory. The new officers were William Spurgeon, Jacob Ross, Jr., Sheldon Littlefield, Samuel Armor, and A. Guy Smith, Orange County Board of Supervisors; James W. Towner, superior court judge; and E.E. Edwards, district attorney. Other officers were Dr. William B. Wall, treasurer; R.T. Harris, sheriff; R.Q. Wickham, county clerk; Fred C. Smythe, assessor; George E. Foster, recorder and auditor; Dr. Ira D. Mills, coroner and public administrator; and Samuel O. Wood, surveyor. John P. Greeley was the first superintendent of schools.

Finding a place to conduct county business was the first problem to solve. Several fine buildings were considered, but the board chose the Billings and Congdon buildings on

John P. Greeley was elected the first Orange County superintendent of schools on July 17, 1889. Courtesy, Fullerton Public Library

A CENTURY OF SERVICE

Decades of rampant lawlessness had come to an end by the time Orange County was formed in 1889. By then, most of the famous outlaws plaguing Southern California were either dead or in jail and law enforcers could easily handle the area's vagrants, drunks, and thieves.

Into this atmosphere came a succession of Orange County sheriffs. Each stamped the office with his own personality and style and made contributions built upon by his successors.

Richard J. Harris, the first elected sheriff-tax collector of Orange County, was more interested in the second of his two titles than the first when he took office in 1889. A businessman from Westminster, Harris had campaigned diligently for the formation of the new county and throughout the years improved the county's tax base. Involved in many progressive business ventures, such as the Santa Ana Cooperative Sugar Company, he was later elected to the office of county treasurer.

During his two-year term as sheriff, Harris arrested many of the tramps and vagabonds that seemed to overrun the county. It was also during his term that the first felony conviction occurred: Modesta Avila of San Juan Capistrano was sentenced to three years in San Quentin for attempting to obstruct a train. She died there after serving two years. The first male to be convicted of a felony was Tom Owens, a farmer who had holdings on the Rancho San Joaquín. He was sent to San Quentin for stealing a horse, and after serving his term was sent back again for stealing a cow.

Harris' most pressing problem was where to put prisoners once they were arrested. This was also the problem of his successor, Theo Lacy, Sr.

Lacy, from Alabama, came to Orange County in 1883. Elected sheriff in 1891, he served until 1895 (he was later elected again and served as

sheriff from 1899 until 1911). The jail Lacy inherited was located on Sycamore Street in Santa Ana between Second and Third. Although it only had three cells, the jail was better than its predecessor; in fact, it was Orange County's first public, capital improvement. Before the new jail was built, prisoners were held in two cells located in the basement of a store owned by jeweler Joseph Hiltbrunner. It was nicknamed "Brunner's basement," and no one knows exactly why the cells were originally constructed.

Built at a cost of $4,000, the new jail was the site of the most sensational crime of the nineteenth century in Orange County—the lynching of Francisco Torres in 1892. Torres had been accused of the murder of a popular resident, William McKelvey, foreman of the Modjeska Ranch. Sheriff Lacy, fearing for the safety of his prisoner, had hoped to take Torres to the Los Angeles County Jail, but the Board of Supervisors ordered him not to. He doubled the guard, but removed the outside guard after three days of quiet. On the fourth night, an unidentified mob broke in, took Torres out, and strung him up from a light pole at the corner of Fourth and Sycamore. It was the last lynching in the state of California.

The third sheriff, Joe C. Nichols, was the first to serve an elected four-year term. His tenure, 1895-1899, was largely uneventful. Nichols was known as the sheriff who provided local citizens with an unusual form of entertainment. As pictures of known criminals arrived, he posted them on his walls then put ads in the weekly newspapers, inviting citizens to come by and view them. Sometimes his walls were covered with pictures and his office was full of visitors.

During Nichols' term the Board of Supervisors set aside $23,000 for the construction of a large, red sandstone

jail on Sycamore Street. Disputes with the contractors caused delays and although its construction date is listed as 1896 it was not dedicated until 1900.

The fourth county sheriff, following Lacy's second stint, was Charles E. Ruddock, who served from 1911 to 1915. A former city marshall of Fullerton, Ruddock was well known for his musical abilities. He was followed in office by Calvin E. Jackson, 1915-1923, who reformed his office to make it more efficient. Jackson also had the dubious honor of incarcerating Bebe Daniels, a popular silent screen actress.

Daniels, arrested for speeding south of Santa Ana in her Marmon automobile, was sentenced by Judge John B. Cox to several days in jail. To make her stay as comfortable as possible, Santa Anans brought in special food and William Spurgeon delivered a suite of furniture to her cell. Each evening an orchestra from the Seal Beach Cafe serenaded her and many people crowded around hoping to glimpse the famous "vamp." The publicity not only put Santa Ana in the national spotlight, but did much for Daniels' career.

Sam Jernigan, sheriff from 1923 to 1931, brought prior experience to the job. Constable of Santa Ana for three terms and chief of police of Orange, he also served as undersheriff prior to his election. Jernigan organized the California Peace Officers Association prior to World War I, and also formed the Orange County Peace Officers Association in 1923. As sheriff during Prohibition, Jernigan had his hands full tracking down bootleggers who used the Orange County coast for their activities. A new jail at 615 North Sycamore Street was built during his term.

His successor, George Logan Jackson, had his hands full in another area. Serving during the Depression 1931-1939, Jackson had to track down gambling dens and confiscate their illegal equipment. He also was the first sheriff in charge of the Night Fruit Patrol, organized in 1929 under the district attorney's office. This patrol, necessary during the Depression, protected farms and orchards from theft. Jackson also saw two disasters during his term, the earthquake of 1933 and the flood of 1938. Both required deployment of men to protect property and to help evacuees find their families. Known for his persistence, Jackson, a successful and popular sheriff, served for a time as president of the California Sheriff's Association.

Jesse Elliott was sheriff during the war years, 1939 to 1947. During his tenure the Sheriff's Reserves were formed, including the first Mounted Reserve Unit, which patrolled beaches and ranches during World War II. These successful reserve units expanded into the Mobil Reserves, Aero Squadron, Harbor Patrol, and Placentia Reserves. A further reorganization created the North Orange County Reserves and South Orange County Reserves for jail and patrol support, and the Industrial Reserves that included experts in explosives, photography, and communications.

In 1947 James Musick was elected sheriff of Orange County. His term, which stretched to 1974, was characterized by growth and change as the small, rural sheriff's department evolved into a twentieth century urban organization. An event that triggered part of that change was the Overell murder case.

On March 15, 1947, an explosion in a yacht in Newport Harbor killed Walter and Beulah Overell, wealthy Los Angeles residents. A few weeks after their seventeen-year-old daughter, Beulah Louise, and her boyfriend, George Gallum, were charged with the murder.

After a long, sensational trial—featuring a special prosecutor brought in

by the state attorney general's office and $75,000 worth of evidence analysis—the two suspects were acquitted. Afterward Sheriff Musick successfully lobbied for a crime lab in Orange County. The case also led to important legislation to control the use of explosives.

As sheriff, Musick obtained funds for a new jail and headquarters facility, constructed in 1967 at the corner of Sixth and Flower streets. In 1971 he became sheriff-coroner and his combined staff swelled to more than 900 employees.

Streamlining the reserves in 1964, Musick reorganized them into Headquarters, Search and Rescue, Aero Squadron, and Technical Service units. Other improvements credited to Musick include the formation in 1970 of a permanent Mounted Unit (in addition to the reserves). This unit is useful for crowd control in rural parks and along parade routes. He also formed the Hazardous Devices Squad in 1971 that handles explosives, firebombs, and hazardous chemicals, and assists other agencies in identifying devices.

Sheriff Musick retired in 1974. He was replaced by the eleventh sheriff of Orange County, Brad Gates.

The only sheriff to be born in Orange County, Gates grew up in San Juan Capistrano and joined the sher-

iff's department as a deputy in 1961. While completing a master's degree in criminology, Gates worked his way up through the ranks of the department. During his term as sheriff-coroner, he designed and implemented the Orange County Mutual Aid Compact. He also instituted the use of helicopters and canines in patrol activity.

Current challenges facing the sheriff's department include whether or not the coroner's office should be separate from the sheriff's, and where to construct new jail facilities to alleviate overcrowding. Another is the day-to-day effort of providing law enforcement to a burgeoning county population. In addition to serving unincorporated areas of the county, the sheriff's department also serves as the municipal police department for a few incorporated cities.

No matter what challenges it must face, the Orange County Sheriff's Department continues to provide a high level of service. Innovative and efficient, the department has an outstanding reputation and continues to be one of the best law enforcement agencies in the country.

The Orange County Jail has seen many outlaws pass through its doors throughout the years. Courtesy, First American Title Insurance Company

English walnuts, shown in this 1900 photo drying in the sun, were harvested by knocking them off the trees. After the appropriate drying time, the nuts were bleached, polished, culled, graded, and sacked. J.R. Congdon claimed to have planted the first English walnuts in Orange County in 1870. He first planted them in San Juan then later moved to Santa Ana. By 1910 the crop was netting nearly one million dollars a year for county farmers. Courtesy, Anaheim Public Library

Fourth Street since they were offered for one dollar per year. The county offices remained there for the next two years, but eventually found larger quarters at a modest rent. The county's first major purchase was a block of land to house a courthouse and county facilities, which would be built at a later time. William Spurgeon offered land for $9,500 but shrewd bargaining got him down to $8,000. The block also contained room for a new jail, built out of necessity in 1895.

The first jail used by the new county was nicknamed "Brunner's basement" because it was in the basement of Joseph H. Hiltbrunner's Santa Ana store. The second, a small board and brick structure with three cells, was built on Sycamore between Second and Third streets in 1890. It was the first building constructed by the county and it cost $4,000. The first case tried by Judge Towner did not need the use of a jail since the alleged horse thief was acquitted. But it was needed for the case of Modesta Ávila, the first felony conviction in Orange County.

Modesta Ávila was a young woman from San Juan Capistrano who made the mistake of opposing the Santa Fe Railroad in a unique manner. Ávila, tired of hearing the train at night and sure it was responsible for keeping her chickens from laying, protested the iron monster by hanging her wash across the tracks. She also had a running feud with the railroad for not paying what she thought adequate for a right-of-way through her mother's property, which might have accounted for her quick apprehension by the local railroad agent. Arrested for attempted obstruction of a train, she was sent to Santa Ana to stand trial. After the first trial ended in a hung jury, the second one resulted in a conviction. She was sentenced to three years in San Quentin where she died after serving two years of her term.

For Ávila, Orange County justice was harsh; for Francisco Torres, it was nonexistent.

In 1892 Torres, an employee of the Modjeska Ranch, was accused of killing William McKelvey, the ranch foreman, over a $2.50 poll tax that had been withheld from his pay. Torres fled, a reward was offered, and a huge manhunt ensued. He was caught and taken to the Sycamore Street jail to be held for trial. The trial never took place. On the night of August 20 a group of masked men dragged Torres from the flimsy jail and hanged him from a telephone pole at the corner of Fourth and Sycamore. The lynching received widespread publicity around the state. It was the last to occur in Orange County and although an investigation took place, the men involved were never identified.

The new county also had its share of robberies, wife beatings, and shoot-outs. One could land in jail for murder or for not trimming his weeds to the proper height. But for the most part Orange County was a safe, prosperous place to live and raise children.

In 1891 the Santa Ana Board of Trade wrote:

Within the next few years the horticultural industry of Orange County will assume proportions that will astonish even the most sanguine. Already the keynote has been sounded, the 'horny-handed sons of toil' have awakened from their slumber and with thoughts of coming wealth, with all its luxuries and pleasures, are working as they never worked before. Acres upon acres of the county's favorite soil are being planted to trees of every description and an air of prosperity is pervading the homes of our many honest and faithful husbandmen.

The words were prophetic and the golden promise took on a new luster.

As seen in this photograph looking west on Fourth Street in the late 1920s, Santa Ana had become a bustling community. The Spurgeon Building, with its clock tower located on the right, was a prominent landmark. Courtesy, Charles W. Bowers Memorial Museum

The Emergence
of a
New Century

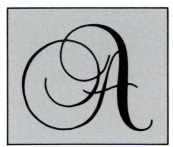

A visit to Santa Ana at the turn of the century was a special event for the entire family. It had a shooting gallery, a skating rink, fine new hotels, and many stores. There was an "opera house," where plays and musical programs were held, and the grounds of the Thirty-Second Fair Association, where you might catch a wild west show or a circus. Or you could wander over to Sycamore Street to see great columns of steel from Pennsylvania and Minnesota, massive slabs of Arizona sandstone, and great earthen ramps on which mules moved supplies. It was the construction of the new Orange County Courthouse, and for eighteen months it was the best show in town.

On April 4, 1900, the first shovel plunged into the earth, marking the

Above: *Frank Eastman is shown at the wheel of his home-made Rural Free Delivery mail carrier. He established the first of three Anaheim routes in 1901, which had previously been covered on foot. Courtesy, Anaheim Public Library*

Facing page: *A local farmer proudly shows off his 1935 season crops. The soil and climate of Orange County helped to produce abundant and sometimes large vegetables and fruit. Courtesy, Charles W. Bowers Memorial Museum*

Right: *The "Hayburners," seen in this 1890 photograph of the Number 21 Streetcar Stables on Fourth Street in Santa Ana, were a popular mode of local transportation. Courtesy, Charles W. Bowers Memorial Museum*

beginning of the courthouse's construction. Designed by Charles L. Strange of Los Angeles, the Richardsonian Romanesque structure was the product of a design competition, drawing fourteen applicants who competed for a prize of $2,400.

The construction of the courthouse was a sight no one wanted to miss. Yet the significance of its construction went deeper than its entertainment value for people confined to tedious jobs or the routine of their farms. The courthouse symbolized the coming of age for the new county. The magnificent new structure, touted by some locals as the finest building in the state, could certainly hold its own among public buildings of other counties. Orange County, California, was a prospering, hopeful land of golden promise and its future, exemplified by its impressive new courthouse, was beginning to shine.

The decade prior to the turn of the century had brought many changes to Orange County. Gas, electricity, and phones were available in the major cities, pavement could be found in

downtown Santa Ana, and an inter-city trolley called the Orange Dummy or Peanut Roaster (because of the heat coming from its engine) connected Santa Ana and Orange. Agricultural production was booming and Orange County farmers proved it by bringing home many prizes from the Chicago World's Fair in 1893.

"Almost upon one's fingers could be counted what we do not or cannot raise, while it would seem to require the very hairs of one's head to enumerate our varied and endless productions," Orange County's promoters wrote at the end of the century. The Santa Ana Chamber of Commerce, responsible for the 1898 brochure extolling the county's potential, was not far from the truth. Most crops grew well in Orange County. The adoption of irrigation

143

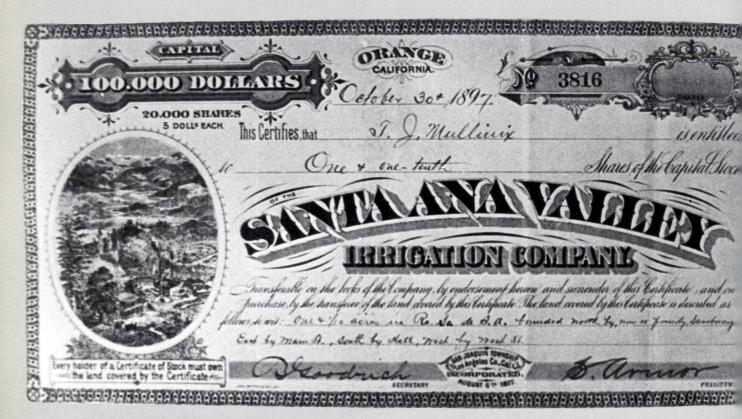

Above: *Dated 1897, this irrigation stock certificate entitled its owner to 100 shares of acres in the Santa Ana Valley Irrigation Company. Courtesy, Charles W. Bowers Memorial Museum*

Left: *Fullerton was another community that benefited from the construction of irrigation ditch lines. Courtesy, Fullerton Public Library*

Facing page: *Peat bog horseshoes were used in the Westminster and Fountain Valley area in an effort to prevent horses from sinking into the watery soil. Courtesy, Charles W. Bowers Memorial Museum*

THE TREASURE OF ORANGE COUNTY

The promise of gold hidden in the earth drew swarms of treasure seekers to California in the 1850s. Many passed through Orange County as they hurried to the goldfields in the north, paying scant attention to the amber hills that hid secrets of their own.

Tucked away in the Santa Ana Mountains were canyons and streams in which the Spaniards had found gold. But quantities were small and sightings infrequent so there were no large-scale attempts to find the source of the gold nuggets that sometimes glittered in the sun. In later years some did take up the pursuit, but only a few met with success.

Orange County's silver, coal, and tin mining booms drew many prospectors to the area for short periods of time. But the lure of gold always beckoned—if it could not be found in its natural state, then the searchers looked for treasure hidden and forgotten by others.

Orange County's earliest tale of hidden treasure involved the visit of the pirate Hippolyte Bouchard, who raided the California coast in 1818. In that year he anchored off Dana Point and sent a party ashore to seek supplies. Warned by lookouts who had spotted the ships, the inhabitants of Mission San Juan Capistrano evacuated. All valuables were buried either on site or at inland mission stations where the villagers awaited the piracy's end. When Bouchard's sailors departed—after burning a few buildings and consuming a great deal of brandy—the villagers returned, but many of the mission's valuables remained buried in the ground, their locations forgotten.

From that day on stories abounded about buried treasure in the Santa Ana Mountains and in the mission grounds. The fact that Franciscans took an oath of poverty and the mission had very few valuables made little difference to the storytellers. According to historian Father Zephyrin

Engelhardt there was only one treasure ever buried at the mission: a $2,000 religious fund was buried for safekeeping by Father José Zalvidea who was going away on a lengthy trip and had no one to entrust it to. When he returned he dug up the money, found it intact, and restored it to its usual place.

Stories of treasure in the mission and surrounding ranch lands have survived through two centuries. Many were passed down in a book called *Capistrano Nights,* a collection of folk tales published in 1930. In this book is a conversation between Father St. John O'Sullivan, resident priest from 1910 to 1933, and an old woman of the parish:

'Are you not afraid to stay in the Mission at night?'

'No,' he said, 'Should I?'

'Why, don't you know that people dig at night for money left in the ground by the old pirates and there are ghosts about?'

'And did you know any of them,' he asked.

'Yes, indeed,' said the woman, who told about a gardener who, as he lay dying from an illness, recounted the fact that there was a treasure on the mission grounds.

'Near the zaguan which you pass through when you go into the old church, the one they call Father Serra's Church, there is a pillar that holds up an arch at the zaguan and it has a mark on it. It was put there many years ago with paint like they used for the decorations in the big church that the earthquake ruined. Go to that spot and dig beneath the mark and you will find the money,' the old gardener had told the woman.

The woman searched and searched but couldn't find the spot. A few years later all the pillars were painted

and if there had been a mark, it was lost forever.

Capistrano Nights is also the source for tales of treasure in the Santa Ana Mountains. It describes a sure way that old-timers had of finding a treasure: if you see a pillar of light rise from the ground then fall back again, be sure to mark the spot, for that is where a treasure is located. But don't dig in the night. Come back the next day or bad luck will follow you.

A cowboy, seeing the strange light while on a cattle drive near the Plano Trabuco, stopped near the ruins of an old adobe and noticed that the light seemed to be coming from a corner of a room. He marked the spot and rode off to find his employer. The next day they returned, dug at the spot, and unearthed a clay pot full of gold coins.

A similar story from Rancho Mission Viejo is about a man named Manuel who stopped to rest at a deserted adobe. His horse, tied to a wobbly fencepost, tried to jerk free and pulled the post from the ground. After catching the animal Manuel went back to the hole and was amazed to see a cache of gold coins in it. The owner of the adobe told Manuel that the gold belonged in the post hole, that he always kept it there.

Another story about gold coins in the ground took place near the mission. A man digging holes for a fence found a clay pot full of gold coins. Not wanting to call attention to his find, he reburied the pot and continued digging in other areas. Later that night he went back to remove his find. Unfortunately he had hidden it too well and could not find it.

Others hearing the story were blamed for the destruction of the Verdugo Adobe, located near the spot where the treasure disappeared. The owner complained that zealous treasure hunters dug so close to his house that his foundations were underminded, causing his house to collapse.

A larger treasure disappeared in downtown San Juan, this one owned by Juan Avila. In 1879 his hacienda caught fire. In the confusion of the night, while neighbors attacked the flames with shovels, blankets, and bucket brigades, Avila called for assistance to help him save his gold.

Several strong men were needed to lift the chest of gold from its hiding place in a secret chamber under Avila's bed. Carrying it out of the burning house, they were directed to deposit it on the ground and return to work. Avila and his servant dug a hole and put it in the ground for safekeeping.

After the fire, when the last ember was dead, Avila went to retrieve his gold. But it wasn't there. Either he couldn't remember where he had buried it, or someone had stolen it in the confusion. Later accounts indicate that Avila may have circulated the story of the lost treasure to keep bandits from bothering him. Others say that the servant, who disappeared soon after the fire, returned years later, dug up the treasure, and was never heard from again. Still others say the treasure is still in the ground, waiting for someone to find it.

One of the most intriguing stories about hidden treasure in the Santa Ana Mountains is told in Don Meadows' book *Orange County Under Spain, Mexico, and the United States.* A man named Marcelino was riding in the hills and happened to see a curious sight. High in a tree was a piece of rawhide with three keys tied to it. They were very old and Marcelino thought they might belong to the mission. He climbed the tree, carefully removed the keys, and tied them to his saddle. He delivered the keys to the mission padres, who thanked him but could not find the locks that fit them. Years later, a visiting priest from Hermosillo stopped by the mission with an interesting story. He had stumbled across a treasure map and wondered if the padres could assist him in locating the starting point. He was to find a large sycamore tree which had three keys attached to the branches with rawhide. Had they ever seen such a tree?

Some who did not wait to stumble on a treasure map or treasure chest looked for gold in the Santa Ana Mountains. Maximo Lopez, a prospector for more than forty years, built a cabin in Lucas Canyon and mined enough gold to buy supplies and meet his needs. Spurred by his success, others staked claims, some motivated by an old story about a "lost mine of the padres" hidden in the mountains. One story, appearing in *Capistrano Nights,* pinpointed the lost mine to Lucas Canyon.

An old soldier, a veteran of the Mexican War, claimed that the padres had used gold from the mine to make many things for the mission churches. According to the old soldier, nobody knew where the mines were except for a few of the oldest Indians, and they would not tell. In his youth he had known an old Indian who supposedly knew where the mines were.

The old Indian did provide clues. It was between the sunrise and the sunset, he said, black above and yellow below. But he would never say exactly where and the old soldier searched for eleven years before finally giving up.

Hidden treasures, lost mines, and the chance of making a new strike all combined to bring hope to those who had little chance for riches. Genuine sources of buried gold were bandits who robbed travelers and village stores and often hid their gold in the ground until they needed it. This tactic may have been responsible for the most spectacular find of the twentieth century.

In 1905 a contractor named George Washington Smith had a crew laying pipe near Old County Park Road. As the digging progressed, someone struck a metallic box near the bottom of the trench. Pulling out the small box, the workers were surprised to find that it contained $5,020 in gold coins. Not one was dated later than 1856.

Lost loot was a phenomenon not only of the nineteenth century. In 1925 the Santa Fe was robbed of $2,500 during a run between Oceanside and Santa Ana. The assailant hid on the roof of the baggage car, kicked in the glass of the sliding door, shot the attendant, lowered himself over the edge into the car, removed the cash, and jumped off the train. He did all this while the train was running at top speed. The money was never recovered and the assailant never caught. Stories persist to this day that somewhere along the tracks a sack full of money is buried.

While treasure hunting is usually an individual pursuit, on one occasion hundreds of people joined in the search. In 1877, responding to reports that a pirate had buried his gold on the shore, hordes of people combed the cliffs of Dana Point hoping to find it. After an exhaustive search the only treasure uncovered was a tarnished silver crucifix. The treasure hunters went home and the cliffs sported a few extra holes.

While most efforts to find it proved futile, buried treasure gave many something to talk and dream about during years of drought and depression. One could always hope that some night a mysterious white light would appear and the golden promise of a hundred folk tales would at last become a reality.

and drainage acts provided necessary improvements and assessed the cost to adjacent property owners in direct proportion to benefits derived; the water problems of earlier decades were nearly ended.

Some areas had too much water. Nearly 10,000 acres of the area west of the Santa Ana River were considered peat lands which were extremely rich, but difficult to work. Residents of the Bolsa swamps employed the Drainage Act of 1881 to get water removed from their area. Once drained, it became useful for many types of crops. D.E. Smeltzer planted celery south of Westminster in 1891, but was initially unsuccessful. His partner E.A. Curtis convinced the Earl Fruit Company to try celery and even brought in Chinese laborers to grow it on eighty acres of peat land near the same location. Although people resented the Chinese to the extent that guards were hired to protect them, the project was successful until 1896, when a blight infested

the crops and caused a decline.

A successful crop started in the 1890s was sugar beets. Sugar beets grew well, but were difficult to market since the closest processing plant was in Chino. In 1896 the Bixby Land Company convinced William A. Clark to start a factory in Los Alamitos and guaranteed him a supply of beets. The E.H. Dyer Company built the plant and operated it the first year. Other plants were built in Huntington Beach, Anaheim, and Santa Ana to serve this early Orange County crop that was productive until the 1980s.

Lima beans and chili peppers were first planted in the 1890s as were grapefruit trees. The boom crop of the 1890s, however, was apricots.

Apricots were grown primarily in El Toro, La Habra, and Santa Ana, although they thrived in other parts of the county as well. The apricots were harvested around mid-June and were usually dried. First they were cut in

Above: *Many Chinese workers were used to work the fields and groves of Orange County. These laborers are seen in about 1895 picking oranges in a Placentia field. Courtesy, Charles W. Bowers Memorial Museum*

Left: *The Holly Sugar Beet Factory, located along today's Freeway 55, processed sugar beets into sugar. The factory was active until 1983. Courtesy, Charles W. Bowers Memorial Museum*

Facing page, top: *Celery was a favorite crop in Orange County until its decline in the late 1890s. This Westminster area farmer is shown with his horse team in about 1890. Courtesy, Charles W. Bowers Memorial Museum*

Facing page, bottom: *On January 13, 1905, the Southern Pacific Engine No. 2215 became hopelessly stuck in the peat bog at Smeltzer when the tracks sank. Five days and five nights of constant work were required by the wrecking crew to get the engine out. Courtesy, First American Title Insurance Company*

Right: *Niguel Regional Park now occupies the site of this scene. Taken in 1916, the photo shows John Osterman's threshing rig in full operation. The Osterman family was prominent in the farming community of El Toro. Courtesy, Saddleback Area Historical Society*

Top, far right: *The growing 1900s citrus industry demanded long hours from these orange pickers. Courtesy, Anaheim Public Library*

Bottom, far right: *A watermelon feast at the 1908 El Toro School picnic has these children in good spirits for this impromptu photo. Courtesy, Saddleback Area Historical Society Collection*

Below: *A local farmer hauls the season's crop of sugar beets near Greenville in 1911. Courtesy, Costa Mesa Historical Society*

Left: *Workers from the Santiago Orange Growers Association are shown packing oranges into field boxes in this 1890s photo. Courtesy, Charles W. Bowers Memorial Museum*

Facing page: *The girls' basketball team of the Santa Ana High School class of 1908 poses with its teddy bear mascot. Courtesy, History Room, Santa Ana Public Library*

Below: *One of the first citrus cooperatives was the Santiago Orange Growers Association, which later became known as Sunkist. Courtesy, Charles W. Bowers Memorial Museum*

halves then put on a redwood tray that was placed over a pit of powdered sulfur, leaving space for air to circulate. A cardboard "house" was put over the stacked trays to prevent spoilage and the fruit usually dried in three to seven days in the open air. After a two-week "sweat" under canvas the apricots were ready for market.

The county's most famous agricultural crop—oranges—took off with the formation of citrus cooperatives. The first, formed in 1885, was the Orange Growers' Protective Union. In 1893 the Southern California Fruit Exchange, which later became Sunkist, was started

Above: *School children and teachers pose in 1908 in front of the original El Toro School, which once stood at First and Olive streets. This building later became a Catholic church and now is an important part of Heritage Hill Historic Park in El Toro. Courtesy, Saddleback Area Historical Society*

Facing page: *One of the earliest and largest orange packinghouses was owned by Dr. W.B. Wall, who can be seen at the far left. The oranges were carefully wrapped in individual tissues and placed in crates before shipping. Courtesy, Charles W. Bowers Memorial Museum*

Above: *This truckload of Chapman's Brand walnuts are in transit to local merchants. Courtesy, Fullerton Public Library*

Facing page: *By 1900 Santa Ana had a population of 4,933 and was growing at a rapid pace. This view is of Fourth Street, looking west from Spurgeon Street. Courtesy, History Room, Santa Ana Public Library*

in Fullerton, assisting farmers in picking, spraying, packaging, and marketing their crops. Other popular fruit and vegetable crops were walnuts, barley, corn, potatoes, pumpkins, tomatoes, apples, peaches, and pears. In addition, the county produced abundant numbers of beef cattle, dairy cattle, hogs, and poultry.

One of the most productive of the industries that blossomed in the 1890s had nothing to do with agriculture. It was oil.

Oil was first discovered in California as early as 1865. Shortly thereafter unsuccessful attempts were made to drill in Brea. In 1882 efforts were revived and a well was drilled at the junction of Tonner and Brea canyons. Oil was found at a depth of 100 to 300 feet and

the company moved its operations deeper into Tonner Canyon and established a settlement called Petrolia near Olinda. By 1884, 5,000 barrels had been recovered.

In 1885 the Puente Oil Company had two high-producing wells in the La Habra area. Oil was shipped to a refinery in Chino. More wells were drilled and by 1903 the Puente Company merged with the Columbia Oil Company, retaining the Puente name. In 1922 sixty-five wells were sold to Shell Oil.

More discoveries were made near Brea in 1897 by the Santa Fe Railroad in partnership with E.L. Doheny, who also promoted the Brea Cañon Oil Company. By 1903 they had thirty producing wells. Other companies such as Fullerton Consolidated, Fullerton Oil Company, Birch Oil, Menges Oil, and Olinda

Facing page, top: *During the oil boom at the turn of the century, wells sprung up rapidly as the demand for oil increased. Courtesy, Charles W. Bowers Memorial Museum*

Facing page, bottom: *One of Orange County's fledgling organizations, the Woodmen of the World, was founded in 1890 as a fraternal aid (insurance) society. This photo was taken in 1898 and shows the Anaheim Chapter in its full ceremonial robes, carrying symbolic axes. Fraternal aid societies performed a very necessary function before the days of Social Security. Courtesy, Anaheim Public Library*

Above: *One of the most important, and sometimes quite prosperous, members of the turn-of-the-century community was the local blacksmith and livery stable owner. This wood frame building housing Spangler's and Johnson's blacksmith shop was once located on Sycamore Street in Santa Ana between Second and Third, and is seen here in 1901. Courtesy, History Room, Santa Ana Public Library*

Above: *The red cars provided an important service to Orange County for more than forty years. Seen here on Fourth Street in Santa Ana in the late 1920s, the red car allowed Orange County residents to travel to Los Angeles and back in one day. Weekend tours became a popular form of recreation and the Pacific Electric Railway Company operated special tour cars on Sundays. Courtesy, History Room, Santa Ana Public Library*

Right: *Santa Ana residents lined the street in 1906 to greet the first red car as it chugged along Fourth Street. Part of the celebration was a "Parade of Products," which included a float from each surrounding town depicting an array of vegetables, fruits, and other products. The most popular float was from the town of Tustin that featured a tribute to that town's burgeoning peanut industry. Courtesy, History Room, Santa Ana Public Library*

Oil Company were formed. The latter was the first company to drill with mud in the bore hole.

Union Oil, one of Orange County's most famous companies, was formed in 1890 by Wallace Hardison and Lyman Stewart, who had been active in Petrolia. They and others pooled their resources and formed Union Oil, buying property near productive oil lands and leasing others. They operated in the Brea Canyon and on the Jose Sansinena property in the hills north of La Habra before 1900. As technology developed and wells could be drilled deeper there were more discoveries and greater success stories. The nearby Whittier Fields were developed by Home Oil, Central Oil, and others. In 1903 Murphy Oil drilled at the north base of the West Coyote Hills owned by Domingo Bastanchury, but was only mildly successful. Gambling, Murphy bought 2,200 acres nearby and by 1906 hit gushers.

Many small companies continued to search for oil, as did the large companies after the turn of the century. In addition to Union, Standard Oil was on the scene in Orange County but was largely unsuccessful until 1911 when it found oil on the Toler, Williams, Yriarte, and Leffingwell ranches of La Habra and in the Coyote Hills. The activity in the

Above: *The second venture into Orange County by the Pacific Electric Railway Company was the establishment of the Santa Ana, Garden Grove, and Artesia line. The construction of this line was completed in 1905. Courtesy, Charles W. Bowers Memorial Museum*

oil fields added to the prosperity and development of several Orange County communities, notably Fullerton, La Habra, Placentia, and Brea.

Growth and prosperity in the boom of the 1880s followed the progress of the railroads. Another real estate boom came after 1900 to Orange County, this time in the form of conveyances called the "big red cars."

The big red cars were the brainchild of Henry Huntington. He envisioned a transportation system linking four Southern California counties together, with Los Angeles at its center. This interurban railway would carry passengers and freight and would be powered solely by clean, quiet electricity. His system would cost less than the cumbersome traditional railroads, and would have connections to more cities. In 1901 he filed incorporation papers for the Pacific Electric Railway Company and began to fulfill his promise.

The link that brought the Pacific Electric into Orange County was its Long Beach line, completed in 1902. The first city to be reached was Bay City, renamed Seal Beach in 1915. In 1903 Phillip A. Stanton formed Bayside Land Company and founded Bay City, which would one day tout itself as an amusement center complete with pier, dance hall, and roller coaster. Prior to this was the founding of Pacific City, subdivided by Stanton in 1901 through the West Coast Land and Water Company. Stanton's company was purchased by the Huntington Beach Company in 1903; it changed the name of the town from Pacific

The Edward Atherton family of Fullerton enjoys a quiet summer afternoon in 1898. Courtesy, Fullerton Public Library

City to Huntington Beach and gave Henry Huntington the right-of-way he needed to extend his line. On July 4, 1904, the first red car pulled into Huntington Beach amidst a public celebration featuring a free barbecue and brisk land sales. Land values skyrocketed. Orange County was off on another boom.

By 1905 the line was put through to Newport Beach, completing one of the most popular excursions in its day. The spectacular ocean scenery, particularly at sunset, drew hosts of travelers and gave many future settlers their first glimpse of Orange County. The Newport Beach Company had been formed by William S. Collins and Charles Hanson in 1904. Huntington bought half of the Collins interests, acquiring parts of the peninsula, all of the then-submerged Lido Island, and a few mainland lots. Two other investment groups, the East Newport Town Company and the Newport Bay Investment Company, completed the development of the community. Balboa, so named by an investor who was vice consul of Peru in Los Angeles, was laid out in 1905 complete with pier and pavilion. On May 13, 1906, the Pacific Electric extended its line to East Newport and on July 4 to Balboa, after promoters of both communities paid Huntington a fee to do so. In honor of the occasion a new hotel was built in Balboa—in just ten days. A few weeks later all three settlements in the area incorporated as the City of Newport Beach.

The Pacific Electric was not the first railroad in the Newport area. In 1888 the McFaddens had built a wharf where the Newport Beach Municipal Pier is today. The wharf was 1,300 feet long, sixty feet wide, and nineteen feet above the water at high tide. Immensely successful, the wharf enabled large ships to take on and unload cargo without having to enter the bay. To improve marketing opportunities for farmers and provide easier access for peo-

The McFadden family helped to establish Newport Beach by building the wharf, which was the forerunner to the present-day Newport Beach Municipal Pier. The McFaddens also formed the Santa Ana and Newport Railroad, enabling easier access for the residents of the outlying farming communities to reach Newport Beach Harbor. Courtesy, Fullerton Public Library

ple to get to the wharf, the McFaddens opened the Santa Ana and Newport Railroad in 1891 with connections to the Santa Fe. By 1892 they had acquired half of the peninsula, divided it into lots that were leased for twelve to eighteen dollars per year, and built a hotel.

At its height, the McFaddens' railroad and wharf had a payroll of 100 and was one of Orange County's largest businesses. In 1896 the McFaddens bought Lido and Balboa islands, built a spur line to the celery fields,

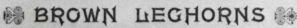

Above: This exquisite antique cash register from the turn of the century was used for many years in an Anaheim clothing store. Courtesy, Charles W. Bowers Memorial Museum

Facing page: Local farmers' wives advertised their homegrown poultry and eggs. Courtesy, Fullerton Public Library

Right: The Fullerton Racket Store advertised the many items available for local residents in this 1900s ad. Courtesy, Fullerton Public Library

and lobbied the federal government for harbor improvements. But the improvements went to San Pedro instead of Newport, so the McFaddens sold their railroad to private parties, only to have it turned over to their old enemy, the Southern Pacific, who immediately disbanded it. Disillusioned, they closed out their holdings and by 1902 had departed from the Newport area, although they remained in Orange County. They were not present to witness the arrival of the red cars.

The next line, straight from Los Angeles via Watts, was the Santa Ana line with stops at Cypress and Stanton (areas that were quickly subdivided) and also at Garden Grove. Cypress (called Waterville) was founded by Simeon O. Walker, who had come to the area in 1896. Stanton, platted as the town of Benedict, was owned by the Pacific Electric Land Company and a syndicate headed by Robert McFadden. Garden Grove, already established with the arrival of the line, profited greatly from having the new freight service.

In December 1906 the first red car pulled into downtown Santa Ana, courtesy of the commun-

Above: The Ellis brothers' 1909 Buick was the second car in the Costa Mesa area. The car was run in the Los Angeles to Phoenix Road Race in 1913, pictured here, and seventy-one years later completed a successful run in the Los Angeles to Indianapolis Road Race of 1984. Courtesy, Costa Mesa Historical Society

Facing page: This woman helped advertise the outstanding quality of the Holly brand pure granulated sugar. Courtesy, Charles W. Bowers Memorial Museum

ity's citizens who paid $22,000 for the right-of-way. Santa Ana celebrated the occasion with a parade of agricultural products featuring floats from other communities. With the completion of the Santa Ana line it was now possible to go to Los Angeles and back in one day. The Pacific Electric also offered special excursions. One popular trip was the Triangle Trolley Trip. For just one dollar a person could travel from Los Angeles to Santa Ana to Huntington Beach and up the Long Beach line back to Los Angeles. Realtors met every stop and land values continued to rise wherever the red cars went.

Fullerton Tribune.

| FOURTEENTH YEAR | FULLERTON, ORANGE COUNTY, CALIFORNIA. THURSDAY MORNING, JANUARY 7, 1904. | NUMBER |

FOR INCORPORATION

Why Fullerton Should Join the Ranks of Thriving Cities.

Taxpayer Advances Cogent Arguments Showing It Would Result in the Greatest Benefit--His Letter.

EDITOR TRIBUNE: Permit me, through your columns, to state my position on the question of the incorporation of Fullerton, and to give my reasons for taking that position.

In the first place we should assume that those opposed to, as well as those in favor of incorporation are actuated solely by a desire to secure that condition which will be to greatest advantage to the community. I can hardly believe that any citizen of the town will consider only his own selfish interests in forming his opinion on the question.

In short, I would oppose incorporation were I not convinced that it will be for the advantage and improvement of our town and community.

Recently I have visited several incorporated towns of this and other counties, among them Ontario, which is no larger, I think, than Fullerton; and I could not help noticing the contrast in the appearance of those towns and that of Fullerton. On the one hand was a general appearance of neatness, of well-kept and lighted streets, of shade trees trimmed and side-walks clear of weeds, giving an

from incorporation. Anaheim, however, is not a fair sample, for that city has had considerable to contend with, having undertaken at the start the erection and maintenance of water and lighting plants, fire department, etc. These things entailed heavy expense from the first, and at the same time there was for a long time in Anaheim a condition of falling values in realty, which added to the difficulty. And still, those of us who remember Anaheim as it was before incorporation and compare that with the present Anaheim, cannot but believe that the improvement has been worth the cost. The fact is that at the present time Anaheim is going ahead of Fullerton in business. Several times a week I pass through that town, and it is easy to see much more mercantile business is done there than here; and I also observe that a large part of that business comes from Placentia, Orangethorpe, and even from Fullerton. Shall we stand by and watch our neighbor forge ahead of us, or will we wake up and by shaping ourselves into a well-regulated, well-improved, up-to-date town, increase our business, growth and prosperity?

But to return to that awful bugbear, taxes. There will be no necessity of any burdensome tax, and I have no fear that the rate will ever be over 50 cents at most, on the county assessor's valuation. Many of the benefits to be had by incorporating will cost comparatively nothing. For example, a little judicious sanitary regulation would not add to our taxes, and yet it

*The front page of the January 7, 1904, Fullerton Tribune car-
ried the day's news as well as local advertisements. Courtesy,
Fullerton Public Library*

The final Pacific Electric line was from La Habra to Yorba Linda. Originating as a branch of the Whittier line at Los Nietos, the new branch went from La Habra to Pillsbury, west of Randolph (later called Brea). By July 4, 1910, it was completed to Randolph and one year later extended past Yorba Linda to Stern. There, it was planned to turn and head toward Riverside County. The new line was completed with great difficulty as Henry Huntington waged a battle with E.H. Harriman of the Southern Pacific to see who would complete a line in this area first. The winner would have an advantage in getting freight business. Although the Southern Pacific resorted to intimidation and other tactics, the Pacific Electric won.

As in previous cases, the coming of the red cars stimulated growth and development along the way. The community of La Habra, informally settled in the 1880s and 1890s, was developed by W.J. Hole, but not formally platted until 1903 by Robert C. Hiatt and Maggie Coy. The town of Brea, originally named for Epos Randolph, Huntington's engineer, was surveyed in 1903, but not formally recorded until 1908. The advertisements appearing after the Pacific Electric station opened curiously announced the formation of a new town. Yet it had been in existence since 1902 with the formation of the Randolph School District. In

This is a view of Spadra Street (Harbor Boulevard) in Fullerton, looking north toward La Habra Hills in 1900. Courtesy, Fullerton Public Library

Facing page, top: *A popular place of lodging was the St. George Hotel of Fullerton. The Amerige brothers were photographed in front of the hotel in this 1889 view. Courtesy, Fullerton Public Library*

Facing page, bottom: *The famous site of the Fullerton Four Corners is shown here in 1888 at the intersection of Spadra Street (Harbor Boulevard) and Commonwealth Avenue. The St. George Hotel in the center dominates this view. Courtesy, Fullerton Public Library*

Above: *Advertised in the late 1920s as Orange County's finest lodging, the California Hotel in Fullerton was later remodeled into a specialty shopping plaza. Courtesy, Fullerton Public Library*

Above: Local parades were a frequent and festive form of entertainment as this one demonstrates progressing along Fourth Street in Santa Ana in 1905. Courtesy, History Room, Santa Ana Public Library

Facing page: To provide a healthy alternative to the town's pool halls, Mrs. James Dean, wife of a Fullerton dentist, established a free reading room above a bank, which was soon to develop into a library. However, as this circa 1900 photo shows, there were still many who preferred a pool hall to a reading room. Courtesy, Fullerton Public Library

1910 it was replatted and its name changed to Brea.

The first Yorba Linda map was filed in 1908 by Dr. Peter Janss of the Janss Investment Company. The land was advertised as citrus land and sold for $150 to $250 per acre. Many Quakers settled in the area, which became known as a prime area for growing avocados with the planting of the first Fuerte grove in 1913 by John T. Wheedon.

Other lines were the Santa Ana to Orange line which followed the route of the Orange Dummy trolley, and a line that connected Fullerton and Laon Junction near La Habra.

The Orange County stage of the interurban promise was complete and Huntington looked ahead to extend his lines to other counties.

The red cars, which brought on another land boom, contributed greatly to the economic growth of Orange County. New freight routes provided new opportunities for farmers; increased population brought stores, hotels, restaurants, service-oriented businesses, and expanded local markets for farm products. Orange County's residents were stable, secure, and satisfied with the quality of life they enjoyed.

Above: *Company L of the National Guard returns to* *Ana at the end of the Spanish-American War in 189* *Ana's early citizens were very patriotic and huge crow* *lined the route as the National Guard departed and* *from duty. Flowers were often strung in their path, a* *mayor made presentations while the merchants gave* *members free merchandise. Courtesy, History Room,* *Ana Public Library*

Facing page: *The men of Santa Ana's famous Comp* *the National Guard pose in front of their tent in Sa* *cisco in 1898. This group fought in the Spanish-Am* *War, helped in the 1906 San Francisco earthquake a* *Long Beach earthquake of 1933, and gave aid during* *ange County flood of 1938. Courtesy, History Room,* *Ana Public Library*

Above: *A sandy Orange County beach provided the ideal resting spot for these afternoon strollers. S.T. Miller, a pioneer and early beekeeper from Bell Canyon, can be seen at the far right near the water's edge. Courtesy, Charles W. Bowers Memorial Museum*

Right: *This early Newport Beach scene from the 1920s shows a number of fine sailing yachts bedecked with flags suggesting the possibility of a forthcoming regatta. Courtesy, Charles W. Bowers Memorial Museum*

Top, far right: *The inviting coastline of Newport Beach provided endless enjoyment for the nearby residents of Orange County. Courtesy, Charles W. Bowers Memorial Museum*

Above: *Two rows of tents line the mesa at Laguna Beach. For many years it was the habit of area families to load their household goods in a wagon and head for the beach to spend two weeks in the summer. Mattresses, bedding, clothing, pots and pans, dishes, and rugs went with the family to the beach. Courtesy, First American Title Insurance Company*

Above: Sporting the latest men's fashions, A.O. Stovall poses for his portrait in 1902. Courtesy, Fullerton Public Library

Facing page: Friends and members of the Forster family pose on the steps of the Forster home in San Juan Capistrano in 1911. The woman with the dog is Ysabel Forster, daughter of Marcos Enrique Forster. The building is the former schoolhouse from Forster City (an unsuccessful boom town near San Onofre), which was moved to San Juan Capistrano in the 1890s and served as the Forster home. Ysabel married Lloyd Patterson and this photo is from the collection of their daughter, Marie. Courtesy, Marie Patterson Swanson Collection

Purveyors of the golden promise, the Santa Ana Chamber of Commerce, had written in 1898:

Orange County, while its population is somewhat cosmopolitan and made up largely of wealthy, educated classes, is an agricultural and horticultural region, and, is therefore, essentially a poor man's county. Nowhere can he live and maintain his family more cheaply and comfortably or find less difficulty in getting on in the world.

While most county residents would like to have thought this of their home territory, it was somewhat optimistic.

In 1900, 60 percent of the population still lived on farms; most were able to eke out an adequate living, yet some survived only marginally. There were many pockets of poverty throughout the county. Vagrancy, a jailable offense, kept the county continually supplied with an adequate labor force to work on public projects. Life was particularly hard for ethnic groups such as Mexicans and Chinese who had different cultures and lifestyles and sometimes experienced persecution by those intolerant of their differences.

Yet even for the poor there were things to enjoy in Orange County. There was a fine new park donated in 1897 by James Irvine in Santiago Canyon, beaches and mountain campgrounds, public schools in every community, and free diversions such as bicycle races and athletic competitions. Life seemed better in Orange County, even for the poor.

Regardless of financial status, Orange County people had a resilience and courage that would see them through the worst of times. They would need it in the decades to come with war, disasters, and depression, and a golden promise that would be always within view, but sometimes out of reach.

Evidence of a strong community spirit was shown by the Santa Ana Breakfast Club, the third to be organized in the state. This 1930 photo, taken two years after the club's organization, shows one of the group's favorite locations for its meetings; Main Street between the Odd Fellow's Hall on the right, and the Fox West Coast Theatre on the left. Courtesy, History Room, Santa Ana Public Library

War,

Boom,

and Depression

In an old church on Second and Main in Santa Ana a young man with high ideals and a future full of promise poured over plans and spent every dollar he earned on a secret project. Pounding and sputtering could be heard all hours of the night from inside the wood-frame building while Glenn Martin, encouraged by his mother, struggled to build the first airplane in Orange County.

On August 1, 1909, he hauled it over to McFadden's pasture to give it a test flight. He had practiced taxiing in James Irvine's bean field and felt confident when he climbed into the bucket seat; with a twist of the propeller he heard the engine sputter to life. The crowd, gathered at the field's edge, cheered when the little craft with its wings of shellacked

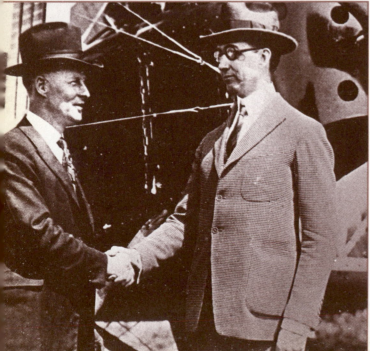

Above: *In 1909 Glenn Martin constructed the first plane to be built in Orange County in an empty Santa Ana church. Courtesy, First American Title Insurance Company*

Left: *A local citizen congratulates Glenn Martin (right) on his historic flight from Newport Beach to Catalina Island. The flight was thirty-four miles long and was completed in thirty-seven minutes. Martin soon formed his own airplane manufacturing company, receiving his first order from the War Department in 1913. Courtesy, Charles W. Bowers Memorial Museum*

Facing page: *Orange County's first successful airplane was buil* by Glenn Martin in Santa Ana in about 1909. This airplane was flown in Martin's historic flight. Courtesy, Charles W. Bowers Memorial Museum*

muslin finally left the ground after several attempts and an engine change. It was the first airplane flight in Orange County and among the first in California.

Martin continued to improve his plane, after moving to larger quarters on First Street. During the next three years he formed his own airplane manufacturing company, gave many exhibition flights, and was the first to fly from Newport to Catalina. He eventually moved to Los Angeles, then to the East Coast to fill orders for the U.S. armed forces.

Martin's metamorphosis from experimental obscurity to technological prominence was symbolic of the changes being wrought in Orange County. In 1910 the population was 34,346, almost double that of 1900, and while three-fourths of the county's income was still derived from agriculture, 60 percent of the population now lived within six incorporated cities: Santa Ana, Anaheim, Orange, Fullerton, Huntington Beach, and Newport Beach. Garden Grove and Tustin were the largest of the unincorporated towns, followed by El Modena, Olinda, and Placentia. Other communities, which could only be called settlements, included Bolsa, San Juan Capistrano, and Yorba, and the crossroad communities of Buena Park, La Habra, Olive, Westminster, Cypress, and Stanton.

Farming communities also existed. Los Alamitos began with the sugar industry; McPherson was born, lived, and died with the raisin industry. Celery was the crop of Smeltzer and Wintersburg, and Talbert (Fountain Valley) began with bean and beet fields. El

Above: *The construction of the Harper Reservoir in 1914 took place on the site that is now the northwest corner of Placentia and Nineteenth streets in Costa Mesa. Courtesy, Costa Mesa Historical Society*

Right: *Shown in this 1920s photo, the interior of St. George's Episcopal Church of El Toro featured natural redwood walls, ceiling, and floor, and had kerosene lamps hanging from the ceiling and on the left side. The establishment of the Episcopal church was part of a plan by Dwight Whiting, Sr., to attract more English settlers to the El Toro area. Courtesy, Saddleback Area Historical Society*

Facing Page: *Eddie Martin participated in his family's tradition of interest in aviation. Courtesy, Charles W. Bowers Memorial Museum*

THE GOLDEN PROMISE

Toro was known for its apricots and Irvine as the commercial center of the Irvine Ranch. Costa Mesa was consolidated from three early settlements, Harper, Paularino, and Fairview, and the coast cities of Alamitos Bay, Bay City, Sunset Beach, Arch Beach, and Laguna Beach were known as resorts.

Orange County was a place of innocence and optimism. But the county, along with the rest of the country, was on the brink of a great many changes. And the reality of war, absent from the American home since 1898, would be the catalyst.

The people of Orange County, like Americans everywhere, read with apprehension about the growing tensions in Europe. Most were certain that the United States would be forced into the war and formed Red Cross chapters and organized drives for Liberty Bonds.

In April 1917 the United States officially entered the world war and by July the first men were drafted. In September a contingent of Orange County servicemen boarded the train and headed for Camp Lewis near Tacoma, Washington. In some cities stores were closed so everyone could gather at the station to wish them well. Santa Ana's Company L of the California National Guard had been called even sooner—eleven days before war was declared. Most saw duty in France, many as replacements for other units. More than 1,600 Orange County residents served in the armed forces. Many did not return.

·On the home front people were not idle. Although news of the war was sparse in hometown papers, people filled their Liberty Loan quotas and rolled bandages, knitted socks, and mended used clothing to send to Europe. Home guards were formed and drilled regularly; households were encouraged to grow more food in personal gardens; and everyone with a relative in service put a flag in the front window. Feelings ran high as news of friends

Above: *Santa Ana celebrated the end of World War I in thi. 1918 "Welcome Home Parade." A Red Cross nurse and "Uncle Sam" carry the American flag with the help of retur. ing soldiers. Courtesy, Charles W. Bowers Memorial Museu.*

Below: *Local Boy Scouts helped to celebrate the end of World War I in this Santa Ana parade. Courtesy, Charles W. Bowers Memorial Museum*

Above: *Three local servicemen from Costa Mesa pause for a candid 1918 snapshot. Courtesy, Costa Mesa Historical Society*

Facing page, top: *Three young women frolic on the water's edge near Dana Point in about 1920. Courtesy, Charles W. Bowers Memorial Museum*

Facing page, bottom: *Dana Point, shown here in about 1920 was named after Richard Henry Dana, a New England autho who, as a young sailor in 1835, transported cowhides from California to New England shoe factories. The hides were tossed over the cliff to the beach, enabling easy transport to the waiting ships. Courtesy, Charles W. Bowers Memorial Museum*

and neighbors trickled home. Residents of German descent did not suffer greatly as long as they did their part; those who were not yet naturalized could not become citizens during the war and were watched more closely for unpatriotic remarks, a jailable offense in some Orange County communities.

On November 11, 1918, the war ended and Armistice was celebrated with parades, picnics, and patriotic speeches. In September 1919 a special victory party was held in Orange County (Irvine) Park at which the governor of California presented victory medals to all World War I veterans. More than 20,000 victory buttons were sold in Orange County to raise money for the event, and people remembered the occasion for many years to come.

The end of the war brought new perspective and new prosperity to Orange County. Prospective home buyers poured into the state, many of them lured south by brochures printed by the Orange County Board of Supervisors and the Santa Ana Chamber of Commerce. With fanfare reminiscent of the boom of the 1880s, several new communities opened their sales offices. Coast Royale near Dana Point opened in 1921 complete with a landing strip to fly in potential customers. In 1923 the San Juan Point Association was formed, planning a new community on the bluffs, complete with a hotel. The grand opening of Dana Point in 1924 drew thousands who came to hear the band concert, partake of the free barbecue, and pay $1,000 for a 60-by-100-foot lot. This development was not an immediate success because it had no paved highway, but was reopened by S.H. Woodruff, who acquired 1,400 acres of the settlement in 1926, put in the utilities, and built thirteen residences by 1928.

Farther south another entrepreneur by the name of H.H. Cotton formed a syndicate and

Above: *Charles C. Chapman was an early citrus producer in the Fullerton area. In 1919 he became the proud owner of one of the most productive oil wells in the state. Courtesy, Charles W. Bowers Memorial Museum*

Facing page: *The town of San Clemente, founded in 1925, built its train station in the mid-1930s. This station depicts the architectural style of the red tile roof and white stucco envisioned by Ole Hanson. Courtesy, Charles W. Bowers Memorial Museum*

bought 2,000 acres of land to develop. He formed a business alliance with Ole Hanson who dreamed of building a Spanish village with white stucco houses and red tile roofs. After convincing Cotton, he filed a tract map and opened for business in a tent on December 6, 1925. By the end of the day he had collected $125,000 and his city, incorporated as San Clemente in 1928, was firmly launched.

Doheny Park, which would become Capistrano Beach, also had its beginnings in 1928 when Edward L. Doheny, Jr., laid out a town on 1,000 acres. When its founder was murdered the following February, the project was taken over by Doheny, Sr., who managed to stay afloat during the Depression and keep

125 employees on the payroll. Doheny was an oilman and oil had its own boom in the 1920s.

On March 11, 1919, the Chapman No. 1 well on the Charles C. Chapman property near Placentia sent gallons of oil into the sky. After two years of drilling, Chapman's patience finally paid off in what would become one of the most productive wells in the state. The new gusher brought even more oil development. Standard Oil leased property from Samuel Kraemer across the street from the Chapman well that paid off immediately. Reportedly the cost of the lease was $250,000. Another five wells were drilled at the same depth and a sixth drilled deeper. Although all

Facing page: *The discovery of oil was not without its problems as seen by this oil seepage in a nearby farmer's field.
Courtesy, Anaheim Public Library*

Above: *The Chapman Building at the corner of Wilshire and
Harbor was a sensation in its day and continues to be a Fullerton landmark. Courtesy, Fullerton Public Library*

were successful, the deeper one was called the Kraemer Zone and became the most productive. Standard was also successful in Huntington Beach where oil was discovered on March 24, 1920.

The discovery of oil had a tremendous impact on the communities near the oil fields. Huntington Beach went from a quiet, "dry" community of 2,000, to an active, boisterous boom town of 8,500 residents in less than a year. The Placentia area almost immediately had a housing shortage and overcrowded schools; the town itself acquired the reputation of being a rough, if not rich, place with more than 900 producing wells around it. It finally incorporated in 1926 with an official population of 800 and a transient population of many more.

The oil and land booms of the 1920s affected many Orange County communities. La Habra grew into a thriving city of 3,500 during this period and added a new development called La Habra Heights, which promoted ag-

ricultural development. It incorporated in 1925. Costa Mesa opened a few land sale subdivisions, started a newspaper, poured new sidewalks downtown, and built 250 new buildings in 1923. In Garden Grove a group of twenty local businessmen and farmers started a company called Garden Grove Home Builders that successfully added many new homes to the community, profited from the boom in the process, and led the way for many other developers.

The boom period of the 1920s found most Orange County communities adding to their housing stock and taking on the trappings of modern cities. Most expanded their downtown business districts, opened banks, and looked toward improving education and cultural opportunities in their cities. The popularity of the automobile added to this prosperity as many advertisements and travel guides promoted motor vacations on the West Coast. With increased emphasis on automobile travel, the need for better roads became a critical

Facing page: *During the 1910s and 1920s, large imposing school buildings were often the center of local activity. After Orange County High School was abandoned in 1954, Chapman College purchased its building. The building in the center, opened in 1905, was moved 200 feet in 1922 to the northeast so that the present building could be constructed. Courtesy, First American Title Insurance Company*

Above: *Culture was alive and well in Orange County when this group of performers called "The Merry Troupers" performed in Cab 71 in Santa Ana in about 1920. Traveling theater groups and vaudevillian troupes frequently came through Santa Ana and Anaheim in the early part of the century. Courtesy, History Room, Santa Ana Public Library*

Above: *A woman and her companion show off their fine automobile on an afternoon outing. Courtesy, Charles W. Bowers Memorial Museum*

Facing page, top: *S.C. Best was the owner and operator of this early 1920s bus. It traveled between Riverside and Santa Ana, stopping in Corona along the way. There were many small bus lines in Southern California in the 1910s and 1920s, some of which were bought by Greyhound Bus Lines in the late 1920s and went on to become part of the huge national bus system inaugurated by that company. Courtesy, History Room, Santa Ana Public Library*

Facing page, bottom: *Motor trips became a favorite 1920s pastime as Orange County's roads expanded and improved. Courtesy, Charles W. Bowers Memorial Museum*

Above: *Along with the growth of car dealerships came an opportunity for other automobile-related businesses such as Oldfield Tires in Santa Ana, pictured here in 1930. Courtesy Charles W. Bowers Memorial Museum*

Left: *The Tustin school bus ran through Laguna Canyon to bring youngsters from Laguna to Sycamore School. Courtesy, First American Title Insurance Company*

Facing page, top: *As the demand for the automobile increased in Orange County, dealers ordered cars by the trainload, as this 1925 photo of a shipment for dealers S. Hill & Son in Santa Ana illustrates. Courtesy, Charles W. Bowers Memorial Museum*

Facing page, bottom: *This Orange County automobile showroom selling early Franklin and Liberty cars illustrates the thriving new automobile industry of the 1920s and 1930s. Courtesy, Charles W. Bowers Memorial Museum*

Above: *Lewis Moulton, owner of the Moulton Ranch, came to California in 1874 and became a sheepherder for the Irvine Ranch. Eventually, along with Jean Pierre Duguerre, Moulton restored the total 26,000 acres of the original Avila land grant into one ranch, the Moulton Ranch. This ranch remained in operation until 1960 when it was sold to a syndicate that developed the land into the communities of Laguna Hills and Leisure World. Courtesy, Saddleback Area Historical Society*

Above right: *Nellie Gail Moulton, wife of prominent rancher Lewis Moulton, was a schoolteacher in El Toro when she met her future husband. She was well known throughout the area for her participation in charitable and educational groups. Courtesy, Saddleback Area Historical Society*

Facing page: *Built in Laguna Beach in 1924, the Wave Street House possessed a unique architectural character similar to a fairy-tale house. Courtesy, First American Title Insurance Company*

concern. In 1912 the people of Orange County had passed a $1.2 million bond issue to pave and improve major inter-city roads throughout the county. By 1915 more than 108 miles of road had been completed. In 1926 a new segment of the Roosevelt Coast Highway opened from Long Beach to Laguna Beach, creating a building boom along the way. By 1929 the road had reached Dana Point and was pushing south through San Clemente.

The popularity of the automobile had a disastrous effect on one Orange County institution, the old Pacific Electric. As automobile dealerships sprang up in every community and travel by car became more convenient and affordable, the reliance on the red cars as a transportation system began to decline. In

Below: *James Irvine, Jr., was a prominent Orange County citizen and owner of the largest agricultural land tract in the area. Courtesy, Charles W. Bowers Memorial Museum*

Above: *City dwellers and farm families alike turned out for this holiday parade. Patriotic holidays such as Memorial Day, Labor Day, Fourth of July, and Armistice Day inspired local bands and organizations to put on elaborate costumes and strut their best. This band posed on an Anaheim Street in the 1920s. Courtesy, Anaheim Public Library*

Left: *The spacious St. Anne's Inn, once a popular place for newlyweds, was built in 1921. In later years it served as a courthouse annex, and was torn down when the new county administration building was built. Courtesy, History Room, Santa Ana Public Library*

1924 the Pacific Electric had 2,700 runs and carried 109,108,650 passengers. It would never again carry that number and experienced a decline thereafter.

The boom of the 1920s created a flurry of activity but soon stabilized. The population shift to the cities was underway, but agriculture was still Orange County's major industry. The largest agricultural area under a single ownership was the Irvine Ranch, which harvested a variety of crops, the most predominant being beans and barley. Oranges, walnuts, and apricots were also harvested, as were limas, peanuts, and chilis. In 1921 avocados were planted there for the first time and by 1930 lemons were added. Similar crops were harvested throughout Orange County and the abundance of the harvests, the product of good climate and hard work, continued to polish the golden promise.

Growth was evident in much of Southern California and with growth came the resurgence of an old problem—water. In 1923 officials from seventy-five cities gathered in Fullerton to discuss the problem of insufficient water. They planned a strategy to urge

Facing page: Judge Cox was an acclaimed foe of all traffic violators. When Bebe Daniels, a famous silent movie star, was apprehended for driving her car at forty-five miles an hour down a Santa Ana street, Cox sentenced her to five days in jail. Daniels did not suffer too much, however; her press agent arranged for the best furniture store in town to furnish the cell and the nearby Rossmore Hotel to send in her meals. Her cell was filled with candy, flowers, and magazines during her stay. Courtesy, History Room, Santa Ana Public Library

Below: Santa Ana was one of the hardest hit areas of the devastating 1933 earthquake. Courtesy, Charles W. Bowers Memorial Museum

Congress to adopt the Swing-Johnson Bill that would insure the construction of Boulder Dam and bring water from Colorado to California. By 1928 the Metropolitan Water District (MWD) was organized with Anaheim and Santa Ana voting to become its first Orange County members. While the MWD was preparing for the future, the present was dealt a resounding blow with the crash of 1929. The crash tempered Orange County's prosperity and tested its resilience. As month by month the news grew worse people began to realize they would be relying on their own strengths to see them through the crisis. And if the Great Depression was not enough to challenge its mettle, a natural disaster soon followed to tax the county's resources. On March 10, 1933, at 5:55 p.m., an earthquake hit. Centered in Long Beach, the quake destroyed many buildings and severely damaged the downtown areas of Santa Ana, Garden Grove, and Anaheim. Twelve persons were killed; luckily, the quake occurred after most people in the hardest hit cities had left their stores

and offices for the day.

Most people survived the earthquake with nothing more than a chimney to replace or a crack to repair; they survived the Depression by planting gardens, helping less fortunate neighbors, and by beseiging their local officials to get recovery funds promised by the Roosevelt Administration into Orange County. The first funds, borrowed from the Reconstruction Finance Corporation, arrived in April 1933. They were used to put 3,133 men to work on public projects for six days. The next funds from the same source arrived in May and a reduced amount came in June. The board of supervisors supplemented the funds by allocating $60,000 of county money for relief work in July.

A series of relief measures was enacted by Congress in the months and years to come and Orange County legislators fought hard to get their fair share. Californians helped themselves by voting bond issues to provide funds that could be loaned to local cities and counties. Four Civilian Conservation Corps camps

Facing page: *Farming was a family business. The Shiffer clan takes a break to pose for this 1930s snapshot. Courtesy, Costa Mesa Historical Society*

Above: *Activities surrounding the citrus industry included the naming of a citrus queen. This young woman was honored with the title in the 1930s. Courtesy, Charles W. Bowers Memorial Museum*

Participants in the Old Timers Picnic pose for their portrait on June 11, 1927, at the Anaheim City Park. Among these descendents of California's first settlers is Francesca Mosserman in the wheelchair, the only surviving pioneer who settled in Anaheim in 1857. Mosserman celebrated her ninety-second birthday just before this picnic. Courtesy, Anaheim Public Library

The quiet village of Laguna Beach, shown here in about
1910, has become one of the most popular and unique beach
cities along the Southern California coast. The Laguna Hotel,
built in 1898, is in the center of the photo. Courtesy, History
Room, Santa Ana Public Library

were established in the county to put young men to work. Three were under the California Division of Forestry and the fourth was under the U.S. Soil Erosion Service.

The National Industrial Recovery Act put forth a system of price- and wage-setting that met with only limited success in Orange County, although many subscribed to it. The legislation's public works administration activities were more popular since assistance was provided to cities and counties to put people to work on large, visible projects. Yet despite these efforts there were still four million unemployed throughout the country at the end of 1933. More relief was needed.

The government responded with several more programs, the most prominent being the Works Progress Administration in 1935. Activities were numerous and varied. Roads, public buildings, bridges, and sewers were built; historic buildings were documented; public art projects were constructed; nearly anything that needed to be done found a willing hand and a federal or state program to support it. One major project, sought for decades, was the dredging of Newport Harbor. It was approved by the federal government, bond funds were approved by the people of Orange County to provide more jobs, and the work was begun in 1935.

Despite the difficulties of the times, Orange County residents still found time to entertain themselves. One of the most creative of those endeavors was the establishment of the Festival of Arts in Laguna Beach. Laguna had little more than a general store when it was "discovered" by artist Norman St. Clair in 1901. Several other artists followed and by the end of World War I Laguna Beach had the reputation of being an artists' colony. The Festival of Arts began in 1932 and one year later held its first "living picture" tableaux. By 1935 the show was taken over by Roy M.

Above: *The early industries of Orange County provided many employment and business opportunities and helped the local communities to flourish. This automobile upholstery factory illustrates the diversity of these new businesses. Courtesy, Charles W. Bowers Memorial Museum*

Facing page: *During the 1910s and 1920s, a popular place to visit was Laguna Beach, with its fledgling artists' colony. The members of the Orange County Historical Society posed in 1927 in front of the old Laguna Beach Hotel. Courtesy, First American Title Insurance Company*

The flood of 1938 destroyed the bridges of the Pacific Coast Highway where the Santa Ana River empties into the ocean. Courtesy, Costa Mesa Historical Society

Ropp, an artist and architect, who renamed it Pageant of the Masters, and operated it in much the same format it has today.

Recovery, both economic and spiritual, was well on its way by 1938 when the county had to overcome yet another disaster. From February 27 to March 3 a series of storms flooded the rivers, reaching a peak around midnight of March 3 when the Santa Ana River breached its banks, taking houses and cars in its wake. Many of the bridges in the county washed out, thousands of acres of agricultural land were damaged or destroyed, 2,000 were left without homes, and nineteen people lost their lives. As a result of the devastation the federal government began the construction of Prado Dam, located in Riverside County, to prevent future devastation. Started in the fall of 1938 under the direction of Kenneth J. Harrison and the Army Corps of Engineers, it was completed in 1941.

Orange County—surviving storms, earthquakes, and financial setbacks—kept its sanity and its sense of humor. Despite the challenges, Orange County was still a place of beauty and a source of pride to the 130,760 people who lived there in 1940. There were still thousands of acres of natural wilderness areas in the Santa Ana Mountains, most of which had become Cleveland National Forest, miles of open fields, acres of orange groves, and forty miles of scenic coast. Orange County was as yet unspoiled and somewhat provincial. But rumblings on the horizon and headlines in the newspapers would soon change the county's image and its development. And the golden promise would be fulfilled.

*This aerial photograph documents the vast destruction of the
1938 flood when the Santa Ana River overflowed its banks.
Courtesy, Charles W. Bowers Memorial Museum*

THE PROMISE FULFILLED
PART III

Servicemen of the Santa Ana Army Air Base and their companions enjoy the festivities surrounding the Christmas holidays in this early 1940s photograph. Courtesy, Costa Mesa Historical Society

World War II
and the
Stirrings of Change

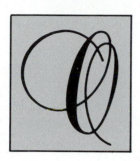

O n December 7, 1941, the Japanese bombed Pearl Harbor and the United States entered World War II. While World War I had seemed somehow remote, World War II entered every home, touched every family, and set the stage for a dramatic change in the face of Orange County.

The war was not unexpected. For years local agencies prepared for the inevitable by forming local disaster committees, inventorying resources, and readying their citizens for coming hardships. Some, like Santa Ana, developed strategies for lessening those hardships.

Taking an option on a little more than 400 open acres, the City of Santa Ana sent a lobbyist to Washington to try to interest the

Above: *This contemporary sketch of the Santa Ana Army Air Base by Scott Kennedy illustrates how the base looked after its completion in the early 1940s. Courtesy, Costa Mesa Historical Society*

Facing page: *Looking southeast from the corner of Harbor Boulevard and Warehouse Road, these photographs document the S.A.A.A.B. as it appeared in the early 1940s (top) and later in 1972 (bottom). Courtesy, Costa Mesa Historical Society*

government in developing a military base in the area. The property, located where Orange Coast College and the Orange County Fairgrounds are today, would be leased to the government for one dollar per year. Santa Ana would pay $6,386 per year on a twenty-five-year lease unless it chose to buy the property for $500 per acre. The presence of the military meant growth, jobs, and economic revitalization. Community leaders felt it was worth it. Santa Ana's effort was successful and the United States Air Corps Replacement Training Center (later called the Santa Ana Army Air Base) was soon on the drawing board.

As early as 1939 Congress had appropriated funds to increase the strength of the nation's air power. Goals were set for numbers of pilots to be trained, and contracts were awarded to aircraft firms, many of them in Southern California, to provide the necessary equipment. Doubtless these factors, along with the availability of the flat, open land, and the inexpensive price, influenced the government's decision to locate its West Coast preflight training center in Orange County—a decision that would have far-reaching impacts stretching beyond the war.

On October 23, 1941, ground was officially broken for the new facility that initially would include 145 buildings and accommodations for 3,000 cadets, 806 enlisted men, and eighty-three officers. In addition, a Headquarters Squadron would be located at Orange County's airport, and a five-acre site in downtown Santa Ana would be used for the West Coast Army Air Corps Training Command Headquarters.

Orange County was also chosen as a site for other military activities. In 1941 the U.S. Naval Air Station obtained a site in Los Alamitos and moved its operation from Long Beach in April 1942. Two years later the navy added a Naval Ammunition and Net Depot at nearby Seal Beach. The navy was also active in the Irvine area, building the Santa Ana Naval Air Station or LTA (Lighter Than Air) station in March 1942. Included on this blimp base were two of the largest clear-span wooden buildings in the world, both 171 feet high, 1,000 feet long, and 300 feet wide, built at a cost of two million dollars each. The blimps, eventually numbering fourteen, were used for anti-submarine shore patrol. East of the blimp base was the U.S. Marine Corps Air Station at El Toro. Established in August 1942, it was originally built on 2,333 acres at a cost of eight million dollars.

As time passed the army expanded Orange County Airport, known as the Santa Ana Army Airdrome, by bringing in sixteen P-38s used for offshore patrol. Other military facilities included a camp at Irvine Park, a radio-monitoring station at Fairview and Edinger, and a series of nineteen aircraft warning stations, located throughout the county. The warning stations were manned twenty-four hours a day by civilian volunteers reporting to the West Los Angeles Filter Center of the Fourth

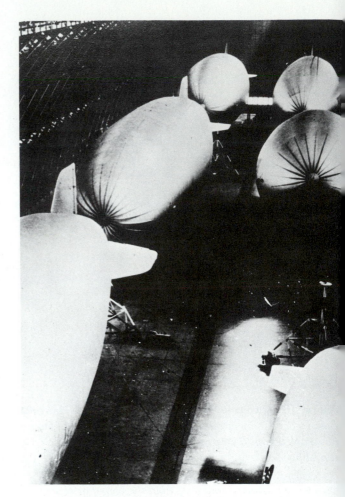

Fighter Command.

The construction and staffing of military installations immediately had an impact on the economy of Orange County. Construction companies hired hordes of workers to meet contract deadlines. Skilled workers from many professions left their jobs for higher paying employment as civilian workers on military bases. Public transportation facilities such as bus and rail lines enjoyed new prosperity, and many new businesses opened, such as restaurants, movie theaters, and ballrooms, to entertain the influx of servicemen to the county. In *The SAAAB Story,* historian Edrick Miller writes, "Orange County cities were overrun by military men. Restaurants, cafes and other business establishments were mobbed. The local Chamber of Commerce's prediction of prosperity for the business community had

Above: *The servicemen of the Santa Ana Army Air Base in the early 1940s used the cafeteria of the Service Club as a gathering place and eating establishment. Courtesy, Charles W. Bowers Memorial Museum*

Facing page: *Blimps circling Orange County and the ocean during the latter part of the war were a normal sight. The prime objective of the huge craft was to provide submarine surveillance along the California coast. As pictured here, six airships could be housed in each hangar of the Naval Air Station in Tustin. Courtesy, First American Title Insurance Company*

Right: *Now listed as a national landmark, these two blimp hangars were built in 1942 on the grounds of the Naval Air Station in Tustin. The wooden doors weigh hundreds of tons each, and slide back and forth like an accordian. The twin hangars are among the largest unsupported wooden structures in the world. In 1951 the station became the first installation in the United States to be devoted entirely to helicopters. Courtesy, First American Title Insurance Company*

This wide variety of orange crate labels from Orange County packinghouses illustrates how well the county lived up to its name. Courtesy, Special Collections, Pomona Public Library

This early Santa Ana milk bottling plant may have been one of the industries in which women sought work during World War II. Courtesy, Charles W. Bowers Memorial Museum

come true."

The war called for extraordinary efforts from ordinary citizens. Women who had never before worked outside the home left their children with babysitters and went to work in aircraft factories and other industries where there were vacancies left by men, now in service. The National Guard—Company L of Santa Ana, Company I of Orange, and Company K of Anaheim—had all been called to active duty months before Pearl Harbor, so State Guard units were formed to protect communication and transportation centers and vital resources. Not only did civilians volunteer as air scanners, but as air raid wardens and as temporary assistants to police and firemen. Like families, communities drew together and became dependent on each other's strengths to help them through the coming ordeal. They were confident, buoyant, and resourceful. They

were also scared.

The attack on Pearl Harbor had brought the war very close to the West Coast. Japanese submarines were sighted in coastal water and had in fact attacked ships near Eureka, San Luis Obispo, Cayucos, Goleta, Redondo, and Catalina. On February 25 people actually heard anti-aircraft guns fired in the night. At 2:27 a.m. planes tracked by Los Angeles radar were reported to be within three miles of the city. Air raid sirens and the sounds of firing guns pierced the darkness as people, awakened by the noise, huddled in their homes and waited for the end. The event was later known as the mysterious Battle of Los Angeles; trackers swore there were at least five planes although their origin was never discovered.

These incidents, along with rumors of hidden ammunition dumps, intercepted short-wave radio messages, and unexplained lights during blackouts, fanned the flames of suspicion and mistrust. People in Orange County, as elsewhere along the California coast, began to feel nervous, particularly after the issuance of the Roberts Commission Report claiming that espionage was a primary factor in the bombing of Pearl Harbor. The report placed blame not on individuals, but on an entire ethnic group—the Japanese-Americans—and called for its immediate internment.

Before that time people in Orange County generally viewed their Japanese neighbors as they did anyone else, although anti-Oriental feeling did exist in some areas. In 1940, 1,855

persons of Japanese descent lived in Orange County. Most were farmers who led quiet lives and kept to themselves. Although many held on to traditions and customs of the old culture, 1,178 were American citizens and contributors to their communities. If anyone's loyalty was at issue, most people were content to leave such matters to the FBI.

But that was not the feeling of the government.

A curfew, effective March 27, 1942, was imposed on all German and Italian aliens, and all persons of Japanese descent, including citi-

Fumigation of citrus groves became easier with the introduction of the caterpillar-like "sausage tents." This tent was pulled along the rows of grove trees enabling the workers to fumigate more trees at a faster pace. Courtesy, Charles W. Bowers Memorial Museum

Lemon Heights, located to the northeast of Tustin, was covered with miles and miles of citrus groves and eucalyptus trees from the 1930s through the 1960s. Each spring the air was heavy with the smell of orange blossoms. Courtesy, Tustin Area Historical Society

ens. Between the hours of 8 p.m. and 6 a.m. hey had to be in their homes; they were also estricted in travel. But that wasn't enough. The Exclusionary Order, issued the following month, directed all Japanese to be moved out of Orange County. Those living in Laguna Beach and southward registered in a San Onofre schoolhouse. The rest registered in Huntington Beach and Anaheim. By May 12 all had to be registered; by May 15 all were shipped to the Poston Relocation Center in Arizona, where they remained until they could apply for relocation to another part of the United States.

The relocation effort, placed in the hands of the War Relocation Authority, moved very slowly. Many opposed having the Japanese in their communities and could not guarantee their safety. By fall a plan had been developed; after proving loyalty, interned citizens could apply for indefinite leave. This aspect of the process was successfully challenged in the U.S. Supreme Court. If loyalty was proven, why was the leave "indefinite?" Military exclusion orders were cancelled and on January 2, 1945, all Japanese of proven loyalty were allowed to return home.

Of the 1,800 Japanese who left Orange County, only 600 returned. Some had sold their land and belongings, accepting the low prices offered on such short notice; they wanted a fresh start in a new area upon their return to society. Those who had not sold often found their property in chaos, their buildings occupied or neglected, and their furnishings removed or destroyed. In some cases, their farms had been turned over to property managers by local committees, but many of the tenants knew little about farming and had allowed crops to deteriorate or die. Sometimes the tenants refused to leave and the returning Japanese, without funds or hope, chose not to enter a costly court battle. The bright promise

that had lured them to Orange County seemed very far away.

As the war progressed, life went on, but it had a new focus, a new purpose. People went to work in the morning and at the end of the day clustered around their radios to hear the latest news. Mail grew increasingly important. Basic necessities could no longer be taken for granted. Rationing was instituted and every housewife felt the pinch at the grocery store.

The first rationed items were sugar, coffee, and shoes. Gasoline rationing, which prompted a lively black market, started in December 1942 and had its own coupon books. People who needed gasoline traded food coupons and cash for more gasoline coupons.

By March 1943 a second ration book was being used for fresh and canned meats, canned fish, processed foods, and dairy products. There were also restrictions on tires and other commodities. Many unrestricted items also grew scarce and difficult to obtain: women lined up for blocks if a department store announced a new shipment of nylon stockings.

The people of Orange County, living in a largely agricultural area, fared better than many. The rich soil touted by boom-period land salesmen was ideal for most who wanted to plant a backyard victory garden. People who raised more than they needed shared with others. A drive into a farming area might find a fruit or vegetable stand with surplus to sell.

The war created special problems for farmers. With the labor supply diminished, farmers looked to high school students to harvest their crops. But citrus ranchers needed more workers than the local community could supply. Meetings were held in 1942 to address the problem and plans were drawn. On February 11, 1943, representatives of nearly all Orange County packinghouses met in Anaheim to hear a plan to import large numbers of seasonal laborers from Mexico. A new organization called

Citrus Growers, Inc., was established and 1,650 workers, called braceros, were brought in to harvest the 1943 citrus crop.

Even with an increase in the bracero program the following year there were still not enough workers to do the job, so the citrus ranchers brought in 1,600 Jamaicans to supplement the work force. Most lived in a tent city in La Habra, with others stationed at Irvine. The Jamaicans, who had marked cultural differences and were not used to rationing, became quickly dissatisfied and returned to their own country.

The third group of replacement workers found for the Orange County citrus industry consisted of 500 German prisoners of war who were held in a camp near Garden Grove. The POWs were used for the 1945 crop through an arrangement with the State Agricultural Extension Service. They remained after the harvest to work at the Santa Ana Army Air Base as cooks, bakers, mechanics, janitors, and other service-oriented jobs.

The largest of the military installations, the Santa Ana Army Air Base, had outgrown its facilities immediately after its establishment. More land was necessary to expand the base that eventually contained 1,283 acres. At its peak the base was like a small city where thousands of people had lived briefly before passing on to another place. It had a library, golf course, hospital, three movie theaters, five stores, a sewer and water system capable of serving 40,000 people, three post office branches, and four chapels. It even had its own newspaper and sports teams.

The preflight training period peaked in late 1943. The following year this activity was phased out and the base became a rehabilitation and redistribution center. In November it was transferred to the Army Air Force Personnel Distribution Command and became the fourth redistribution center for war veterans, with the job of processing returnees to either send them back to the war or to send them home.

The base gained the reputation of a resort hotel because of its climate, excellent facilities, and nearness to recreation areas. These were important to the returning veteran who, in the words of Costa Mesa and Santa Ana Army Air Base historian Edrick Miller, had "four things on his mind—back pay, furlough, good chow, and women and not necessarily in that order."

The war ended August 15, 1945. Many bases, including the Santa Ana Army Air Base, served as deactivation centers, processing thousands of returning servicemen. By November 15 the Santa Ana base had shut down permanently as a military facility. The City of Santa Ana used it as temporary housing for veterans and their families who had sensed the golden promise of Orange County and wanted to make it their permanent home.

By spring of 1946 the Santa Ana Army Air Base, which had served hundreds of thousands of men and women, was for sale. The once bustling, self-contained city lay vacant and silent, yet somehow expectant as if distant echoes would breathe life into it once again. Gone were the marching feet and nervous laughter of cocky young men who hid their fear behind masks of conceit. In their place were empty streets and row upon row of vacant buildings.

Many of the buildings escaped the wrecker's ball. Some were relocated to parts of Costa Mesa as homes, churches, restaurants, and businesses; others became part of the Orange County Fairgrounds. A good portion was used by schools. Orange Coast College opened on the site in 1948 with 500 students; that same year on another part of the land, the Southern California Bible College was established as the first four-year college in Orange County. There was talk of reactivation, but it never occurred. Other bases established in Orange County were used; some changed their names

Workers in this sheet metal department toiled long hours as the demand for their product increased. Courtesy, Charles W. Bowers Memorial Museum

and activities. All marched to a slower pace than in the frenetic years of World War II.

The war changed Orange County forever. New buildings stood where beans had grown; new businesses remained as permanent fixtures in downtowns. But the greatest change would come later. The war had brought hundreds of thousands of people into Orange County, however briefly. They had sampled the sunshine and had felt the ocean breezes; they had seen productive fields and growing cities. All around them they saw opportunities for a better life for themselves and their families.

Some fell under the spell of the golden promise and vowed to return.

Above: *These soldiers arriving at the Santa Ana Army Air Base in 1943 may have decided—as did many—to stay in Orange County after the war's end. Courtesy, First American Title Insurance Company*

Right: *This poster features the Santa Ana Army Air Base. Courtesy, First American Title Insurance Company*

FROM BUCKETS TO BATTALIONS

In 1801 a boy entered a store room at Mission San Juan Capistrano to get tallow. Preoccupied by the bats he noticed hanging from the rafters, he accidentally overturned a lighted candle. The resulting fire—the first recorded structure fire in the history of Orange County—destroyed the building, 12,500 pounds of tallow, and 1,000 bushels of wheat and corn.

Such costly damage, unfortunately, was common in the nineteenth century, since the county's frontier fire fighting methods were weak and ineffectual. Water was usually too far away and manpower too scattered to bring a fire under control. But as communities grew in Orange County, so did fire fighting resources. In 1871 the county's first group of volunteer firemen was organized in Anaheim.

Two spectacular fires—one destroyed a private home and the other the Planters Hotel—prompted the organization of the Anaheim volunteers. Within two weeks of operation, the department had ordered a two-wheel Studebaker hose truck with 500 feet of hose. The hose could be attached to a water main on Center Street (now Lincoln), which was fed from an elevated tank. Although better equipped to fight fires, Anaheim still suffered from conflagrations. In 1877 a large section of the downtown was destroyed, and in 1890 the rebuilt Planters Hotel burned again. To become more effective, the fire department went through many reorganizations and in 1883 was called the Confidence Fire Company No. 1 with Fred Rimpau as chief.

In 1915 the old fire equipment was replaced with a motorized Seagrave Chemical Hose Wagon. By then Anaheim had a population of 3,000, a better water system, and a bell to call volunteers. In 1926 a full-time fire department was organized with Rudolph Nyboe as chief. The town trash collector and building inspector, Nyboe also kept his eye on the water level in the nearby Santa Ana River. Nyboe, chief until 1950, saw many changes as the city grew.

Another early fire department was organized in 1883 in Santa Ana. An election was held and residents voted a property tax of ninety cents for every $100 assessed valuation to pay for the department. C.E. Berry was the first chief and the first station was located on Sycamore between Third and Fourth. The funds were used to buy a Chemical Climax Fire Engine and a hook and ladder wagon, both purchased in San Francisco for $1,400. Other supplies included two dozen rubber fire buckets, four torches, six chiefs' trumpets, one cord and tarrall, and twenty-five pounds of chemicals. Volunteers were equipped with black hats and bright red shirts trimmed with blue.

What they didn't have in Santa Ana was a bell to call the volunteers to duty. In 1885 another election was held to vote for funding for the bell, belltower, and a year's operating funds (about $550). The firemen lost the election (51-54), and shortly thereafter the entire department resigned. A year later the fire department was reorganized with Adam Forster as chief. Perhaps the formation of the Santa Ana Gas Company hastened the reestablishment of the fire department, since some people feared the gaslights would burn the town to the ground. Feelings ran so high that the city fathers even agreed to purchase the bell.

Santa Ana functioned with existing fire equipment and water from local wells or cisterns. In 1890 $60,000 was approved by the voters to form a municipal water department including operable fire plugs. The new plugs improved fire fighting efficiency—as long as people did not use water at the time of a fire. To discourage this practice, a twenty-five-dollar fine was levied on persons caught using water during a fire.

Squabbles about payment for fire fighting service were solved by paying each person answering a call two dollars for a fire and one dollar for a false alarm. New bond issues provided new funds for higher pay and also for many upgrades throughout the years.

The most sensational Santa Ana fire occurred in 1906. When a man thought to have leprosy was discovered in Santa Ana's Chinatown, the city government decided the only way to stop the disease from spreading was to burn down the entire settlement of small wooden buildings. Although the plan was to be kept secret, word leaked and several hundred people gathered to watch the spectacle. Afterward, the displaced Chinese were given food and shelter and were allowed to remain in the community.

The first full-time paid fire chief of Santa Ana was John Luxembourger, who was appointed in 1918. He had four paid firemen, thirty-five volunteers, and motorized equipment. The department continued to progress as the city grew, adding stations and equipment as needed.

Early communities that approached fire fighting in a different way were Fullerton and Orange.

Fullerton was incorporated in 1904 with little thought given to fire prevention. At the outbreak of fire, a ringing church bell awoke a man at the livery stable who then mounted a horse and rode through town, shooting a six gun to arouse the citizenry. When such an event occurred in 1907, the people who gathered to form bucket brigades found the bakery, post office, barber shop, rooming house, and second-hand store ablaze. Fullerton had no fire fighting equipment, so a rider was sent to alert Anaheim's volunteer fire fighters. Unfortunately, when they arrived, their hose did not fit the town's only hydrant and all was lost.

The following year the chamber of commerce organized and financed Fullerton's first volunteer fire department. Thereafter the city obtained a water source and new hydrants. O.S. Erickson, the first elected chief, had a team of hardworking volunteers. All equipment was made in local shops and young men were "conscripted" into service by shopkeepers who guaranteed their wages while they were away fighting fires. By 1914 the department had a motorized truck and full-time driver. Fullerton was the site of the first meeting of the Orange County Fireman's Association, formed in 1913.

In Orange the volunteer fire department was organized in 1905, along different lines. Twenty-nine volunteers paid $100 for a share of the company, forming the Orange Volunteer Fireman's Mutual Association. E.T. Parker was elected chief. The group bought its own equipment and facilities, divided the city into fire districts, and conducted its own drills. In April 1907 the group bought a hook and ladder wagon and five years later was the county's first fire fighting organization to purchase a horseless carriage, a Seagrave pumper.

The motorized firetruck, with its paid, full-time driver, ended heated disputes among local cowboys who, when the firebell rang, would race to the fire hall, fighting with each other along they way to see who would have the privilege of driving the ladder wagon or hose car. The lucky driver always received fifty cents for his efforts.

Progress in Orange also included a modern alarm system and new equipment. William Vickers was the first full-time fireman. On call twenty-four hours a day, Vickers paid eight dollars a month rent for his living quarters at the fire hall.

In other parts of the county, cities developed their own fire departments in their own ways. Huntington Beach organized its department in 1909 and had a fireman's ball to raise funds for equipment. The Newport Beach fire department was organized in 1910, replacing its active volunteer service,

after a fire destroyed the city council's meeting room. Brea's fire department, formed in 1917 at the time of incorporation, was totally volunteer until the 1930s, when a full-time chief, Judge Charles Kinsler, was hired. With public donations, Laguna Beach organized its twenty-one-man volunteer fire service in 1919. Garden Grove formed its volunteer group in 1926—after two spectacular fires in 1922 and 1924—and had E.J. Tobias as its first chief.

La Habra's fire service began in 1916 when volunteers raised $1,200 to purchase a small Model T Ford pumper and other fire fighting equipment. The volunteers sold their assets to the newly incorporated city of La Habra in 1925 and reorganized under the city's sponsorship.

Seal Beach discovered it had forgotten to form a fire department when it suffered from a fire soon after incorporation in 1915. It quickly purchased some used hose, appointed the water superintendent as fire chief, and did the best it could. For a number of years, Seal Beach relied heavily on assistance from nearby Long Beach. But in 1928, when a Long Beach fire truck was damaged during a Seal Beach fire, Seal Beach was told to organize its own department. The following year the Seal Beach Volunteer Fire Department was formed and the city purchased all new equipment.

Other fire service agencies began with new cities. San Clemente formed its fire department soon after incorporation in 1928 with James Bennett as the first fire chief. Westminster relied heavily on individual efforts until 1932, when it formed a volunteer organization under the leadership of the county. A civilian fire department of paid personnel was organized in 1943 for El Toro Marine Corps Air Station. Headed by B.C. Ray, it was one of the first full-time fire departments with a fully paid staff in the county. The Buena Park Fire Depart-

ment was born from the joining of the Buena Park Volunteers and the West Anaheim Volunteers in 1953. Costa Mesa incorporated in 1953 and two years later organized its fire department under the direction of Ralph Lee. Prior to that a volunteer unit operated under the direction of the county. Stanton organized its volunteers in 1952. Six years after its 1956 incorporation the city hired its first paid staff under the direction of Paul T. Harrison. Fountain Valley was the last of the city departments to be organized, completing its formation in 1964 under the direction of H.C. Lawson.

As the cities struggled to pull together effective fire fighting teams,

the Orange County Fire Department assisted many communities with fire services and training. It had its beginnings with the Orange Ranger Unit of the State Division of Forestry, and with a man named Joe Scherman.

When Scherman was hired in 1930, he had eighteen back pumps, eighteen axes, sixty shovels, and sixty canteens. That same year the State/County Cooperative Agreement was signed by the Board of Supervisors, and Scherman received funding for three fire engines and was assigned the duty of setting up a county fire department. During the Depression he developed volunteer organizations in many small communities, as well as new roads, firebreaks, lookouts, telephone lines, and stations. By 1939 there was a fire control budget of $23,000.

With increased funding, personnel, and stations, the county organization continued to grow. Several cities elected to contract with the county for fire protection, among them Tustin, La Palma, Cypress, San Juan Capistrano, Yorba Linda, Placentia, Los Alamitos, Irvine, and Villa Park. In 1963, when Scherman retired, there were twenty-two stations, 103 full-time and 419 volunteer personnel answering more than 1,400 alarms per year. In 1979 the Orange County Fire Department severed its ties with the state, becoming the third largest fire agency in California. Larry Holmes was appointed the first chief.

Today the Orange County Fire Department has a team of more than 600 full-time and volunteer personnel, as well as a staff of specialists in search and rescue, hazardous materials, paramedic services, and emergency preparedness. Among its goals and objectives is to become the finest county fire department in the state. Through hard work and dedication, the Orange County team is destined to achieve its goals.

This restored 1912 Buick fire truck was donated by Sam Tustin, son of founder Columbus Tustin. Courtesy, Tustin Area Historical Society Museum

This aerial view of Newport Beach, taken in 1950, shows the Balboa Peninsula as a growing community with only a few vacant lots. Boat docks jut into the bay and the Balboa Pavilion can be seen in the upper left-hand corner of the photograph. The Balboa Pier is in the upper right-hand corner. Courtesy, History Room, Santa Ana Public Library

The 1950s Boom
and the
Impacts of Growth

hether seeking an ideal vacation spot, or a location for a home or business, you will find not only a hearty welcome, but also much to make life richer.

—*The Majestic Empire of Orange County, California, 1953*

The war was over. Servicemen put away their uniforms and scoured the classified sections of the newspapers looking for homes, jobs, and opportunities. All three were scarce. Many returned home only long enough to pack their belongings and head for a new place where they could begin again. Thousands of servicemen had passed through Orange County during the war and remembered the warm climate and open spaces, the sandy beaches and suntanned girls, the thriving businesses

and busy towns. To them, Orange County was a place of golden sunshine, rich in promise, where a young family might get its start.

Promotional materials encouraged this idea by advertising low rents, cheap power, and ample transportation. The rhetoric of past promoters was still present, despite the new focus. Though offers of cheap land and rich soil no longer found their way into the promotional slogans, there was still pride in agricultural accomplishment. *The Majestic Empire of Orange County, California,* a brochure published in 1953 by the county's Associated Chambers of Commerce, boasted:

Orange County is one of the ten wealthiest agricultural counties in the United States— citrus fruits lead in production, followed by avocados, truck farms and field crops, including such specialties as lima beans, peppers, asparagus, celery, and berry crops.

But years of agricultural dominance were coming to an end. Land was needed for houses and businesses, and it was developed just as fast as crops could be disked under or orange trees pulled out. Land sales were fairly smooth, since the citrus industry was suffering acutely from an incurable disease called quickdecline and from stiff competition from Florida. A human tsunami swept over Orange County in the 1950s, taking much of the old culture with it. When it receded the promise of the past was gone and reality glittered in its place, especially for those who held the most precious commodity of all—land.

Above: *The Holiday Stage stock company brought summer theater to Orange County in 1946. Tustin High School Auditorium played host to well-known actors and actresses from Hollywood as well as many newcomers to the acting field, such as John Alvin, above. The Holiday Stage was considered second only to Pasadena in the quality of its productions. Courtesy, Tustin Area Historical Society Museum*

Facing page: The lure of Orange County promised sunshine and recreation to the many families who settled here after World War II. Courtesy, Charles W. Bowers Memorial Museum

Right: This 1964 photograph features Newport Center, Corona del Mar, and Fashion Island. Courtesy, First American Title Insurance Company

In 1950 much of the land was still used agriculturally. The Cleveland National Forest comprised more than 60,000 acres in the northeastern part of the county while the Irvine, Mission Viejo, Reeves, Starr, and Moulton ranches took up another 175,000 acres in southern Orange County.

Most of the growth began in the northern, western, and central portions of the county and gradually spread south. In 1950 the population was 220,000 with 68 percent living in urban areas. By 1960 the population was 704,000 with 96 percent living in urban areas. In 1956 alone the population of Orange County jumped by 34 percent.

The boom of the 1950s and early 1960s was an outgrowth of a period of phenomenal prosperity. Orange County had been "discovered" not just by people, but by industry. In the 1950s it remained more of a "bedroom" community for workers commuting to Los Angeles County on a growing network of free-

Above: *This aerial photograph shows the downtown area of Costa Mesa in the 1950s, looking west from the corner of Nineteenth and Newport. Courtesy, Costa Mesa Historical Society*

ways. According to the 1960 census, 68,000 residents worked outside of Orange County. That figure quickly changed as more industries found their way to the land of golden promise.

"High tech" companies specializing in manufacturing and research had certain criteria for ideal working conditions. The area had to have adequate housing, many job opportunities, reduced travel time to work, ready access to open space and recreation, and higher-than-standard cultural, educational, and recreational opportunities. It also had to have low levels of unionization. Orange County fit the bill.

The state's program of freeway building also contributed to the development of the county. Howard Seelye and Don Smith of the *Los Angeles Times* wrote in 1976:

The completion of the Santa Ana Freeway

Facing page, top: *For those who don't believe it has ever really snowed in Orange County, this photo taken in 1949 is proof. The children were delighted and wasted no time in making snowmen and having snowball fights. Courtesy, Tustin Area Historical Society*

Above: *The area surrounding the Bayshore-King's Road, today's Pacific Coast Highway, was widely developed by the late 1950s. Courtesy, Charles W. Bowers Memorial Museum*

Above: *Charles TeWinkle was elected Costa Mesa's first mayor in 1953 at the time of the city's incorporation. Courtesy, Costa Mesa Historical Society*

Facing page: *The archway over North Spadra Road greeted many visitors to Fullerton. It was later destroyed as part of a road-widening project. Courtesy, First American Title Insurance Company*

triggered a massive population buildup which staggered the more settled cities, created a host of new towns and wiped out many of the county's orange groves and open fields.

The boom period was a time of great exhilaration and excitement. Politicians predicted unsurpassed prosperity; developers filed tract maps as fast as they were drawn. Yet the rapid change did not please everyone. Vested traditions clashed with the new reality; longtime residents stood stunned as bulldozers swept away trees, hills, and history. They shook their heads in dismay, feeling frustrated and helpless, and unhappily chalked it up to progress.

Others took action.

Knowing they were unprepared to deal with "growing pains," many communities incorporated either to protect themselves from encroaching urbanization or to give them the tools to handle rapid change. Eight new cities incorporated during the 1950s; all were in north-central Orange County, where the greatest growth was occurring.

Buena Park and Costa Mesa both held successful elections in 1953. Buena Park became a city to counter the threat of annexation from Anaheim and Fullerton, and because it needed more police protection as a result of a growing population. Costa Mesa residents who opposed oil drilling in their community led their fight for incorporation.

Growth also promoted incorporation of Dairyland, later called La Palma, not because of intra-community growth (there were 500 residents and 15,000 cows at the time), but because growth from neighboring communities threatened to end use of land for dairy farms. Farmers feared that residents of subdivisions built near their operations would complain about flies and odor and try to close down the dairies. Incorporation seemed the most reasonable way to protect themselves and their livelihoods.

Similar reasons were given for the 1956 incorporation of Cypress. The small dairying community felt pressured by residents of Buena Park who favored annexation. The same year saw the reincorporation of Stanton; the "big red car" crossing had been in existence for forty-five years, first incorporated in 1911, deincorporated in 1921, and becoming a city for the second time to avoid annexation by Anaheim.

A third incorporation attempted in 1956 would have combined Westminster, Barber City, and Midway City. After the latter's withdrawal the two remaining communities incorporated in 1957 as the City of Westminster. Fountain Valley incorporated that same year, primarily to keep developers out of the community. The movement was spearheaded by the residents of Talbert village, who opposed annexation by Santa Ana. The new community expanded its boundaries a year later through annexation, and eventually changed its policies toward development.

While most of the growth occurred in metropolitan areas such as Santa Ana, Anaheim, Costa Mesa, and Fullerton, some unincorporated areas grew particularly fast as well. Garden Grove joined the incorporation movement of the 1950s to keep pace with the growing needs of the community, but was not successful until its third try in 1956. By then the population was 41,238 (up from 2,100 in 1940) and 90 percent were new residents. By 1965 Garden Grove reached the staggering population of 113,800 requiring a network of fifty elementary schools, eleven intermediate schools, and six high schools.

In the 1960s there were four incorporations. Los Alamitos incorporated in 1960 almost entirely along its original township boundaries; San Juan Capistrano became a city in 1961, fearing annexation from San Clemente and wanting to keep its own identity; and Villa Park incorporated in 1962 to remain separate from Orange and to insure that residential community standards were observed. The fourth city to incorporate had one of the longest

241

Above and facing page: Residents of Leisure World enjoy the many activities available in this retirement community. Courtesy, Beatrice Hohenegger

battles in county history—Yorba Linda.

In 1953 Yorba Linda residents had a fight on their hands. Upset by proposals that would permit oil well drilling near their homes and plagued by farm animals in residential areas, they wanted strict zoning laws. Incorporation was suggested as a possible way to get local control, but it was not considered seriously until three years later when Placentia expressed an interest in annexing Yorba Linda. Committees of residents and businessmen studied the proposed incorporation plan and several alternatives, but took no action. In 1961 a decision was made to incorporate, but the attempt failed. In 1963 the residents of Yorba Linda again filed incorporation papers just ahead of Placentia who filed for an annexation. The incorporation documents took precedence, but again the attempt failed.

The matter was taken to the courts with charges that the county was preventing the incorporation. Rulings were made against the community and appeals were filed. In 1967 the California Supreme Court upheld Yorba Linda's right to hold an incorporation election. The vote was taken and the new city was formed.

Some areas waited too long to incorporate and lost their chance. One was the 1,200-acre tract of 3,500 homes called Rossmoor, built by developer Ross W. Cortese near Los Alamitos. Its commercial acreage was annexed by Seal Beach before Rossmoor could incorporate. Cortese is better known in Orange County for two other projects. Called Leisure World, these developments were open only to persons fifty-two years of age or older. The first was built in 1961 on a 541-acre tract near Seal Beach; the second was built in Laguna Hills near El Toro. Both featured golf courses, swimming pools, shopping centers, an internal transportation system, and a secure, walled environment with guards at the gates to keep intruders out.

Above: *Snow White and the Seven Dwarfs lead a group into Sleeping Beauty's Castle, which is the center of Disneyland's Magic Kingdom.* Courtesy, History Room, Santa Ana Public Library

Facing page: *Since its opening in 1955, Disneyland has continued to delight and attract children of all ages.* Courtesy, Walt Disney Productions

Other adult-only developments followed, but none were as large, comprehensive, or expensive.

While growth and its impact was the major topic of conversation in Orange County, politics followed close behind. The county soon gained a reputation as being politically conservative. The *Los Angeles Times* reported that:

In the late 1950s and early 1960s there emerged a conservative zeal which labeled the county as the hotbed of far-out, ultra-conservative, gimlet-eyed reactionaries—an image it has still not lived down.

In 1960 the Democrats had a stronghold in Orange County, as they had since the rise of Franklin Delano Roosevelt. But in the 1940s the Republicans gained some ground with the election of Sam L. Collins of Fullerton to the California State Assembly, who eventually became speaker of the assembly, and Willis Warner of Huntington Beach, who spent twenty-four years on the Orange County Board of Supervisors guiding the county through its growth years. Though Democrats held the majority of registrations, Republicans continued to win elections.

This period also saw the rise of arch-conservative organizations such as the John Birch Society, which claimed to have 5,000 members in Orange County. The county's ultra-right views were nurtured in Washington, D.C., by Congressman James B. Utt of Tustin. Each year, he introduced a measure in Congress called the Liberty Amendment, designed to eliminate income tax and to get government out of private business. Until his death in 1970, he vigorously attacked communism, welfare, civil rights, and the United Nations. While some supported his views, others did not, causing a split in the Republican Party in Orange County for many years.

Facing page, top: *The Monorail and the Matterhorn are two of the many popular attractions in Disneyland. Courtesy, Walt Disney Productions*

Facing page, bottom: *Thirty-one years after its opening in 1955, Disneyland, Walt Disney's Magic Kingdom, continues to be the nation's most popular amusement park. Courtesy, Walt Disney Productions*

Right: *The Charles W. Bowers Memorial Museum, located at 2002 North Main Street in Santa Ana, houses a fine collection of Orange County historical artifacts. Courtesy, Charles W. Bowers Memorial Museum*

Below: *Walter and Cordelia Knott pose in front of the original berry stand they built when they started their business in the 1920s. Cordelia made and sold boysenberry pies and jams and eventually started serving chicken dinners using her best china. Now a multimillion-dollar business, Knott's Berry Farm is owned and managed by the descendants of Walter and Cordelia. Courtesy, History Room, Santa Ana Public Library*

Above: *Sailing has always been a favorite recreational activity in Orange County, as seen in this view off the coast of the Newport-Balboa area in the 1940s. Courtesy, Charles W. Bowers Memorial Museum*

Facing page: *In 1955 the Reverend Robert Schuller and his wife Arvella moved to Orange County from the pastorate of the Ivanhoe Reformed Church in Chicago to conduct worship services. Schuller selected the Orange Drive-In Theatre as a worship center. On Sunday, March 27, 1955, about fifty cars pulled into the theater to attend the first sermon delivered from the snack bar rooftop. Courtesy, Robert Schuller Ministries*

Politics alone did not put Orange County on the national map. The single most important contributor to Orange County's nationwide reputation was a place, not an idea, and it represented the epitome of the golden promise. It was Disneyland.

On July 17, 1955, Governor Goodwin Knight joined the citizens of Anaheim in opening the Magic Kingdom. Created by Walt Disney after twenty years of planning, Disneyland opened in what was then a remote part of Anaheim surrounded by orange groves. It started with four theme areas—Fantasyland, Frontierland, Adventureland, and Tomorrowland—and contained room for future expansion. In 1959 additional attractions were completed, and it quickly became the most popular amusement park in Southern California. Walt Disney and his team of planners and engineers had counted on that. What they hadn't foreseen was the tremen-

dous impact the park would have on Anaheim. Within months of Disneyland's opening, land values skyrocketed, orange groves disappeared, and motels and restaurants sprang up. The once-remote area soon caught up with the rest of the city and threatened to overwhelm it. Anaheim, the golden dream of the vineyard colony, became the golden mecca of the tourist industry. The oldest incorporated city in Orange County, Anaheim soon became the biggest.

Disneyland was not the only tourist attraction in the county. Buena Park had its own popular attraction. Knott's Berry Farm had humble beginnings as a roadside berry stand in the early 1920s. Walter and Cordelia Knott expanded their business by selling pies and jams, and later opened a restaurant that served chicken dinners. To amuse the patrons while they waited for a table, Walter added entertainment such as wagons, mining equipment, and a

Above: *In the late 1950s an A-frame backdrop was added to the back of the snack bar roof to create a more church-like atmosphere. Ushers walked from car to car with collection baskets, and Sunday School classes were held in the drive-in's recreation area near the screen. Dr. Schuller and the Garden Grove Community Church moved into their new walk-in drive-in church on Chapman Avenue in 1961. Courtesy, Robert Schuller Ministries*

Facing page: *This impressive four-story brick building, the Holly Sugar Factory, was a well-known landmark along the Newport Freeway until it was demolished in 1983. Built by the Santa Ana Cooperative Sugar Company in 1912, it served the thousands of acres of sugar beets which covered Orange County between the 1890s and the 1960s. Courtesy, History Room, Santa Ana Public Library*

small railroad. Next came a ghost town, followed by more rides and a small theater. Soon the amusements outgrew the restaurant and the park rivalled Disneyland.

Other destinations attracted residents as well as tourists. The Bowers Museum in Santa Ana, opened on February 15, 1936, housed Orange County's finest treasures and attracted thousands of visitors each year. Mission San Juan Capistrano, under continuous restoration since 1910, and Laguna Beach, with its reputation as an artists' colony and its annual Pageant of the Masters, also had their share of visitors. There were also miles of beaches, many of them state parks, and colorful Newport with its thousands of pleasure boats tied to moorings, and the Balboa Pavilion's surrounding "fun zone."

In an evaluation of Orange County's growth and attraction, an article in *Orange County Illustrated* observed:

Freeways have proved to be a potent tie that binds, but even more binding has been the Orange County idea. For Orange County now is more than a geographical location, more than a convenience for cataloguing disparate interests of unrelated cities. Orange County is a way of life, conducted joyously on a new and higher standard.

Quality, not quantity, would be the issue of the future. And the golden promise would be challenged once again.

Formed in 1967, Air California became one of the largest air carriers on the West Coast. Courtesy, City of Anaheim, Public Information

C H A P T E R   X I

New Immigrants, New Opportunities

I n 1967 the gleaming jets of Air California took off from Orange County Airport for the first time. Their orange-striped bodies streaking over the waters of Newport Bay symbolized the new cadence set for Orange County as it rushed headlong into the 1970s.

The focal point of the late 1960s and 1970s was still growth, but the perspective had changed. People were thrilled when the new University of California, Irvine, was dedicated in 1964; they gave an enthusiastic welcome to the California Angels who moved to the Anaheim Stadium in 1966; and they were impressed by plans for the new Dana Point Harbor the same year. But they began to complain about the acres of houses that looked exactly the same, schools that were on double sessions, the

Above: *The Anaheim Baseball Team in 1907 attracted interest despite the lack of a proper facility, such as today's Anaheim Stadium. Courtesy, Anaheim Public Library*

Facing page: *The fifty-million-dollar Anaheim Stadium is a multi-purpose complex, hosting concerts and consumer shows as well as many major sporting events since 1966. Courtesy, City of Anaheim, Public Information*

increasing number of smoggy days, and the loss of open fields, groves of oranges, and mesquite-covered hillsides that were part of Orange County's attraction. As their concerns moved from issues of quantity to quality, they began to protect what they valued.

Orange County was a series of neighborhoods, most of them new, without cohesiveness or common roots. Yet issues could bring them together and make them, for a time, a community. One such issue was the initial expansion of Orange County Airport.

The tiny Martin Brothers Airport, which had served the needs of rural Orange County, was originally located near the intersection of Main Street and Newport Avenue in the 1920s and 1930s. But the new highway linking Santa Ana and Corona del Mar forced it to move to county land adjacent to Lane Road, later called MacArthur Boulevard. The Martins had just built the first hangar when the army took over the facility for its own use during World War II. With government control new runways and taxiways were built. These were still used after the war when the county reacquired the property.

Crop dusters and private planes shared the dusty runways until Bonanza Airlines made Orange County a regular stop. But the airport was woefully inadequate as a commercial facility; in 1961, at the urging of Supervisor William J. Phillips, an airport study assessed the needs of the facility. The study found that the airport was not keeping pace with the needs of

Early orange grove sites were replaced by tract housing development such as the Mesa del Mar tract of Costa Mesa, which is pictured here in 1966. Courtesy, Costa Mesa Historical Society

the rapidly-growing area it served. It recommended two runways, a tower, and various other improvements, all totalling $6.3 million. Despite opposition from Newport Beach and a big price tag, the county ordered the work and by 1967 had a refurbished airport, a host of new companies lured by the proximity of the modernized facility, and a new airline—Air California.

It also had a set of new problems.

Airport studies indicated that the newly completed improvements were already obsolete, that the county was still losing passengers to Los Angeles International and other airports, and further expansions would be necessary. The people of Newport Beach who lived under the flight path, inundated by noise and concerned about the safety of their homes, resisted the expansion and began preparing for a fight—one that would take them into the 1980s.

Orange County Airport, later named for fa-mous county resident John Wayne, was not the only facility in the county. There were small airports in three other communities, but these were for private planes and did not have the traffic that made Orange County Airport the fourth busiest in the United States. Pressuring the airport was the seemingly unending growth that was spreading south and east into the county's agricultural areas.

As the freeway moved south, growth followed. By the late 1960s and early 1970s the old communities of El Toro, San Juan Capistrano, and San Clemente were sprouting houses where acres of orange groves and scenic hillsides once were. San Juan Capistrano, alarmed by its growth rate, actually banned residential construction for a time, and eventually adopted limits on building permits issued each year. No other city took as strong an action, but many people took hard looks at what their communities had become and were not always pleased at what they saw.

An August 1964 article in *Orange County Illustrated* expressed concern about what Orange County was becoming:

It is not just the bad architecture and the jerrybuilt which we deplore; it is what it represents. Civilizations are judged centuries hence on what they have built—and for good reason. Where people live determines in a major way what kind of lives they lead. Many of us came to Orange County because we wanted the type of environment it offered us. Are we to destroy the very things we sought?

Potential congestion was also a concern. In 1970 an eighty-page study conducted by the University of California, Irvine, and Project 21, a group studying community issues, determined that open space preservation was necessary for psychological as well as physical well-being. The study recommended preserving ag-

This 1971 view of the San Diego Freeway looking south provides an interesting study in contrast between the older agricultural lifestyle and the newer urban developments. The old Segerstrom Ranch is pictured in the upper left-hand corner and the bustling city of Costa Mesa is on the right. Courtesy, Costa Mesa Historical Society

riculture, even as just a holding zone or area where future development might occur, using school playgrounds for public recreation, and designating floodplain areas as greenbelts—all of this to preserve a modicum of open space in a rapidly urbanizing area. Some developers had already incorporated these ideas into their existing plans. One was the Irvine Company.

In the 1950s the Irvine Company, which controlled the Irvine Ranch, had taken a new direction. It made the transition from agriculture to urbanization with the development of residential tracts around Newport Bay and in the coastal areas, and had leased land for industrial development to Ford Motor Company (Aeronautics Division) and Collins Radio Company. But the major planning of the ranch, which represented one-sixth of the

land area of Orange County, came later. It was spurred by a single development—the construction of the University of California, Irvine.

In 1957 the Regents of the University of California commissioned William Pereira and Associates to seek potential sites for campuses in Southern California. After a two-year

The rolling hills of the Moulton Ranch are seen here as a backdrop for the Daguerre Ranch on Salt Creek in 1952. At the turn of the century, many such modest farms dotted the still-pastoral countryside. Courtesy, Tustin Area Historical Society Museum

study, the site chosen from a potential list of twenty-one was in the San Joaquin foothills east of Upper Newport Bay on land controlled by the Irvine Company. The report submitted by Pereira outlined the need for master planning of the 10,000 acres surrounding the university. This job was taken on by Pereira and the Irvine Company's own planning staff.

In 1960 the Irvine Company hired Pereira to develop a master plan of its remaining 88,256 acres. The company directors favored paced, orderly development. Instead of a sea of houses, they wanted a balanced community that respected the integrity of Irvine's agricultural traditions. The majority of the land was to continue producing strawberries, tomatoes, asparagus, citrus, and cattle, and the annual spring roundup would still take place in Bom-

mer Canyon.

Building was to be done in phases and would include a golf course, shopping areas, parks, and greenbelts. Irvine was to be built for people and the directors hoped it would become a model copied throughout the world.

Industrial development began in and around the ranch with the opening of the 3,000-acre Irvine Industrial Complex in 1964. The quickly expanding complex, built near Orange County Airport, included four industrial parks that attracted "high tech" research and development industries. In 1964 the population of Orange County reached 1,056,900; of the 319,000 people employed, 29 percent worked in manufacturing, and most of these worked in electronics. While Orange County was not big in mainframe computer or semiconductor production, it had a high concentration of small and medium-sized companies. Run by the people who founded them, many of these companies located in Irvine or points south, while the larger, defense-oriented industries generally located closer to Los Angeles.

Keeping pace with industry development was the growth of shopping centers. South Coast Plaza was developed in Costa Mesa by the C.J. Segerstrom family on sixty-six acres of bean fields in 1967. The Segerstroms came to Orange County in 1898 and prospered as dairy farmers in addition to growing lima beans. When land became too valuable for agricultural use, the Segerstroms focused their many talents on land development. In 1968 Fashion Island opened at Newport Center, continuing the trend for large-scale shopping centers built away from traditional town centers. This trend eventually contributed to disuse and decay in many of the county's older downtowns, forcing them toward redevelopment.

Orange County was riding a tide of prosperity that seemed unending. But in 1970 the war in Vietnam ended and the aerospace industry entered a period of decline.

The recession and inflation of the 1970s ended the county's spiraling growth rate. With defense spending down, both large and small companies dependent on government contracts laid off workers and cut back production. Unemployment and lower in-migrations affected the housing industry that continued to build despite warnings that the recession would not quickly disappear. But many employers—Hughes, McDonnell-Douglas, Northrop,

This is a 1966 view of the Pacific Coast Highway as it heads south to Corona del Mar. Courtesy, Costa Mesa Historical Society

Rockwell International, Beckman Instruments, and others—shifted focus and survived until their markets could be rebuilt.

Another entity that had been quietly rebuilding its "markets" during the late 1960s was the Democratic Party. During the 1960s a few Democrats were elected to office, notably Richard T. Hanna, William Dannemeyer (now a Republican), and Ken Cory. In 1968 Robert Battin was elected to the Orange County Board of Supervisors, triggering a major revitalization of the Democratic Party in Orange County, even though a Republican and Yorba Linda native, Richard M. Nixon, had just been elected President of the United States. Led by the strategies of Fred Harber and using the funding resources of Richard O'Neill and Dr. Louis Cella, Orange County by 1974 once more had a two-party system, with both parties electing candidates.

The construction of the South Coast Plaza was underway in this 1966 aerial. Situated at the corner of Bristol and Sunflower, the plaza has become one of the most popular shopping complexes in Southern California. Courtesy, Costa Mesa Historical Society

In the midst of this rise in fortune the Democrats suffered two setbacks. The first was the loss of Harber and Supervisor Ron Caspers in a boating accident off Baja California. The second was a number of political scandals alleging misuse of staffs and funds, and illegal registrations of candidates. Indictments came, along with trials. Some were exonerated and others convicted. As the Republicans began to emerge from the shadows of Watergate, the Democrats began to decline.

In the mid-1970s the growth issue was raised again, but in a new way. The federal government, opening its doors to refugees from the Vietnam War, designated the U.S. Marine Corps' Camp Pendleton as a relocation center. After thousands of volunteers prepared the new arrivals for assimilation into a new culture, the refugees left the camp to live in new communities throughout the United States. Many went no further than Orange County, most of them settling in Westminster, Garden Grove, and Huntington Beach. Assisted by the Immigrant and Refugee Planning Center, started with private funds from Fluor Corporation and the United Way, many immigrants started their own businesses and actually developed small communities within larger ones. Others found employment only as low-income laborers; they could only afford to remain in Orange County by doubling up on housing or turning to welfare. The Indochinese community in Orange County soon grew to more than 87,000, and is still the highest concentration of this ethnic group in the United States. While most of the Asians were considered law-abiding, tensions grew because of overcrowding, cultural differences, and an increase in gang activity in the most congested areas.

Tensions grew in the Hispanic community for the same reasons, and continued to mount as illegals poured across the border seeking a better life in the land of golden promise. The bracero program that brought many workers to California legally ended in 1963 but workers continued to come. Wages earned in one day often equaled a week's pay in Mexico. Many ran the risk of deportation and paid the $300 or more to be smuggled across the border into opportunity-rich Southern California.

Hispanics, the largest (287,000) and one of the oldest minorities in Orange County, enjoyed a cultural resurgence in 1976. It was the year of the American Bicentennial and the 200th anniversary of settlement in Orange County.

The year 1976 dawned with a flurry of books on local communities, a film on the history of Orange County, and renewed interest in historic preservation. Buildings scheduled for demolition received instant reprieves, memberships in historical societies doubled, and everyone lined up for the greatest show in town—the Freedom Train.

The train chugged into Anaheim on January 9. People stood in line for hours near Anaheim Stadium to see American history memorabilia, ranging from the Golden Spike to Wilt Chamberlain's basketball shoe. The next stop in Orange County was San Juan Capistrano, where lines snaked through five blocks. The town's main street closed down to provide food booths and entertainment for those waiting in line.

The bicentennial did more than renew interest in American heritage; it turned diverse groups into cohesive communities. People planned celebrations around the traditions of ethnic groups that had settled in their area; they became experts on genealogy; and they raised funds to restore and furnish buildings that were surviving examples of their community's heritage. To help them select worthy buildings, the Orange County Chapter of the American Institute of Architects surveyed important structures in Orange County, many of them in the path of development.

As the bicentennial passed and Orange County moved toward the decade of the 1980s, the activities inspired by the heritage celebration continued. A new respect for the traditions of the past lingered, long after the colorful flags of Spain and Mexico had been put away.

Orange County entered the 1970s with a concern for the environment; it entered the 1980s with the same concern and a new challenge to the golden promise.

The San Juan Capistrano depot still functions as an Amtrak stop and a restaurant. Photo by R. Gibson

Above: *The large Mission Revival Railroad Station, shown here on its moving day in 1981, was originally built by the Union Pacific in 1923. It is now part of the Fullerton Transportation Center and is listed on the National Register of Historic Places. Courtesy, Thirteenth Street Architects.*

Right: *One of Orange County's first rehabilitations of historic buildings took place on Fourth Street in Santa Ana. Workers pulled off the building's 1950s facades to reveal the building's 1933 face, which was added to the 1886 structure after the 1933 earthquake. The building is now part of the Downtown Santa Ana Historic District. Courtesy, Thirteenth Street Architects*

Sculptor J.R. Terken stands proudly next to his nine-foot bronze statue of Richard Henry Dana, which is now at Dana Point Harbor. Courtesy, Pamela Hallan-Gibson

Orange
County
Today

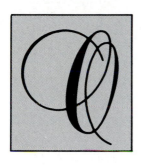range County today is a place of paradox.

Strawberry fields are cultivated next to multistoried financial buildings; 20,000-square-foot mansions overlook acres of low-income housing; and cities with multi-million-dollar businesses must fight urban blight.

Orange County is the home of the ultramodern Crystal Cathedral and adobe-walled Father Serra's Chapel; of planned communities built next to sprawling cattle ranches. With the thirtieth largest economy in the world (according to Bank of America), Orange County has areas where several families crowd into one-bedroom apartments and people are afraid to go out at night.

The county has been called a "ghetto for millionaires." Anyone

Above: *The Lido Village offers a spectacular view of Newport Bay. Photo by Jeff Marks*

Facing page, top: *Agriculture thrives side by side with modern industry in this photo by Jeff Marks*

Facing page, bottom: *The construction of luxury hotels attests to the importance of tourism as a growing industry in Orange County. Courtesy, City of Anaheim, Public Information*

viewing its scenic coastline dotted with 12,000 yachts, its gated retirement communities with homes priced at $350,000, and its luxury hotels clustered near the airport might easily get that impression.

But millionaires do not live in Buena Clinton, a thirty-nine-acre postwar apartment complex in Garden Grove, which has been called the "worst slum in Orange County." And millionaires do not live on mattresses under freeway bridges, or in tents in county parks, or in cars on public streets. Pockets of poverty plague most of Orange County's twenty-six cities, and solutions seem difficult to find.

The Orange County Survey, an annual poll taken since 1982 by the University of California, Irvine, indicates that most county residents are far from poor. Fifty percent of all Orange County families make more than $36,000 per year and 75 percent of those responding to the poll have had at least one year of college. The survey also points out that affluence is not necessarily tied to political conservatism. While only 17 percent consider themselves liberals, an overwhelming 70 percent support the Equal Rights Amendment and abortion, two issues usually identified with the liberal camp. At the same time a majority of the same group opposes gun control, supports school prayer, and advocates the death penalty.

No matter what their beliefs, most Orange County residents have an affluent lifestyle—in the eyes of the rest of the world, at least. There are cases where an income of $40,000 per year qualifies a family for low-income housing, and there are places in Orange County where persons will line up for days for a chance to buy a new home for the bargain basement price of $120,000.

Other areas purposely project an image of affluence. One is the planned community of Mission Viejo.

Known as the home of Olympic swimmers and prize-winning Rose Parade floats, Mission Viejo is a master-planned community of 55,000 people. Built in southern Orange County around 1966, the community rests on part of an old land grant bearing the same name. The land was developed by the Mission Viejo Company, now a subsidiary of Phillip Morris Incorporated.

With two golf courses, an equestrian center, several tennis and swimming facilities, and a man-made recreation lake, Mission Viejo advertises itself as the fulfillment of the California promise. If that promise includes a strong sense of community identity, then Mission Viejo has met the requirements.

The ties are not so strong across Interstate 5 in the diverse communities of Laguna Hills.

Golfing and yachting are two of the more popular leisure activities to be enjoyed in the increasingly affluent communities of Orange County. Photos by Jeff Marks

All built by different developers, the different neighborhoods are lost in a checkerboard of suburbia, the only ties being the schools that the children attend. New interest in future incorporations may change this as neighborhoods examine whether it is in their best interests to become one city.

Rancho Mission Viejo, lying east of its developed namesake, still contains 42,000 acres of undeveloped land. It still operates primarily as a cattle and agricultural business as it did when purchased in 1882 by an early Richard O'Neill and James Flood. Guided by Tony Moiso, son of Alice O'Neill Avery, who, with her brother Richard O'Neill, inherited much of it, the ranch is being master planned to move slowly but surely into the twenty-first century. Under development is the new community of Rancho Santa Margarita.

Since the image of affluence may keep some buyers away, Santa Margarita will feature a mix of housing aimed at first-time home buyers, seniors, and families. Other communities are doing the same. Irvine advertises itself as an area of "affordable" housing, in addition to offering a quality lifestyle. The motivation for this effort partly comes from the City of Irvine, incorporated in 1971 as the twenty-sixth city in Orange County, which has an agreeable relationship with its creator and major developer, the Irvine Company.

The push for affordable housing is a counteraction to an unfortunate by-product of Orange County's own success, a success some feel will drive away industry. In the 1950s and 1960s industries were attracted to Orange County's acres of inexpensive, open land, its gleaming new freeways, and its thousands of tract houses in a wide range of prices. But in the 1980s commercial land is nearly unavailable in the north county areas and outrageously expensive in the south; freeways are choked to the stopping point at rush hour;

and the median price of a single-family home is $150,000 and climbing. Not only is it difficult for first-time home buyers to find affordable housing, it is equally difficult for rich executives from other parts of the United States to find comparable housing at an affordable price.

Alarmed by the inflated housing market, fed in some cases by massive speculation in the 1970s, and fearing an industrial flight to less affluent areas, the Orange County Board of Supervisors adopted a new housing policy. The policy required a developer of an unincorporated area to designate at least 25 percent of a project as "affordable housing" that would sell for $70,000 to $110,000. In exchange, the developer would receive higher density allocations and smoother processing as his project made its way through the maze of bureaucratic approvals.

Opponents of the new policy attacked it as "social engineering" and doubted its workability. Established residents fought proposals to locate the housing projects next to their homes; human rights advocates said it would do nothing to create housing for the elderly and poor, the groups with the greatest need. Frustrated by roadblocks and pressured by developers, the county rescinded its action and is currently looking at other ways to meet housing needs.

Housing is only one problem that threatens the county's industrial base. The other is transportation.

In 1960 it was possible to live in Los Angeles and Riverside counties and have a reasonably comfortable drive to Orange County to work. In the 1980s the drive is still possible if you leave at five in the morning for your 8 a.m. job.

Most of the county's freeway system was built during the 1950s and 1960s when the cost was one million dollars per mile. Recession during the 1970s halted the freeway pro-

Right: *The possibility of affordable housing continues to draw prospective buyers to new Orange County developments such as Anaheim Hills. Courtesy, City of Anaheim, Public Information*

Below: *New home construction is on the rise to meet the increasing demand for single family dwellings. Courtesy, City of Anaheim, Public Information*

gram, as did Governor Edmund G. Brown, Jr., who favored public transportation rather than freeway improvement. The system not only halted, but deteriorated. At today's costs freeway building has slowed down and the county can no longer count on the state to pay the full price. Yet the need remains.

The 1980 census indicated that three-fourths of Orange County's residents who drive to work drive alone. Efforts to encourage car pools or the use of public transportation have failed for the most part. However, there has been a new interest in rail transportation, promoted in part by the upgrade of Amtrak stations.

In 1982 the Orange County Survey found that two-thirds surveyed were dissatisfied with existing transportation systems; in the 1984 survey three-fourths indicated displeasure. In 1982 13 percent said traffic congestion was a great problem for them; in 1984 the figure rose to 25 percent. The solution offered by the persons polled was to widen existing

freeways.

In 1984 Orange County voters were asked to approve a one-cent sales tax that would be used to add lanes to existing freeways, build new transportation corridors, and provide money to local communities for street improvements. An additional portion of the money would be set aside for public transportation—buses and a future light-rail system would be first built in the congested north county areas and later expanded into the south county. But in June 1984 Orange County voters overwhelmingly defeated the proposal. Today transportation improvements continue to be a major concern.

With the defeat of the one-cent sales tax measure, the Orange County Transportation Commission hopes to find new revenues for highways. One method will be to seek assistance from cities in implementing "bridge and thoroughfare fees." These fees will place an assessment on all new residential and commercial developments benefiting from the construction of new transportation corridors, notably the San Joaquin Hills Corridor, linking San Clemente to Costa Mesa, and the Foothill-Eastern Corridor, being built east of Interstate 5 from San Clemente to Santa Ana. The county is also actively seeking funds at the state and federal levels. Whatever the outcome, the traffic problem will not disappear in the next decade, despite the fact that Orange County's yearly growth rate is now only nine-tenths of one percent.

The slower growth rate has given Orange County residents time to get to know one another. The 1984 Orange County Survey indicated that most residents have now been here more than ten years and 68 percent currently own their own homes, implying a more stable society. County residents are involved in their communities through service clubs, cultural organizations, and political issues. Some of

The Anaheim Convention Center hosts numerous and varied events. Courtesy, City of Anaheim, Public Information

these activities cross city lines, such as the drive to raise more than sixty-five million dollars for the Orange County Performing Arts Center that is being built on five acres donated by the Segerstrom family in Costa Mesa, United Way campaigns that contribute funds to several social service organizations, and many county-wide private groups that have special charitable purposes. Some, like El Viaje de Portolá, get together once a year to commemmorate a special event, in this case the expedition through Orange County made by Portolá in 1769. In 1988 the group will celebrate its twenty-fifth anniversary with a trail ride along the same route. There is also support for institutions like the Newport Harbor Art Museum, the Laguna Beach Museum of Art, and the Bowers Museum in Santa Ana.

Orange County has support groups for everything from private galleries to public libraries, from the county-sponsored Marine Science Institute at Dana Point to the privately-owned Los Angeles Rams football and Angels baseball teams that occupy Anaheim Stadium. Issues also band people together to push their point of view. But there was no support group for one environmental issue that emerged in the 1980s that crossed city and county lines. It was the proposal by American High Speed Rail Corporation to link Los Angeles and San Diego with the "bullet train."

From its inception the bullet train met with skepticism and concern. People liked the idea of getting somewhere faster, but they didn't want elevated trestles blocking ocean vistas, overhead electrical lines in an era of underground utilities, or the noise of seventy-eight trains per day whizzing next to residential areas. Despite efforts by the corporation to quench all concerns, lawsuits were filed and anti-bullet train brochures were mailed. Even bumper stickers appeared with the message, "Stop the Speeding Bullet." The massive

The modern Anaheim Civic Center houses many community service offices. Courtesy, City of Anaheim, Public Information

funding required to fulfill the rail system's environmental requirements killed the project completely. The bullet train, lodged in a wall of bureaucracy, remained an idea on paper that faded as rapidly as it had appeared.

Not all transportation fights were as intense or as short-lived. One lengthy battle was the fight involving the expansion of Orange County Airport.

The opening of the modernized airport in the late 1960s solidified opposition from Newport Beach residents. As more flights were added and more airlines used the terminal, residents living under the flight path became increasingly concerned. Efforts were made to reduce jet noise on takeoff and alternative airport sites were examined, but rejected. The only feasible solution to the airport's mounting problems was another expansion. Unfortunately, this was not the answer the residents sought.

Orange County in the early 1980s generated ten million air passengers annually. Yet the airport was only capable of handling 2.5 million per year, forcing the rest to use Los Angeles or Ontario airports. The Board of Supervisors, wanting the overflow market, announced an airport expansion. A lawsuit was promptly filed and the courts ordered a new Environmental Impact Report, completed and approved in 1985.

The expansion is now underway. When it is completed, there will be facilities for as many as seventy-four commercial flights per day. The increase in jets has prompted a search for new technology to quiet jet engines. Additional sites will still be studied, including the joint use of the Marine Corps Air Station at El Toro, an idea the federal government has resisted. Meanwhile, people will keep fighting as long as their quality of life is at stake.

Unpopular issues can bring together people of divergent backgrounds, and popular events do the same. The most popular event of the 1980s had people of all income levels lining the streets waving American flags—it was the Olympic Torch Run.

The torch run was the precursor of the Olympic Games, and although they were officially held in Los Angeles, many competitions were held in Orange County.

Following a route that began in Greece and made its way throughout the United States, the Olympic flame wound its way to the Twenty-third Olympiad in Los Angeles in the summer of 1984. Passing this flame from torch to torch was a series of runners that entered Orange County on July 25. Mile by mile the torch instilled a new sense of identity in the thousands of spectators lining the streets. The moment gave each witness a feeling of excitement, exhultation, and renewed patriotism. Throughout Orange County the same phenomenon occurred as if each person was caught in a moment of time with everything past and future erased.

But past and future are still very much a part of Orange County.

Two hundred years have gone by since the Franciscans hoisted their belongings onto the backs of mules and set out for a land of golden promise. In their fifty years of dominance they turned arid bottomland into productive fields, set cattle to graze on chaparral-covered hills, and taught Indians the tools of survival in a Western European culture.

The Mexican period that followed built upon the ruins of the mission spirit. Land held in trust for the Indians was granted to rancheros, who expanded the production of cattle and built up trade. The Mexicans freed Indians from mission control and established settlements, and when the Americans took over, there was a more stable, if feudal, economy in what would some day be Orange County.

The Americans and their proof-of-ownership

The modern and beautiful University of California Irvine campus is captured in this photograph by R. Gibson.

requirements took the county in new directions. Drought, disease, and debts broke up the vast ranchos into smaller units allowing colonists, such as the vintners of Anaheim, to reach for their golden promise. The availability of land spurred the booms of the 1870s and the 1880s, encouraged the settlement of future great cities, and stimulated the formation of the County of Orange in 1889.

Progress marked the turn of the century as communities improved their quality of life and new crops thrived in the rich soil and moderate climate. Oil production continued along with agricultural production and the end of World War I found Orange County in another land boom. The Depression reached every home, as did World War II, but Orange County bounced back in the biggest of the booms, the land rush of the 1950s. But quantity didn't always equal quality; residents began to push for the lifestyle they had hoped for in the land of sunshine, beaches, and full employment.

The coming of the 1980s has brought new prosperity and new promise to Orange County. There are problems to solve and work to do, but many willing hands and intelligent minds are there to help. In 1985 unemployment was at a new low and quality of life at a new high; new cities are now being built and old cities are being revitalized; economic development continues to prosper, and people still view Orange County as one of the most desirable places to live in the United States. As the "most California county" looks forward to its centennial in 1989, there is new spirit, new hope, and a confident feeling that not only does the golden promise still beckon, but for many, it has been fulfilled.

One of the most inspiring events of the 1984 Olympics was the Torch Run, shown here as it made its way through Orange County. Courtesy, City of Anaheim, Public Information

HAUNTING LEGENDS

Orange County has its past, present, and future, but it also has another dimension, one that transcends every other time frame. It is the county's supernatural element. Documented in folklore, it is often embroidered and always entertaining.

Many of the legends center around Mission San Juan Capistrano. The mission is a place of beauty and activity by day, where throngs of tourists wander through the peaceful, well-tended gardens, tasting the flavor of the past. But at night the mission's beauty changes as shadows shift with the angle of the moon. In the eerie silver light, it is easy to believe that the spirits of the old padres haunt the ancient grounds.

One such spirit is a hooded monk, who supposedly appears from the depths of the inner courtyard, attached to a place that had significance in his life. He walks about at night, his sandals echoing through the stillness as he melts into the shadows. Never get too close, legend warns, for if you peer into the empty hood the fearful sight will turn your hair white and stop your heart.

The mission is also the setting for stories of a headless soldier and of bells that ring mysteriously in the night. The most poignant ghost story of the mission involves a young girl.

In 1812 an Indian girl named Magdalena fell in love with a young man named Teófilo. Although forbidden to see one another—for Magdalena was thought to be too young—Magdalena and Teófilo were resourceful and found ways to be together. But they were not careful and their tryst was soon discovered.

Magdalena's punishment was to walk in front of the other members of the mission parish carrying the penitent's candle. On December 8, 1812, the day of her repentance, the ground began to tremble and people ran screaming out the church doors. Unable to escape, Magdalena was killed in the earthquake that destroyed the Great Stone Church. Teófilo later found her body, the candle still clutched in her hand.

On dark nights when there is barely a fingernail of a moon, it is said that a face can sometimes be seen in a window of the church ruins, illuminated by a candle—the ghost of Magdalena, still doing penance for her forbidden love.

A number of Orange County's ghost stories originate outside the mission walls in San Juan Capistrano, the area's oldest community. One that has transcended several generations is the story of La Llorona, "the crier."

La Llorona was a woman of ill repute who lived many generations ago. As she gave birth to unwanted children she would drown them in Trabuco Creek. After she died, the legend goes, her penance was to walk the creek banks looking for the children she had murdered. On dark nights when the wind rustles through the trees it is best to stay clear of Trabuco Creek. Those are the nights that La Llorona moans and sobs for the infants forever lost from her.

Another famous ghost, less formidable than La Llorona, is the White Lady. She is said to be a ghost with black hair swirling about her shoulders, wearing a long white dress. Pretty and flirtatious, the White Lady is sometimes seen with a large black dog.

Stories of the White Lady can be traced back to the nineteenth century. The legend may have started after a young girl who fit that description poisoned herself on the front porch of her ex-lover. The incident occurred in the 1890s on Los Rios Street in San Juan. The White Lady was first sighted on that street, and sightings continued well into the twentieth century.

A young man, walking home from a high school dance, reported seeing a girl in an old-fashioned dress and a dog near the large pepper tree in front of the Rios Adobe. He walked on, only to see her appear again in front of him. He passed her once more, turned a corner, and there she was again, across from his house. Running at full speed he entered his house and locked the door behind him. His father looked out the window, then turned and said, "Don't worry son, she won't hurt you."

The same ghost supposedly appeared in the 1960s in a house near Los Rios Street, materializing from a thick white fog. She appeared again in the late 1970s in the new home of a stewardess who lived a few blocks away. This time the White Lady stayed.

Plagued by poltergeist activity, the stewardess was unaware that her intruder was the White Lady until the night the ghost materialized, again in a white fog. Although the ghost disappeared, other incidents apparently occurred. Objects moved by themselves, and one morning the stewardess awoke to find her Christmas tree knocked over, the ornaments smashed. To rid herself of the ghost, she conducted a seance and asked the White Lady to go away. The ghost did leave, for a time, but has occasionally returned.

Another ghost that won't depart from its earthly resting place is in the Yorba Cemetery in Orange. She is Orange County's most well known ghost and is called the Pink Lady.

The Pink Lady is supposedly Alvina de los Reyes, a young woman who died in a buggy accident in 1910 at the age of thirty-one. She was coming home from a party, wearing a beautiful pink ball gown, when she died. It is in such a dress that she is said to appear on June 15 of even years. Legend has it that she rises from her grave, looks over the graves of her family members, then disappears, as if reassured that all is well.

In years past crowds have gathered in the tiny cemetery, waiting for the event. One observer actually captured

...hosts whirl in time to the sounds of a ...altz in Disneyland's Haunted Mansion. ...dvanced technology is a major contribu- ...r to the "magic" of Walt Disney's en- ...anted kingdom. Courtesy, History ...om, Santa Ana Public Library

the shape of a person on film, although he had seen no one. The cemetery is now owned and maintained by the county, and such gatherings are discouraged.

Old cemeteries are popular places to conduct psychic experiments. A few years ago a research group spent the night in the old San Juan Capistrano cemetery, which dates back to the mid-nineteenth century. A tape recorder was left on during the night, and persons were stationed nearby to prevent tampering. In the morning the tape was played and on it were two voices. One said, "I'm scared," and the other, "I have to give you my name."

While most of Orange County's ghosts and spirits are not vocal, many can be heard walking around the places they haunt. Such was the case in an Anaheim home. There, the spirit of a man who had died in World War I could be heard walking around above the ceiling. The Rios Adobe in San Juan Capistrano reportedly has a ghost, believed to be a long-dead ancestor. This ghost occasionally walks around the house at night and has been heard by several family members.

The ghost of Knott's Berry Farm, on the other hand, can be seen but not heard. He is believed to have been a wardrobe attendant who was killed on his way to work and can still sometimes be seen sorting costumes. The ghostly appearance of an old stagecoach that races through Santa Ana Canyon, crossing freeways and distracting motorists, has turned up in accident reports, but only happens when atmospheric condi-

tions are just right. Several people have reported seeing the phantom stagecoach, which follows an old stage route now covered with houses and asphalt, but its appearances are not predictable.

A group sighting also occurred at a house in Garden Grove where psychics were once taking a tour. As they walked up the stairs they felt as if they had been kicked in the back of the knees. As they neared the top of the stairs, a portrait on the wall appeared to bleed. Many in the group witnessed the incident, but it has not reoccurred.

Seeing a supernatural phenomenon is rare. Feeling a supernatural presence is more common. In a cabin in the old mining town of Silverado researchers experienced the presence of two spirits, one good and one evil. The researchers found that at one time a man and his daughter had occupied the house. The daughter was a kind, loving soul, but the father was an evil man who had made his daughter's life miserable. The daughter's grave lies on a hill behind the house.

Another evil spirit was reportedly found in a condominium in San Juan Capistrano. An upstairs bedroom had a window that would not remain closed. No matter what was done to secure the window the family always found it open. The children often awoke crying in the night, and were finally moved from the room. Sometimes a strange shadow appeared on the wall, as if a man was standing with his head bowed.

When the spirit was contacted it was found to be that of a man

hanged from a tree that once stood at the level of the upstairs window. The ghost was exorcised and has not returned.

Many incidents have been reported throughout Orange County which defy explanation. Other incidents, however, do have explanations, often surprising ones.

There was a grove of trees on Rancho Mission Viejo that even the bravest cowboy carefully avoided, for on many occasions a low-pitched moaning could be heard coming from it. One particularly hot summer day a lone rider approached the grove at noon, noting the inviting shade it offered. He had heard the stories, of course, about how the grove was haunted, but he swallowed his fear and stopped to rest under the spreading branches.

No sooner had he sat down when the moaning started, low at first, then higher as the breeze picked up. Afraid but curious, he threw back his head and looked high into the branches where the sound was coming from. Instead of a demon with burning eyes and sharp fangs, he saw an empty bottle among the leaves. The bottle was lodged at just the right angle so that when the wind blew it emitted the low moaning sound that had been scaring riders for a dozen years.

Real or imagined, explainable or unexplainable, Orange County's ghost stories add a dimension to its folklore. They have provided mystery and suspense for two centuries and will continue to be a source of entertainment in the years to come.

SPRING ETERNAL

ORANGE COUNTY CALIFORNIA

LANGDON SMITH

VALENCIAS

PALA
BRAVE
BRAND

GROWN IN U·S·A

PACKED BY

BRADFORD BROS., INC.
PLACENTIA
CALIFORNIA

Sunkist

Above: *This orange crate label, featuring a proud American Indian, displays a common and appealing motif. The idealized brave had a strong association with the "golden West." Courtesy, Anaheim Public Library*

Previous page: *Romanticized portrayals of daily life such as this woodland scene, promising an idyllic rural existence, did much to attract new residents to Orange County. Courtesy, Anaheim Public Library*

Facing page: *The 1922 Valencia Orange Show featured displays, contests, and products centering around Valencia oranges, first developed in Orange County in the 1890s. Held in Anaheim in May 1922, it was the first of many successful shows. Courtesy, Anaheim Public Library*

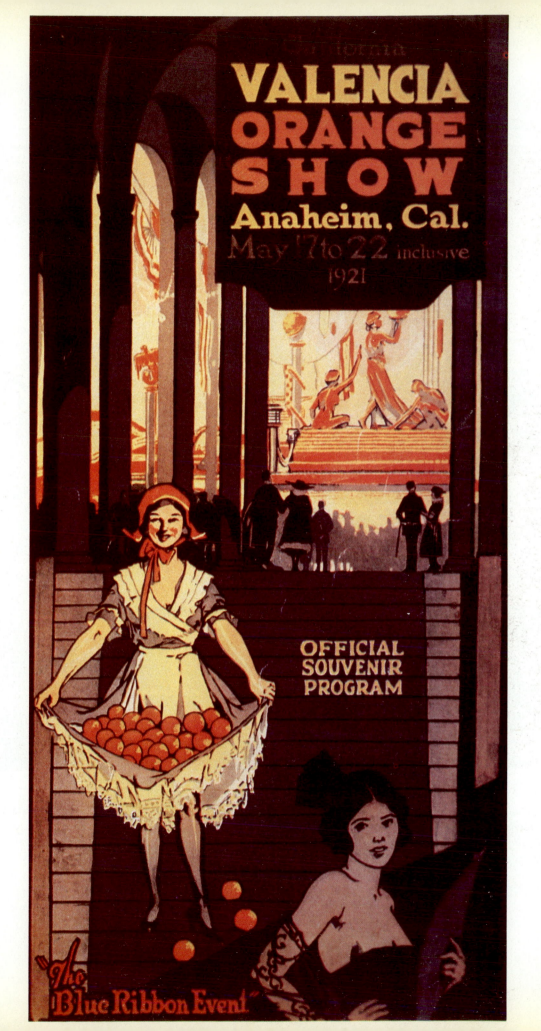

MIRACLE BRAND
BRADFORD BROS. Inc.
PLACENTIA ORANGE COUNTY CALIFORNIA
GROWN IN U.S.A.

Above: *This romantic orange crate label, featuring a genie bearing a tray holding three huge oranges, drew from and added to the mystique surrounding the "miracle" that gave Orange County its name. Courtesy, Anaheim Public Library*

Facing page: *The creator of this orange crate label chose two carefree puppies playing under an orange tree, appealing to a sense of peace and well-being of life in Orange County. Courtesy, Anaheim Public Library*

Facing page: *Orange County's most famous early celebrity was Madame Helena Modjeska, an internationally acclaimed actress. This portrait was painted at the home she and her husband built in verdant Modjeska Canyon, which they christened* Forest of Arden, *after the setting of Shakespeare's* As You Like It. *The house and grounds are today preserved as a private residence. Courtesy, Anaheim Public Library*

Above: *The beauty of contrast was not lost on the artist who painted this scene of an Orange County orange grove with a snowcapped peak in the background. Courtesy, Anaheim Public Library.*

Above: *Oak Canyon Nature Center offers peaceful respite from the urban center that Anaheim has become. Courtesy, City of Anaheim, Public Information*

Facing page: *On a clear day, pleasure craft of all types fill Newport Harbor, as weekend sailors escape to one of Orange County's most popular and refreshing berths. Photo by Jeff Marks*

Facing page, top: *The Newport Environmental Preserve maintains a part of the Southern California coastline in its original state, an increasingly important reminder of the natural beauty of the sea and its environs. Photo by Jeff Marks*

Facing page, bottom: *Lido Marina Village in Newport Beach offers the appealing combination of ocean breezes, shopping, and fine dining in pleasant, tree-shaded surroundings. Photo by Jeff Marks*

Above: *The quintessence of Newport Bay is captured in a spectacular sunset over calm blue water, after a day of play in the surf. Photo by Jeff Marks*

Facing page: *Scenes such as this view of the beach at dusk have helped to make Laguna Beach a popular retreat for many Orange Countians as well as visitors from surrounding areas. Photo by Jeff Marks*

Above: *Laguna Beach manages to radiate the ambience of a small beach town while keeping in touch with its neighboring communities to the north, south, and east. Photo by Jeff Marks*

Above: *Residents of Orange County's coastal communities have become avid sailors, taking advantage of an abundance of marinas and related facilities in order to enjoy the splendor of the sea. Photo by Beatrice Hohenegger*

Left: *Orange County's famous citrus crop continues to appear throughout the county, graphically illustrated here in Laguna Canyon. Photo by Jeff Marks*

Facing Page: *Containing some of California's finest surfing spots, the beaches of Orange County continue to attract large numbers of devotees to this exciting, and sometimes dangerous, sport. Photo by Beatrice Hohenegger*

Above: *Keeping pace with the rest of Orange County, Anaheim is constantly developing and building toward the future. Courtesy, City of Anaheim, Public Information*

Facing page: *Anaheim's penny carnival continues to delight children of all ages. Courtesy, City of Anaheim, Public Information*

Right: *Boysen Park in Anaheim is an exciting and creative place to play, picnic, and enjoy the sunshine. Courtesy, City of Anaheim, Public Information*

The Santora building in Santa Ana is known for its Spanish
Renaissance architecture. Constructed in 1929, it has been
the home of many types of businesses, including Mrs. Daniger's
Tea Room, a popular stopping place for Hollywood stars en
route from San Diego to Hollywood. Courtesy, Thirteenth
Street Architects

Given to the county by James Irvine in 1897, Irvine Park has remained a popular spot for more than eighty years. In 1983 the park underwent a major restoration, preserving many of the buildings that have been added since the 1890s. Courtesy, Thirteenth Street Architects

Above: *Ruby's Cafe, at the end of Balboa Pier, maintains the appearance and menu of a typical 1950s diner. The white lacquered walls and red leather upholstery compliment the cherry cokes and old-fashioned hamburgers. Courtesy, Thirteenth Street Architects*

Left: *Modjeska Park, named for Madame Helena Modjeska, offers a peaceful retreat in the bustle of downtown Anaheim. Courtesy, City of Anaheim, Public Information*

Facing page: *The Newport Center reflects the clean style and open spaces that characterize Newport Beach. Photo by Jeff Marks*

Above: *The Orange County Airport, in keeping with the character of the county, presents a peaceful facade of carefully tended flowerbeds and lawns. Photo by Jeff Marks*

Right: *Although officially held in Los Angeles, many of the games of the 1984 Olympics took place in Orange County, generating much excitement, here evidenced by crowds at the Anaheim Convention Center. Courtesy, City of Anaheim, Public Information*

Facing page: *The Crystal Cathedral in Garden Grove is the home to what was originally Dr. Robert Schuller's drive-in church. The cathedral, made entirely of glass supported by a steel framework, is one of the more awe-inspiring buildings in Orange County. Photo by Beatrice Hohenegger*

Essentially a "people planned" community, Irvine has a reputation for being a very pleasant place to live and work. The offices of the Irvine Industrial Complex, pictured here, literally reflect the goal of open space and a nearness to the land. Photo by Jeff Marks

CHAPTER XIII

Partners

in

Progress

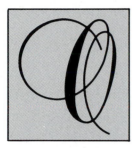

range County businessmen have provided leadership in all facets of community life since the time of the county's organization nearly a century ago. For the county as an entity, 1889 marked a new beginning for the 782 square miles that were created from the lower third of Los Angeles County.

During the county's first decade much of the incredible wealth of the region remained untapped. Businessmen formed water cooperatives and developed irrigation systems on both banks of the Santa Ana River. With the settlement of the water question, Orange County was now unrestrained to realize its full economic potential.

The foundation of wealth in Orange County was agriculture. Orange groves were first planted in the 1870s. As early as the mid-1880s growers were shipping to eastern markets. So successful were those citrus pioneers that when the county was organized in 1889, oranges provided the new county's name and its official seal.

With the dawn of the new century, town roots were firmly planted as agribusiness diversified. The 1900s were destined to see all aspects of Orange County life branch out and flourish.

The arrival of interurban trolley cars, the automobile, and the radio ended the isolation of the rural farming communities. At first change was barely perceptible—then county residents began to feel the impact of a new mechanized world.

The valencia orange remained king of the agricultural commodities.

Peak production occurred in 1929, when more than ten million boxes were shipped from county packinghouses. Barley, lima beans, chili peppers, tomatoes, and strawberries all reached record production levels in the first half of the twentieth century.

With the onset of U.S. participation in World War II, Orange County began to lose its rural identity. As farmland gave way to factories, the county acquired a new industrial profile.

In the postwar years Orange County embarked upon a swift transformation, becoming an integral part of the Los Angeles metropolitan area. Orange groves were uprooted as tract homes spread south, following the freeway tentacles. Residential developments and multimillion-dollar industrial plants became a common sight.

As towns grew so did the demand for services, retail goods, and recreation facilities. The population boom of the 1960s underscored the need for a University of California, Irvine campus (1965), South Coast Plaza (1966), and the dedication of a county airport (1967).

Throughout the 1970s urban planners looked to Orange County for lessons in the development of the planned community. As residential tracts were completed, developers channeled their resources into new high-tech office and industrial centers. Trends in the 1980s indicate that Orange County is destined to become an important Pacific Coast business and cultural center.

The organizations whose stories are detailed on the following pages have chosen to support this important literary and civic project. They illustrate the variety of ways in which individuals and their businesses have contributed to the area's growth and development. The civic involvement of Orange County's businesses, institutions of learning, and government, in cooperation with its citizens, has made the county an excellent place to live and work.

*Brea Canyon oil field received its name from the pits of tar
that were common during the days of Spanish rule. Courtesy,
First American Title Insurance Company*

BOWERS MUSEUM

Contrary to visitors' speculations, the Bowers Museum, at the corner of Twentieth and Main streets in Santa Ana, is not an old mission. Nor was it the private residence of the Bowers family. The building was constructed in 1932 as a museum, the result of a trust left to the City of Santa Ana by Charles W. Bowers.

Charles Bowers migrated to Orange County from the Midwest in the late 1800s, involving himself in land development and citrus cultivation. He inherited land that constituted a segment of the original Yorba-Peralta Spanish Land Grant of 1810, causing the perpetuance of stories and legends about early California and the rancheros. Bowers keenly desired the preservation of Orange County's historical heritage, and in 1924 he created the trust that provided for the museum.

After Bowers and his wife, Ada, passed away, their Victorian home

A trust left to the City of Santa Ana by Charles and Ada Bowers allowed for the construction of the Bowers Museum.

was razed, and the Spanish-style adobe museum was erected. Although construction was completed in 1932, the museum did not officially open until February 15, 1936, because of the Depression.

In 1934 the museum's first curator, Bessie-Beth Coulter, applied herself to the task of obtaining exhibit material reminiscent of early California history. Her efforts over twenty-five years provided the museum with a solid local history base that remains an inherent fiber of the Bowers Museum.

In 1957 and 1961 small additions

for workroom space and storage facilities to house the growing museum collection were built. In 1974 a major expansion plan increased the museum space by 12,000 square feet. The added footage boosted the caliber and size of exhibits the museum could host; traveling shows from other museums and institutions such as the Smithsonian Institution Traveling Exhibition Service (SITES) highlighted the show schedule.

Exhibits of particular acclaim have been international doll shows; paintings by European masters, including Picasso, Homer, Klee, Hopper, and Dufy; Fayum mummy portraits; "In China" photographs; western art; whale skeletons; and Mickey Mouse memorabilia. The museum's own permanent collection prompts displays of California history, American Indian artifacts, and African, pre-Columbian, and New Guinea sculptures, masks, and totems.

The Bowers Museum sponsors a variety of lively events—preview openings for members with complimentary hors d'oeuvres and entertainment, lectures, workshops, films, and cultural programs. Tours are given by the docents, a guild schooled in presenting information on the current exhibits to the public. The mini-museum, traveling trunks, and mobile museum are outreach programs that are taken into schools and the community.

The ambience of the museum courtyard beckons local business people to brown bag their lunches amidst the large old trees, giant cacti and Indian grinding stones. The arcades buffer the noise of street activity while housing displays of antique vehicles.

The Bowers Museum continues to grow in its prominence in the community and in its development of expansion and exhibition ideas for the future. Charles Bowers accomplished his aim.

Entrance to the Bowers Museum, located at the corner of Twentieth and Main streets in Santa Ana.

CARL KARCHER ENTERPRISES, INC.

The first Carl's Jr. in Anaheim was located at Lincoln and Janss.

"Carl had the stamina and vitality to oversee the evolution of his company from a single hot dog cart to a multimillion-dollar corporation."
—Irv Mills, longtime employee

The saga of Carl Karcher Enterprises, Inc. (CKE), is a story of opportunity in America. It is a chronicle of hard work, courage, and perseverance. Carl Karcher is an individual gifted with a rare ability of vision, but who also has the resolute character to make a dream reality.

Carl Nicholas Karcher was born to Leo and Anna Karcher on January 16, 1917, in Wyandot County, Ohio. He was one of eight children. Coming from a large family was an influence in his decision to leave school after the eighth grade to devote full time to the family farmstead. The years of the Great Depression were difficult for farm families. Karcher often dreamed of heading west to California, the land of opportunity. In 1937 he departed for Anaheim, doing as he had envisioned.

In 1939 Karcher married Margaret M. Heinz of Anaheim. The responsibilities of family life prompted him to seek a business venture to supplement his income as a bakery deliveryman. He noticed the large consignment of hot dog buns ordered by the multitude of hot dog stands that were springing up around Los Angeles. In 1941, in partnership with his wife, Karcher purchased the hot dog cart of Louis Richmond for $326.

By 1942 Karcher owned two more carts and hired two employees while continuing his full-time job with the bakery. Three years later he opened Carl's Drive-in Barbecue, for many years a favorite among Anaheim diners. Karcher served as cook until he was drafted into the Army. After the war he returned to assume full control of his restaurant business.

The year 1946 was an important one as Karcher introduced the hamburger to the menu. By the onset of the 1950s his restaurants were doing a big business, and in 1956 he opened two smaller versions of his Anaheim restaurant and called them Carl's Jr.

In 1960 there were four Carl's Jr. restaurants in Orange County. Throughout the decade restaurants were added in rapid succession. Employees were loyal, and so were customers.

In the late 1960s the firm underwent some major administrative changes after incorporation in 1966. Henceforth, the company was known as Carl Karcher Enterprises (CKE).

The year 1968 is considered the "era of new beginnings," since it was the first year of the firm's upscale, fast-food concept, featuring upholstered booths and carpeting. The new fast-food concept proved so popular that CKE surged forward, adding as many as forty-five units each year. The CKE advertising campaigns of 1968-1972 paid immediate returns.

The phenomenal growth continued in the 1970s. In 1981 Carl Karcher Enterprises, Inc., formerly privately held, began selling stock to the public. CKE moved into the Arizona market in 1982, having previously expanded from California to Nevada. In 1984 the company initiated a franchise program in California.

A modern-day Carl's Jr. restaurant.

DISNEYLAND

Disneyland has been called an "enchanted kingdom" that defies description and must be seen to be believed. Most visitors agree a single visit to Disneyland is not enough. Things change. More entertainment areas are added. Attractions are updated to keep pace with change and progress. And always, there are the adventures that could not be explored on previous visits to the park.

When Disneyland opened in July 1955, a year and a day after groundbreaking, the public was offered a well-organized blend of fun, food, and family enjoyment. Those looking for good, clean entertainment found it in this $17-million theme park spread over seventy-six acres of what just a short time before was orange groves.

Opening day visitors were entranced by five "lands"—Fantasyland, Adventureland, Frontierland, Tomorrowland, and Main Street, USA—and eighteen delightful attractions. Although the park met with immediate success, Disneyland continued to grow.

Eleven years after the park's debut, a sixth land was opened, New Orleans Square, representing the Queen City of the Mississippi with startling splendor and authenticity. Bear Country, a lighthearted look at America's Northwest wilderness, opened in 1972, becoming the park's seventh theme land.

Set amid the rustic beauty of an authentic-looking gold-mining town of a century ago, Big Thunder Mountain Railroad opened in September 1979 at a cost of $15.8 million. Climbing aboard open-air ore cars, guests find they are cargo on a "runaway" mine train. Before their

Walt Disney, the man behind the dream, takes advantage of a quiet, reflective moment to stroll the grounds. © 1985, Walt Disney Productions

splashing return to the little boom town of Big Thunder, visitors survive a host of threats along their journey, including swarming bats, a raging waterfall, and an underground earthquake and ensuing avalanche.

In 1983, after a two-year, $55.5-million renovation, a new Fantasyland opened. Transformed into a quaint Old World village, Fantasyland now presents the wizardry of space-age special effects, recreating scenes from classic animated features within carefully aged cottages and castles—the homes of some of Walt Disney's most beloved characters.

Thus, Walt Disney's $17-million investment is now a $285-million entertainment complex, boasting fifty-four major attractions and a worldwide reputation as a healthy diversion from the trials of the day for children of all ages. With its seven lands as a nucleus, guests on a single visit may brave the wild inhabitants of a jungle cruise, glide into the ocean's depths in an "atomic" submarine, or brave an adventurous trip in their own flat-bottomed bateau for a plunge backward in time to when pirates ruled the Spanish Main.

Those interested in journeying out of this world can enter the Haunted

Nearing completion, Main Street, USA, and Sleeping Beauty's Castle rise up from the ground where an orange grove stood just months before. © 1985, Walt Disney Productions

Mansion, where apparitions drift through walls and lifeless statues sing and dance, or take a simulated voyage to the planet Mars and back in just a matter of minutes.

Visitors who prefer a more leisurely pace may stroll through a bit of Americana in days gone by. An old-fashioned ice cream parlor, silent cinema, and general store keep alive this delightful nostalgia.

Guests may also discover old and new eras of transportation as they board putt-putting horseless carriages, a soaring Skyway, horse-drawn trolleys, or the silent Disneyland Monorail System, gliding on highways in the sky. On the futuristic People-Mover, guests can experience the sensation of tremendous speed in the Superspeed Tunnel.

Space Mountain, a high-speed, thrill-filled rocket adventure into "superspace," made its debut in 1977. Within the 118-foot-tall structure, voyagers experience the excitement of a speeding, twisting journey through unexplored deep space. This futuristic complex includes an amphitheater, restaurant, and space-age arcade.

Some Disneyland visitors like to just "walk around," enjoying an ever-changing panorama of beauty and color and experiencing the excitement of discovering a new attraction. Those who visit the Main Street Opera House may enjoy "The Walt Disney Story," featuring "Great Moments with Mr. Lincoln," an "Audio-Animatronics" salute to our nation's sixteenth president.

The Matterhorn bobsleds offer a thrilling, high-speed adventure through wind-whipped grottoes and icy caverns aboard colorful bobsleds. Constructed in 1959, the Matterhorn has been a favorite of millions of Disneyland guests. After major additions were made inside the mountain in 1978, bobsledders found a host of exciting new experiences, including

President Dwight D. Eisenhower and his wife, Mamie, are among the hundreds of dignitaries who have visited the Magic Kingdom in its thirty-year history. © 1985, Walt Disney Productions

chilling temperatures, drifting fog banks, and the hulking presence of the Abominable Snowman.

America Sings, in the Carousel Theater, allows fun seekers to enjoy 200 years of America's most memorable music through the comical antics and songs of more than 110 humorous animals, who come to life through the wizardry of Audio-Animatronics.

At the same time visitors are being entertained, batteries of Disneyland artists, sculptors, painters, carpenters, electricians, technicians, and cleanup crews are working behind the scenes to make each guest's visit even more enjoyable. More than 500 arts and crafts are represented by the men and women who apply their expertise maintaining and improving the Disney dream.

Employees in the park's dining facilities cater efficiently to as many as 60,000 people a day during the peak summer period at Disneyland. One food center may satisfy the appetites of as many as 4,000 persons in a single hour.

Equally important is the wardrobe

department, which outfits as many as 7,000 persons in a single day, utilizing nearly 700 different types of costumes amounting to more than 500,000 individual articles of clothing.

Some of the best professional landscapers in the business continually give loving care to 500,000 trees, plants, and shrubs that are an integral part of the Disneyland show. Adding their own special touch to the park are the custodial personnel, who polish, clean, dust, scrub, sweep, and tidy the grounds, almost around the clock.

All of these individuals are vital cogs in the big wheel that makes Disneyland tick. They are the meticulous partners of the late Walt Disney, one of the world's greatest dreamers who had an extra-special talent. He knew how to make a dream come true. Just ask the 250 million people who have visited Disneyland.

The Disneyland Monorail System was the first in the United States to provide regular daily service. © 1985, Walt Disney Productions

BIRTCHER

The groundbreaking of Allergan Pharmaceuticals joined Birtcher with one of Orange County's oldest manufacturers. Fayette and Ron Birtcher built the facility as part of the 45-acre Santa Ana Industrial Park. From left to right are Richard Hausman, Fayette Birtcher, unidentified, Keith Herbert, Gavin Herbert, Sr., and Gavin Herbert, Jr.

The history of Birtcher, a tight-knit family organization that has evolved into a nationwide development, investment, and property management company, is an Orange County success story. It is based on strong family ties, a conservative business approach, development foresight and expertise, and sound fiscal management. In June 1985 Birtcher was ranked by *Corporate Design & Realty,* a major commercial/industrial development publication, as the seventh-largest developer in the United States and the ninth-largest in all of North America of 100 firms surveyed. The company's quiet growth has paralleled the industrial growth of Orange County, as illustrated by the four generations of Birtchers who have been involved in one particular piece of property that has become an Orange County landmark.

In 1909, when Orange County was little more than miles and miles of citrus fields, Justus Birtcher moved here from Philadelphia to earn his living as a carpenter. From 1916 to 1919 his son, Fayette, worked in the Holly Sugar factory in Santa Ana, located near what is now the 55 Freeway. The Birtcher dynasty was beginning to take shape as Justus became one of Orange County's largest building contractors. In 1938 Fayette purchased sugar beet properties across from the Holly Sugar factory and erected industrial facilities on the site. He continued his father's legacy as one of Orange County's leading developers, and built the first residential housing in Orange County after World War II—Emerald Terrace in Laguna Beach.

As Orange County steadily grew, so did Fayette's company. Ron Birtcher, Fayette's eldest son, joined the development firm in 1951, bringing his construction and marketing expertise to the expanding roster of projects. In 1961 his younger brother, Art, also joined the development team, adding his skills in accounting and finance to the Birtcher business operations. After Fayette's retirement in 1965, Ron and Art assumed positions at the helm of the company, each with his own responsibilities as general partner: Ron guides the design, construction, and marketing activities, while Art supervises all financial, investment, and administrative matters. The story of the evolution of the Holly Sugar factory continued with fourth-generation Brandon Birtcher, Ron's son, who joined the firm in 1976.

In 1982 Brandon acquired the Holly Sugar property on behalf of the family, and was involved in the conversion of what had once been Orange County's largest employment facility into the county's largest single-phase high-tech "campus" that employs more than 1,500 people. The distinctive Orange County Tech Center, home to a variety of industrial companies, features the county's first child care facility incorporated into a business center. It is now a landmark in the local industrial community. Through four generations on this very site, Birtcher has been a part of the changing Orange County skyline.

Of course, the Birtcher story branched into many more chapters as the years rolled by. Since the 1950s, when the company was called Mar Crest Corp. and was based in Corona del Mar, the scope of the operations has followed a steady course of growth and prosperity. From 1953 through 1969 Fayette and his sons pioneered the method of concrete tilt-up construction, which has since become standard in the industry. In the 1950s Birtcher also pioneered the concept of land leases as a financing tool in structuring office and industrial developments to meet the needs of the county's growing population.

In 1969 a partnership was formed that expanded Birtcher's operations into the national arena. The Southern Pacific Railroad Co. conducted a nationwide search for a company to become its partner in the development of railroad properties within the Southwest. Birtcher was selected for its conservative business approach and fiscal management. The new Sequoia Pacific partnership developed between three and three and one-half million square feet a year in twenty-two states. One of the partnership's most notable projects was the Pacific Design Center in West Hollywood, built in 1976. This 750,000-square-foot facility quickly became a landmark known as the "Blue Whale" because of its striking blue-hued exterior and mammoth size, housing more than 200 wholesale showrooms for design trade manufacturers.

In 1977, when Southern Pacific reduced its development activity, Birtcher acquired the partnership's interest in all its active properties, which included office centers in Houston and Santa Clara. Birtcher

The Holly Sugar factory in Santa Ana employed both Justus and Fayette Birtcher in the early 1900s.

Once the major employer in Orange County, the former Holly Sugar factory was replaced in 1985 by the fourth generation of the Birtcher family, in order to accommodate the county's expanding high-tech industries. Photo by Lloyd de Mers

then continued its development momentum under the name Birtcher Pacific, opening a network of regional offices in areas targeted as high-growth centers. Birtcher has since opened offices in Washington, D.C., Seattle, Portland, Dallas, Denver, Palm Desert, Chicago, and Phoenix, while maintaining national corporate headquarters in Orange County. In 1984 Birtcher dropped "Pacific" from the company name to more accurately reflect its national scope and prominence.

Since 1974 Birtcher has developed more than thirty-four million square feet of space in cities throughout the country. It has entered into joint ventures with landowners, life insurance companies, pension funds, personal estates, and individuals to develop projects worth hundreds of millions of dollars. Its clients have included twenty-eight *Fortune* 500 companies as well as major national financial institutions. On an annual basis since 1980 it has had more than one billion dollars in projects under development. Emerging as an instrumental force in the redevelopment of downtown Los Angeles, Birtcher has received city endorsement for its development of the giant Los Angeles Wholesale Produce Market, incorporating distribution facilities and offices into the largest United States mart of its kind.

In addition, the Birtcher Investments division has experienced significant growth and achieved national prominence. Established in 1983, Birtcher Investments is headquartered in Orange County. Its first public investment fund closed in October 1985, after having raised $97.2 million. Out of 154 firms that are ranked nationally, Birtcher ranked eleventh after only one year in the business.

Three generations of the Birtcher family, all of whom have been active in developing Birtcher into one of the top ten commercial development and investment companies in the United States. From left to right are Fayette Birtcher, Ronald Birtcher, Arthur Birtcher, Wendy Birtcher, and Brandon Birtcher (not pictured, Baron Birtcher).

Birtcher is also diversifying its activities. In 1985 it acquired franchise rights from another Orange County family business to open thirty-one Carl's Jr. restaurants in Texas.

The Birtcher family is deeply involved in every facet of the company's operations, including land acquisition and planning, building design and construction, and fiscal and property management. Fourth-generation Birtchers, the children of Ron and Art, are continuing the tradition as company executives. Brandon works with Ron in construction and marketing. Baron, who joined the firm in 1980, supports Art in the finance and investment division. Wendy joined the investment division in 1984 and is working closely with the company's projects as an investment analyst.

While growing into a national organization of enormous scope, the Birtchers have roots deep in Orange County soil. Since 1959 three generations of the family have lived next door to one another on a private seven-acre ranch in south Orange County. The family is extremely active in state and national politics, as well as Orange County's arts, charities, civic organizations, and community churches.

The pioneering tradition begun in the early 1900s by Justus and Fayette E. Birtcher continues to evolve, guided by new Birtcher leaders. Their ability to see a piece of land and envision its potential, then transform that vision into the reality of office, industrial, or retail facilities, has opened the doors for many thousands of jobs in Orange County. As the industry of Orange County—and the nation—moves forward, Birtcher will undoubtedly be at its leading edge.

DISNEYLAND HOTEL

The Disneyland Hotel in Anaheim has experienced tremendous growth, rising from a 100-room motel to an 1,100-room resort hotel and convention center. This phenomenal expansion has contributed to the growth of both Anaheim and Orange County as a Southern California vacation and commercial center.

The hotel began in 1954 as a vision of two California entertainment entrepreneurs: Walt Disney and Jack Wrather. Disney asked his friend Wrather to build a hotel in the groves of orange trees across from his now-famous theme park—Disneyland. Wrather, convinced that the hotel and park would grow to be a leading resort and attraction, acquired sixty acres of orange groves adjoining the park.

The hotel's first 100 rooms opened on October 5, 1955, just three months after Disneyland had successfully opened with a crowd of 30,000. The first rooms featured balconies and an orange tree on every patio. The newly opened hotel was designated the "Official Hotel of the Magic Kingdom."

In 1960 Disneyland Hotel was linked to the park via a monorail system. That same year the hotel unveiled the Embassy Ballroom, where Orange County society dined and danced in the county's first ballroom facility.

The eleven-story Sierra Tower North, completed in 1961, was Orange County's first high rise. The Disneyland Hotel claimed another first when the thirteen-story Bonita Tower was added in 1979; it became the first solar-energy hotel in the nation.

Seaports of the Pacific, which opened in 1970, has remained the hotel's showpiece. This 3.5-acre, multimillion-dollar water wonderland features a 55,000-square-foot inland marina, shops, restaurants, swimming pools, Koi fish ponds, a sandy beach, and waterfalls. A dazzling display of cascading fountains, lights, and music, known as Dancing Waters, is the focal point of this aquatic playland.

Disneyland Hotel has evolved into a world-class resort. Amenities include sixteen restaurants and lounges and sixty-one shops and services. Unique among the hotel's services is the Youth Club. Children from around the world enjoy supervised games, dinner, movies, and arts and crafts in the summer and during winter holidays. Convention facilities include 79,000 square feet of exhibit halls and three ballrooms. There are fifty-four meeting rooms and 160,000 square feet of meeting and banquet space.

The year 1985 marked the thirtieth anniversary of Disneyland Hotel. The astonishing growth of the little hotel in the orange grove to its position as the most complete resort in Southern California is one of Orange County's unparalleled success stories.

Disneyland Hotel in Anaheim has grown from a 100-room motel on sixty acres of orange groves in 1955 to an 1,100-room resort hotel and convention center.

DELOITTE HASKINS & SELLS

When Deloitte Haskins & Sells opened its first public accounting office in Orange County two decades ago, the area was a thriving farming region. Bean fields dotted the countryside. Strawberry farmers harvested prize-winning crops. Orange and lemon trees lined the streets of Anaheim and Santa Ana. Ranch land extended as far as the eye could see. Saddleback Mountain, then as now, towered in the background.

But the partners at DH&S knew that development was coming. No longer would Orange County be merely a bedroom community. The county was about to take on a new identity. Homes and stores would be built to accommodate the people, buildings would rise to meet business needs, and new services would be required.

The firm became part of that development, part of that thriving community. DH&S opened its first office in Santa Ana in 1966 with four employees. Two years later it moved to larger quarters.

Deloitte Haskins & Sells prospered along with the county and moved to its present location in the South Coast Plaza Town Center in 1979. There are now over 175 Orange County residents employed at that location.

The firm has anticipated the county's needs by specializing in services to the real estate, high-technology, health care, and banking industries, as well as providing tax services. As one of the oldest and largest Big Eight firms in the area, DH&S offers a full range of public accounting and consulting services to Orange County business. Its local resources are supplemented by a network of practice offices, serving an almost endless variety of clients, public and private, large and small, around the world.

Deloitte Haskins & Sells also encourages the growth of Orange County through its involvement in various community organizations. Employees coach Little League teams, volunteer for community groups, and advise fledgling companies on how to improve their business practices. The firm also supports organizations, such as the Bowers Museum, that have enriched the cultural life of the community.

C. Stephen Mansfield, partner in charge.

Deloitte Haskins & Sells is part of the growth and good living that symbolize Orange County—working with area residents to build an even better community.

RANCHO MISSION VIEJO

Sired by Spain, mothered by Mexico, and reared with Irish pluck, no parcel in Orange County enjoys a lengthier heritage than does the 40,000-acre Rancho Mission Viejo, whose destinies have been guided by Richard O'Neill, Sr., and his descendants for over a century. Incorporating two former Mexican grants and portions of a third, the ranch's legacy began with the first Spanish expeditionary force into Alta California.

On July 22, 1769, Capitán Gaspar de Portolá, with sixty-three men and two priests, stepped across the ranch's southern border into local history. Here, in Cristianitas Canyon, the baptism of two Indian babes brought Christianity to California and the earliest place name to Orange County. Following a night's bivouac near the ranch's Campo Vaquero off the Ortega Highway, the explorers spent a day and a night on the mesa above O'Neill Park. The loss there of a soldier's gun inspired the name Trabuco (Spanish for "blunderbuss"), which survives today as the oldest ranch name in the state.

Six years later the ranch witnessed the first attempt to found Mission San Juan Capistrano. After the mission was relocated in 1778, its departure from San Juan Canyon endowed that area with the name "Mission Viejo," and historians with a dilemma that has lasted ever since. While the exact whereabouts of the "Old Mission" remains a mystery, the name has prevailed for over two centuries.

In 1821 Mexico won its independence from Spain and a new flag fluttered over the province. Following secularization of the missions, huge estates were granted by the Mexican governor to a few prominent citizens. Among those lands in Orange County were the ranchos Trabuco (22,184 acres), Mission Viejo (47,432 acres), and Los Potreros (1,167 acres). Acquiring title to each was an astute

Richard O'Neill, Sr.
1825-1910

English trader named John Forster, who changed his name and citizenship and wisely married the governor's sister. Eventually "Don Juan" Forster would own even Mission San Juan Capistrano itself.

For his part, Forster's brother-in-law, Governor Pío Pico, amassed a barony of 133,440 acres in San Diego known as the Rancho Santa Margarita y las Flores, and gambling debts that nearly matched his estate. In 1846 Pico's high-rolling reign ended with the American invasion. Pursued

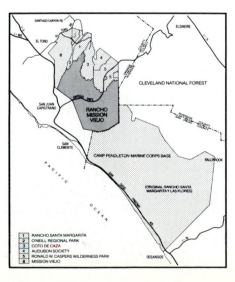

1 RANCHO SANTA MARGARITA
2 O'NEILL REGIONAL PARK
3 COTO DE CAZA
4 AUDUBON SOCIETY
5 RONALD W. CASPERS WILDERNESS PARK
6 MISSION VIEJO

and in exile, Mexico's last governor hid out in the old adobe on Trabuco Mesa, then fled the country. More pliable than his in-laws, Forster welcomed the Yankee intruders and continued to prosper under statehood. Sixteen years later he picked up Pico's mortgages and the Rancho Santa Margarita y las Flores to stretch his holdings from Oceanside to Aliso Canyon.

It was a storybook beginning without a storybook end. By 1881 the cost of fencing 205,000 acres had drained Forster's capital; a series of droughts destroyed half his cattle; and ill-fated promotions to attract settlers dried up the last of his credit. When he died a year later, Don Juan's estate teetered precariously between a half-dozen heirs and a half-dozen banks.

Left with no choice, his sons had to sell.

Sizing up the ranch was a bandy-legged Irish cattleman whose name was Richard O'Neill, Sr. Born in Brigown Parish, County Cork, in the heart of Ireland's dairy country, he had traveled far in his fifty-seven years and had missed several fortunes in the process. O'Neill vowed not to miss another. Somehow, the sight of Santa Margarita's slat-sided cows dining on parched stubble reminded him of his own odyssey.

As a lad his family had fled Irish poverty to resettle on the rock-bound coast of New Brunswick. There, in St. Andrews, the elder O'Neill, Patrick, found small demand for his skills as a butcher in a village devoted largely to fish. For his apprenticed son, it was a hard-scrabble life. By the time he was twenty Richard swore that he had cleaned his last

Under Richard O'Neill Rancho Santa Margarita y las Flores, covering 359 square miles, stretched from Oceanside to Aliso Creek. The name is being revived in current Rancho Santa Margarita development.

Orange County's greatest wheat field in 1909, Trabuco Mesa will be the setting for the forthcoming urban village of Rancho Santa Margarita.

cod. Alone, he made his way down into Massachusetts to slave again in a Boston butcher shop. Here news reached him of the wondrous gold strike in California.

O'Neill caught the next ship.

But weary months of grubbing along the Sacramento brought only a handful of dust and the conviction that California's real gold lay only in business. Returning to San Francisco, Richard resolutely opened a small meat market near the docks Here his fortunes began to brighten. Successive shops found better locations, and bought him a home for the love of his life, an Irish wife, who bore him four children.

Most fortuitous, perhaps, was his early friendship with James C. Flood, another Irish immigrant. A former carriage-maker turned saloon-keeper, Flood bought O'Neill's meat for his Auction Lunch, and dabbled in stocks at the Mining Exchange across the street. While O'Neill's successes led to a modest meat-packing plant, Flood's fortunes soared astronomically. By clever stock manipulations he managed to corner the Comstock Lode, America's most famous silver mine.

Tempted by Flood's success, O'Neill also took a flier at the market. The result was instant disaster. To fend off complete ruin and save rent, he moved his California Meat Company next door to his home, and started over from scratch. If the atmosphere taught his family a lesson in humility, it also brought them one of pride. By shear toil and tenacity—some say bull-headedness—they saw their father scrap back to redeem

both his debts and reputation.

Impressed by O'Neill's grit, his friend James Flood asked him to look into a run-down ranch he had repossessed in Merced County. Richard danced at the opportunity. He knew good beef, and within two years he knew how to raise them. So dramatic were the changes he wrought that the ranch was sold out from under him at a handsome profit. As a tribute to O'Neill's skill as a manager, the new owner put him onto the Forster deal.

A week's survey in the saddle convinced Richard of the potential of Rancho Santa Margarita y las Flores, and that no way in the world could he float it. The heirs wanted $250,000 for the property; the banks nearly doubled that price with their notes. Still, God willing, he would have it! With Irish spunk he approached the one man he knew with that much cash—his old friend, the new "Silver King of Nevada."

Flood sized up the proposition, then sized up its suggestor. Tapping the ash from his cigar, he said, "Buy it!"

Attesting to their mutual respect, the deal was struck with a handshake. Both men were to become equal partners, Richard to work out his half at $500 a month as resident manager. With a purchase price of

$457,000, it should have taken him thirty-seven years. Knowing that he hadn't that many left, O'Neill vowed to trim the time with his share of the profits. Proof that he managed to do so is seen in the fact that he won full title to half the ranch in just twenty-four years!

It was an arduous quarter-century. After installing his brood in the Santa Margarita's adobe ranch house—a relic from Pico's times—O'Neill took stock of its cattle. Holdovers from California's hide and tallow trade, they were small, tough, and rangey. Even his vaqueros admitted that "They're good for almost anything but eating." To upgrade his herds, O'Neill imported shorthorns from Texas, then put in feedlots and crops to sustain them through the dry years. Mother Nature promptly responded with the two wettest winters in history.

Happier was the arrival of the Santa Fe. By 1888 it ran the length of the ranch. Recognizing that the railroad was a great cattle saver, O'Neill fought for his own sidings in order to ship his beef to better markets. During the 1890s he reintroduced cattle

This turn-of-the-century photo depicts John Baumgartner, Sr., branding a calf. Rancho Mission Viejo still grazes from 3,000 to 6,000 cattle annually.

Rocket-testing facilities of TRW on Rancho Mission Viejo represent one of many leases, which run from ornamental plants to aerospace.

Members of the O'Neill family—Marguerite M. O'Neill with her children, Alice O'Neill Avery and Richard J. O'Neill, and Mrs. Avery's sons, Anthony R. and Jerome J.—dedicate a plaque at O'Neill Park, June 18, 1950.

on Rancho Mission Viejo that heretofore had grazed mostly sheep. He commissioned a tourist hotel at San Juan Hot Springs, which boomed with unexpected visitors, then suffered through a mining boom in Lucas Canyon, which sparked more brushfires than profit. He waged war on squatters and wild hogs in the San Mateo, and leased out Trabuco Mesa to see it become Orange County's biggest wheat field.

Those who knew Richard O'Neill, Sr., remembered him as an honest rancher, a man who drove both his men and a hard bargain. Perhaps his cowboys and tenants would have

been less loyal had they not met a man who drove himself twice as hard.

Broken in health, O'Neill was past eighty in 1907 when James L. Flood, son of the "Silver King," made good his father's promise. Richard had, indeed, earned his half of the ranch by his labor. Four months later O'Neill deeded his interests in the spread to his son, who assisted him as manager. In 1909 Jerome became so in fact.

Jerome O'Neill shared Richard's robust spirit, but in a frame handicapped by an early bout with polio. Loved by his cowboys, they joshed that "the señor wasn't fully dressed until he was in the saddle." Once astride a horse, they claimed, "he could ride like Satan himself."

Hard-driving like his father, but tempered by more insight and humor,

San Juan Hot Springs on Ortega Highway became Orange County's most popular spa. The first hotel was built there in 1890 by Richard O'Neill, Sr.

Jerome brought the ranch new direction. In return, nature brought him a host of problems—everything from thistles to ticks, while the Depression sent him such man-made ones as rumrunners and rustlers. Even so, during his nineteen-year tenure, the ranch prospered as never before. Fields of blackeyes and sugar beets now vied with grain crops and 15,000 head of cattle to become the big money-makers.

Under Jerome the ranch reached its greatest extent—230,000 acres. In 1923, to consolidate their interests, Jerome and James L. incorporated under the name Santa Margarita Company.

Ironically, what began as a second-generation friendship ended abruptly in 1926 when both men died just two days apart.

Never married, Jerome established

Anthony R. Moiso, Alice O'Neill Avery, and Richard Jerome O'Neill.

trusts for his sister, Mary (Mrs. John Baumgartner), and younger brother, Richard. While the Baumgartners loved ranching, Richard Jr. felt more at home in San Francisco banking circles. The next dozen years saw a succession of interim managers whose efforts were largely dissipated by water litigation and ill-advised sales on the Rancho Mission Viejo. Among them were Bell Canyon (today an Audubon sanctuary and Casper's Park), the three-mountain potreros, and Gobernadora Canyon (now Coto de Caza).

As the 1930s closed, the Flood heirs, little disposed to ranching, elected to sell. An epic division of the Rancho Santa Margarita y las Flores followed in 1940, the Floods and Baumgartners taking the lower portion, while Richard O'Neill, Jr.—by luck or foresight—retained the Orange County parcel. Owing to World War II, within three years Marine Corps condemnations had absorbed the entire San Diego property for Camp Pendleton.

By 1941 what remained of the historic Rancho Santa Margarita y las Flores became known as the Rancho Mission Viejo, much reduced, but still a substantial 52,000 acres. Living but two years to enjoy it, Richard Jr. died, passing his interest to his widow, Marguerite, and their children, Alice and Richard. A seventh-generation Californian of Spanish descent, Marguerite also brought the Rancho Mission Viejo's heritage full circle.

For over thirty years trusts established by Jerome O'Neill hamstrung full family control of the ranch. During the mid-1940s it was "Ama Daisy," as Marguerite is fondly recalled, who personally "took on the bankers" to thwart several attempts to liquidate it completely. As tough-minded as she once was beautiful, she lived an astonishing 102 years, and is still venerated as the family heroine. By Daisy's dedication and devotion, she made possible the remarkable strides of the past two decades.

Today Rancho Mission Viejo is jointly owned by members of the O'Neill family while its operational entity, Santa Margarita Company, is headed by Anthony R. "Tony" Moiso, great-grandson of Richard J. O'Neill, Sr.

Forced to modify its pastoral ways in the mid-1960s by Orange County's population explosion, the ranch's

Reviving a tradition begun in mission times, in 1971 the ranch set out seventy-one acres of wine grapes. Several varieties of wine are now being marketed locally under the brand name San Juan Creek.

first residential venture was with the 10,000-acre planned community of Mission Viejo—since sold to Philip Morris, Inc. Subsequently Moiso and his planners have faced an array of challenges—from creating new water districts to coping with freeways. Upcoming is their most impressive opportunity, the urban village of Rancho Santa Margarita. Far from neglecting the ranch's commercial activities, Moiso has diversified them from dry farming and mining to everything from race horses to aerospace.

Keeping pace with their personal achievements, the O'Neills have met their civic commitments with generous land donations for roads, schools, and parks, and made personal ones to such things as the restoration of Old Mission in San Juan Capistrano and supporting local historical museums.

Moreover, the ranch has retained its 200-year heritage by hosting such events as El Viaje de Portolá, spring round-ups, and annual fandangos. Most important, the family has kept faith with its founder. Today the ranch remains the last large-scale cattle operation in Southern California.

Having observed its own centennial of ranch management, the O'Neill family salutes Orange County by pledging to preserve the best of the past as it plans for a still brighter future!

C.J. SEGERSTROM & SONS

The Segerstrom family of Orange County represents an outstanding example of the emergence of the private landowner as a skilled urban planner and developer. Drawing upon an agrarian heritage, the Segerstroms have emerged from caretakers of the land to the creators of a multimillion-dollar real estate partnership—C.J. Segerstrom & Sons.

The American odyssey began for Charles John Segerstrom in 1882 when his family departed its native Sweden. Following an arduous transoceanic voyage, the Segerstroms lived one year in Chicago, moved to Wisconsin for two years, and then to St. Paul, Minnesota. In St. Paul, Charles John "C.J." devoted thirteen years to the railroad.

In 1898 Segerstrom and his family relocated to California, anxious to make use of farming techniques learned in the "old country." In 1900 the family settled in the Greenville area of Orange County (then known as Old Newport). Included among the various agricultural operations of the Segerstroms during their first fifty years in Orange County were two of California's largest dairy farms, which were sold in 1942.

As early as 1918 Segerstrom realized that the family's acreage was better suited to the cultivation of lima beans than to growing alfalfa dairy feed. Through methodical individual land acquisitions, ranging in size from a few acres to 600 acres, the Segerstroms had become the nation's largest independent producers of lima beans by the 1950s. "Grown by Segerstrom" became synonymous with the hallmarks of pride and quality.

Planned development for industrial use began in 1948 with the purchase of seventy-five acres, which included 110,000 square feet of warehouse buildings, and a 2.5-mile-long railroad line, which was a portion of the World War II Santa Ana Army Air Base land and partially a reacquisi-

Jewel Court at South Coast Plaza Mall.

tion of Segerstrom land acquired for the military site.

In the mid-1950s the overflowing population of Los Angeles forecast a boon to the fortunes of Orange County. Segerstrom holdings were located in the midst of this burgeoning development. The farsighted conceptual planning of Segerstrom was ready to begin.

The decade of the 1960s proved to be extraordinary in the Segerstrom annals. Segerstrom Center was incorporated in 1961 to develop the United California Bank Building in Santa Ana—Orange County's first fully air conditioned multistory office building. In keeping with the family's philosophy of community responsibility, in 1963 the Segerstroms pre-

sented to the city of Costa Mesa the historic Estancia Adobe and surrounding five acres for perpetual use as a park and recreation area.

The year 1967 marked the grand opening of South Coast Plaza—Orange County's first enclosed regional shopping mall and crown jewel of the Segerstroms' holdings. Just as their dedication to uncompromising quality had produced a superior agricultural product, that same commitment ensured that South Coast Plaza would be a retail center of distinction. Indeed, South Coast Plaza has grown to become a retail institution of world renown. The Segerstroms

South Coast Plaza Mall and Town Center—Orange County's burgeoning central business district. Photography by Aerial Eye Inc.—Irvine.

have personally supervised the selection of high-quality tenants for South Coast Plaza. Every attempt is made to be certain that tenant aims parallel the Segerstroms' focus on superior retailing selection and service.

After six years of increasingly successful operation, South Coast Plaza was expanded in 1973 with the addition of Bullock's and sixty specialty shops of national prominence. Also in 1973 South Coast Plaza Village, a collection of international restaurants and unique shops, was opened. Growth continued from 1977 to 1979 with the additions of Saks Fifth Avenue, I. Magnin, and the first Nordstrom store in California.

The master-planned South Coast Plaza Town Center progressed steadily forward, capitalizing on the success of South Coast Plaza—which achieved over $450 million in gross sales in 1985. As the Orange County high-rise office market developed, the Segerstroms planned and constructed office buildings in the area east of the mall to answer the changing needs of professional and corporate businesses. Thus, the Segerstroms

created a cosmopolitan hub from suburban Orange County land. South Coast Plaza Town Center's master-planned three million square feet of multistoried commercial and cultural buildings founded the basis for an Orange County central business district—South Coast Metro.

Commitment to building a quality development has gone far beyond the bricks and mortar of the business structures. The Segerstroms have translated a strong support of the cultural arts into the cultural lodestone of Orange County. In 1975 the Segerstroms contributed the site for construction of the Fourth Step South Coast Repertory Theatre and, subsequently, strategically placed major works of sculptural art for public enjoyment throughout the area. One such commission is Isamu Noguchi's "California Scenario," a 1.6-acre garden sculpture that has commanded worldwide attention following its opening in 1982.

Complementing the area's dominant role in the arts was the contribution of five acres of land and over seven million dollars by the Seger-

strom family toward construction of the Orange County Performing Arts Center. Central to the performing arts complex is the dramatic 3,000-seat, multipurpose hall designed to accommodate symphony, opera, musical theater, and ballet.

Segerstrom operations are managed by cousins Henry and Harold Jr., both grandsons of founder Charles John Segerstrom, and Ruth Segerstrom, Henry's mother. The Segerstrom story is exceptional in that the family completed a land-use transition from agriculture to internationally recognized quality urban development. It is the story of a close-knit family whose members elected to stay and develop their own land, reinvesting in Orange County, working with the community to build and develop projects to the best standards of quality for the future and good of the area where they live.

McLEAN CADILLAC

McLean Motor Company, more commonly known as McLean Cadillac, was established in Santa Ana on April 14, 1939, by Russell G. "R.G." McLean. Since that time the dealership has grown steadily and will always remain as a landmark business in the history of Santa Ana.

The foundation for that growth was provided by R.G. McLean, who had worked in the automotive business since 1916. His first job was with Speck Buick Company in Sunnyside, Washington. Over the next fourteen years he gained experience in several positions within that dealership. In May 1930 R.G. and his family moved to Southern California. Four years later he purchased a Buick dealership in Riverside. The following year this became a Studebaker dealership. He sold this venture in 1939 and that same year secured the Oldsmobile and Cadillac franchises in Santa Ana.

With the onset of World War II the automobile business came to a standstill. Many dealerships were to close their doors, never to reopen. R.G. McLean, however, kept the dealership going, and by 1949, with the aid of his son, R. Thomas "Tommie" McLean, sales started to escalate.

During the early 1950s the business experienced the first of its growing pains. In 1953 R.G. embarked on a program to secure surrounding land for expansion. One year later a spacious service facility was in operation. This was the first of many building and remodeling projects that stretched into the late 1960s.

Changes occurring at McLean Motor Company during this time included the liquidation of the Oldsmobile franchise. Since 1960 McLean Motor Company has been exclusively a Cadillac franchise.

As R.G. approached retirement, Tommie McLean assumed more responsibility for the direction of the

This late 1940s photograph shows McLean Motor Company's used-car lot, located at 111 South Main. Today this same location is the site of a popular Taco Bell restaurant.

business. R.G. remained active in the dealership until his death in 1972, at which time the younger McLean became president.

Tommie guided McLean Cadillac through some of its most successful years. The early 1970s witnessed unprecedented growth in the automotive and particularly the Cadillac markets. Tommie McLean's two sons, Michael and Bruce, entered the business during that time, thereby continuing a family tradition in one of the most respected automotive dealerships in Orange County.

In December 1982 R. Thomas McLean passed away, leaving Michael T. "Mike" McLean as president and Bruce R. McLean as vice-president. Marcia Griffin, Tommie McLean's daughter, is also an active member of the firm's board of directors.

The McLean family has for many years maintained strong ties with the community. R.G. initiated this tradition, which has been continued by his son and grandsons.

In the post-World War II years R.G. was instrumental in the establishment and building of the Boys Club of Santa Ana. He later joined the industrial division of the chamber of commerce, an organization whose chief purpose was to attract new business to the Santa Ana community.

R.G. also remained a dominant figure within the automotive world.

The headquarters of McLean Motor Company, located at Main and Second streets, in the late 1940s.

He was twice elected by his peers to serve on the National Cadillac Dealer's Council, while also being a staunch supporter of the Orange County and Southern California Motor Car Dealer's associations. Two months before his death R.G. was honored for his dedicated service to the community and industry with the *Time* Magazine Quality Dealer Award, an honor presented each year to the outstanding dealers in the nation.

his contributions to the organization.

In the late 1970s Tommie was a member of the board of directors and president of the Santa Ana City Center Association. In addition, he was a founder of the Economic Development Corporation of Santa Ana and served as a two-term president. He also served as a member of the Redevelopment Commission of Santa Ana, as well as on many other special committees and commissions. So great was his contribution to Santa Ana that shortly after his death the city council proclaimed January 17, 1983, as R. Thomas McLean Day, in recognition of his years of dedicated

Three Generations of Caring

For forty-three years there's been a McLean behind every Cadillac

McLean Cadillac
201 North Main Street
Downtown Santa Ana
Sales and Leasing (714) 543-9421
Service and Body Shop (714) 972-8050

As this 1982 advertisement states, there has been a McLean behind every Cadillac sold by McLean Cadillac for over forty years. Pictured (from top to bottom) are Russell G. McLean, R. Thomas McLean, Michael T. McLean, and Bruce R. McLean.

In 1956 the firm remodeled its facility and installed its present facade. Photo taken in 1962

Tommie McLean developed this sense of community responsibility at an even earlier age. While still in his twenties he joined the Santa Ana Police Reserves. In the late 1970s Tommie helped develop the nationally recognized Santa Ana Businessman's Community Oriented Policing Program. During the ensuing years he was director of the Motor Car Dealer's Association of Orange County and director of the Southern California Motor Car Dealer's Association. In 1972 he became director of the Boys Club of Santa Ana. He served as president of the Boys Club in 1976-1977 and was posthumously given the Man and Boy Award for

service to the community.

Mike and Bruce McLean represent the third generation of the family active in community affairs. Mike is a past president of the chamber of commerce and is currently on the board of directors of the Boys Club of Santa Ana, TODOS, Santa Ana Rotary Club, and immediate past president of the Motor Car Dealer's Association of Orange County. Recently, Mike has served as chairman of the board for the Exploratory Learning Center Foundation. Bruce was on the Orange County Transportation Commission-Citizens Advisory Committee for several years and has served as the treasurer of the Santa Ana City Center Association as well as belonging to other community groups and charities. Bruce also is a distinguished past president of the Santa Ana Kiwanis Club.

McLean Motor Company has been a highly visible landmark in the Santa Ana community, both for its dedication to quality service and its commitment to community involvement. What started in 1939 as a small Cadillac/Oldsmobile dealership with a staff of seventeen has evolved into McLean Cadillac as it is known today—a business with more than 100 employees situated on four city blocks in the heart of a major metropolitan area.

In 1986 McLean Cadillac will relocate to a more spacious headquarters at the Tustin Auto Center, directly next to the Santa Ana Freeway (I-5) between Redhill and Myford avenues.

After forty-seven years of service to the residents of Orange County, McLean Cadillac retains its original goal: to provide quality transportation while striving to maintain the highest professional standards in the sales and servicing of these automobiles.

ST. JOSEPH HOSPITAL

The Sisters of St. Joseph came to California as teachers. It was during the 1918 flu epidemic that the order became involved in nursing, and by 1919 it was staffing its first hospital in Eureka.

In 1922, anticipating the growth needs of Southern California and at the invitation of Archbishop John Cantwell, the congregation moved their motherhouse to Orange where they purchased the old Burnham estate on ten acres of land on Batavia Street.

St. Joseph Hospital of Orange opened September 18, 1929, the second of what would be nine Sister-owned institutions. Doctors came from as far south as San Juan Capistrano and north from Brea and La Habra. Dr. Herbert A. Johnston of Anaheim, considered by many to be the father of the hospital, played an instrumental role in convincing the Sisters that a modern facility was needed in the county.

Sister Elizabeth Lirette, with no training or hospital experience, was made administrator in 1929. Faith in God was of prime importance during her administrative years. "He's been running the business a long time and He knows what He's doing," she said.

The original hospital building (top) was constructed in 1929. Today it is the Northeast Building and part of the large medical complex (above) that comprises St. Joseph Hospital.

The 1930s were a period of growth for St. Joseph Hospital, of getting the word out that a new country hospital was available with modern-day equipment. There were few doctors and fewer regulations to get on staff. Although operating room procedures were primitive by today's standards, St. Joseph Hospital was accredited by the American College of Surgeons in 1931.

In the early days the Sisters were actively involved in all phases of hospital life, just as they are today. The executive board minutes of 1932 read that "the Sisters would inaugurate a special rate for patients who were too poor to pay the regular room rates

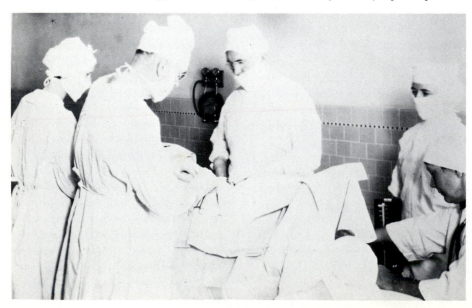

Although operating room procedures were primitive by today's standards, St. Joseph Hospital was accredited by the American College of Surgeons in 1931.

and who were ineligible for the county hospital. In six-bed wards such patients would be charged $3.50 per day. Private rooms were $5 per day, while children under four were to be hospitalized at $1.50 per day."

The 1940s were a time of struggle and survival. World War II called doctors away from St. Joseph as fast as they could join the medical staff. Nurses were also in short supply. While doctors were recruited from area military facilities to help keep the doors open, the hospital volunteered to open its own school of nursing to provide additional nurses for both military service and stateside hospitals. The nursing school played an important role during World War II and was later expanded to include cadet training.

As the war ended not only did St. Joseph's doctors come home, but many more who had worked at the facility decided to stay in the pleasant climate of Southern California. Sister Rita Rudolph recalled that "as the population began to grow, the

The Sisters of St. Joseph came to California as teachers but, due to the 1918 flu epidemic, became involved in nursing. Here they inspect the construction of St. Joseph's original building in 1928.

census became higher and the shortage of beds was getting to be a constant worry." The school of nursing was discontinued in 1948, and the building was converted into a much-needed medical wing, increasing capacity by seventy beds.

The 1950s marked a period of rapid growth for St. Joseph Hospital. The focus was on building services, adding staff, expanding and creating departments, adding new equipment, and finding more efficient ways of doing things. There were indeed times of controversy, but much of the 1950s reflected a banding together. Doctors, nurses, employees, community members, volunteers, businesses, government, and the Sisters joined forces to begin a building fund campaign in 1956. Eventually, the goal to fund a new wing became a much larger one: the funding of a new hospital.

The 1960s were explosive, innovative years—a time of "miracle medicine." For St. Joseph Hospital that included fund raising, expansion, and breakthroughs in heart surgery, in specialized intensive care areas, and in treatment of emotional problems.

Ground was broken for the new St. Joseph Hospital in March 1962. On September 12, 1964, the new, 290-bed facility was dedicated. Next door the 104-bed Children's Hospital opened, making "Choco the Bear" a household word in Orange County.

The 1970s witnessed a rise in new technology, expanding departments, and many "firsts" for the facility. On September 25, 1976, a new $5.6-million wing was dedicated. At the end of construction CHOC and St. Joseph were licensed for 710 beds—making them the third-largest private hospital complex in the state.

The late 1970s marked two significant milestones in the history of St. Joseph Hospital. On April 10, 1978, Jason Lee Dehaven of El Toro was the 100,000th baby delivered at the

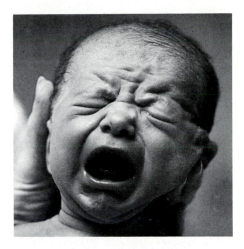

In 1978 Jason Lee Dehaven of El Toro was the 100,000th baby born at St. Joseph.

institution. In 1979 St. Joseph Hospital celebrated its golden anniversary—fifty years of service to the Orange County community.

In the 1980s new milestones have been reached. In 1983 the Lederhaus quadruplets, three boys and a girl, were the first set of quadruplets to be delivered at St. Joseph Hospital. On the technological front a new outpatient laser laboratory was opened in 1984 for treatment of eye problems and other outpatient therapy.

Throughout the years buildings have been remodeled, services have been added or changed, and physicians have come and gone, but the quality care of St. Joseph Hospital has remained constant. The institution will continue to operate under the philosophy of the Sisters of St. Joseph of Orange: "From its beginning the hospital has been operated with special emphasis on the importance of fairness in its dealings and with respect for human life and dignity. These spiritual considerations shall continue to act as a decision-making balance to the demands of economic and legislative forces. The institution shall seek out appropriate ways to further enhance its Catholic witness to the healing ministry of Christ."

SMITH INTERNATIONAL, INC.

At the turn of this century the oil industry was a rough yet rewarding way of life for men rugged enough to work the crude rigs of that era. At a time when America was evolving from an agricultural economy to an industrial giant, hard work, ambition, and timing were an unbeatable combination.

In 1902 a twenty-year-old Alabama native with an eighth-grade education opened a blacksmith shop in Whittier, California. Herman C. Smith's Carriage and Wagon Shop served some unusual and unexpected customers. Oil had been discovered nearby in Montebello and Santa Fe Springs. Smith was soon sharpening and repairing, modifying and improving bits and other tools used in drilling oil wells.

By the 1920s oil exploration and development activity in Southern California was booming, and Smith was growing right along with it. To accommodate the increase in business, Smith opened a larger facility, the H.C. Smith Manufacturing Co. In 1929 he decided to sell the company and "retire" at age forty-seven to his avocado ranch near the coast.

The life of a country gentleman, however, soon wore thin. Even though the oil industry was in the midst of a recession (the price of oil had dropped to ten cents a barrel), Smith went back into the business with the purchase of Allen Brothers Oil Tools of Compton. The new H.C. Smith Oil Tool Co. was incorporated and opened for business with fifteen employees on January 18, 1937.

The first few years were difficult. During the early part of World War II, drilling activity was cut back sharply. In California alone, drilling was reduced by 90 percent. Smith began to look beyond the oil industry for sales prospects and was soon successful. After a bleak 1942, the company teamed up with the California

H.C. Smith, founder of the company known today as Smith International, Inc.

A salesman's company car at Signal Hill, circa 1925. Because of their heavy-duty construction and suspension, Cadillacs were used to deliver oil tools to the rig site.

Institute of Technology to develop and produce the first five-inch combat rockets. Parts for the B-29 were also manufactured by Smith.

Following 1943 Smith phased out its involvement in war supplies and again geared up for oil tool production. By the early 1950s the oil industry was again expanding rapidly. Smith now served customers in Canada, Mexico, and South America as well as in the United States. In 1959 Smith became a public corporation, ready for the next stage of growth.

One year later, as Smith Industries International, Inc., the company began an aggressive program of acquisitions and internal development. In the early 1960s, for example, one of its "skunk works" projects focused on developing a new method of turning the drill bit. The result was a unique positive displacement downhole "mud" motor which revolutionized directional drilling techniques and led to the creation of a new division, Dyna-Drill, in 1964.

In 1967 Smith merged with another company, Drilco Oil Tools, Inc., of Midland, Texas. Two years later Smith stock was moved to the "Big Board" on the New York Stock Exchange and the firm moved its headquarters to Orange County. Soon

after, plans to move the Smith Tool division into a master-planned 68-acre manufacturing complex in Irvine were formulated. The move was completed in 1975. A forge facility was added in 1977. Along with Smith Tool, the company currently has two other operations based in Orange

H.C. Smith examines his 1902 blacksmith tools.

In the early 1950s Herman C. Smith, founder, posed with his company's largest and smallest oil drilling tools.

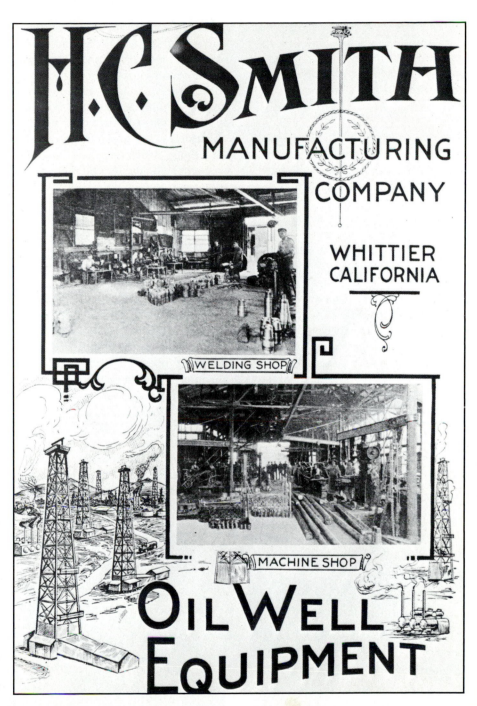

County.

Today Smith International, Inc., is a *Fortune* 500 corporation with 7,000 people worldwide. Despite the inevitable ups and downs of the oil business—the booms and the busts, the embargoes and the gluts—H.C. Smith's original business purpose and philosophy still guide the firm that

bears his name. Six decades ago he described his vision in the company's 1926 catalog:

"Believing oil to be one of the greatest sources of wealth of this country, and realizing the needs of oilmen for better and more efficient machinery, we have dedicated ourselves to the

The first page of the firm's 1926 catalog, in which H.C. Smith published his business philosophy and purpose.

task of creating and perfecting tools and equipment that will lessen the burdens and increase the efficiency of this basic industry."

HOAG MEMORIAL HOSPITAL PRESBYTERIAN

"Medicine, like all knowledge, has a past as well as a present and a future; and . . . in that past is the indispensable soil out of which improvement must grow."
— Alfred Stille

The movement to build Hoag Memorial Hospital Presbyterian began in the 1940s as a response to the fact that no facility existed along coastal Orange County. In one year alone 770 people were injured along the coast, and many lost their lives because they did not receive treatment in time.

The Reverend Raymond Brahams of Community Presbyterian Church in Laguna Beach lost a friend in an auto accident on a treacherous coastal road. The pastor responded to the loss by organizing a group of men whose goal was to build a hospital for coastal residents. The committee, comprised of seven Presbyterian church members and a Laguna Beach physician, met for the first time in 1944 and established the Community Presbyterian Hospital of Laguna Beach.

The committee set out to accomplish its first task—to find a suitable location for the hospital. Several sites in Laguna Beach were investigated, but the high cost of real estate forced the group to look elsewhere. The search took a positive course when the group learned of a piece of property in Newport Beach, described as being "on the bluffs near the Arches at the junction of Newport Boulevard and Coast Highway."

The Reverend Brahams and the committee could foresee that the sweeping view of Newport Bay and the Pacific Ocean would be therapeutic for recuperating patients. Dallas "Shorty" Blue, a Newport Beach city councilman, owned the land and agreed to the sale. His price was more than fair: $20,000 for the twenty-acre area.

The first organization to lend its wholehearted support was the Newport Harbor Chamber of Commerce, which sponsored the first fund-raising event in conjunction with the Newport Harbor Assistance League. The event, which raised more than $19,000 in twenty minutes, allowed the committee to purchase the twenty acres of land.

Fund-raising activities began in earnest once the land had been purchased. Thanks to a number of generous donations, such as $100,000 given by aviator Glenn Martin, the group raised $590,000.

The Hoag Foundation, established in 1940 by George Grant Hoag, Sr., his wife, Grace, and their son, George Hoag II, provided the $500,000 needed to complete the project. The committee agreed that the facility would be named Hoag Memorial Hospital Presbyterian.

The facility's first administrator, Robert Bacon, was appointed in 1950. Working closely with his wife, Winifred, he took on the exhaustive job of overseeing the institution's

As the population of Orange County increased, Hoag Hospital made plans to expand. In 1967 president of the board George Hoag II, administrator Winifred "Winnie" Bacon, and actor John Wayne, who was honorary chairman of the hospital's fund-raising efforts, met to discuss plans for a proposed multistory patient tower.

The September 1951 ground-breaking ceremonies for Hoag Memorial Hospital Presbyterian drew more than 300 people from all over Orange County. From left to right, Councilman Dallas Blue, the original owner of the twenty-acre site upon which the hospital was built; George Grant Hoag II; Mrs. George G. Hoag; Harry Welch, a Newport Beach-area fund raiser; and George Grant Hoag III.

construction. Unfortunately, Bacon died unexpectedly shortly before the long-awaited ground-breaking ceremony.

Winifred Bacon, also a capable and talented professional, was asked by the board of directors to continue her husband's work. Her career as Hoag Hospital's administrator was to span fifteen years of growth and change.

On September 15, 1952, Hoag Memorial Hospital Presbyterian opened as a 75-bed facility. The seven patients admitted on the first day were welcomed by a staff of sixty-eight physicians and sixty employees. That night the number of patients increased to eight with the birth of a baby girl.

The hospital's reputation as an outstanding medical facility spread rapidly. In 1953, after only one year of operation, the institution received full accreditation from the Joint Commission on Accreditation of Hospitals (JCAH).

It wasn't long before the sleepy beach towns of the 1940s had become the thriving communities of the 1950s. In the midst of this gigantic population explosion was Hoag Hospital.

In 1959 a four-story structure was built, adding 150 beds plus a 6,000-square-foot laboratory, a medical library, a new obstetrics and gynecology section, and a new delivery room.

Still strained to capacity by an overabundance of patients, Hoag Hospital once again made plans for expansion. The next step was to build a Pediatrics Pavilion, a gift of the Hoag Foundation. The project,

By October 1972 work had begun on a ten-story patient care tower. Today this Newport Beach landmark stands as a testimonial to the fund-raising efforts of Hoag Hospital's 552 Club support group and to the generosity of countless Orange County residents and organizations.

completed in 1966, added forty-six more beds, but the shortage continued. This situation was remedied temporarily as the hospital leased bed space from a nearby convalescent facility.

In the 1970s the time was ripe for Hoag Hospital's most ambitious project: the construction of a ten-story patient care tower, a five-story parking structure, and a new power plant. Costs were estimated at thirteen million dollars.

The James Irvine Surgical Center was built in 1972. It was the first outpatient surgery center in California. Working at full capacity since the day it opened, the center was an innovative way to provide the safety of hospital care without the expense of a hospital stay.

Since 1975 Hoag Hospital has been one of five paramedic base stations in Orange County, serving Newport Beach, Costa Mesa, and Irvine. Hospital staff and paramedics are equipped to handle any emergency.

By the 1980s Hoag Hospital had come full circle. Accidents still occur along foggy coastal roads, but no longer is treatment delayed by distance. Within minutes ambulances arrive on the scene. Countless lives have been saved because of immediate treatment.

In the minutes of a meeting of the planning committee, which met for several years before the hospital opened in 1952, there was an expression that was repeated again and again: "Class A hospital." At the committee's insistence and with the generous support of the Hoag Foundation, that is what was created. Throughout the years this insistence on excellence has never changed, and Hoag Memorial Hospital Presbyterian continues to provide exemplary health care in an increasingly technological, but always humanitarian, environment.

Today Hoag Memorial Hospital Presbyterian is a 471-bed facility serving the medical needs of Orange County residents.

RUTAN & TUCKER

The law firm of Rutan & Tucker has Orange County roots reaching back to the turn of the century. A.W. Rutan, the firm's namesake and founder, practiced law in the county for sixty-six years, beginning in 1906. Across those years Rutan developed a diverse and faithful clientele based upon his reputation for integrity and quality legal services. Rutan & Tucker has carried on his tradition, still enjoying the confidence of many of Rutan's clients, while it has expanded the practice, both in numbers of lawyers and in areas of legal expertise, to keep pace with the dynamic business growth of Orange County. Today Rutan & Tucker stands as the largest and one of the oldest law firms in Orange County and has public and private clients spanning the range from agrarian to high technology.

Back in the early days of the twentieth century Rutan's practice included agriculture-related clients such as water companies, irrigation districts, citrus packinghouses, and bean growers' associations. Orange County was then the lima bean capital of the world and a leader in citrus cultivation in the United States, and Rutan's knowledge of water law was a cornerstone of the development of the county's early economy. In 1933

he co-authored the Orange County Water District Act, which has served as a model for groundwater management throughout the state and the nation. The firm continues an active water law practice.

In 1936 Rutan linked legal expertise with James B. Tucker, a former Utah Superior Court judge who had ventured to California. Rutan and Tucker opened offices on the sixth floor of the First National Bank Building in Santa Ana, located at Fourth and Main streets. In the late 1940s H. Rodger Howell and James B. Tucker, Jr., joined the firm, and in 1950 the firm of Rutan, Tucker, Howell & Tucker opened its doors. Later that same year Judge Tucker passed away.

Milford W. Dahl, a Rutan & Tucker founder, recalls a conversation with Rodger Howell over coffee in a booth at the Santa Ana Woolworth's store one day in the early 1950s. They contemplated changing trends in the county, especially the transition from agriculture to industry, land development, and construction. The men foresaw that these changes in the county would bring the need for more sophisticated legal services. They conceived the idea of an Orange County-based full-service law firm to meet legal challenges created by those changes for individuals, local governments, and corporations in the county.

On January 1, 1955, the Rutan firm was joined by other prominent Orange County attorneys to become the firm of Rutan, Lindsay, Dahl, Smedegaard, Howell & Tucker, commencing with six partners and two associates. The new firm captured the vision of its founders of a modern, multidiscipline law firm, offering ex-

Rutan & Tucker's first office was on the sixth floor of the First National Bank Building, on the corner of Fourth and Main streets in Santa Ana. Courtesy, Bowers Museum

Alexander Wallace Rutan, founder.

pertise in corporate law, civil litigation, probate, tax, water, and public law. In order to accommodate the new firm, a two-story office building was constructed on land owned by the firm near the Orange County Courthouse on what is now Civic Center Drive in Santa Ana.

In 1956 James R. Moore became the first associate attorney to join the new firm directly upon graduation from law school. Establishing a pattern since followed by many others, Moore advanced to membership in the firm and now serves as chairman of its real estate department and as a member of the firm's management committee. In the years that followed, the firm continued to expand into new areas of legal expertise, along the way hiring experienced attorneys, such as trial expert Garvin F. Shallenberger and eminent domain specialist Mike McCormick. Like Moore, both Shallenberger and McCormick became partners, department heads, and managing committee members.

In 1964 the name of the firm reverted to Rutan & Tucker. By 1967 the firm had outgrown its two-story office building and spilled into overflow mobile office trailers and an adjacent home. The firm moved to

Rutan & Tucker moved to this handsome Central Bank Building at 611 Anton Boulevard in Costa Mesa in 1981.

temporary quarters while a new high-rise facility was erected and in 1969 Rutan & Tucker occupied three floors of a new ten-story office building constructed at the site of its previous law offices.

During the 1950s and 1960s Rutan & Tucker participated in Orange County's explosive growth by providing legal counsel for the formation of several cities and water districts and for the development of roads, utilities, housing, and commercial and industrial facilities. As the county became the headquarters for major businesses, the firm expanded its business litigation and advice capabilities. Members of the firm have served on various city councils and planning commissions in the county, and are involved in numerous civic, cultural, and charitable organizations. Befitting the firm's position in the legal community, its members also have been prominent in bar association activities, some advancing to the positions of board member and president of the Orange County and the state bar associations.

A.W. Rutan died in 1972. He had contributed sixty-six productive years to the practice of law, was a dynamic force in the agricultural development of the county, and participated in its transformation to a modern metropolitan center. He was gifted with a rare mix of ethical and intellectual attributes. By the time of his death at age ninety-two, Rutan had come to personify the ideal attorney for the then-45-lawyer firm. Attorneys at Rutan & Tucker still attempt to emulate the qualities manifested by A.W. Rutan through his long practice in Orange County.

In 1981, having once again outgrown its offices, Rutan & Tucker moved to its present location, occupying handsomely appointed offices in the Central Bank Building near South Coast Plaza. The firm's present quarters include space for future expansion as Rutan & Tucker expects to pass the 100-attorney level in the near future.

During the 1970s and 1980s the firm has continued to grow, not only in numbers of attorneys, but also in diversity and depth of legal expertise. Evolving from its strong foundations in real estate advice, civil trial practice, probate law, corporate finance, and water and public law, the firm has added or developed expertise in such diversified special fields as labor law; bankruptcy; banking and commercial law; corporate, individual, and property taxation; municipal finance; redevelopment law; and cable television regulation. The firm now guides business and governmental units through capital development programs; advises corporations on mergers, take-overs, and securities offerings; counsels developers and financial institutions on sophisticated real estate ventures; and represents public- and private-sector clients in complex litigation matters including environmental pollution, computer technology, product liability, securities, and professional sports franchises.

Proudly, with eighty years of accomplishment behind it, the largest of Orange County's law firms continually strives to enhance its quality, each year seeking out top law graduates from across the nation, grooming and training them to carry on the proud traditions of integrity and legal excellence established and nurtured by A.W. Rutan.

ST. JUDE HOSPITAL

The history of St. Jude Hospital is one of never-ceasing expansion and progress in an effort to meet the needs of the north Orange County community. Beginning as Fullerton General Hospital, this ten-bed facility has grown to become a major hospital and rehabilitation center capable of providing a variety of medical services.

In 1900 Fullerton General Hospital began in a large, wood-frame house on the corner of Pomona and Amerige avenues. Twelve years later, with the financial support of the civic community, construction began for a main wing. However, due to the advent of World War I and financial circumstances, the expanded hospital did not open until 1921.

Intended plans for the new Fullerton General Hospital were never realized. The average number of patients remained low throughout the 1920s. And, with the onset of the Depression, the fate of the facility was uncertain.

A very important event occurred in 1922 that to this day holds significance for the operation of St. Jude

Fullerton General Hospital, the precursor of St. Jude Hospital. Photo circa 1902

Hospital. It was in the spring of that year that the Sisters of St. Joseph, at the invitation of then-Archbishop John Cantwell, moved from Eureka to Orange. Reverend Mother Francis Lirette appointed Sister Marie Ange Demers as the first religious administrator of Fullerton General.

The years from 1931 to 1945 were prosperous times for Fullerton General Hospital. During that period the medical staff was reorganized, new equipment was purchased, laboratory facilities were added, and the hospital was renovated and incorporated. A maternity wing was completed, and the total number of patients increased dramatically (from 670 in 1939 to 1,635 in 1945). In 1938 the institution played an important role in the community by admitting nearly 100 people as a result of the flooding of the Santa Ana River.

Due to a shortage of bed space in 1946, Fullerton General Hospital was forced to refuse patients. Expansion plans for a new 75-bed facility were thwarted by traffic problems and the new fire and health regulations, and the Sisters of St. Joseph of Orange found it increasingly difficult to operate Fullerton General Hospital. Regrettably the facility closed on August 29, 1953. Reverend Mother

Mary Felix expressed the disappointment felt at the time: "It is with deep regret that we have been unable to overcome obstacles so that we could have a new hospital to move into before we were forced to close Fullerton Hospital. Despite our unceasing efforts, time has run out, and our better judgment dictated to our desires."

Four years later, however, the Sisters formally opened their new 125-bed St. Jude Hospital, located at what is now the corner of Harbor Boulevard and Bastanchury Road in Fullerton. Archbishop James Francis Cardinal McIntyre of Los Angeles dedicated the new facility with 2,000 local residents in attendance. St. Jude Hospital was noted as being one of the newest and best medical facilities in the state. Unfortunately, within three days of its opening every bed was filled, and, once again, patients were turned away.

It was fortunate for St. Jude Hospital that Sister Jane Frances was its administrator at that time. Sister Jane Frances first came to Fullerton General in 1941, when she served as assistant secretary and lab and radiology technician. Cognizant of the lack of sufficient space, she immediately initiated an expansion program for the hospital. On May 9, 1961, Sister Jane Frances was joined by city officials and by Eric Hansen, the first baby born at St. Jude in 1957, for ground-breaking ceremonies for the new west wing. Following five years of grant applications, fund-raising projects, and spiraling building costs the west wing was finally dedicated in 1962. St. Jude Hospital was now a 250-bed quality health care facility. By 1964, however, the hospital was again plagued by a lack of bed space.

Largely due to the foresight of Sister Jane Frances, a new five-story North Tower was dedicated in 1971. This rehabilitation center is a prototype in Orange County and includes

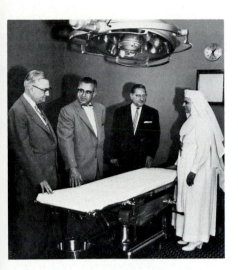

The operating room at the new St. Jude Hospital gets a last-minute inspection in 1957. From left to right are James A. Woods, M.D., chief of staff; Ramiro Fernandez, M.D., executive medical board vice-president; John A. Larson, M.D., staff president; and Sister Augustine, the hospital's first surgery supervisor.

neuromuscular and cardiovascular units, a cardiac rehabilitation department, and a well-respected oncology unit. As a result, a wide variety of in-patient rehabilitation programs are now offered at St. Jude Hospital. The completion of the North Tower increased bed capacity to 304.

In 1974 Sister Jane Frances became president and coordinator of the Sisters of St. Joseph of Orange Health System, overseeing the operation of a number of Sister-owned hospitals. Later she would be honored as one of the Association of Western Hospitals' "Women of the West." It was also in 1974 that Ronald W. Harper was appointed the hospital's executive vice-president. In 1981 St. Jude Hospital opened a new 106-bed facility in Yorba Linda.

St. Jude observed its twenty-fifth anniversary in 1982. The success of the hospital can be attributed to the dedicated efforts of its medical staff

St. Jude Hospital is located in Fullerton.

and nurses, administrators and support personnel, guild volunteers, and advisory board. The financial support provided by such groups as St. Jude "5" and Damas de Caridad, was critical in the realization of twenty-five years of service.

St. Jude Hospital offers an impressive list of medical programs, units, departments, and services with a specialized interest in health education. Along with future expansion plans this demonstrates the hospital's continuous outreach and commitment to the people of north Orange County,

Sister Jane Frances (second from left) joins religious and civic officials at the 1961 groundbreaking ceremonies for St. Jude Hospital's west wing expansion project. Wielding the shovel is Eric Hansen, the first baby born at St. Jude Hospital.

and reflects the philosophy maintained by the Sisters of St. Joseph of Orange: "We are compelled to pursue excellence in the care of the whole person—body, mind, and soul—in the spirit of love and concern, serving all people as we would serve Christ."

THE PACIFIC MUTUAL LIFE INSURANCE COMPANY

In 1868 the need for a Pacific Coast life insurance company prompted leading western financiers and industrialists to underwrite The Pacific Mutual Life Insurance Company of California. Since its Sacramento birth more than 100 years ago the firm has been directed by executives of strength and imagination. A list of founders reads like a "who's who" in the annals of California history. Prominent among this group of early supporters were Leland Stanford, Charles Crocker, and Mark Hopkins.

Pacific Mutual Life's first headquarters was established in the D.O. Mills & Company building. From 1868 to 1912, even after the relocation of the home office to San Francisco and later Los Angeles, Pacific Mutual Life's Sacramento office remained at 1007-1009 Second Street, near the corner of J Street.

The organization of the company was the vision of two experienced life insurance agents—Simon Schreiber and Josiah Howell. In each of the first six years of the firm's existence, agents had sold in excess of one million dollars of new insurance on American lives. Also during those embryonic years Elizur Wright, "the father of American life insurance," served as a consultant to the fledgling concern. A number of milestones were reached including the introduction of the arithmometer in 1873—the first calculating machine to be used in the West.

In 1881 company president Dr. George A. Moore transferred the home office to San Francisco. Dr. Moore retired in 1905 after a quarter-century of distinguished service. The assets of the firm had grown eightfold during his tenure. Insurance on the lives of policy owners stood at nearly sixty-two million dollars. Pacific Mutual Life agencies were now firmly rooted in forty states and territories.

On March 12, 1906, Pacific Mutu-

The Pacific Mutual building at Montgomery and Sacramento streets in San Francisco was officially opened on January 10, 1893. The structure was destroyed by fire on April 18, 1906, following the San Francisco earthquake.

An example of a million-dollar policy issued by Pacific Mutual in 1918.

al Life and Conservative Life of Los Angeles were consolidated. The new management elected to maintain the home office in San Francisco, fortuitously adding fireproof vaults for the storage of company records. Five weeks later the city by the bay was jolted by an earthquake of terrifying proportions. Within a few hours the financial district, including Pacific Mutual Life's home office, was gutted—"a stark silhouetted skeleton against a backdrop of bleak devastation." Owing to the bravery of a resolute employee, Rich J. Mier, the firm's securities were rescued. When the vaults had sufficiently cooled some six weeks later, vital documents were found preserved intact.

In their first post-earthquake meeting, the board of directors officially voted to establish the home office in Los Angeles. Staff was immediately dispatched to set up operations in the former home office of Conservative Life.

The ensuing three decades were under the direction of George I. Cochran (1906-1937). Cochran's first order of business was to oversee the construction of a new headquarters adjacent to Pershing Square. The classic six-story structure was completed in 1908. The building was expanded in 1928 and became a distinctive landmark in downtown Los Angeles.

The Great Depression that followed the stock market crash of 1929 reversed the upward trend of insurance sales. By 1935 the stagnant economy brought Pacific Mutual to the brink of insolvency. Under the leadership of Asa V. Call, the com-

Pacific Mutual's headquarters was located in Los Angeles adjacent to Pershing Square from 1908 to 1971.

pany went through a reorganization blueprint initiated by the California Insurance Commissioner. Call successfully stemmed the tide of reversals to achieve full restoration of the firm. Asa Call joined the company's board of directors in 1932. A year later he became vice-president and general counsel. Call was promoted to executive vice-president, president, and subsequently chief executive for seventeen years, from 1942 to 1959. Call, more than any other, exemplified Pacific Mutual's "right man in time of crisis."

In 1948 Pacific Mutual energetically moved into the group insurance and pension market, in which it is today a nationwide leader.

Another milestone was reached in 1956. Pacific Mutual became the first private enterprise west of the Mississippi to install and fully utilize a large-scale electronic data-processing system called Univac I. Scores of other firms profited tremendously from Pacific Mutual's pioneering efforts.

In 1972 the company designed and constructed a specialized insurance operations center, facilitating the move to its current corporate headquarters in Newport Beach.

With a heritage born on the frontier 118 years ago, Pacific Mutual continues to play a vital role in Orange County's history today. Currently The Pacific Mutual Life Insurance Company is directed by Walter B. Gerken, chairman of the board and chief executive officer, and Harry G. Bubb, president. The board of directors includes a number of very prominent West Coast business executives. The firm ranks among the twenty largest mutual life insurance companies in the nation from the standpoint of both assets and total life insurance in force. Pacific Mutual's products include a wide variety of life, pension, and health insurance plans. As part of America's swiftly growing financial services industry, Pacific Mutual's portfolio contains innovative and contemporary insurance and investment services.

Pacific Mutual also provides jobs for many Orange County workers and operates nationwide with a network of 2,700 employees and agents and a system of fifty-six field offices.

The hallmarks of Pacific Mutual's history—decisive management, fiscal soundness, business community support, and a commitment to the welfare of its individual policy owners and business clients—remain essential to the company's vision for the future.

In 1972 Pacific Mutual moved to its new corporate headquarters building in Newport Beach.

ANAHEIM MEMORIAL HOSPITAL

In the early days of Anaheim Memorial Hospital lawyers were as much involved in planning as were the doctors and administrators. A severe recession in 1957 prolonged the opening of the institution (constructed 1956-1957) until February 1958. More than any other individual, it was longtime administrator James W. McAlvin who steered Anaheim Memorial through its turbulent early growth years to its current position as a dynamic community hospital.

After gaining approval of a creative reorganization plan engineered by investor Max Simon and Drs. Denmark and Johnson, administrator McAlvin prepared the new 72-bed facility for an opening in 1958. The nonprofit corporation would retain the name of Anaheim Memorial Hospital. Principles of the Seventh-Day Adventist Church would apply in the day-to-day operation of the facility.

Interestingly, the closing at about this same time of two area institutions, Anaheim Community Hospital and Cottage Hospital of Fullerton, helped to ensure the success of the fledgling Anaheim Memorial Hospital. Ralph Steen, owner of Cottage Hospital, proposed that Anaheim Memorial purchase equipment and supplies from Cottage Hospital and employ all of its personnel at their

Anaheim Memorial Hospital opened in 1958 as a 72-bed facility.

The busy emergency care center monitors forty calls a day as a paramedic base station and boasts accreditation by the American Heart Association as a "First Hour" treatment center for cardiac emergencies.

prevailing wage. The offer to accept a two-year note in payment made the proposal a difficult one to refuse. According to McAlvin, "This truly was a godsend because although his equipment was old, most of it was usable. But even more important was the fact that we inherited a cohesive staff of nursing personnel and other supportive employees."

Prominent among early board actions was the election of Dr. John Wood as the first chief of staff. The immediate heavy usage of the hospital guaranteed that vendor commitments could be met and credibility established.

The first Anaheim Memorial Hospital Guild meeting was held on September 5, 1958. This supplemental arm of the institution's professional services carved out its role as a strong hospital support group. The guild soon became involved in fund raising and was instrumental in the establishment of the hospital gift shop. Today the organization has evolved into three branches: the Guild, the Junior Volunteers, and the Guardian Angels.

At the outset of the 1960s the local economy had rebounded strongly as Anaheim entered an era of explosive growth. Anaheim Memorial had grown from about a dozen doctors to

a medical staff of 250. *The Record,* a hospital publication, reported 31,000 admissions since opening day.

A modern pathological department was developed when Dr. Frank Kendrick joined the staff in 1963. Dr. Kendrick's dedicated involvement in the carefully planned growth of Anaheim Memorial stands as a powerful testimony to the incalculable benefits derived from the many volunteer hours contributed by staff members.

In 1964 Anaheim Memorial became truly a community hospital. For the first time in its seven-year history the board was composed of local civic leaders. Prominent figures in this shift in board policy were George C. Beck, Richard L. Johnson, and Newton Curtis. Johnson was the financial genius who was deemed "born for the task of leading the board."

By 1965 it was apparent that hospital facilities were inadequate to keep up with the area's burgeoning growth. It was generally agreed that the institution would move up—rather than grow out. The "fast-track" approach was developed to accommo-

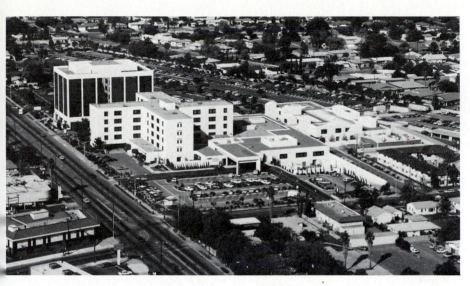

Currently, Anaheim Memorial Hospital is a 240-bed nonprofit, nonsectarian community hospital staffed by 940 dedicated health care professionals.

date the first-phase development of an ambitious twenty-year expansion program.

The focal point of the expansion program was the Clyde Cromer Tower dedicated in September 1969. The five-story, cross-shaped building has become, literally, the "backbone of the hospital." The newly added eighty-eight beds increased capacity to 164 beds. New ancillary services were housed in the tower including emergency, laboratory, X-ray, surgeries, recovery, central service, pharmacy, and physical therapy. As a part of this first-phase expansion, extensive remodeling of the hospital's original building was also completed. The original structure was demolished in 1979 to make way for a new addition.

The 1970s ushered in a number of pioneering efforts for Anaheim Memorial. An Acute Care Center was opened in the tower in 1972, bringing worldwide attention to the facility. The center was designed to provide critical care during the time of greatest loss of life among cardiac patients. This essential half-step saved countless lives. The reputation of Anaheim Memorial as an innovator was firmly established.

In 1975 Anaheim Memorial assembled the first all-female paramedic team in the United States. The Anaheim Fire Department now handles all paramedic responses, but its program had its roots in that group of pioneer nurses.

That same year the hospital initiated a Tumor Registry that led to the establishment of an oncology department in 1977. Another milestone was reached when the Hemophilia Foundation approved Anaheim Memorial's treatment center in 1976—the first of its type in Orange County.

In 1978 Anaheim Memorial celebrated its twentieth year of outstanding community service. In its first two decades the institution was firmly entrenched among the nation's leaders in the treatment of cardiac disease and cancer, specializing in emergency service given with professionalism and compassion.

Currently, Anaheim Memorial Hospital is a 240-bed nonprofit, nonsectarian community hospital. The institution boasts a staff of 940 dedicated health care professionals. Anaheim Memorial is fully accredited and enjoys the support of many civic-minded men and women whose generosity enhances the hospital's programs and services. Key administrative staff members include Pete Gray, acting chief executive officer; R. Graham Nash, vice-president, AMH Foundation; and Ellen Wentzel, vice-president of nursing.

In 1984, 367 open-heart surgeries were performed at AMH, the largest number performed in any Orange County hospital. This procedure is one of many offered at the Heart Center that encompass preventive as well as therapeutic modalities.

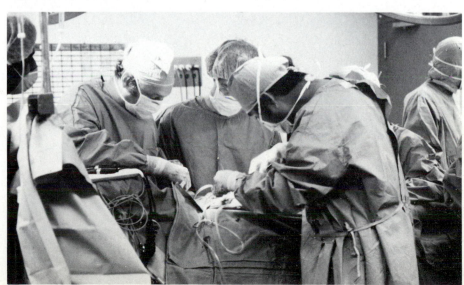

FIRST AMERICAN TITLE INSURANCE COMPANY

First American Title Insurance Company is one of the oldest companies in the title industry. It is among the three largest title insurance firms in the nation; its phenomenal growth nationwide has occurred primarily since its corporate expansion program began in 1957.

In the early years First American literally grew up with Orange County. Its list of founding fathers reads like a "who's who" in Orange County history. Board members C.E. Parker, D.M. Dorman, Thomas L. McKeever, Frank Ely, and George A. Edgar were among Orange County's leading citizens and steered the company on a steady course into the twentieth century. These pioneers helped to record and insure the property lines of Orange County; along the way they were instrumental in shaping its destiny.

In 1889 Orange County was created out of the southern coastal townships of Los Angeles County. At that time two title firms served the newly formed Orange County: Santa Ana Title Company and Orange

This turn-of-the-century office, leased in 1895, was the firm's third location in downtown Santa Ana and boasted the only curved-glass windows in town.

County Abstract Company. By 1894 Parker had completed the consolidation of the two firms as Orange County Title Company, predecessor of First American Title Insurance Company.

One of the first tasks undertaken by the Orange County Abstract Company was the abstracting of the complete record of all Los Angeles County documents pertaining to Orange County. A staff of six worked full time, six days a week for two years to transcribe by hand the land records—some dating as far back as 1834. The records of many of these early transactions were painstakingly translated from Spanish. This gargantuan task proved to be a brilliant stroke of foresight. Today First American has remained the only title firm in the county in possession of these complete records.

From its inception First American and its staff members have played a number of important roles in the development of Orange County. C.E. Parker, a pioneer horticulturalist in the environs of present-day Orange, furnished Orange County nurserymen with some of the areas first plantings of oranges and walnuts. In addition, Parker played a key role in the first use of electricity and the telephone in Santa Ana.

Indicative of First American's continuing role in the county's progress, the company issued the original abstract for the first courthouse site on September 11, 1893, and in 1966 became the title insurer for the new courthouse building. At that time the $22.2-million policy was believed to be the largest title policy ever issued

Board members of the Orange County Title Company, predecessor of First American Title Insurance Company, in the 1890s included (left to right) George A. Edgar; Frederick Stephens, secretary; D.M. Dorman; C.E. Parker, president; Thomas L. McKeever; and (standing) Frank Ely and Charles Riggs.

in Orange County.

The principal business of First American is the issuance of title insurance and related services. The title policy is an insured statement of the condition of ownership of real property. The policy protects the client against title defects, liens, and encumbrances existing at the date of issuance. Policyholders generally are purchasers of real property or lenders who make loans secured by real property. In the event of a challenge that calls into question the terms of a title policy, the firm provides legal defense for the policyholder and promptly pays all valid claims or losses up to the amount of the policy.

First American has insured more Orange County property than any other firm. Orange County landmarks such as Disneyland, Knott's Berry Farm, University of California-Irvine, and numerous other clients have depended upon the company for title protection and ancillary services.

By the 1950s First American was a thriving but small localized title firm. Stockholders had inherited shares from early investors that had accrued substantial value. Many persons in the First American community inquired about purchasing stock, but shareholders were reluctant to sell. In 1954 shares outstanding totaled only 1,950 and stockholders' equity was $1,620,193.

Wholesale changes were authorized when the board embarked upon an extensive expansion program in 1957. In December of that year assets totaled $2,138,927, and stockholders' equity had risen to $1,844,152.

The year 1964 marked an important milestone in the history of the company. Under the new First American name, its stock became available on the national over-the-counter market in December of that year.

The firm was reorganized in 1968 and again the name was changed,

synonymous with the development of Santa Ana and Orange County. The current president, D.P. Kennedy (C.E. Parker's grandson), continues to guide the national corporation within the founding family's tradition that was started by Parker in 1889. First American's national headquarters and the Orange County Title Division still operate from the same city block in Santa Ana that the firm has

D.P. Kennedy, president and chief executive officer.

First American's nationwide operations are headquartered in First American Square. The beautiful colonial complex, built in 1976, occupies an entire block in downtown Santa Ana.

this time to The First American Financial Corporation. A new, wholly owned title insurance subsidiary, First American Title Insurance Company, was formed to handle the existing title business. From December 31, 1968, total assets of the insurance firm have increased from $18.322 million to $197.341 million as of December 31, 1984.

For nearly a century First American and its predecessors have been

occupied since the turn of the century.

The year 1985 marked the ninety-sixth year of title insurance service. First American Title Insurance Company, along with its parent concern, The First American Financial Corporation, operates through a network of more than 1,900 offices or agents in all fifty states. It also provides title services abroad—in Guam, Mexico, Puerto Rico, and England.

CASE-SWAYNE COMPANY, INC.

Throughout its 43-year history Case-Swayne Company, Inc., has profited from generations of experience in the food industry. Today the firm ranks among the leading food processors on the West Coast. Since 1943 Santa Ana has been its home base. As the agricultural landscape of Orange County was being transformed to accommodate the population growth in the 1960s, the company shifted its emphasis from "commodities" to "specialties." The ability to change with the times more than any single factor has made the Case-Swayne Company an Orange County corporate success story.

The business was founded by Paul Case and Amos Swayne in 1943. The exigencies of World War II created a sharp demand for canned foods; the major portion of the firm's early business was large government contracts. The partners drew heavily upon their early experience with a major Northern California food processor, and for a time operated a cannery in Portland, Oregon. Almost from the outset plans were made to locate a plant amid the agricultural abundance of Orange County. The new Santa Ana facility opened in the latter part of 1943.

"From the company's beginning in 1943, we've had a tradition of adjusting to market demands, constantly challenging procedures. The founders were entrepreneurs, willing to try new products and untapped markets," says Keith Swayne, Amos Swayne's son.

In the years prior to the 1960s the company packed beans, juices, and potatoes from local fields, selling the bulk of production to the government. By the late 1960s Santa Ana-Anaheim-Orange had become the second-fastest-growing metropolitan area in the country. The real estate boom rapidly turned the rich agricultural zones into housing tracts. Local produce supplies simply were no lon-

Paul Case, co-founder.

Amos Swayne, co-founder.

ger available in the volume needed to sustain the business.

"At one time Orange County was geared to agriculture. But, with the real estate boom and the sharp reduction in military procurement in the early 1970s, Case-Swayne had to change course. Otherwise we would have seen our product sources dry up here, our competitors in Northern California becoming more efficient, and ourselves out of business," says Swayne.

As one development threatened the very existence of Case-Swayne, another opportunity appeared on the horizon to rescue its fortunes. In the true entrepreneurial tradition of the company, management found fresh markets in restaurants and fast-food chains. Case-Swayne serviced its first proprietary packing customer in 1969, a "No. 10" sauce for a Mexican fast-food chain.

By the early 1970s the firm had recognized the industrywide trend to meet a demand in food-service consistency. Case-Swayne zeroed in on the restaurant market, becoming a leading innovator with the copyright pack. "Our proprietary business does not simply copy a food-service item;

it is a total concept that includes product development, reformulations, package design, and innovations such as converting sauces into dry mixes," says John Morton, vice-president of sales and marketing. "Our proprietary products include specially formulated bean items, portion-packed condiments, dry seasonings, and liquid sauces in both cans and plastic pouches."

The copyright pack involves translating the customer's formula into a processed product. To Case-Swayne the catch phrase "the secret's in the sauce" is not to be taken lightly. In the highly competitive fast-food industry, maintaining a popular taste often is the key factor in the success of a franchise operation. The "secret recipe" is guarded by a strict nondisclosure agreement to protect the customer's formula. "In this arrangement, customers use Case-Swayne as their technical service group. We may start with one product, then expand our role to other areas of the menu," says Carrie Nishikawa, director of technical services.

When Keith Swayne became the company's chief executive in 1977 gross sales grew dramatically. He

Case-Swayne opened this facility in Santa Ana in the latter part of 1943.

The company is still the largest West Coast canner of white and sweet potatoes. The Santa Ana plant and support facilities consist of approximately 151,000 square feet of floor space. Specialty products are processed year-round, while commodity packs are seasonal with the exception of dry beans. The company has additional production capacity in Bryan, Ohio, and also maintains distribution facilities in Atlanta, Georgia; Dallas, Texas; San Martin, California; Kent, Washington; and Phoenix, Arizona.

Case-Swayne is still a privately held corporation with little interest in going public or undergoing a vast expansion. Of its 250 employees, about 85 have been with the firm for at least ten years; one-half of those have accrued more than twenty years of service. Critical to the success of Case-Swayne has been its reputation for integrity in dealing with both the customer and the employee.

brought an aggressive "people-oriented" approach. A number of new employees were brought in because doing business had become a more complex proposition. The company's sales increased from fourteen million dollars in 1977 to more than thirty million dollars in fiscal 1984.

A decade ago Case-Swayne's product line division was 80 percent commodity products (beans, potatoes, carrots, peas, green beans) and 20 percent specialty products for its food-service customers. Today that ratio has reversed to 30 percent commodity products and 70 percent specialty products.

The firm's shipping warehouse.

DATAPOWER INC.

Datapower Inc. was founded by Richard Gregg in 1969. Gregg, a Santa Anan, began Datapower with three employees in a 1,200-square-foot building at Broadway and Warner in Santa Ana. Initially the company manufactured custom power supplies for computers. Since that time Datapower Inc. has diversified its product line to include electronic ballasts and, in 1985, automated test equipment.

The first expansion came in 1972, when Datapower increased its work force to twenty-five and moved to a building on Pomona Street. Two years later the number of employees doubled, and in 1978 the firm relocated to its present facility at 3328 West First Street in Santa Ana. The company purchased the ten-acre site from the Archdiocese of Los Angeles.

When Gregg passed away in February 1979, his widow, Suzanne, assumed control of the firm. In August of that year Frederick J. McKee became the new president of Datapower Inc. McKee was a founder and past president of M&M Computers and vice-president of EECO, Inc., of Santa Ana. McKee established Datapower Inc. as a publicly owned corporation following his purchase of the firm in 1981.

Today the company designs, manufactures, and markets power supplies for computers and their components, in addition to industrial and telecommunication equipment. Those power supplies, which are used to convert alternating electrical current into direct current, comprised a substantial amount of the firm's net sales in 1985. Datapower Inc. provides both custom and standard power supplies to clients for installation in their products. Increasing complexity of power supply requirements along with engineering and economic considerations have created an attractive market for independent manufacturers such as Datapower.

Frederick J. McKee, president and chairman of the board.

Although power supplies comprise the majority of the firm's business, Datapower Inc. is also involved in the design, production, and marketing of solid-state electronic ballasts. Electronic ballasts are devices that aid in the operation of fluorescent and high-intensity lighting systems. These ballasts are not only much smaller than the conventional magnetic ballast, but also have a longer life and are more energy efficient. Datapower currently holds five U.S. patents on its electronic ballast products. Recently the firm has introduced two new products relating to the automated test equipment market: the in-circuit test system and the automated power supply tester. These revolutionary products are marketed through a nationwide sales organization.

Today Datapower Inc. employs 215 workers in its 88,000-square-foot facility in Santa Ana, the majority being involved in manufacturing and testing. Total sales for 1985 were more than fifteen million dollars. In addition to the chairman of the board and president, Frederick J. McKee, other principals of the firm include vice-presidents William O. Fordiani, Terry W. Busby, Jerre A. McMahon, and Gerald A. Felper. Datapower Inc. has for a number of years been actively involved with the Santa Ana Chamber of Commerce.

BOB BLACK OLDSMOBILE

Few women in the United States hold the position of president and chief executive officer of an automobile dealership; Anne Black of Orange County is one of that select group. She assumed the duties and responsibilities of those offices in 1973 following the untimely death of her husband, Robert R. Black.

Bob Black had originally opened an Oldsmobile agency in 1960 at 626 West Seventeenth Street, Santa Ana, shortly after his arrival with Anne and their five children in Orange County. Their relocation from Milwaukee, Wisconsin, where Bob Black had also owned an Oldsmobile dealership, enabled him to satisfy a longtime ambition to merchandise automobiles in Southern California. During the first few years the new agency employed twenty-one sales and service personnel, with a payroll of approximately $250,000.

Gradually Bob Black Oldsmobile outgrew its Seventeenth Street facility, and at about the same time that its lease expired in 1966, the dealership moved its corporate headquarters, showroom, and service center to a modern, five-acre, 30,000-square-foot complex at 2345 North Grand Avenue, Santa Ana. At the new site Bob Black continued to provide sales, leases, parts, service, and repairs to both new and former customers, with repeat business comprising 50 to 60 percent of the company's sales and leases. In 1967 Bob Black employed thirty-five people; by 1985, under Anne's leadership, sixty-three employees earned an annual payroll of more than one million dollars.

Prior to inheriting the family business in 1973, Anne had a long list of community service and administrative experience to her credit due to her long-term involvement with the Red Cross, Community Chest, PTA, Girl Scouts, Boy Scouts, and the Santa Ana Children's Home Society. Such service and experience in the community helped her to continue to develop Bob Black Oldsmobile to its current level of prosperity.

In addition, dedicated sales and service teams, representing many years of practical experience in running a car agency, proved to be invaluable business assets. David

The original Bob Black Oldsmobile dealership was located at 626 West Seventeenth Street in Santa Ana within five miles of its present five-acre complex at 2345 North Grand Avenue in Santa Ana.

McDowell, Anne's brother-in-law, has been with the firm since 1962 and currently serves as business manager. Tom Fiedler, service manager, has worked for the Black family for forty-five years, having begun his employment in Wisconsin before the Blacks relocated to Orange County.

Maintaining the tradition of a family-owned and -operated business, two sons now participate in the firm—Brady as fleet manager and Robert as the dealership's general manager. Being one of the few women in the United States to successfully operate an automobile dealership has given Anne Black a tremendous sense of achievement and satisfaction, and her ability to meet the challenges presented to her is reflected in the tremendous success experienced by Bob Black Oldsmobile.

STEFFY BUICK CO.

John A. Steffy, founder of Steffy Buick Co., was born on May 16, 1897, in Westminster, Maryland. Following military service in World War I Steffy entered the automobile business, and spent his entire career in that field.

Between 1921 and 1951 Steffy was employed by General Motors Corporation in various executive capacities, including market analysis, business management, and sales administration. Such work assignments required frequent and extensive travel throughout the United States and Canada, and eventually the desire to domicile himself, his wife, and their three sons as an integral part of a single community prompted Steffy to retire from General Motors, relocate to Southern California, and open his own Buick dealership in Anaheim in 1951.

Once he and his family were settled and their business was established in Anaheim, Steffy participated in various civic and business organizations. He served as director of the Anaheim Chamber of Commerce, president of that city's United Fund Drive, and president of the Community Chest; he also held memberships in the Lions Club, the Elks Lodge, the Tamasha Club, the Santa Ana Country Club, and the Palm Springs Ranch Club.

The couple's eldest son, Robert, was a career officer in the U.S. Air Force; William is a practicing attorney in Michigan; and Richard is the current president of the family's auto dealership. Richard Steffy, Jr., has also joined in the operation of this three-generation firm.

Widowed in 1940, John A. Steffy married Grace C. Van Norman in 1945. She was active in the Assistance League of Anaheim, the Ebell Club, the Claretian Guild of Orange County, is a charter member of Providence Speech and Hearing, a life member of Children's Hospital's Jack

The Steffy Buick Co., in 1951, at its first location in Orange County at 410 South Los Angeles Street, Anaheim.

John A. Steffy (now deceased) opened his Buick dealership in Anaheim in 1951.

and Jill Guild, a charter member of Damas de Caridad of St. Jude Hospital, Angelique Guild, and is a life member of St. Joseph Hospital's Guild.

Over the past thirty-four years Steffy Buick Co. has experienced continual growth and development, just as Orange County has, in spite of fluctuating interest rates, competition from imports, fuel shortages, municipal redevelopment, zoning changes, and arterial highway modifications.

Today and in the future Steffy Buick Co., with its staff of approximately thirty-five and its modern facilities at 953 South Anaheim Boulevard, plans to continue the family tradition begun by its founder of providing quality new and used automobiles to all of Orange County.

THE IRVINE COMPANY

The corporate evolution of The Irvine Company in the 1980s is the latest chapter in a homegrown epic of Orange County progress. The wealth and influence of the organization originated in the ingenious use of ranch land by one of Orange County's pioneer families—the Irvines.

The original Irvine Ranch consisted of 120,000-plus acres that were consolidated in 1876 by James Irvine, Sr. A native of Ireland and a veteran "Forty-niner," Irvine became sole owner of the property, purchasing his partners' holdings for $126,000. The elder Irvine died in 1886; title to the ranch passed to James Jr. "J.I." on his twenty-fifth birthday in 1893. The following year J.I. incorporated and henceforth did business as The Irvine Company.

Historically the Irvine Ranch embraced one-quarter of the land known after 1889 as Orange County. Prior to the master-planned developments of the 1960s, the primary business of the company was agriculture. By the 1920s Irvine's "fabulous spread" was the state's leading producer of lima beans and barley.

The Agricultural Division has remained one of The Irvine Company's seven operating divisions. Although relegated to a minor role, the Agricultural Division still oversees the irrigation of nearly 14,000 acres consisting of citrus and avocado orchards and various row crops. The year 1985 marked the end of cattle grazing on Irvine Company land.

The firm embarked upon a new era in 1962, when it began development of its master plan for the Irvine Ranch's remaining 90,000 acres. Since that time, according to business writer Tom Self, "The Irvine Company has provided homes for 80,000 in fifteen communities. The Irvine Business Center, which was the largest planned industrial site in the world, became home to 3,600 firms employing more than 90,000."

Newport Center is currently under development on 622 acres in the city of Newport Beach overlooking Newport Harbor.

In the 1970s the success of the General Plan brought national attention to the city of Irvine, which was incorporated in 1971. UC Irvine, which was started on a 1,000-acre parcel donated by the company, now has 12,000 students and is expanding toward a goal of 30,000 by the year 2000.

Ownership of The Irvine Company remained with the family-controlled James Irvine Foundation until 1977. That year the Irvines sold their interest to a consortium headed by Alfred Taubman and Donald Bren. In April 1983 Bren acquired majority interest.

Bren, a successful Southern California home builder, moved swiftly to change the firm's direction, placing a high priority on luring high-technology firms onto Irvine Company land.

Today The Irvine Company continues to plan and build on the 68,000 acres remaining from the original Irvine Ranch. Thomas H. Nielsen, an Orange County native, has served as president since 1983. The firm has 1,450 employees and is committed to developing a wide spectrum of high-quality commercial, industrial, and residential projects in Irvine, Newport Beach, Tustin, and Orange.

The Village of Woodbridge is a community planned for an ultimate 25,000 people in central Irvine.

WESTERN MEDICAL CENTER/SANTA ANA

Orange County health care has come a long way since 1848, when President James K. Polk signed the Treaty of Guadalupe Hidalgo in which Mexico ceded California to the United States. Clear skies, sunshine, and gold attracted increasing numbers of adventurous settlers to California, and among those pioneers were the region's first physicians.

Most of the early medical practitioners in what was to become Orange County were educated graduates of leading medical schools, and many had surgical experience in the Mexican War. They had no hospitals or nurses, and whiskey was often the only available anesthetic.

Typhoid, diphtheria, tetanus, and smallpox threatened area residents in the 1860s. Physicians made their way on horseback, riding dusty trails with medical equipment packed in saddlebags. It was not until 1902 that Orange County had its first hospital—the Santa Ana Valley Hospital.

In 1902 a group of local physicians decided to improve the quality of Orange County health care by creating Santa Ana Valley Hospital. The new institution had twelve rooms and

more patients than it could handle. The first of many additions was completed in 1905 to serve the county's growing population. By 1927 a major renovation was needed. It took the form of a new, relocated hospital facility with forty-two beds instead of the earlier twenty-five. In 1950 a new $500,000 wing was built, and thereafter only minor expansion took place until 1975 and the "main event"—the unveiling of a new, selectively staffed, superbly equipped Santa Ana-Tustin Community Hospital (SATCH).

In 1975 WESTMED/Santa Ana became the first hospital to create a departmentalized medical staff structure where physicians, nurses, and technicians could develop highly specialized skills, benefiting patients and encouraging more concentrated medical research. WESTMED/Santa Ana, a $70-million facility with 327 beds, is just one of United Western Medical Centers' nonprofit hospitals,

This 1910 photograph shows the Santa Ana Valley Hospital nursing staff gathered in front of Orange County's first hospital.

which include WESTMED/Anaheim and WESTMED/Bartlett.

WESTMED/Anaheim became a member of United Western Medical Centers' family in 1982. With 248 beds and a central location near Disneyland, it is the largest health-care center in Orange County's largest city. It provides a wide variety of affordable, quality acute care capabilities including cardiology and cardiovascular services, intensive and coronary care units, an ambulatory care center for treatment that does not require hospitalization, and an adult psychiatric unit with a special geropsychiatry section for older patients. The 24-hour emergency room has expanded service with All Care, a low-cost, walk-in treatment center for minor illnesses and injuries.

WESTMED/Bartlett is a 241-bed subacute care and rehabilitation center located in central Santa Ana. It is the largest nonprofit, nonsectarian facility of its kind in California. WESTMED/Bartlett has pioneered the use of multiple nursing stations to better serve the individual needs of the patients and offers physical and occupational rehabilitation as well as speech therapy. The facility actively reaches into the community with programs such as Meals on Wheels, which was recently honored by the Santa Ana City Council for delivering 115,000 meals to elderly area residents since 1979.

There are now five medical institutes affiliated with United Western Medical Centers: Southern California Infertility Institute, Regional Allergy and Clinical Immunology Institute, Orange County Rheumatology-Arthritis Institute, Respiratory Disease Management Center, and the Orange County Regional Head and Neck Institute.

WESTMED/Santa Ana is a pioneer in medical technology utilization. The first hyperbaric chamber, the first high-energy linear accelera-

Western Medical Center/Santa Ana is the direct successor to Santa Ana Valley Hospital, Orange County's original health-care facility.

hospitalization. United Western Medical Centers value their place in the history and tradition of the Orange County health-care field and are determined to continue their heritage of innovation and concern for the health of the community—it is a matter of legacy.

Western Medical Center/Anaheim became a member hospital of United Western Medical Centers in 1982.

tor, the first fully computerized cardiac catheterization laboratory, and the first trauma center have earned WESTMED/Santa Ana a reputation for innovation. The Rehabilitation and Conditioning Center (RACC) is one of only ten health centers in the nation to offer medically supervised exercise programs in conjunction with a hospital. The RACC provides physical therapy, pain management, biofeedback, nutritional counseling, and prenatal and postpartum programs.

United Western Medical Centers also bases the MedAir air ambulance at WESTMED/Santa Ana. That service was created in 1981 to helicopter patients and accident victims quickly and safely to the nearest hospital equipped to care for them. MedAir is one of only four air emergency services in Southern California.

There is a future as well as a past for United Western Medical Centers. Because of the increasing burden of health-care costs, WESTMED hospitals are creating and expanding outpatient services to give patients the care they need, without unnecessary

Western Medical Center/Bartlett is a major health-care and rehabilitation center in Santa Ana.

CHERRY DIVISION OF TEXTRON, INC.

The origin of the Cherry Division of Textron, Inc., can be traced to the aircraft industry prior to World War II. It was at that time that the industry began the mass production of aircraft. Carl W. Cherry's invention and patent of the aircraft-quality "blind" rivet in 1940 was indispensable to America's war effort.

The act of installing rivets in aircraft was often a problem; difficulties were encountered in riveting assemblies where access to the work was restricted. Midgets were used to buck rivets because of their ability to climb into narrow areas. These individuals performed an important service when no other method was available. Later, intricately shaped bucking bars were used but they provided only a partial solution. Many of the restricted areas remained inaccessible.

In the late 1930s Carl Cherry became interested in developing a type of rivet that could be installed on only one side of the material. His interest stemmed from conversations he had with his stepson, who was employed as a riveter at Douglas Aircraft. Cherry knew that in order for

the rivet to be suitable for aircraft production, it had to be an aluminum alloy. Following experiments conducted in his kitchen, he developed the idea of drilling a hole through a solid rivet and expanding it. This was accomplished with the use of a steel mandrel that had a head similar to a finishing nail. The feasibility of this concept resulted in the issuance of the initial patents in 1939 and the formation of the Cherry Rivet Company in Los Angeles the following year. The purpose of the venture was to produce the new Cherry blind rivet.

Lockheed Aircraft placed the first major order for Cherry blind rivets in April 1941, for use in the production of the Hudson bomber and the P-38 fighter. Shortly thereafter Boeing, Douglas, and Consolidated used the new rivets in practically all of their military airplanes, including the Boeing B-17 and B-29; Douglas A-

Edmond B. Buster, general manager and then president from 1957 to 1985.

20, A-26, C-47, and C-54; and Consolidated B-24 and PBY. Cherry rivets were literally "off and flying!" In addition, the firm's rivets were used in the field repair of aircraft worldwide.

Following World War II Cherry Rivet Company continued to improve the quality of blind rivets when it patented a series of proprietary fasteners. The fasteners met with tremendous success and are used on almost all commercial, military, and private aircraft and space vehicles produced in the United States. Furthermore, Cherry fasteners are widely employed in domestic uses such as automobiles, trucks, and buses, and in the electronics and metalworking industries.

In 1951 the Townsend Company of New Brighton, Pennsylvania, purchased the Cherry Rivet Company. The firm then constructed a new manufacturing facility at 1224 East Warner Avenue (then Dehli) in Santa Ana. The original building contained 87,000 square feet on a sixteen-acre tract located in the midst of orange groves and bean fields. During that time the Cherry Division of Townsend employed 175

The Cherry Division of Townsend's new home, at 1224 East Dehli Road in Santa Ana, as it appeared in 1952. Note the orange groves and bean fields, which have since disappeared.

workers. Textron, Inc., acquired Townsend in 1959, and in 1983 Cherry became a separate division of Textron, Inc.

Edmond B. Buster, past president of the Cherry Division of Textron, Inc., was involved with the company for nearly thirty years. Buster's long and impressive career dates back to World War II, when he was supervisor of manufacturing engineering at Douglas Aircraft. At the war's end he was one of the founders of the Pacific Rivet and Machine Company, and in 1946 he became its president. In 1952, when the firm was sold to the Milford Machine and Rivet Company, Buster acted as vice-president/general manager of Milford's Pacific Division. Two years later he served as vice-president/sales manager for S&C Electric in Chicago. Early in 1957 Buster was named vice-president/general manager of the Cherry Division of Townsend.

Buster is directly responsible for the company's role as the leader in the fastener industry. The success of the CherryMAX, the firm's current best-selling fastener, exemplifies his emphasis on research and design for a diverse marketplace. Today the manufacturing plant at the Cherry Division of Textron, Inc., contains 286,000 square feet of floor space, over three times the size of the original facility. However, the present structure is still not large enough; the company leases additional buildings in Anaheim and Costa Mesa. The Cherry Division employs a work force of more than 1,000. Estimated sales for 1985 exceeded eighty-four million dollars.

Buster retired from the company in 1985 and will always be remembered as an innovator and pioneer in the fastener industry. In addition to his efforts at Cherry, Buster is a well-known philanthropist throughout Or-

Cherry/Textron, at 1224 East Warner Avenue in Santa Ana, as it appears today. About the only recognizable thing remaining is the old barn still standing in the background. All the "open" areas have been cleared for industrial development in the near future.

ange County. Some of the many posts he has held include chairman of the board of trustees of Children's Hospital, president of the St. Joseph Hospital Foundation, chairman of the advisory board of Cal State Fullerton, chairman of the board of trustees of UCI College of Medicine, and member of the executive committee of the Boy Scouts of America. For his service to the community he has received the Ernest Coulter Award from Big Brothers, the Manager of the Year Award from the Society for Advancement of Management, and the Humanitarian Award from the National Conference of Christians and Jews.

SIGNAL LANDMARK PROPERTIES, INC.

Although Signal Landmark Properties, Inc., was not organized until 1968, the company has had a long and colorful association with the oil industry in Southern California. The firm was created to manage the myriad of real estate and land holdings of the Signal Oil and Gas Company, forerunner of the parent corporation—The Signal Companies, Inc., now Allied-Signal Inc.

Signal Landmark Properties, Inc., through its major development subsidiaries, Signal Landmark, Inc., and Signal Development Corporation, builds and markets residential, commercial office, and industrial structures primarily in five Southern California counties: Orange, Los Angeles, San Bernardino, Ventura, and San Diego. In addition, the company owns extensive acreage on the big island of Hawaii on the Kona-Kohala coast.

With more than 12,000 homes built and sold during the past twenty years Signal Landmark, Inc., has become one of the most successful community developers in Orange County. More than any single factor, the key to Signal's success has been the desirable locations of its developments.

A number of these desirable locations are properties that formerly

The Bolsa Chica area, pre-oil field development, circa 1938. The salt ponds can be seen in the center.

were associated with oil production. Signal Oil and Gas Company was organized by Sam Mosher in the early 1920s. As early as 1924 Mosher had been interested in the potential of offshore oil in the vicinity of Huntington Beach. Mosher made overtures to Hancock Oil in 1937 to join with Signal in a partnership to participate in a working agreement with the City of Huntington Beach in the event that the state opened offshore tracts for leasing. A joint subsidiary was formed under the name Southwest Exploration Company, 65 percent owned by Signal and 35 percent by Hancock. Hancock was eventually absorbed by Signal in a merger in 1958.

Mosher's move proved to be a farsighted one, though for many years competing companies blocked any move to open the tidelands to drilling. A decade later a compromise with Standard Oil of California was approved by the state legislature that culminated in the passing of the State Land Act in 1938. This act made it possible for oil companies to submit bids for legalized tidelands operations on a sliding-scale royalty basis. California was the last of the oil states to permit the leasing of its tidelands.

At the time of the bidding no one in the industry could fathom the extraordinary richness and depth of the Huntington Beach offshore reservoir. Bob Pyles was the drilling superintendent when Southwest's first well, State Number One in the Main Zone, was "spudded in" on October 12, 1938, and completed one month later. Many of the technical strides in the art of whipstocking were made on the Southwest Exploration lease, which in years to come would add another 835-acre block of offshore

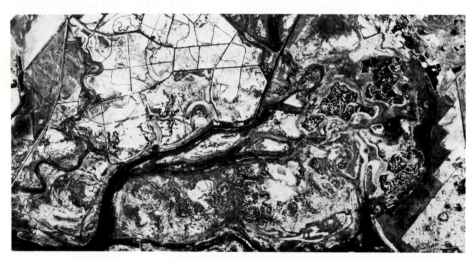

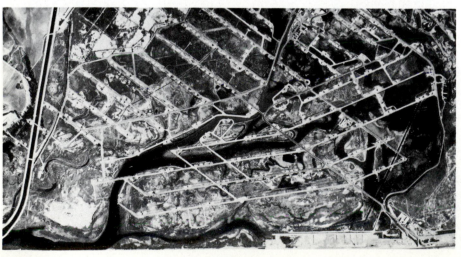

The Bolsa Chica oil field, around 1965, showing well access road pattern and Wintersburg flood control channel (left).

The Bolsa Bay project area, showing the ecological park (foreground) and Huntington Harbor (extreme left) in 1983. Future plans envision an ocean entrance, 1,300-slip marina and commercial complex, and 5,700 residential units.

land, plus two square miles held in Signal's name. It was this operation, which together with the Wilmington Field, established the firm as an industry pioneer and leading exponent in directional drilling.

In the years after 1939 Signal's earnings from Orange County oil grew steadily. The company added the Bolsa lease in 1940 that included the area known today as Bolsa Chica. By the middle of 1963 a total of 188 wells had been completed on the original Bolsa lease for a total production of sixty-one million barrels of crude and fifty-two billion cubic feet of gas.

The formation of Signal Properties in 1968 was a natural outgrowth of the company's interest in land "for its own sake," the oil properties, and the residual holdings under the management of the real estate section.

One year later Signal acquired Shattuck & McHone Enterprises, builders of "Landmark Homes." Following a reorganization in 1970 the corporate name was changed to the current Signal Landmark Properties, Inc. That same year the company purchased the Bolsa Chica acreage it had so successfully leased.

Signal Landmark Properties rapidly developed a life of its own, concentrating on the "upper scale" of California development. Of the dozen or so properties inherited from oil boom days, all but a few have been sold or developed. The first development (1968) of this type was the Hancock Refinery site in Signal Hill, consisting of more than 100 acres. The property was converted into an industrial park and residential condominiums. Other oil properties that have been developed or are in the environmental review process are Newland Refinery Site (500-plus acres), Huntington Beach; Newport Onshore Oil Facilities Site (forty acres), Newport Beach; and the Bolsa Chica Oil Field (1,900-plus acres), Huntington Beach. The preliminary development

plan for Bolsa Chica was approved by the California Coastal Commission in late 1985 after a decade of negotiations with governmental agencies and environmental advocates. The Bolsa Bay plan envisions an ocean entrance, 1,300-slip marina and commercial complex on 75 acres, up to 5,700 residential units, and an ecological park and restored salt marsh covering 915 acres.

Signal Landmark Properties, Inc., is headquartered at the Skypark V Office Complex located in Irvine near the John Wayne Airport. The firm's chief executive is Norman V. Wagner II who, as president, directs a full-time staff of fifty professionals. In addition, the firm utilizes the expertise of dozens of consultants and subcontractors.

Currently, Signal Landmark Properties, Inc., and its subsidiaries have sixteen projects in various stages of development in Southern California. Throughout the oil production years (1920s-1960s) and the real estate boom of the 1970s, Signal has been and remains a highly visible partner in progress with Orange County.

MARTIN LUTHER HOSPITAL MEDICAL CENTER

Martin Luther Hospital Medical Center, located in Anaheim, was established by the Orange County Lutheran Hospital Association in 1960. Ground-breaking ceremonies were held in March of that year for a 144-bed facility. The hospital was dedicated on October 30, 1960, and two months later the first patient was admitted. This facility became the first voluntary hospital in Orange County to provide cobalt therapy.

In the late 1960s an intensive care unit was established at Martin Luther. In 1969, in an effort to meet the expanding needs of the north Orange County community, the hospital acquired ten acres of land on which to construct a new eleven-story, 168-bed facility.

The 1970s represented a period of building expansion, hospital growth, and community support and involvement. In 1975 a newer and larger facility, Martin Luther Hospital Medical Center, was opened housing a number of new services. These included a twenty-bed hemodialysis unit, with inpatient/outpatient dialysis services provided by the Artificial Kidney Foundation of California, Inc., a coronary care unit, a gastrointestinal laboratory, oncology services, a cardiac rehabilitation unit, speech pathology and audiology departments, a full-body CAT scanner, a five-bed special care nursery, a full-service emergency department and paramedic receiving center, an alcoholism recovery service, and a seven-bed telemetry unit. Telemetry equipment has been responsible for increasing the number of available critical care beds through the monitoring of ambulatory patients.

In addition to the hospital's Guild, which began its service in 1960, it was in 1970 that Heartbeats, a fund-raising support group of physicians' wives and community leaders, was organized. Both these groups have been responsible for donating funds for necessary capital improvements and the purchase of new equipment.

Our nation's bicentennial in 1976 marked both the first anniversary of the new hospital building and the organization of the Martin Luther Hospital Foundation. To celebrate this event more than 1,000 people attended a Baby Fair, illustrating the institution's commitment to perinatal care.

In 1978 and 1979 Martin Luther Hospital Medical Center instituted several community-oriented programs. These programs included health fairs and estate-planning seminars, CPR

Martin Luther Hospital on opening day, December 12, 1960.

Today Martin Luther Hospital Medical Center's eleven-story facility is a landmark in northern Orange County.

instruction, poison prevention, and groups for widows/widowers and oncology patients and their families. At the same time the Autumn AMBROSIA (Annual Medical Benefit Reflecting Our Service In The Area) fundraising dinner-dance was established. This event has become increasingly popular, benefiting several hospital programs. Because of MLHMC's commitment to the National Hospital Voluntary Cost Containment program, hospital expenses (per patient day) were significantly reduced.

MLHMC celebrated its twentieth anniversary in 1980. That same year ground was broken for the Parry Professional Building on the site of the original hospital, and the Tincher-Lewis Health Education Center was dedicated. Community programs continued to expand as the Anaheim and East Anaheim Rotary Clubs supported poison prevention in the schools. Noteworthy is the fact that the women's treatment center, which handles pregnancy, birthing, and child care education, regularly administers classes for well over 1,000 couples each year.

The opening of the sports rehabilitation center in 1981 represents a commitment by MLHMC to address the growing outpatient needs of the 1980s. The skilled professionals at Martin Luther are equally at home in the fields of sports medicine and perinatology. Martin Luther was also chosen as one of seven hospitals from more than 300 nationwide that served as demonstration sites to adapt successful management skills used by business and industry to hospital settings. This program was funded by a $800,000, three-year Kellogg grant.

In 1982 there were several firsts for MLHMC. Significant among these was the recognition that the special care nursery became the first in Orange County licensed as an intermediate intensive care nursery. In addition, the outpatient surgery center was opened, and a celebrity golf tournament to benefit critical care ser-

vices was made an annual event.

As Martin Luther Hospital grew along with the surrounding community, twenty-four beds were added in 1983, bringing the total to 200. Obstetrics and gynecology continued to expand as two floors were designated for that department. For the first time the health fair was televised, enabling the hospital to reach an expanded community. That same time the annual celebrity golf tournament, now co-hosted by Dodger pitcher Orel Hershiser, was named for Don Sutton, Orange County's own major league pitcher and future hall of famer.

The following year witnessed the establishment of Resources for Employee Assistance and Comprehensive Health and founding of the Personal Assistance Link (PAL), an automatic dialing system that puts elderly and disabled persons in immediate contact with the hospital's emergency department. Additionally, Martin Luther was honored by being named an official hospital for the XXIIIrd Olympiad to provide health care for the handball competition. Also during the Olympic year the first annual Anne Kiyasu Memorial 5K-10K Run benefiting employee education was initiated and In-Home Health Care services were established. These were among others of the community outreach programs that have helped to ensure the success of Martin Luther Hospital Medical Center.

MLHMC celebrated its silver anniversary in 1985. In its rise to the forefront of a complex and dynamic health care industry, the hospital has remained a model health care institution, creating a friendly and cheerful environment for the north Orange County patient. Terry A. Belmont currently serves as president and executive director of Martin Luther Hospital Medical Center and directs a staff of 900 dedicated health care professionals.

TRAMMELL CROW COMPANY

Responding to the dynamic growth potential of Orange County, in 1974 Trammell Crow Company began an aggressive move into one of the economic hearts of the county—the greater airport area. The firm first built the 303-room Registry Hotel on MacArthur Boulevard, across from the John Wayne Airport, followed by the development of Douglas Plaza, in partnership with the McDonnell Douglas Corporation. The company, in the ensuing years, continued to develop, lease, and manage various projects throughout Orange County including Bradley Plaza (Orange), Clauset Centre and Clauset Park (Santa Ana), Inwood Park and Crow Distribution Center (Irvine), and Cambridge Center (Anaheim).

Today Orange County is the home of one of the fastest-growing divisions of Trammell Crow Company. William H. Lane, Jr., is the partner-in-charge of the firm's Orange County Division. In 1985, under his leadership, the company completed the sale/lease-back and joint venture, with Fluor Corporation and Winthrop Financial Associates, of the Fluor Corporation World Headquarters facility and adjoining property in

Trammell Crow Company, headquartered in Dallas, Texas, has contributed much to the skyline of that city through its many realty projects.

Irvine. Trammell Crow Company has exciting plans for the Fluor property. It plans to convert this superb facility into a world-class, multitenant, multipurpose complex. Initially, new office structures, a health club, a multi-cinema theater, hotels, restaurants, and various retail stores will be added to the complex. Ultimately, the firm hopes to make it the premier mixed-use development in Orange County.

Orange County is one of four divisions of Trammell Crow Company's Southern California Region guided by regional partner Thomas A. Bailey (the other divisions are San Diego, Los Angeles/Riverside, and West Los Angeles/Ventura). Trammell Crow Company, headquartered in Dallas, is recognized as one of the top real estate investment firms in America; it develops, leases, and manages commercial projects (176 million square feet) in eighty-six cities through fifty-five offices, including Orange County. This firm, with gross assets in excess of $7.5 billion, is involved in a broad range of developments including office buildings, industrial buildings, and shopping centers. The company also has many affiliates involved in residential, trade mart, hotel, medical, and agricultural projects, including Crow Residential Companies and The Dallas Market Center Company. Nationwide, some of the more prominent Trammell Crow Company projects include the LTV and Diamond Shamrock Towers in Dallas; the Galleria in Atlanta; the Commerce Distribution and Business Center in Los Angeles; the Imperial Bank Tower in San Diego; and 601 Montgomery in San Francisco.

The firm's Orange County offices are located in the Fluor Tower in Irvine.

SANTA ANA NISSAN/DATSUN

Flexibility and an awareness of changing conditions are two characteristics of the business life-style of Robert E. Wilde, founder of Santa Ana Nissan/Datsun. For the past forty years Wilde has actively participated in Orange County's evolution from an economy based primarily on agriculture to one focused increasingly on business and technology.

Raised in Orange County, Wilde began his career there after World War II. In 1944 Wilde married Jeanette Klatt, daughter of pioneer ranchers Carl and Lena Klatt, who had come to Orange County from Illinois in 1909. Wilde helped manage the Klatt ranches near Seventeenth Street and Tustin Avenue in Santa Ana and Tustin, where orange groves thrived for many years under his supervision.

By the 1950s, however, it became apparent to Wilde that use of the family's property solely for agricultural purposes was no longer economically feasible. The fact that others shared his realization was reflected in the changing land-use patterns throughout Orange County during that period.

In 1970 Wilde purchased the second-oldest Datsun franchise in the United States. Then known as Clean Car Center, it was a dealership that had been founded in 1958 in Santa Ana on a quarter-acre of land near Main Street and Warner Avenue. The dealership employed just twenty people at the time of Wilde's purchase.

Wilde changed the name of his newly acquired franchise to Santa Ana Datsun. He also relocated the agency to family-owned ranch properties on Seventeenth Street, where other commercial development had already been completed. There, on a 3.8-acre site, Santa Ana Datsun opened for business in a newly constructed facility with offices, showrooms, and service and parts departments conveniently housed in 53,300 square feet of floor space. That year the agency recorded sales of two million dollars.

Wilde and his son, Raymond, who also participates in the family business, recall that in 1970 only six car models and one pickup truck model were available to offer their customers, whereas in 1985 twenty-five car and sixteen truck models were offered for sale. This variety of products, coupled with the labor of the Wildes and their seventy-four employees, has helped to increase 1985 sales figures to twenty-five million dollars.

Frank Klatt, standing in the middle of what is now Seventeenth Street west of Tustin Avenue, looking west. The right side of the street is the approximate location of Santa Ana Nissan/Datsun today. Klatt is the brother-in-law and brother, respectively, of owners Robert and Jeanette Wilde.

As part of Wilde's ongoing commitment to community service, he has loaned Datsun vehicles to several educational and religious institutions in Orange County and has sponsored numerous youth-oriented sports programs. In 1984 the Motor Car Dealers Association of Orange County submitted the name of Robert E. Wilde as its nominee for *Time* magazine's 1984 Quality Dealer Award (TMQDA). He was one of sixty so nominated throughout the United States as a result of his long-term involvement in Orange County civic and community organizations and in the National Automobile Dealers' Association (NADA).

The Santa Ana Nissan/Datsun dealership shortly after its grand opening in July 1972.

HUNTINGTON BEACH COMPANY

The history of the Huntington Beach Company is linked to the early development of the city of Huntington Beach. In 1903 the firm came to Huntington Beach, then known as Pacific City, and embarked on a program of economic development and community growth.

The Huntington Beach Company's first improvement was to arrange for an extension of the Pacific Electric Railway to serve the area. On July 4, 1904, 50,000 spectators attended the opening of the rail line to Huntington Beach; the depot was located at Main and Ocean. This widely celebrated event was important in that the railroad furnished access to the town and paved the way for its expansion.

With the support of its namesake, Henry E. Huntington, Huntington Beach was headed for certain success.

Huntington was responsible for the formation of the Pacific Electric Railway Company in 1901. Three years earlier Henry, along with his uncle Collis Huntington, had purchased their first electric railways in Southern California. These trolleys, the "Big Red Cars," provided a comfortable and convenient alternative to the trains of the Southern Pacific Railroad. When Huntington incorporated the Los Angeles Inter-Urban Railroad in 1905, trolleys began to serve the Southland. Largely due to the extension of the railroad, many areas were opened for settlement.

The expansion of Huntington Beach from a seaside village to a town site was accomplished with the support of the Huntington Beach Company. This business was responsible for many town improvements including the subdivision of lands;

Huntington SeaCliff, a planned community built by the Huntington Beach Company on a former oil field, contains crafted homes situated on a championship golf course.

the grading and paving of streets; the installation of curbs, electric lights, and telephones; and construction of a water system.

J.V. Vickers, the first president of the company, believed in the future of Huntington Beach. In his enthusiasm for the town and its beauty, he planted rare trees from around the world and personally supervised their maintenance. Many of the trees are still visible around the city.

Huntington Beach incorporated in 1909 as a city of 1,000 residents. The town council encouraged development. In about 1920 the Standard Oil Company of California leased

500 acres from the Huntington Beach Company. Well A-1 brought in 100 barrels per day, and Huntington Beach became the second-largest oil producer in the state.

Oil provided the stimulus for growth. Soon thereafter the town became a center of the petroleum industry. As the population increased, Huntington Beach realized new prosperity. From 1920 to 1945 oil was responsible for 85 percent of the city's tax revenues.

The Huntington Beach Company has long been familiar with the importance of planning and land use. Until 1960 the city was predominantly comprised of farmlands and oil fields. However, the findings of a Stanford Research Institute study indicated that oil would become a declining economic factor. In fact, from 1945 to 1960 oil was responsible for 50 percent of the city's tax revenues, a decrease of 35 percent over the previous estimate. The firm realized that an intelligent urban planning policy would be necessary to accommodate the burgeoning population and changing economy.

A key to the Huntington Beach Company's long-term planning was to achieve a compatible mix of people and industry. The firm used oil revenues as seed money for residential and commercial development. In preparation for this development, it removed unsightly oil equipment. Miles of pipes were placed underground and other oil-producing machinery was clustered within walled "islands."

In 1960 residential and commercial construction proceeded. Standard Oil formally agreed to drill inside enclosed islands, thus ensuring the integrity of developing communities. The Huntington Beach Company built a planned community called Huntington SeaCliff. This impressive development was constructed on a former oil field and contains crafted

In the early 1920s the Standard Oil Company of California leased 500 acres from the Huntington Beach Company. Soon the town became a center of the petroleum industry. Shown are city streets covered with oil following the collapse of a tank.

homes situated on a championship golf course. Responding to this residential complex, then Huntington Beach Mayor Dr. Donald Shipley stated, "City government feels Huntington Beach Company has improved the environment more than any other industry in the city. . . . "

In its eighty years in Huntington Beach, the firm has seen a seaside village evolve into a city of 180,000 people. It will continue to maintain its oil operations in a productive and environmentally responsible manner, in addition to building homes, recreational facilities, and commercial structures. More important, the Huntington Beach Company will enhance the beauty and economic health of the city while remaining sensitive to community needs.

Roger Work is vice-president and general manager of the Huntington Beach Company. He directs a staff of twenty full-time employees and a host of subcontractors and consultants. The corporation has been a staunch supporter of the Huntington Beach Chamber of Commerce from its inception. Since 1904 the firm has been an active participant in the city's Fourth of July celebration and is a member of the Urban Land Institute.

FOUNDERS K CORPORATION

Founders K Corporation is a business that evolved from a 1979 merger of two California firms (Upper K Ranch Corporation and Founders K Corporation), both of which are owned by the descendants of two prominent pioneer Orange County families—the Kraemers and the Yorbas.

The Kraemer and Yorba families and their ancestral landholdings in Southern California were first brought together on September 30, 1886, by the marriage of Angelina Yorba and Samuel Kraemer. The lands of Angelina Yorba had been in her family's possession since 1810, when her great-grandfather, José Antonio Yorba, received Rancho Santiago de Santa Ana in a Spanish land grant from Governor Arrellaga of California. Rancho Santiago originally contained 62,000 acres and was one of the earliest and largest of the Califor-nia land grants. Though now reduced in size, Rancho Santiago is believed to be the only existing land grant still farmed by the descendants of the original Spanish grantee, José Antonio Yorba.

Eastlake Village, with its sixteen-acre private lake, is a master-planned residential community developed by Founders K Corporation on 865 land-grant acres at Fairmont Boulevard and Esperanza Road in the city of Yorba Linda.

This site plan of Eastlake Village in Yorba Linda shows the village's major streets, locations of existing and proposed dwellings, and the community's lakefront recreation center on Village Center Drive.

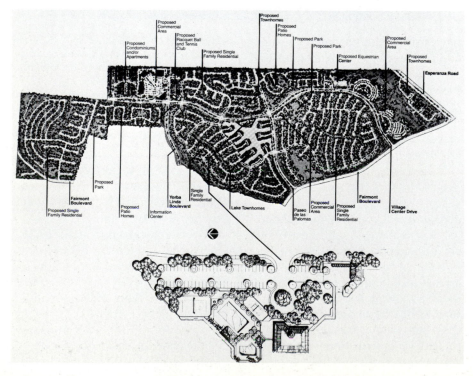

Samuel Kraemer had inherited property from his father, Daniel Kraemer, who had initially purchased 3,900 acres on April 27, 1865, for $4,200. The Kraemer-Yorba estates stretched from Riverside County to Newport Bay. Within the boundaries of the couple's land were located what are now the cities of Placentia, Yorba Linda, Costa Mesa, Santa Ana, Orange, Tustin, and portions of Newport Beach and Anaheim. Farm crops and cattle/horse herds thrived on their holdings, and the discovery of oil in Placentia further added to the power and prosperity of the families.

From the union of Angelina and Samuel were born five sons and three daughters, all of whom married, had children, and passed their land down from generation to generation. Today

their grandson, Gilbert U. Kraemer, Jr., serves as president of Founders K Corporation. Other family members holding corporate positions are Harold W. Muckenthaler, vice-president; Lawrence O. Kraemer, Jr., treasurer; Richard J. Francuz, secretary; and Rosemary Kraemer Raitt and Jack Martin Roth, directors.

The 1979 merger that gave birth to the present Founders K Corporation was brought about by the third and fourth generations of the Kraemer-Yorba family for the purpose of consolidating their real property interests and resources into a coordinated, unified commitment to develop their remaining historic land grant acres with the greatest possible efficiency and economy. Today development of such land, particularly in the cities of Placentia and Yorba Linda, as well as ranching and farming, are the corporation's major areas of focus. In the near past it was the original Founders K which greatly developed Placentia, while Upper K Ranch was instrumental in extending the eastward boundaries of Yorba Linda to the San

This commercial office building at 101 South Kraemer Boulevard, Placentia, is owned by Founders K Corporation and illustrates the manner in which the corporation has developed some of the Kraemer/Yorba land-grant acreage for nonagricultural use.

One of the focal points of Eastlake Village is its 8,060-square-foot lakefront recreation building which features bi-level decking and numerous windows for viewing the village's lake against a background of Yorba Linda's rolling hills.

Bernardino/Riverside County lines.

A major land development project of the new Founders K Corporation consists of an 865-acre tract in eastern Yorba Linda. This development features a sixteen-acre man-made, stocked lake with boat ramps; 2,350 luxury town homes and single-family one- and two-story, three- and four-bedroom detached houses; three parks; eight acres of equestrian amenities; and 75 acres of commercial development.

This unique master-planned residential community, named Eastlake Village, is being constructed by means of a 1976 joint venture agreement with Shapell Industries, Inc., a Delaware corporation. A subsidiary of Shapell, S&S Construction Company, has built the project's new recreational facilities and residences in several phases of the development

since formal ground-breaking activities took place on April 13, 1984. The estimated value of this master-planned community development, when completed, will approximate $500 million.

Eastlake Village is located at Fairmont Boulevard and Esperanza Road among the Yorba Linda hills where 8,000 head of cattle once roamed and grazed near the now-razed, two-story adobe casa of Bernardo Yorba, the third son of California's first Yorba, José Antonio. Bernardo's once-thriving livestock, field crops, and citrus groves have been replaced by sailboats, swimming pools, supermarkets, and other amenities of California suburbia, but his heritage endures throughout Orange County.

Founders K Corporation is headquartered at 842 Alta Vista in Placentia. The facility serves as a link between the firm's diverse and widespread business interests, which now include cable television and out-of-state ranches in addition to real estate development, farming, ranching, and oil production in Southern California.

AIRCAL

From its early years the history of American aviation has been closely connected with Orange County. Dating back to the first decade of the twentieth century, Orange County has been home to some of the greatest aerial daredevils, including Glenn Martin, Eddie Martin, and Bessica Raiche.

In modern times another pilot, Major General (USAF retired) William Lyon, may one day be counted among the superstars of Orange County aviation. Although Lyon is an Air Force veteran with almost fifty years' flying experience, he will be best remembered for his daredevil rescue of Orange County's airline—AirCal. The airline officially changed its name to AirCal after Lyon and his partner, Orange County developer George L. Argyros bought the

The 140-passenger Boeing 737-300 is the newest member of AirCal's fleet of thirty-five modern jets serving major cities throughout the western United States and Western Canada.

company in 1981.

Air California began operating in January 1967 as an intrastate carrier regulated by the California Public Utilities Commission. The airline had been organized by a group of Orange County businessmen who were unsuccessful in convincing an established carrier to provide service between Orange County Airport (now John Wayne Airport) and the San Francisco Bay area.

A 22,500-square-foot terminal, completed in 1967, was immediately serving 30,000 passengers per month, almost as many as it was designed to service in a year. The major portion of the passenger increase stemmed from the inauguration of direct flights from Orange County to San Francisco by the Orange County-based Air California. The new airline operated five flights a day with Lockheed Electras.

In 1970 Air California was added to C. Arnholt Smith's Westgate-California conglomerate, which some years later declared bankruptcy. The airline continued to operate "semi-

independently" under the aegis of the U.S. Bankruptcy Court and remained a viable and profitable entity.

Throughout the 1970s the Orange County Airport and Air California grew in spurts matched only by the jump in local real estate prices. As early as 1972 the Orange County facility ranked as the fourth-busiest airport in the United States. Air California had posted a profit for each year since 1972 and was, according to writer Thomas Self, "the only airline besides Delta to do so."

The year 1981 proved to be the turning point in Air California's brief history. A number of serious bidders mounted attempts at a takeover of the airline. Emerging from the pack of combatants were Air Florida Systems and William Lyon. Self adds, "During the dogfight that followed, Lyon was joined by Argyros (Arnel Corporation), and they won the bid at $61.5 million. The two builders put up thirty-five million dollars of their own money and backed a loan from Wells Fargo Bank for the remainder." The partners were firmly

William Lyon, chairman and chief executive officer.

George L. Argyros, vice-chairman and chairman of the executive committee.

David A. Banmiller, president and chief operating officer.

committed to winning because "an Air Florida takeover was not in Orange County's best interests."

Lyon's recent successes at AirCal have tended to complement his life-long accomplishments at The William Lyon Company. Self summarizes: "His building company is distinguished by its longevity and a consistent winning posture in an up-and-down industry, and it has amassed a net worth in excess of $400 million."

In 1980 Lyon became acquainted with George Argyros, another California developer and owner of the Seattle Mariners baseball team. Their entry into the airline business seemed at first an inopportune move. By the end of 1981 the industry had been hard hit by the PATCO (air traffic controllers) strike, recession, spiraling fuel prices, and ruinous fare wars. AirCal lost money for the first time since 1972.

In 1982, with losses soaring to $35.6 million, longtime president Robert Clifford retired. Devoting full time to the airline, Lyon assumed the positions of president and chief executive officer. He and Argyros immediately decided that "get tough" decisions were necessary if the company was to survive.

During the first months of 1983 Lyon "trimmed the fat" from the budget. He negotiated a 10-percent pay cut and wage freeze with payback provisions from future profits, and structured a profit-sharing plan for employees once profitability was returned. The work force was cut 20 percent, with even deeper cuts made in management. Austerity measures also included the pulling out of four unprofitable markets: Monterey, Fresno, Las Vegas, and Phoenix.

In 1983 AirCal took another important step and completed a financial restructuring that boosted equity by $62.3 million and reduced overall debt by $75 million. The privately held AirCal went public and sold 2.5 million shares for $27 million, applying $26 million to debt reduction.

AirCal's turnaround began gradually in mid-1983. The key element in the company's continuing success of 1984 was "a more aggressive marketing posture—one which often takes direct aim at PSA." At the start of a fare war with PSA, Lyon redeployed the company's resources. David A. Banmiller, AirCal's marketing chief and assistant to the president, concentrated on the lucrative San Francisco to Los Angeles market. Starting

in 1983 with five flights daily, AirCal increased its share of the market to the sixteen to eighteen daily flights it makes today. "Ten years ago we were one-tenth the size of PSA. Today we are approaching 60 percent," says Banmiller. In July 1985 AirCal reported a second-quarter net profit of $8.772 million, the highest quarterly profit in its eighteen-year history, and its eighth consecutive quarterly profit. Banmiller was named president and chief operating officer in May 1985.

The mood is positive at AirCal's headquarters on Birch Street straddling the southeast perimeter of John Wayne Airport. The history-making AirCal turnaround was engineered by William Lyon, a dedicated management staff, and the spirit of cooperation on the part of more than 2,100 employees. States Lyon, "AirCal has been the biggest challenge of my life. Nothing in building or in the military holds a candle to it."

Today AirCal is the number one airline at many of the airports it serves and has earned national attention for its aggressive marketing strategies, the comfort and convenience of its equipment and facilities, and its consistent record of growth and profitability.

CAMINO REAL SAVINGS BANK

Mervyn A. Phelan purchased Camino Real Savings and Loan Association in July 1985.

Thomas M. Phelan, president and chief operating officer, heads the firm's property management company and oversees the operations of thirty bank locations and more than 5,000 guest rooms.

The Orange County chapter in the annals of Camino Real Savings Bank is in part a story of the Phelan Group—a diversified hotel and real estate firm based in the city of Orange. Although the FSLIC member was purchased by Mervyn A. Phelan "in his own behalf rather than through his other business enterprises," it was Phelan's more than twenty years of success in finance and real estate that led to his acquisition of Camino Real Savings and Loan Association.

Mervyn A. Phelan was born in 1941, a fifth-generation Californian. The Phelans were ranchers and were prominent in the settlement of Whittier (Los Angeles County) following the breakup of Pio Pico's El Ranchito in the 1870s.

Phelan started his business career in 1962, buying a small apartment project. With his brother, Tom, as a partner, Phelan began to purchase residential units operating under a motel license. The Phelans soon realized that these units, equipped with kitchenettes, could in depressed times provide a "hedge against inflation." Even when tourist occupancy declined, the units were in demand by a local populace in need of temporary affordable housing.

In the ensuing years the Phelans zeroed in on the "affordable" motel/apartment market. At the center of the Phelan approach has been the residential unit with kitchenette: a novel concept that in effect has stabilized the standard motel operations. Typically, in a society on the move, the firm's California clientele has included family vacationers, long-term guests (especially during winter months), and relocating business and military personnel.

The Phelan Group of companies consists of PHI Enterprises, a publicly traded corporation; a management company; and five related service corporations. The firm completed a move in November 1985 to a new expanded headquarters located at 625 City Drive South in Orange.

Mervyn Phelan, chairman, along with brother Thomas, president and chief operating officer, have in twenty years steered the organization to a prestigious position in real estate development and property management. The Phelan Group now owns and operates thirty hotel, resort, and apartment complexes including more than 5,000 guest rooms throughout California and Arizona.

Most visible among its properties are the Ha'Penny Inns which, according to Leventhol & Horvath, rank twenty-fourth nationally among budget motel chains. In 1984 the company selected four of its Ha'Penny Inns for conversion to Executive Lodges. According to Kirk Allen, executive vice-president of marketing, "The most compelling reason for the conversions is our ability to provide an array of amenities and services desirable to most business travelers at rates that are significantly lower than those currently found in the marketplace. Executive Lodge accommodations blend comfort and value, thereby appealing to companies mindful of travel expenditures."

It was this strong financial posture, as well as a keen awareness of the need for affordable housing, that spurred Mervyn Phelan's interest in entering the banking business. With the July 1985 purchase of Camino Real Savings and Loan Association, Phelan had reached a longtime personal goal. "We can provide expert financial services to the lodging industry. This special expertise is rare in the banking world," Phelan comments.

Camino Real Savings and Loan Association and its Hispanic heritage is a unique story in the banking industry. The institution was organized in 1969, opening its doors for business in January 1972. More than two years of lobbying efforts were rewarded when a federal charter was granted to the institution, making it the first Latino-chartered savings and loan in the nation.

Currently the headquarters of Camino Real is located in San Fernando, with branch offices in Sylmar, Canoga Park, Sepulveda, and the City of Commerce. A branch application is pending for an Orange County location; the first local branch is scheduled for a 1986 opening in the city of Orange.

The awareness of the need for more affordable housing, coupled with access to real estate assets, made the Phelan takeover a perfect match with Camino Real's Hispanic heritage. One of Phelan's first priorities was the formation of the Advisory Committee for Hispanic Affairs. This committee reports directly to the board of directors with recommendations for financial programs that meet the particular needs of Hispanic communities statewide. "It is especially satisfying to own an institution that is rich in early California heritage, yet it serves the interest of all Californians," says Phelan.

In September 1985 Camino received approval for a name change to Camino Real Savings Bank. "The name change is simply a matter of better defining Camino's business expansion and diversification, and is just one element in our overall growth strategy," Phelan explains.

Mervyn Phelan is an aggressive, innovative businessman who, for more than twenty years, has been a partner in Orange County's progress. In addition to active roles in the Phelan Group and Camino Real Savings Bank, Phelan was a co-founder of the California Hotel and Motel Association and served on the planning commission that created the city of Villa Park.

In 1985 the Camino Real Savings Bank became a major commercial sponsor of the *Californian,* the state's official tallship. Under sponsorship of the bank, in November of that year the *Californian* set sail from Dana Point for Mexico City with seven tons of medical and shelter supplies for earthquake victims.

The Californian *is a full-scale recreation of the 1849-vintage cutter* Lawrence. *She has been proclaimed the state's official tallship and represents California in special events up and down the Pacific Coast. Under the sponsorship of Camino Real Savings Bank, on November 10, 1985, the* Californian *set sail for Mexico City with seven tons of medical and shelter supplies for earthquake victims. Photo by Gary Felton*

WORLD TRAVEL

Travel is an integral part of the American way of life. In 1980 there were more than 935 million trips taken for vacation, pleasure, or business. In Orange County alone, three million passengers pass through John Wayne Airport annually, with the use of local airports projected to triple by 1995. The development of World Travel of Santa Ana is an Orange County story—testimony to the phenomenal growth of the travel industry.

Never were conditions in Europe more interesting. And probably not for many, many years to come will foreign exchange be so favorable. For little more than it would cost you to remain at home we offer you life in excellent European hotels. Don't postpone. Enroll now!

The above description referred to one of the first World Travel programs billed as Cooperative Educational Tours. The package featured eight countries in fifty-eight days for $760, all inclusive. It was an incredible travel value, not withstanding the fact that the year was 1938. That year marked the creation of World Travel Bureau, and summer tours to Europe were a specialty.

In December 1939 Harry Jackson completed the purchase of the files, desk, chairs, supply rack, mailing list, and Trans Pacific Appointment for the sum of $150. The "Jacksonian era" of World Travel had embarked on a course bound for success.

Jackson was born in Kansas and raised in Colorado. A schoolteacher and former tour bus operator at Pikes Peak, Jackson yearned for a career in travel. The takeover of World Travel Bureau in 1939 turned a dream into reality.

Harry Jackson's son, Tom, virtually grew up in the business. In 1948 Tom enjoyed his first tour to South America. Five years later he issued

Three generations of the Jackson family have been involved in the operation of World Travel. Pictured, from left: Scott Jackson; Jennifer Jackson; Harry Jackson, founder; and Tom Jackson, president.

his first ticket. After an eventful twenty-five years Tom assumed the role of president of World Travel. Harry Jackson has continued his involvement in the firm under the title of director emeritus.

In 1979 World Travel became the first agency in Orange County to install SABRE. This airline reservation system functioned as the leading edge in the industry-wide move toward automation. When American Airlines inaugurated service from John Wayne Airport in June 1983, a partnership between these first-class giants of the travel industry was a natural. This cooperative affiliation has made it possible for agents at sixteen World Travel offices to write tickets and boarding passes for any American

Airlines flight.

World Travel, founded in 1938, is the largest and longest continually family-owned travel bureau in Orange County. In 1985 sales surpassed the $30-million mark. Tom Jackson, current president, is a certified travel consultant and a founding member and past president of Associated Travel Nationwide (ATN). In local circles, Tom is active in the Santa Ana Rotary Club and the Performing Arts Center in Orange County.

KRAFT, INC.

An array of Kraft products manufactured at the Buena Park facility.

Kraft, Inc., of Buena Park observed its twenty-seventh anniversary in November 1985. The celebration commemorated the 1958 opening of the plant and the production of its first salable product: the marshmallow.

In the late 1950s Kraft Foods of Chicago began searching for a centralized location to consolidate three factories in the western region of the country. Prior to the Buena Park opening, Kraft products were manufactured primarily at three locations: Chehalis, Washington, and Oakland and Los Angeles, California. The decision was made to consolidate those three locations into one facility.

A 200-acre site was selected among the orange groves and dairy farms of northern Orange County. Located approximately forty miles from downtown Los Angeles, company planners were convinced that the Los Angeles/Orange County area was destined to be "one of the fastest-growing areas in the United States." At the outset

of construction activity a number of the principals concerned with the project expressed amazement "that Kraft would build a plant out here in the middle of nowhere."

The Buena Park facility was at the time the largest Kraft plant constructed from "the ground up." The original building employed the tilt-up concrete technique and consisted of 420,502 square feet. The finished goods warehouse was expanded by 58,000 square feet in 1967. A 2,801-square-foot addition to the marshmallow department was completed in 1972, bringing the current Buena Park facility to a total of 481,303 square feet, or approximately eleven acres under roof.

Highlights of the early years included a visit by television star and recording artist Perry Como. Como visited the facility during the time that Kraft sponsored the popular "Perry Como Show."

Kraft products manufactured and distributed from the Buena Park facility include marshmallows, salad dressings, barbecue sauces, margarine, shortening, and cooking oil. In 1959,

the plant's first full year of operation, total production amounted to 136 million pounds. The tonnage for 1984 was 281.7 million pounds, a 25-year increase of 207 percent. Company planners had accurately predicted that a Buena Park location would straddle one of the fastest-growing markets in the United States.

The Buena Park plant manager is Thomas J. Burke. Burke has served as chairman of the Food Division of the United Way drive and for many years has been a member of the executive board of the Urban League.

Today Kraft's corporate headquarters is located at Kraft Court in Glenview, Illinois. The Buena Park operation employs more than 600 full-time workers. The years ahead promise even greater opportunities for those who make their living at Kraft, Inc., in Orange County.

The familiar Kraft margarine, Parkay, comes off the assembly line.

365

LEASON POMEROY ASSOCIATES, INC.

Leason Pomeroy Associates, Inc., (LPA) is a nationally recognized Orange County-based design firm founded in 1965. Since its inception the company has continually broadened its expertise and has experienced tremendous growth in the scale and scope of its projects.

On the leading edge of its industry, LPA has provided planning, architectural, and interior design services for office buildings, research centers, retail developments, hotels, and mixed-use projects. In twenty years LPA has branched out to additional offices in Los Angeles and the San Francisco Bay area. A fully equipped data and design computer system is an effective coordinating tool in the Orange office.

LPA was founded by Orange County native Leason F. Pomeroy III, FAIA. Pomeroy serves as corporate president and oversees all business development activities. During a career spanning more than two decades Pomeroy has gained acclaim for expertise in architecture, planning, urban design, and historical preservation.

The firm's corporate headquarters is located at 44 Plaza Square in the historic Orange *Daily News* building fronting the plaza. Although remodeled on several occasions, the ivy-clad

The Landmark, located in Sacramento, California, is one example of the work of Leason Pomeroy Associates. © 1985 Ronald Moore Photography

facade still silhouettes the original building forms constructed in 1890.

Leason F. Pomeroy has been a state director of the American Institute of Architects and a member of the Urban Land Institute. As chairman of the Historic Design Preservation Task Force, City of Orange, Pomeroy was a central figure in the development of strict design guidelines for the preservation of the city's historic landmarks.

LPA is the largest design firm in Orange County and has successfully completed hundreds of innovative projects throughout the United States. "We do business in forty mar-

kets across the country, working for a variety of developers from Reston, Virginia, to Orange County, California," states Leason Pomeroy. "What we bring to the table is the knowledge of trends and business pressures that affect our clients in each market."

Pomeroy is joined by three other partners and a support team of eighty-five specialists who contribute to the design dialogue. "Members of the firm stimulate our design efforts by constantly debating the design issues. We owe a lot to their talent and ingenuity, their imagination and productivity," says Pomeroy.

In the forefront of Orange County's architectural development, LPA has been commissioned by The Irvine Company and The Koll Company to design the 415-acre Irvine Technology Center. The center is an integral part of the internationally marketed Irvine Spectrum. LPA's challenge is to provide a uniform architectural style for the continuing development of this landmark business park.

The firm intends to maintain a steady growth while focusing upon the principle: "Architecture is still an art form," states Pomeroy. "While design considerations are paramount, we ultimately have to provide a marketable, leasable project."

Another of the firm's projects was the California Center in 1984. © 1984 Wolfgang Hoyt Esto

GREAT AMERICAN
FIRST SAVINGS BANK

The lobby of the Great American First Savings Bank office in Laguna Beach features an art exhibit that was planned into the interior.

It all started when Congress passed the Home Owner's Loan Act of 1933, which authorized the formation of the Federal Home Loan Bank system, of which the savings and loan associations were a major part.

Several of Laguna Beach's business leaders realized the need for a local financial institution to serve the needs of Laguna Beach and its surrounding communities. At that time there was only one small local bank in Laguna, making it necessary for residents to go to Santa Ana, some twenty miles away, for most of their financial needs.

Under the inspired leadership of Andrew S. Hall, a Laguna real estate broker, a group of farsighted businessmen applied for and were granted on March 15, 1935, the first federal savings and loan charter in Orange County. On May 1, 1935, First Federal Savings and Loan Association of Laguna Beach (whose name was changed in 1938 to Laguna Federal Savings and Loan Association) opened its doors with three employees and assets of $4,735 in a small office at 260 Park Avenue.

Spearheading the group's organiza-

tion with Hall were original board members L.F. Mallow, pharmacist; Dr. B.B. Mason, one of Laguna's first doctors; Joseph Jahraus, lumberman; H.G. Heisler, who worked with the Southern Pacific Railroad; Arthur C. Peterson, editor of the *South Coast News;* and William A. Wolf, mining engineer. Despite the modest beginning, the unselfish dedication of this community-involved board propelled Laguna Federal toward its status as the largest federal savings institution in Orange County. Assets exceeded $406 million at the time of its merger with San Diego Federal Savings in 1982.

As diversified as the men who founded the bank were the customers who came to be its loyal patrons, seeking loans for hilltop and canyon dwellings, summer cottages and mansions, and beachfront and hillside homesteads. The savings needed to finance these homes came not only from the local community but from every state in the country, as well as many foreign nations.

From its earliest years Laguna Federal served an artistic community in a beautiful niche of the Southern California terrain. The tempting weather, landscape, and life-style lured visitors from all over the world, which in turn stimulated the bank's business and reputation, causing a growth that

pushed it to several successively larger offices around the Ocean Avenue/Pacific Coast Highway block. In 1961 the institution settled into its current home, a handsome New Orleans-style, three-story structure that accommodates not only customer traffic but also sightseers who come to view the art exhibit space that was planned into the interior.

Championing the bank's unbroken record of service to the local citizenry is Lorna Mills, president since 1957. She has served the institution since 1936, when the office staff numbered three, the posting was done by hand with pen and ink, and savings accounts were initiated at the teller's window in a matter of minutes.

Making the transition from real estate loans to unsecured loans for automobiles and business ventures and from simple passbook accounts to certificates and higher-yield, long-term savings, Laguna Federal has achieved an enviable high-reserve position with an excellent branch network.

In June 1982 Laguna Federal merged with San Diego Federal Savings, California's oldest federal savings institution, which was founded in 1885. The consolidation reinforces the strength of each, operating with $10.6 billion in assets and providing twenty offices in Orange County. The combined institutions are today known as Great American First Savings Bank, a shareholder-owned state savings bank with 161 offices in California and Arizona.

In 1961 Laguna Federal settled into its current home, this handsome New Orleans-style, three-story structure.

FLUIDMASTER, INC.

The story of Fluidmaster, Inc., of Anaheim is an outstanding example of another type of Orange County progress. Progress in this case was centered around an inventor and his invention—the number one toilet tank replacement valve on the market today.

How is it that a relatively small plant, which began production in Orange County in 1958, has been able to revolutionize an entire industry? The answer is rooted in the genius of two men: Adolf Schoepe and Fred Schmuck.

The annals of Fluidmaster begin with the career of Adolf Schoepe, known affectionately to the Fluidmaster family as "Mr. Schoepe." Schoepe was born near Cologne, Germany, in 1904. In 1927, at the age of twenty-three, he boarded a ship bound for America. Being an adventurous spirit he came to California after stops in St. Louis, Tulsa, Akron, and Seattle. "Schoepe was one of the immigrants that America could really be thankful for. He knew how to make things work," says Fred Schmuck.

The Fluidmaster building, at 1800 Via Burton in Anaheim, was first occupied by the firm in 1961.

Schoepe's inventive mind sought exciting opportunities in modern industries. He was in on the ground floor in some of the country's most compelling new fields. He helped build airplanes for Boeing and dirigibles for Goodyear.

In the early 1940s Schoepe was ready for a more direct route to success. His first business venture was rebuilding buses in partnership with his friend Karl Reinhard.

The year 1946 marked a number of milestones in the career of Schoepe. From his factory in Southgate, he perfected a new door lock and received a U.S. patent. That same year the partners purchased a dead orange grove in Anaheim. The new site would be ideal for their new company—Kwikset Lock.

Before the end of the company's first decade Schoepe had led Kwikset Lock into a position as the nation's largest manufacturer of lock sets. The financial success of Kwikset was unparalleled in the history of the industry. The firm was also a showcase for modern management techniques, and was honored by many management societies for its progressive employee practices.

Never being one to rest on past achievements, Schoepe became intrigued with a new type of toilet ball cock. The traditional one employed float ball and rod that worked against

the incoming water pressure to squeeze off the flow by sheer force. Schoepe's model was a valve that worked with the pressure. "It used the incoming water pressure to shut itself off. By the time Schoepe got through tinkering with it, it shut off quickly and positively without the typical leaks, squeaks, and whistles," says Fred Schmuck.

Schoepe loved California, and in order to stay there after merging Kwikset Lock with American Hardware (thus parting ways with an incredibly successful company), he moved swiftly to establish Fluidmaster and improve the inner workings of the toilet tank. He was intent on doing for his new company—Fluidmaster—what he had accomplished for Kwikset.

Fluidmaster, Inc., began production in 1958 on Orangethorpe Way. In the early years of the company many in the industry expressed doubts, including Schoepe. "Even when you doubt yourself you make up your mind you're going to do it," he says.

The company stayed in cramped, rented quarters for four years. Between Christmas Day, 1961, and New Year's Day, 1962, employees pitched in and moved Fluidmaster to its present location on land Schoepe owned. The corporation's "functional facility" at 1800 Via Burton in Anaheim has met the firm's needs for more than twenty-five years.

In the early years Fluidmaster conducted extensive market research.

Adolf Schoepe in his office overlooking the Kwikset Lock plant in 1948.

The research showed that the majority of Americans were vociferously dissatisfied with the present performance of toilet hardware. The task for Schoepe became one of how to gain public acceptance for his "nifty product."

Fortunately for Fluidmaster, Fred Schmuck had joined the company in 1958. The former World War II test pilot and national sales manager for U.S. Radiator was "an engineer by education and a marketing man by necessity." Schmuck, whose official title is senior vice-president, corporate development, was a natural choice to head Fluidmaster's marketing program.

Schmuck went to work and designed a Fluidmaster marketing program that stressed quality above

The Fluidmaster plant in 1975.

price. He organized a network of independent sales representatives rather than hiring company salesmen. He did away with "deal making," since all representatives used standardized price lists. "We sell to everyone under the same terms. Defined volume discounts are the only discounts offered," says Schmuck.

What Schoepe did in product development, Schmuck accomplished in the marketplace. His major coup was gaining the acceptance of the plumbing wholesalers. Gradually Fluidmaster made inroads. Under Schmuck's direction, the firm created the appropriate advertising and public relations messages for each of their main audiences.

Today Fluidmaster is a study in efficiency and cost effectiveness. To the untrained eye the toilet tank repair valve has changed little since 1958. However, the product, plant layout, and production procedures today bear little resemblance to the original.

Since 1977 Fluidmaster toilet valves, marketed as Model 200A and Model 400A, have outsold all other competitors in the replacement market combined. The firm has never experienced layoffs, and gross sales for 1985 were estimated to be more than twenty million dollars.

Adolf Schoepe has been a leader in the Anaheim and Orange County Chambers of Commerce, the Boy Scouts of America, and the State Committee to Employ the Physically Handicapped. Fred Schmuck has been active in the Anaheim Chamber of Commerce, United Fund, Junior Achievement, the Better Business Bureau, and the Boy Scouts of America.

A recent photograph of Adolf Schoepe (left) and Fred Schmuck and an array of company products and awards for excellence received by Fluidmaster.

BANK OF AMERICA NT & SA

Every few years a local newspaper runs a comprehensive feature on the history of Yorba Linda. Included in most of these articles is the tale of how Bank of America came to this still-rural Orange County town.

By now the bank's story has been told enough times that it is firmly entrenched in local folklore. For five years between 1940 and 1945 the merchants and residents of Yorba Linda fought with federal agencies to let the bank build a branch there. After countless letters, telegrams, phone calls, and some personal visits to federal offices by townspeople, the Controller of the Currency authorized Bank of America to transfer its charter from San Juan Capistrano to Yorba Linda.

For a quarter-century Bank of America was the only financial institution in Yorba Linda, and its role in the community was a primary one. A story that appeared in a 1948 issue of *Coronet* magazine shows that the bank was able to attract important businesses to Yorba Linda.

"One day an eastern furniture manufacturer asked Bank of America's help in finding a location for an assembly plant," wrote *Coronet* reporter Keith Monroe. "Promptly they escorted them to Yorba Linda—and now a $400,000 building is under construction." The article also noted that the 200 jobs at the assembly plant were drawn exclusively from the community.

As the town grew, the bank's service increased. By 1975 the branch had evolved from a small office with two tellers into a full-service unit with two drive-up teller windows. Today the Yorba Linda branch has fifteen employees and a Versateller automated teller machine.

The history of Bank of America in Yorba Linda illustrates the powerful impact the institution has had on other Orange County towns and shows the general pattern of the in-

stitution's involvement in the region. While most of the county still consisted of orange groves and other small pockets of rural-based businesses, Bank of America founder and president A.P. Giannini saw the potential of Southern California as a home for new industries. He began to expand the bank's branch system in that part of the state with the opening of the first Orange County BofA branch in 1925 at 801 North Main Street in Santa Ana. Since then, the bank has figured prominently in developing the infrastructure that is the foundation of one of the world's most dynamic economies. Over the past sixty years BofA has led on nearly 400 bond issues totaling nearly two billion dollars in county and local municipal improvements. Bond issues led by Bank of America in Orange County have been for the improvement of education, housing, water and flood control, sanitation and sewage, transportation, libraries, municipal improvements, and other general purposes.

In the 1950s Bank of America backed the first color motion picture of an entertainment visionary named Walt Disney. The feature, *Snow White and the Seven Dwarfs,* introduced Disney's revolutionary animation techniques that placed him at the vanguard of the film industry. Bank of America continues to be a principal lender to many of Disney's operations and ventures.

Long before Orange County had become nationally recognized as a desirable place to do business, Bank of America was busy promoting its merits in other parts of the country. For example, in 1957 Don Smith, a vice-president and industrial finance officer, traveled with Orange County Supervisor William Phillips of Fullerton, Costa Mesa City Manager Robert Unger, and Art F. Adair, president of the Newport Harbor Board of Realtors, to the National

Walt Disney (left) and Bank of America board chairman Louis B. Lundborg in front of a fantasy palace being built for "It's a Small World," a hit of the New York World's Fair. Bank of America sponsored the show.

Electronics Conference in Chicago where the group promoted Orange County to the electronics industry.

The trip was important enough to the Southern California economy to receive coverage from a number of newspapers, including the *Los Angeles Herald Examiner.* The group used the trip as a starting point for the organization of a countywide industrial committee composed of county, city, chamber of commerce, real estate, banking, and other representatives. The committee's goal was to bring new industries to the county.

While the value of the trip to the electronics convention was difficult to measure, the effort illustrates what can result from years of combined effort on the part of banks, businesses, and governments. Such efforts have made high-technology and electronics-related businesses the industrial base of Orange County today and the main catalysts that drive its future.

In 1985 there were 114 Bank of America branches, six corporate banking offices, and several loan- and item-processing centers in the coun-

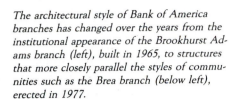

The architectural style of Bank of America branches has changed over the years from the institutional appearance of the Brookhurst Adams branch (left), built in 1965, to structures that more closely parallel the styles of communities such as the Brea branch (below left), erected in 1977.

1980s, the region provided a desirable geography that helped insulate its residents and business from that economic storm," explains Dr. Duane Paul, senior economist for Bank of America in Southern California. "During this period, while other economies suffered setbacks, the Orange County . . . region achieved modest gains in service, trade, and light manufacturing. The region's location— close to two major ports, freeways, and the commercial center of Los Angeles—and its developed industrial structure, which helped see it through the recession, will continue to drive its growth as trade with Pacific Rim countries rises."
—Curtiss Olsen

The old Main Office building, at Eighth and Main streets in Santa Ana, was torn down and replaced in 1965. Here security guards keep a watchful eye out as safe deposit boxes are moved to interim quarters next door.

ty. "Bank of America's Orange County- Los Angeles Coast Region, which also includes southwest Los Angeles, Long Beach, and parts of Whittier and Downey, is a key area of economic activity," says senior vice-president Jim McDermott, regional head.

"Orange County boasts one of the world's most powerful young economies," says McDermott, who has been with the institution for more than twenty-five years. "Characterized by a combination of location, industry, and climate, the spirit and life-style within this area are truly 'entrepreneurial.' The 3.8 million people of Orange County are also a key to Bank of America's presence here. They're innovative, energetic, and collectively possess an unequaled level of education, work experience, and spending power," he notes.

Past Bank of America leaders in Orange County also acknowledged the economic potential of the region. In 1974 BofA vice-president H.H. Jackson, then head of the Orange County region said: "We feel there is

a great future in . . . Orange County, and Bank of America is continually making plans for that future." Jackson cited as an example the City of Fullerton. It has grown from a rural town, whose main enterprise was food processing, into a burgeoning residential city with some large commercial and industrial centers.

"During the recession of the early

RICHARDSON NAGY MARTIN ARCHITECTURE/PLANNING

When the fragrance of citrus still scented the air in Orange County, the architectural team of Thomas & Richardson moved to Tustin from Long Beach. The year was 1958, and in the early days you could figure the drafting board probably held blueprints for single-family dwellings. Throughout the early 1960s Orange County's initial development boom afforded the firm opportunities to participate in the evolution of substantial planned housing developments. The firm's extensive involvement in the innovative master-planned communities of the Irvine Ranch attracted national and international attention to its capabilities.

Within a short time the two-man partnership burgeoned into a planning and architectural design company, adept in every aspect of residential and commercial building. Restructured into Walter Richardson Associates in 1969, the firm took its present title of Richardson Nagy Martin Architecture/Planning in 1974, and currently emphasizes innovative solutions to high-density and environmentally sensitive project requirements that have been repeatedly recognized with awards.

Today the drawing boards of RNM represent projects ranging from moderate-cost residential developments through total planning and detailed architectural work for large-scale, multiuse shopping, office park, and

From left to right are Ralph Martin, Walter Richardson, and Huba Nagy.

recreational complexes. A sampling of assignments encompass a major mixed-use community in western Australia, planned residential communities all across the United States, and master planning for The Irvine Company's newest Village of Westpark and the coastal sector between Corona del Mar and Laguna Beach.

RNM has pioneered ideas with the "zero-lot-line" and "z-line" configurations, motor courts, and, in recognition of the symbiosis of structure and environment, has incorporated conceptual landscape architecture into its growing list of expertise. The company maintains a regional office in Dallas, Texas, presided over by president Thomas K. Benedict. Extensive project sites are found in Florida, Arizona, Colorado, and Canada.

Walter J. Richardson, FAIA, is a recognized international authority in the field of architecture. A graduate of U.C. Berkeley and past president of the Orange County Chapter of the American Institute of Architects, Richardson heads seminars and addresses and frequently contributes articles to builder-related periodicals.

Huba S. Nagy, AIA, is a masterful architectural designer. His European background inspires a unique aesthetic blend of spatial efficiency, adaptability, and design that combines the best features of different styles and eras of architecture.

Nationally respected planning authority Ralph J. Martin, AICP, draws on his experience of creating city master plans, redevelopments, and planned communities to expertly implement imaginative yet practical solutions in planning design.

Richardson Nagy Martin is a team of innovators, paralleling technical skills with an ever-present goal of providing people with compatible living space. The firm has achieved outstanding recognition for excellence, receiving seventy-four Gold Nugget Awards from the Pacific Coast Builders Conference and over thirty other regional and national design awards in the past decade, as well as the 1985 Professional Achievement Award presented by *Professional Builder* magazine. Aurora Awards, Decade '70 National Housing Awards, and AIA Awards also share the wall space of the Newport office.

Richardson Nagy Martin Architecture/Planning shares its success with the community by contributing design services to worthy charitable projects and through major donations to the Orange County Performing Arts Center.

Bayside Cove, a 58-unit luxury water-oriented condominium complex on Bayside Drive in Newport Beach, was just one of the firm's many projects.

FHP, INC.

Robert Gumbiner, M.D., president of FHP, Inc.

In 1959, when health and accident insurance were a rarity, a physician in Long Beach pondered the advantages of a prepaid health plan to eliminate unexpected catastrophic costs for patients. That doctor, Robert Gumbiner, was met with skepticism for what was considered a radical idea. Today Dr. Gumbiner is president of FHP, Inc., one of the country's largest health maintenance organizations, with twenty-five health care facilities in Orange and Los Angeles counties, Utah, Arizona, New Mexico, and Guam, serving over 300,000 medical and dental plan members.

The first to qualify as a multistate health maintenance organization under the HMO Act of 1973, FHP provides a broad range of benefits meeting the high medical, fiscal, and facility standards set by the federal government. The successful strategy of FHP is simple: to offer a high-quality, comprehensive range of services at an affordable price. These services include primary and specialty care, hospitalization and emergency care, dental and vision care, physical therapy, and psychological counseling. FHP places special emphasis on wellness through its health education programs, including stress management, nutrition counseling, aerobics, weight and smoking control, and CPR, aimed to keep members healthy.

FHP contracts with private hospitals to provide prepaid hospital and emergency care, and recently completed construction of its first 117-bed acute care hospital located in Fountain Valley, next to its corporate headquarters. The membership base encompasses federal, state, county, and city government; school districts; manufacturers; unions; and Medicare recipients.

FHP has pioneered a prepaid alternative to traditional Medicare in the state of California called the FHP Senior Plan. By contracting directly with the federal government, FHP adds its benefits to Medicare, at no cost to the recipient. FHP led the nation in dedicating a fully equipped, multiservice medical facility to this plan. The Senior Healthcare Center sprang to life in an extensively restored roller skating rink in Long Beach. The thoughtfully conceived center efficiently meets patients' needs while making them feel comfortable and cared for in a warm, artistically designed environment. Five other Senior Plans are in operation in Anaheim, San Pedro, Santa Monica, mid-Wilshire, and downtown Los Angeles, giving FHP California's largest prepaid Medicare plan enrollment.

In 1972 the Archdiocese of Guam enlisted Dr. Gumbiner's assistance in finding a solution for Guam's troubled health care system. The discussions that followed led to the founding of an FHP Medical Center in Tamuning. Its successful growth has enlarged the medical staff to include a large number of specialists. FHP has recently expanded its Pacific Rim presence to include the islands of Saipan and Palau.

In Washington, D.C., a full-time FHP representative evaluates health care legislation and informs lawmakers of FHP's views on health issues, maintaining an up-to-date exchange of health news and regulations. The viewpoints of FHP members are tapped by the availability of a "hot line" that receives suggestions and complaints with a promise of a response within seventy-two hours.

The professional management of FHP, Inc., is guided by a keen-minded board of directors. Major policy determination and long-range planning are dedicated to growth through diversified membership and innovation while always keeping abreast of the changing needs of its members.

FHP's new 117-bed hospital, located in Fountain Valley.

ROBERT BORDERS AND ASSOCIATES

Robert Borders, planning practically for the future in adolescence, billed himself as a "railroadsman." The plan proved a credible asset in one regard. It propelled him full steam ahead with his true pipe dream, to become an architect.

Growing up on the prairie in Wyoming didn't confine Border's ambition. Following service in the Navy he came to California and began his education with a dollar given him by a co-worker who sensed his abilities. That was the price of tuition at Long Beach City College and the start of studies that took him through the University of Southern California School of Architecture.

Borders opened a small office in his home in 1967 and eased himself into a word-of-mouth clientele that today still includes some of those original clients. Robert Borders and Associates offers a clever twist. The firm will not only draft a client's dream plans, it is equipped to design interior and graphics materials as well as provide all furnishings for the completed space.

A spectrum of visual and dimensional projects have challenged the firm over the years. Renovating the cactus gardens and courtyard of Sherman Gardens and extensive involvement with Leisure World in Laguna Hills made early history. Borders was instrumental in master planning for the City of Cypress, and has left an imprint all over Orange County in residential and commercial projects, from apartments and condominiums, spas and restaurants, to shopping centers and financial institutions.

The company penned the plans for the remodeling of Via Lido Plaza, Wendy's restaurants, Newport Mesa Christian Center, American Savings Computer Center, and a 600-acre camp in the San Jacinto Mountains for the Girl Scout Council. The state and U.S. governments have employed Borders' services, and recently the

firm assumed planning for 75,000 square feet of interior space for Columbia Pictures. The footage features a triangular shape with projection and screening rooms, and required a flexibility of design that would allow for easy reconfiguring of the space to meet special needs.

Expertise in planning, remodeling, and interior designing for savings and loans has culminated in the firm's latest project: headquarters for Butterfield Savings in Santa Ana. To reflect the association's new directions, Borders designed an elegant and contemporary office space with custom furnishings and complementing graphics, thereby providing a full-service package to the client.

It is no surprise that the firm bears many awards for its efforts, among them City Beautiful Awards from Santa Monica and Glendale and the American Savings Plaza Master Award. Borders, a member of the AIA, is registered to practice in California, Arizona, Wyoming, Michigan, and Nevada, and sits on the architectural advisory board of several local colleges.

Borders fuels the morale of his employees with a zesty sense of humor and claims, "We're all important to-

One of the firm's projects was the Laguna Federal Savings and Loan Association's headquarters in Laguna Hills.

Robert Borders, founder.

gether. We're one big team." Perhaps it is the easy-going atmosphere that keeps the employee turnover rate so low. Don Richmond and Joe Petitpas go back a long way in the company, and other principals, Dick Bannister and Steve Tiner, are backbone to the structure. Boasting a wealth of ideas, decades-old clients, and veteran staff members, Robert Borders and Associates just keeps rolling along.

TAYLOR BUS SERVICE

Taylor Bus contracts with sixty school districts, busing students to and from school and on chartered field trips.

Taylor Bus Service is a school and charter bus transportation company that originated thirty-seven years ago in Orange County from a simple good neighbor act. A woman, with a small handicapped child needing to be driven to therapy sessions, graciously offered to drive a neighbor's child who also required treatment. Soon she had located several handicapped children in the neighborhood, and in order to transport them all, she bought a station wagon. When a second vehicle was needed, she made a deal with the local parents, bought another wagon, and hired a driver.

That woman, Mrs. Taylor, expanded her act of goodwill into a full-fledged busing operation, servicing special-education programs for the handicapped, developing a large charter operation, and increasing the fleet from two station wagons to 100 buses. After twenty-three years of running the bus service, she sold the company to a Japanese syndicate based in Hawaii, and in 1972 the business was purchased by its present owner, Tom Berthold.

Today Taylor Bus Service is the largest privately owned bus contractor in the country. Its over 1,300 vehicles include small vans equipped to carry several wheelchairs and passengers, economy transit buses for youth activities and shuttles, and deluxe highway coaches. The firm contracts with sixty school districts and public agencies in eleven western states. The charter service also accommodates groups such as the Boy Scouts, Leisure World, and church groups. Taylor Bus will even suggest fun places for groups to visit. Shopping tours with a lunch or dinner stop, and excursions to Tahoe, Reno, and Northern California wineries represent just a few of the routes traveled by the company.

Fourteen facilities within the state, including the corporate office in Anaheim, maintain full repair, servicing, and washing capabilities. Qualified mechanics are on duty from 5:30 a.m. to 11 p.m. Fixing potential problems before they become reality, and careful inspections have earned Taylor Bus the lowest road failure rate in the nation for any sizable fleet operator. Although California has stricter requirements than most states for school bus drivers, Taylor employees complete an additional eighty hours of training, a comprehensive program instrumental in maintaining its status as the lowest-accident-rate contract carrier in the state.

The privately owned company has 1,100 employees who are kept informed of policy and work toward a common goal of responsible and safe transportation. In an industry where turnover is generally high, Berthold hasn't lost a manager in ten years. He believes he has a good crew of people and that his prices are competitive. As a result, the firm is ready to roll into a few new states. A school district contract in Atlanta, Georgia, heads the list of new territories for the growing Taylor Bus Service.

Taylor Bus Service offers chartered excursions to points of interest, with stopovers at famous eating places such as the Reuben E. Lee in Newport Beach.

IRVINE RANCH FARMER'S MARKETS

Eating an apple need never be an ordinary experience again. Jon Hubbard, owner of the Irvine Ranch Farmer's Markets, has spent the last two-plus decades building a produce market phenomenon that has turned shopping for fruits and vegetables into an incomparable blending of eye and appetite, transforming one open-air fruit stand into a string of marketplaces for exotic and luscious foods.

Jon Hubbard's family has been cultivating in Orange County since 1890, first on their own land in Fountain Valley, and then as tenant farmers on a 1,000-acre spread of the Irvine Ranch. As a youngster, Jon pulled a red wagon door to door in Corona del Mar, selling ripe strawberries and fresh asparagus for nineteen cents a pound. When the Hubbards opened an eight- by twelve-foot lean-to to sell edibles roadside, Jon helped out to raise money for law school. The stand was so successful that managing it and the farm captured Jon's favor over jurisprudence, and, thus, a tradition was begun.

In 1971 the first free-standing Irvine Ranch Farmer's Market opened in Irvine with an orientation toward natural foods and, of course, the sale of the finest produce available. By 1976 the growing health and fitness craze was becoming a way of life and was not without influence in the food industry. Hubbard sensed the middle- to upper-income wage earners were searching for good food just as he was searching for a particular emphasis for his carefully tended market. The idea to combine natural and gourmet foods hit like a thunderbolt, and, seizing the creative image, Hubbard added a butcher, a baker, international foods, and a visual drama to his nine markets that is worth beholding.

No fewer than 600 varieties of produce, artfully piled in color-coordinated aisles, permit Hubbard's statement, "We offer everything that Mother Nature grows." In addition to prize-winning specimens of the expected apples, tomatoes, and squashes, the bins display French green beans, Italian broccoli, Finnish potatoes, and Chinese gooseberries. Cactus leaves, plantains, and peppers in four colors are the norm, and there are more kinds of mushrooms than most people know exist.

Assisting Hubbard in market operations are his father, Jack Hubbard, who serves as corporate supervisor; his mother, Sylvia Hubbard, credit manager; and his sister, Kathy, vice-president. A brother-in-law and several nieces and nephews, from box boys to managers, see to it that only the freshest produce gets sold. Corn purchased at the ranch market in the afternoon was probably picked in the field that morning. After twelve hours the Hubbards take the corn off the stands, as the sugar turns to starch and the corn is no longer sweet.

Most of the produce comes directly from the Irvine Ranch or is trucked in daily from the San Joaquin Valley. Each night produce buyers are at the Los Angeles Terminal Market picking the choicest fruits. They often phone Hubbard in the early hours of the morning for his advice on selections.

Chancing a new concept, Hubbard agreed to open a market on the ground floor of an eight-story shopping mall in West Hollywood called the Beverly Center. What seems like acres of produce initially meet the shopper's eye, followed by vistas of gourmet groceries and seventy-four feet of meat cases, which house prime beef, lamb, and pork cuts; 150 varieties of seafood from the distant waters of Chile, Spain, and New Zealand; and poultry specialties that include pheasant, quail, squab, and Canadian geese. Three hundred wine labels range from the modest Gallos to $199-a-bottle Reserve Cabernet. Several hundred cheeses arranged by country of origin are often the substance of customer samples. At the Irvine Ranch Farmer's Market, perishables account for well over half of total sales, compared to less than 25 percent at regular stores.

In addition to the pasta primavera (one of sixty Italian salads) and chocolate-covered strawberries, the L.A. branch market adds another extravagance, transporting groceries by conveyor belt up to the second-level parking lot, where, at the flash of a claim check, attendants hustle shopping bags into customers' cars. Refrigeration units keep foods cold

while patrons tend to other shopping errands, and a valet is also available.

Instrumental in refining the success of the Beverly Center market are what Hubbard calls the "real experts"—the customers. Patrons, appalled at the thought of a second shopping (and parking) stop, asked for the general necessity items usually left to other stores. To meet that request Hubbard eased into an inventory of a few frozen foods, soft drinks, and paper goods, although he will

A tradition was established with this Hubbard family vegetable stand in Irvine. Photo circa 1960

not acquiesce on the sale of cigarettes.

From a special brand of New York cold cut to a place to sit and have a sandwich, Hubbard has listened and implemented the ideas of his patrons. The L.A. branch market, sales leader of the nine stores, on a good Saturday moves 10,000 ears of corn and 4,400 pounds of grapes, and approaches $360,000 in weekly sales.

Hubbard's most glorious fete to date is the Mediterranean-style market at the Atrium Court in Newport Beach. The 63,000-square-foot showplace evolved after Hubbard's visits to Harrod's in London; and markets in Paris, Munich, and Berlin also provided inspiration. Interlaced with the gourmet food stands is an array of concessions for dining on the premises. One can choose from sushi, Mandarin Chinese or Mexican food, or a salad bar. There are vintage wines on tap, freshly squeezed juices, and a soda shop offering cherry sodas, sorbetto, tofutti, gelatto, and homemade ice cream. Sweet fanciers will find a Belgian chocolate shop and a French bakery with twenty-five types of truffles. The presence of a flower shop and a Ma Cuisine cooking school, with classes by renowned chefs from around the world, delight and surprise shoppers. The cosmopolitan market idea drew skepticism from some initially, but traffic to the center has increased 20 percent since its opening. Sales for the first six months peaked at ten million dollars.

Entrepreneurial grocers nationwide have come to gawk, take notes, and carry ideas back home. Developers in New York, Colorado, and Texas court Hubbard for future prospects in their own states. *Progressive Grocer* listed Irvine Ranch Farmer's Market

Irvine Ranch Farmer's Markets' first venture into a shopping mall was in the eight-story Beverly Center in West Hollywood.

One of the most glorious markets to date is in the Atrium Court building in Fashion Island, Newport Beach.

on its 1985 Honor Roll of Outstanding Independents, and *Time* magazine called the Beverly Center branch one of the "world's most glorious supermarkets, with a breathtaking produce section."

Hubbard repeats with fervor that the market's image and prime profit maker is produce, and adheres to strict standards on the fundamentals. "We're not trying to be anything but a farmer's market with a lot of goodies and fun things on top," he says. Hubbard is a man enjoying his proud accomplishments, and is content with one new store per year so as not to expand faster than quality control will allow. And for now he is content just to build in his local homeland, Southern California.

COVINGTON TECHNOLOGIES

Originating in Anaheim as Manco Development in 1962, Covington Technologies has metamorphosed from a modest contracting company to a major real estate development and technological firm. The two Covington brothers got started in business in 1958 by selling both their homes and using the equity to buy several small lots. The construction of four-unit buildings on the lots provided the brothers with a home, as well as income from the rental of the other three units, popularizing a concept known as "home and income building."

Today Covington offers the owner-investor of a home and income unit a complete optional package of services that includes on-site management, accounting services, grounds maintenance, and unit rental. Renters can choose from among diverse floor plans and elevations, and each unit features a full line of amenities. The company's attention to detail and adherence to a policy of quality construction has made it one of the country's largest four-plex developers, and has made the name "Covington" synonymous with well-built four-plex units.

The year 1968 witnessed a name change to The Covington Brothers, and in 1972 the transition from a private to a publicly held company was completed.

Covington entered the affordable housing market in 1975 and has since satisfied thousands of home owners throughout California, Arizona, and Nevada with quality, well designed single-family homes, condominiums, and income-producing units.

Cobblestone Village, a development of single-family homes in Sunnymead, attracted 287 buyers for the affordably priced homes before the project had its grand opening. The development captured the National Grand Award from *Professional*

Builder Magazine in the prestigious "Smarter House for the Money" competition.

Another example of Covington's diverse product types is the Oasis Country Club development in Palm Desert—an innovative, dream-come-true, resort home complex, environed among golf greens, tennis courts, and desert sunsets. A lavish clubhouse hosts an elegant restaurant and a pro shop. This exemplary development received five distinguised Major Achievements in Merchandising Excellence (MAME) awards from the Building Industry Association.

President Robert B. Fitzpatrick (left) and chairman Loran D. Covington.

The name "Covington" has become synonymous with well-built four-plex units.

The emergence of Covintec U.S.A., the manufacturing and product sales division of the firm, prompted a name change to Covington Brothers Technologies. Covintec produces the innovative Therml Impac Panel, an economical building component that integrates structural integrity, insulation, sound absorption, and fire-resistant properties. The panels reached peak production in this country when the price of lumber materials skyrocketed. The panel, however, is most cost effective when competing against masonry products. The company has sold machinery packages for the manufacture of its Therml Impac Panel to groups in China, England, Venezuela, Mexico, and Korea; and interestingly, the steel wire forms used in producing

the panels are popular in the fashion industry for use as display props.

In 1981 the company was renamed Covington Technologies. Loran D. Covington presides as chairman of the board, and Robert B. Fitzpatrick serves as president. Their team leadership continually addresses the implementation of high standards in affordable housing. This commitment to quality has resulted in a solid reputation with the consumer as well as with joint-venture partners.

In addition to its corporate headquarters in Fullerton, the firm maintains offices in Orange County, Los Angeles, San Diego, Rialto, Palm Desert, and Sacramento.

DYNAMIC AIR ENGINEERING, INC.

In 1942 the United States Air Force urgently needed a compact, lightweight, high-pressure fan for the first aircraft gasoline combustion heater required on the new B-25 and A-26 aircraft. Dynamic Air Engineering came into being with its design and production of the required air-moving machine, meeting specifications of airflow pressure, space, weight, power input, and satisfactory operation from sea level to 25,000 feet, which no other fan or blower on the market at that time could do. Dynamic's high-efficiency, high-pressure Vaneaxial aircraft fan, involving a unique propeller design and a new type of motor, proved to be exactly what the Air Force needed.

In the four decades since then Dynamic Air Engineering has designed and manufactured thousands of high-pressure axial flow fans in varied configurations and performance requirements for the aircraft, missile, and electronics industries. In addition, the firm contributes to technological improvements for seagoing vessels,

Dynamic Air Engineering is headquartered in Santa Ana.

ground support equipment, and weather reconnaissance units at altitudes above 100,000 feet.

With the evolution of pressurized aircraft, new problems of in-flight and ground heating, cooling, and defogging of flight-deck windows needed solving. Dynamic Air specialized in the development of a lightweight and economical air-conditioning system for executive aircraft such as Cessna's 340 and 310 and Beech's Baron. The electrically driven unit, which cools and dehumidifies simultaneously, is housed conveniently behind the bulkhead, not in the engine compartment, and the separation of the condenser and evaporator allows for easy removal for winter weight reduction. The system is as light as sixty-three pounds, accommodating a small, twin-engine plane or four-place helicopter. The company's proximity to John Wayne, Fullerton, Van Nuys, and Burbank airports permits installation and service assistance on-site.

Since its wartime beginning, the firm has maintained a leadership position in solving environmental problems related to pressurization. To assure optimum performance and re-

liability, Dynamic Air manufactures all of the motors, fans, blowers, and housings for its systems. A design review team takes advantage of new technology for product improvement, such as increased weight reduction, and runs tests on the new models in its engineering laboratory.

Dynamic Air has designed and manufactured custom air-conditioning systems for new commuter aircraft for American and European customers.

Overseeing the challenging and changing technological business is the firm's president, Nancy Glascock, whose stint with Dynamic Air began in 1942. Hired as the company's first secretary/bookkeeper, she worked her way up to the vice-presidency. After sixteen years of decision making alongside the corporation's founder, Harry Glascock, she married "Papa G," as he was called. When he passed away in 1972, Nancy assumed the presidency. A compliment to the couple's sound guidance, Dynamic Air Engineering is credited with using sound engineering experience to modify specifications and thus greatly improve the thermal efficiency of thousands of air-moving systems.

ST. JOHN KNITS

In 1962 a young woman named Marie St. John announced her engagement to Bob Gray. As a means of funding their honeymoon trip to Hawaii, Marie, an accomplished knitter, suggested to Bob, a fashion salesman, that he attempt to sell fifty of her dresses to pay for the trip. The idea resulted from Marie's appearance on the "Queen for a Day" television show where a contestant won a knitting machine. Marie gave the machine the once-over and decided to invest in one for herself. The orders she drew for her dress designs from envious friends sparked the idea to market a small quantity.

Skeptical but willing, Bob approached a buyer for Bullock's Wilshire and sold thirty-six dresses. The same day he sold forty-eight more to another store. Instead of being pleased with the orders for eighty-four dresses, Marie actually wept, estimating that it would take her a full year to fill the orders.

Encouraged, however, by the success of the impulse idea, the couple, despite each working at full-time positions, tackled their spontaneous entrepreneurship, enlisting the help of Marie's parents and the use of Bob's mother's garage to launch their own designer knits company. With a payroll of two, one knitter and one crocheter, the neophyte business, dubbed St. John Knits, began.

In the formative years the St. John image focused on a few simple and classic styles. All the knitting was done on one type of knitting machine, and the handwork was crafted with only one stitch. Today up to five types of knitting machines are employed, and dozens of handwork stitches provide superb detailing. With a design crew hovering around twenty, St. John Knits premieres four fashion collections each year. The timeless designs are seldom repeated, and each season's selections, all of fine yarns and colors, complement

The Irvine headquarters of St. John Knits.

Marie Gray, co-owner and designer for St. John Knits, turned her knitting skills into an internationally acclaimed high-fashion industry.

the previous designs without outdating them.

A consistent facet of the business since its first day and dress is the care that goes into each garment, making St. John Knits a very special purchase. The yarns combine wool and rayon, and the comfort and durability stem from a construction technique of knitting each dress piece individually to a desired pattern shape, rather than cutting the piece from knitted fabric. The pieces are crocheted together, not sewn, and the highlighting final trims are crocheted into the finished garment. Each dress reflects Marie's concept of what a St. John Knit should be—chic, comfortable, and durable.

In the world of contemporary fashion, heads turn to glimpse St. John ensembles. The meticulously crafted originals make their debut quarterly in the high-ticket fashion stores of Saks Fifth Avenue, Neiman-Marcus, I. Magnin, and Nordstrom. The multimillion-dollar company has showrooms in Orange County, New York, Chicago, and Dallas, and a glance at the sales ledgers shows accounts in Switzerland, Germany, England, and Japan.

St. John's resemblance to a clothing empire is the direct result of the courage, skill, and plain old-fashioned hard work of the Grays over the years. Marie's bold and intuitive sense of color and sleek line design, in tandem with Bob's astute marketing and business expertise, have groomed the onetime garage operation into one of the nation's fashion pacesetters.

Each year has proven progressively bigger and better for St. John Knits, despite little advertising in the early years and no on-the-road salesmen. The firm's reputation evolved out of a commitment to customer satisfaction, not quantity sales, and from exposure in fine stores where fashion ideas radiate.

Nowadays St. John Knits are portrayed in fashion and social maga-

This slim, classic, three-piece suit is the hallmark of St. John.

A typical St. John knitting factory.

zines. Like the product, the advertisements need few words. The elegance of design and color reflect innovative styling, rich detail, and subtle ornamentation that need no explanation. The once strictly classic styles have expanded to include garments for the younger career woman, evening wear, and a line of sweaters for men. St. John Knits also manufactures its own belts, buckles, and buttons, and may expand to include accessories and children's clothing in the future.

In addition to rearing a phenomenally successful business, the Grays have also managed to raise a family, and it looks as though the company will remain in familiar hands for a long time to come. Son Michael, who has been with the firm for ten years, functions as the executive vice-president. Daughter Kelly is the exclusive photography model for St.

John apparel.

The family input is strong, cohesive, and vivacious. The Grays perpetuate nothing-but-success teamwork for the 24-year-old business. The more informal family of St. John Knits includes a grand total of 1,300 workers in production plants in San Ysidro, the San Fernando Valley, Orange County, Los Angeles, and San Diego. The corporate office is located in Irvine.

What's the toughest aspect of the fashion business? According to the Grays it is keeping abreast of women's taste. That is a challenge, certainly, but no stumbling block for the forces behind St. John Knits, a carefully supervised, adeptly run business that promises an exciting future of still larger, more creative endeavors that continue to be well received in the fashion industry.

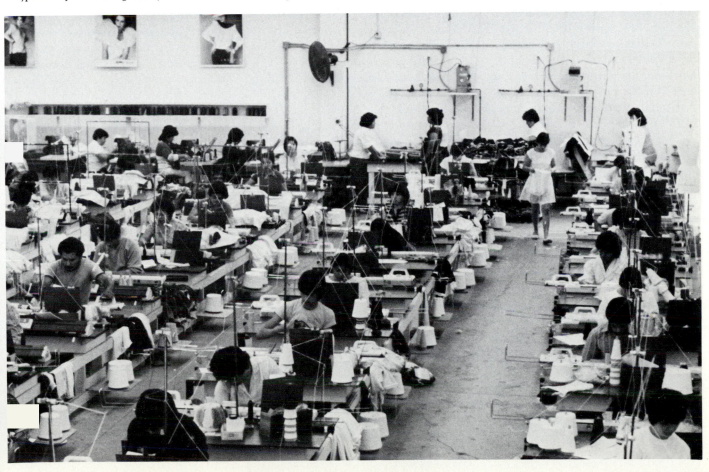

OSTERKAMP TRUCKING INC.

From a one-man hay-hauling service for dairymen, to a $20-million contract carrier transportation concern, Anthony "Gus" Osterkamp has fueled success into his trucking enterprise with a straightforward philosophy: "Give the customer whatever it is he wants." That philosophy, combined with plenty of hard work, has accompanied his step-by-step growth to a highly respected plateau in the trucking industry.

The youngest of ten children of Dutch immigrant parents, Osterkamp survived jostling rides on the family dairy trucks beginning at the age of nine months. At the age of three, his older brothers awakened him in the early morning hours to steer a hay truck through the fields, and at age six, he drove his first truck-trailer.

With an understandable adeptness for handling trucks, Osterkamp passed class one licensing at age eighteen. With only a used Kenworth truck, he began a business hauling hay for local dairymen. As demand increased, the Kenworth became collateral for the purchase of three sets of flatbed trailers, and two owner-operators were hired. By the late 1960s eleven sets of flatbeds, six tractors, and three owner-operators served the venture's first major client, U.S. Gypsum Company, and annual revenues passed the million-dollar mark.

The size of the fleet continued to grow, as did the number of client accounts. Presently, hundreds of Osterkamp's flatbeds and hi-cube vans

(maximum-load trucks) haul building materials, lumber, paper and forest products, glass bottles, and general commodities through forty-eight states for companies such as Certainteed Corporation, Kimberly Clark, Weyerhaeuser, U.S. Gypsum, Masonite Corporation, and Kerr Glass Manufacturing Company. Central dispatch works out of Orange, with other strategic terminal sites in Chowchilla, El Centro, and Ukiah, California.

The high momentum of vice-president and general manager Fred Steiner, comptroller Gene Segrist, and operations manager Cliff Phillips exemplifies Osterkamp's belief that the trucking concern has progressed because of knowledgeable management and teamwork from within. The 150 owner-operators paid to haul Osterkamp Trucking trailers have a vested interest in the success of operations and therefore take pride in

Anthony H. Osterkamp, Jr. (better known as Gus), president of Osterkamp Trucking Inc., directs the firm's operations from its terminal in Orange.

the equipment, treat the customers well, and maintain a high safety record on the road. Customers stay with the firm because it acquires the right equipment to satisfy their needs, and talented people at all levels of operation continue this commitment.

Gus Osterkamp eagerly faces the challenges created by deregulation in 1980. As vice-president of the California Trucking Association, he is involved with legislative issues and new ideas that will benefit both the trucking industry and consumers. He is chairman of the Size and Weights Committee and a member of the board of directors of the American Trucking Association Irregular Route Common Carrier Conference.

The aura of Gus Osterkamp's firm is that of a highly service-oriented business, priding itself on the people involved with it. Directed by a man with plenty of know-how, it's a company with feeling and dedication that performs a cut above its competition.

"Gus" Osterkamp in front of the truck his father, Tony, used to haul hay to his dairy from local Orange County farmers.

COLDWELL BANKER

Colbert Coldwell and Benjamin Banker solidified a business partnership in 1913. They were brought together by a mutual respect for each other's admirable skills in the real estate market and successful honest dealings.

Coldwell, at the time of the San Francisco earthquake, was working for a real estate firm. The quake had caused an agitation in property buying and selling, and Coldwell resolved to start a business that would deal squarely with customers rather than pocketing huge profits by taking advantage of the uninformed—a rampant practice in the real estate field at the time.

Combining business acumen with two associates, the firm of Tucker, Lynch & Coldwell opened for real estate services at 53 Post Street in 1906. Two years later Benjamin Banker entered California to sell meat-slicing machines for a Chicago concern. He quickly recognized the potential in real estate sales and made the transition.

When Coldwell and Banker met, they took a liking to each other, and Coldwell offered Banker a position.

He soon became Coldwell's leading salesman. In fact, his commissions were so high that Coldwell offered Banker a partnership in order to share the company expenses as well as the profits. Partners Tucker and Lynch eventually sold out to Coldwell and Banker.

By continuing a policy of not competing with its customers, Coldwell Banker became the most respected firm in the West. Adhering to ethics while making money for others in turn brought great financial resources to aid in the company's growth. The first Los Angeles branch opened in 1922. By 1928 the firm had reached its twenty-third year, despite a natural disaster and uncertainties of the times. It now boasted five offices—three in Northern California, two in the South.

The 1930s and 1940s brought drastic economic changes everywhere and Coldwell Banker was no exception. But the company had met the challenges of the time and continued to stay solvent and successful by flexibility, determination, and leadership.

By the 1960s Coldwell Banker had not only assumed domination over the northern part of California but over the Los Angeles area as well. This was prodded by the acquisition of a major Southern California real estate company, Forest E. Olson. Coldwell Banker went on to acquire other firms and is now the largest full-service real estate company in the country. In addition to the residential brokerage services, Coldwell Banker offers escrow, mortgage, title, and insurance services.

In 1981 a new turn accentuated Coldwell Banker in the American marketplace. The firm was acquired by Sears, Roebuck and Co., allowing Sears to offer a wealth of services to consumers in the area of real estate, and providing Coldwell Banker with representation in the Sears Financial Network Centers nationwide. The merging is a boon for home buyers who can take advantage of the Sears Home Buyers Savings Program. A similar program for sellers was recently developed, offering substantial savings and advice to sellers from Sears and other companies.

As Coldwell Banker continues to grow, so do the challenges. But the successful visions, strength of leadership, and high ideals of Colbert Coldwell and Benjamin Banker have left a legacy that still prevails within the company today.

Colbert Coldwell, a co-founder of Tucker, Lynch & Coldwell—the San Francisco predecessor of Coldwell Banker.

Benjamin Arthur Banker joined the firm in 1913 and within the year became a full partner.

383

FORSUM/SUMMERS & PARTNERS

You might say Forsum/Summers & Partners is in the business of "land art," since the landscape architectural firm envisions, drafts, and sculpts aesthetic exterior environs to enhance model homes, high rises, industrial and recreational parks, golf courses, and master-planned communities. From sprinkler and shrubbery selection to fences and fountains, the four-man partnership combines sound knowledge of water, soil, and climate in its softscapes, with artistic sensitivity in well-chosen hardscapes. From the firm's office in Dana Point, design plans have taken shape for developers, builders, cities, and communities, both in and outside California, since 1969.

In the early 1960s, when Rey Forsum formed R.W. Forsum Associates, the bulk of the company's business stemmed from Leisure World in Laguna Hills. The 3,000-acre project called for layouts of recreational clubhouses, tennis courts, bowling greens, and equestrian trails. To meet the water needs of the development project, Forsum implemented an innovative irrigation system, which at the time was the largest automatic system of its kind.

As demand for the company's expertise in water systems and landscape design grew outside the county, the partnership expanded to include its current members, John Summers,

The firm's expertise enhances the entry to this private residential community in San Clemente, California. Courtesy, Renee Carver

Jim Pekarske, and Pat Murphy. The division of duties within the firm falls neatly to each partner's individual expertise, from preliminary conceptual design through cost estimating, implementation, and supervision, to plant material selection and irrigation analysis. This collaboration of strengths provides clients with comprehensive architectural and consulting services.

All in a day's work for Forsum/Summers & Partners is mapping the layout of converging streets on a given tract, and then designing them with lights, entry walls and gates, benches, and plant materials. Public and private gardens benefit from the firm's counsel on fountains, trellises, walkways, pool design, and sculptures—always designed in-house.

The architectural group's influence is more subtly appreciated in slopes requiring extensive erosion control, irrigation design, and the selection of

The four partners in the landscape architecture firm are (left to right) Pat Murphy, Rey Forsum, John Summers, and Jim Pekarske.

environmentally compatible plant materials. A Xeriscape Award—for preservation of water through choice of drought-tolerant plants—from the California Landscape Contractors Association, M.A.M.E. awards from the Building Industry Association, and Professional Landscape of the Year Award from the California Landscape and Irrigation Council spotlight the long-running reputation of Forsum/Summers & Partners and its out-of-doors artistry.

The veranda of this residential estate in Tustin Hills overlooks a fourteen-foot-high Carrara marble statue and formal pool with fountain. The landscape architecture was designed by Forsum/Summers & Partners. Courtesy, Renee Carver

NEAR-CAL CORPORATION

Since 1964 Near-Cal Corporation has carried on a tradition of construction in Orange County. Four generations of the Johnson family have labored, managed, and administered in the construction industry. Originally from the New Jersey area, third-generation builder and chairman of the board Harold "Hap" Johnson moved to California after serving as a commander with the Army Corps of Engineers during World War II. He founded Near-Cal Corporation in Santa Ana and, with a team of dedicated people experienced in preplanning through assignment completion, has built many commercial, industrial, and public facilities in Orange County.

The Near-Cal philosophy is an ad-

Harold "Hap" Johnson (second from left), founder and chairman of the board, with sons (left to right) Carl, president since 1983; Dwight, vice-president/field operations; and Donald, superintendent.

herence to projected schedules and budgets, utilizing high-grade materials and qualified craftsmen. That is a commitment not to be broken by fourth-generation brothers Carl Johnson, president of the company since 1983; Dwight Johnson, vice-president/field operations; and Donald Johnson, superintendent. Part of Near-Cal's secret is to hire quality superintendents who are on the site full time, and to back them up in the office with a team of experienced project managers and job coordinators who handle all the necessary paperwork that pertains to the project. They follow this up with weekly superintendents' meetings, and separate weekly meetings with the owner and architect to go over the job and to troubleshoot any unforeseen problems.

Near-Cal's longevity stems from

Downey Savings, one of many repeat clients for Near-Cal Corporation of Anaheim.

being competitive in the marketplace, with 70 percent of the firm's business coming from bid-type situations. Very often Near-Cal's participation begins with the conception of a project, working with the owner and architect to help with cost and design restrictions. Remodelings, additions, and complexes for supermarkets, medical offices, banks, motels, and shopping centers, such as Harbor Plaza in Fountain Valley, show the company's diversity. Columbia Savings and Loan, Downey Savings and Loan, GTE, and Southern California Edison are all repeat customers for the business, which has been centered in Anaheim since 1973. Future growth looks promising for Near-Cal, with annual sales in excess of twenty million dollars.

President Carl Johnson is a member of the American Society of Civil Engineers. He also serves on the board of directors of the local chapter of the Associated General Contractors, and is instrumental in trying to set up a project management program at UCI for graduate students in the civil engineering department.

BUENA PARK LUMBER AND HARDWARE

Arni Nelson, founder of Buena Park Lumber and Hardware, with son Richard in the early 1900s in Buena Park. Nelson's original business was a bicycle shop.

When visiting Buena Park Lumber and Hardware, don't be misled. The sprawling home center on Beach Boulevard, between Manchester and Orangethorpe, didn't always look like it does now. The lumberyard was conceived by Icelandic immigrant Arni Nelson in 1904 as a small but efficient bicycle shop nestled in a tiny farm village now known as Buena Park. Situated on Grand Avenue (now Beach Boulevard), the store carried ice cream as well as bicycles.

The business flourished, and Nelson, infused with optimism, decided wisely to expand and relocate his business less than a block south to the Old Lily Creamery, today a historic site. It was there that the foundation for one of the Southland's most noted lumberyards was laid.

Business continued to prosper as Nelson became immersed in the lumber trade. He married and had a son, Richard, the first heir to Buena Park Lumber. Horse-drawn wagons transported timber from San Pedro Harbor and Anaheim Landing. Electricity brought a new and dynamic dimension to business and industry everywhere, including the yard. A mill was added around 1914, expanding not only its volume, but also its reputation. Southern Pacific Railroad installed a spur track in the yard for easier access to valuable lumber cargoes from the Pacific Northwest.

The 1920s and 1930s saw change abound in Buena Park. As the demographics of the area evolved, so did Buena Park Lumber. Arni later sold the yard to Richard, who, having grown up at the core of the yard's operations, possessed a great deal of business acumen.

By the mid-1920s father and son owned and operated a hardware store, lumberyard, and bean warehouse, all of which were merged by the end of the decade. During those years almost limitless energy and productivity punctuated the lives of both men. Though Richard's life was steeped in the activities of a lumber and hardware business, he devoted a generous portion of every day to his family that included his wife, Ellen, and their sons, Jim and Bud.

The 1940s saw continued growth, particularly with the introduction of plywood into the marketplace. Richard's two sons showed promise in following in the footsteps of their father and grandfather, and by the 1950s brothers Jim and Richard "Bud" Nelson had assumed ownership of the store. When the Santa Ana Freeway and Disneyland opened, thousands of visitors entered the county daily, adding to the firm's business. Soon Buena Park Lumber would enlarge its premises, its payroll, and its profits.

The company was a modernized lumber and hardware firm by the 1960s, catering to the industrial and contracting markets. Computerization achieved more efficiency, but did not help with the need for more space. After the Nelson family purchased the abandoned Uddo Taurmino Cannery next door, the firm expanded and opened its doors to an airier, much larger facility in 1976. A special contractor's sales office was added, targeting an identifiably important market: professional builders.

By the 1970s Buena Park Lumber and Hardware had become a corporation, but was still painstakingly tended by the Nelsons. Beginning in 1976 nearly each year was climaxed by the company winning the industry's Home Center of the Year Award. The store was remodeled in 1984, and is today a 22,000-square-foot visual feast for its shoppers.

The Nelsons, with their penchant for turn-of-the-century antiques, have created an unparalleled shopping environment for their customers that seems almost noncommercial. Ornate carvings, railroad memorabilia, and timeworn lanterns and flasks have been arranged decoratively throughout the store. Shades of Buena Park's history appear everywhere with the use of dramatic facades, displays, and dioramas. As one of the county's oldest and most reputable lumber and hardware centers, Buena Park Lumber and Hardware stands singularly apart from the chain home centers so prevalent today.

The Nelsons, Arni and son, Richard, had a hardware store, lumberyard, and bean warehouse in operation at the time of this late 1940s photograph.

NORTHROP CORPORATION

"Anaheim's quest for additional industry to bolster its economy reached a new goal today when Northrop Aircraft Company announced plans to build a branch factory in Anaheim. . . . "

So began a story in the *Anaheim Bulletin* of June 20, 1951, the first public announcement that Northrop would move a major production unit to Orange County. This was the first aerospace firm to locate in the county, then predominantly a farming and orange-growing community.

Northrop's decision to expand and to build the Electro-Mechanical Division resulted from a major government contract to produce optical range finders for the U.S. Ordnance Corps. Bulldozers immediately began clearing the land, and construction was rushed because of the pressure of the Korean War.

Northrop Aircraft Company, Inc., was formed in 1939 to produce aircraft needed by the Allies in World War II. Its founder, John Knudsen Northrop, proved his multidimensional engineering talents early with such achievements as the design of a

small sport biplane with foldaway wings, the *Vega;* the world's fastest military seaplane; the first all-wing plane; and the famed *Black Widow* night fighter.

Although it started in aircraft production, the company—which became Northrop Corporation—expanded into the design, development, and manufacture of electronic components and systems. Now part of Northrop's Electronics Systems Group, the Electro-Mechanical Division has become a major designer and producer of sophisticated passive sensor systems that greatly expand the usefulness and combat effectiveness of helicopters, missiles, and aircraft by enabling them to track and identify objects under adverse conditions.

Northrop's Electro-Mechanical Division also supplies the U.S. Navy's Fleet Ballistic Missile programs with test and readiness units which are used on the *Polaris, Poseidon,* and *Trident* submarines. Over the years division employees have won over twenty-two commendations and quality awards for their work on these programs. Since the opening of the Anaheim facility in 1951, more than 3,000 jobs have been created in the community.

John K. Northrop, pioneer aircraft designer, standing in front of the B-35 Flying Wing.

Northrop Corporation is now a diversified advanced technology company, specializing in the fields of aircraft and electronics. Based in Los Angeles, the firm employs 47,000 people and its worldwide operations extend into seventy countries.

Northrop's F-5 fighter is the most widely used American supersonic aircraft in the world. The company's newest fighter is the multirole F-20 *Tigershark,* and it has proven itself to be the most reliable and maintainable supersonic tactical fighter aircraft in the world. Northrop is also the principal subcontractor for the revolutionary F/A-18 strike fighter. The U.S. Air Force selected Northrop as the prime contractor for research and development of the Advanced Technology Bomber.

Northrop Corporation's Electro-Mechanical Division in Anaheim in 1959, then known as Northrop Nortronics.

STEINBRUGGE, THOMAS & BLOOM, INC.

The task of a structural engineer, stated simply by John Steinbrugge, is this: "We make buildings stand up." Not so simple is the deciphering of engineering and dynamics problems inherent to today's complex building projects. The 22-year-old firm of Steinbrugge, Thomas & Bloom, Inc., intrinsically designs earthquake stability into new and old structures of modest to monumental size. Housing facilities, athletic clubs, churches, and shopping centers nationwide incorporate the exacting elements of ST&B's structural planning. Waterfronts, bridges, banks, and a 76-story commercial building illustrate its successful strategies.

Schooled at Oregon State University, John Steinbrugge joined a firm in Long Beach shortly after World War II. In 1950 innovative work on a lima bean-processing plant for the Irvine Ranch brought him to Orange County, where he solved one of his first engineering puzzles.

Today Steinbrugge and his partners, Donald Thomas, a USC graduate, and William Bloom, a graduate of California State Polytechnic University, work conjunctively with civil

John Steinbrugge, founder of Steinbrugge, Thomas & Bloom, Inc., a structural engineering firm, has contributed to the design of many Orange County building projects such as Douglas Plaza, South Coast Repertory, and the Crystal Cathedral.

and geotechnical engineers, mechanical engineers, and architects on some of the county's most impressive structures, collaborating on columns, beams, floors, and roofs. Devising the curtain wall portion or exterior cladding of buildings is one of the firm's fortes.

ST&B designed the glass-and-aluminum covering for the Crystal Cathedral, meeting the challenging criteria of preventing the fall of the glass in the event of an earthquake. In Brea, The Union Oil Company

contracted with ST&B for its $30-million research center.

The firm's consultations on structural designs have served architects in all fifty states and in Arabia, Indonesia, Panama, Honduras, and Japan. ST&B has contributed specialized planning to over three billion dollars worth of construction. The company's experience in research and design has led to its active participation in the Earthquake Engineering Research Institute and the American Arbitration Association, which requires serving on a panel to hear two sides of a construction issue and determining a resolution.

The 25-man staff of Steinbrugge, Thomas & Bloom, Inc., looks to a future of designing larger and increasingly complex structural assignments. Noting that its business publicity is scarce unless a building falls down, the Newport Beach structural engineering firm is content to maintain a behind-the-scenes profile.

A recent project of Steinbrugge, Thomas & Bloom, Inc., is the Laguna Hills Financial Office Building.

Construction of the Irvine Bean Growers' building in 1949 brought John Steinbrugge to Orange County.

CENTURY AMERICAN CORPORATION

Century American Corporation is an Orange County-based real estate development company. Roger C. Hobbs, president, grew up in the city that is now home to his business, and, like his parents before him, attended Orange High School. While completing two college degrees at the University of Southern California, Hobbs pursued a real estate agent's and broker's license, working in a full-service real estate office by the age of nineteen.

Within two years after graduation, Hobbs founded Century American, incorporating in 1976 and unveiling to the community his first residential development project, Orange View Heights. Just ten years later, the progress of Century American is distinctly carved in the county by the building of over 1,000 homes.

Century American's successful development of "jewel box" in-fill sites—pockets of land overlooked by larger builders because of inherent problems requiring detailed design or neighborhood public hearings—turns abandoned industrial and school sites into shining opportunities for first-time and move-up home buyers. Barry A. Cottle, executive vice-president, has been with the company since its founding, and strategizes land acquisition, interfaces with city and county agencies, and negotiates with property owners to obtain the sites. Senior vice-president and chief executive officer Thomas P. Hobbs heads all administrative, marketing, product design, and construction functions, while Thomas Heggi, C.P.A., administers the company's financial transactions.

Century American builds for a broad, moderate-income market, creating and pricing homes for those who most need housing, and proving that the American dream of home ownership is still viable. The full portfolio of Century American assignments ranges from the jewel box sites to custom and luxury town homes, from neighborhood developments and restorations to master-planned communities in Los Angeles, Riverside, San Diego, and Orange counties. Sales volume to date exceeds $150 million.

Attesting to the diversity of Century American's achievements are the multifaceted awards the company has received. Highlighting its restoration finesse is the City of Orange Grand Prize for the most beautiful office complex, a project that blends the refurbishing of a fifty-year-old Spanish-style structure with the addition of a twin building in the similar rancho style, and the Fullerton Gold Award for renovation of the Pacific Electric Depot at Harbor and Commonwealth. An architectural award of merit from the City of Fullerton was bestowed for the Century Plaza office complex; and Anaheim Beautiful chose Century American as the winner of its annual multiresidential landscape design award for Stanford Court, an Anaheim town home neighborhood.

Century American Corporation has been invited to participate in the creation of a new master-planned community called Rancho Santa Margarita, situated on the northern section of Rancho Mission Viejo.

Five thousand acres at the foot of Saddleback Mountain will be the site of housing units, a man-made lake, business park, and a downtown center with hotels and restaurants. Century American's involvement concerns Floramar, a town home neighborhood which will be next to the lake. The firm is also working on The Villas, a similar town home project in San Diego in a new master-planned community called EastLake.

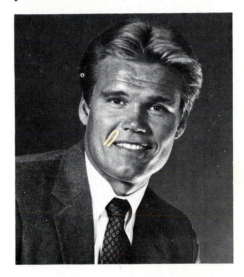

Roger C. Hobbs, president of Century American Corporation.

Century American's corporate offices are situated at 1428 East Chapman Avenue in the city of Orange.

HOBBS TRUCKING COMPANY, INC.

In the late 1920s, when Orlo "Pappy" M. Hobbs started his trucking business, he brought a multitude of experience with him. During his early years Hobbs had trained wild horses in Idaho, operated a dairy farm in Santa Ana, sold Moon and Paige automobiles in the City of Orange, patrolled as a deputy sheriff during a citrus pickers' strike, and, as a grower of citrus crops used some of the first mechanized farm tractors in the county.

As an independent teamster, Hobbs used horse-and-mule teams pulling wagons to haul local crops from Orange County farm fields and citrus groves to packinghouses, and from the packers to various domestic markets and to the Los Angeles Harbor for export. Using horse teams, winches, and cables, Hobbs helped to relocate one of the old Orange Union High School buildings, at the site that later became the Chapman College campus in Orange.

Hobbs' first truck was a Model T Ford, followed by a Model A and a 1936 General Motors vehicle— simple forerunners of Hobbs' current fleet of modern diesel truck-tractors and semitrailers with statewide hauling ranges and the capacity to transport such diverse items as 104-foot-long stuctural steel beams, huge rolls of newsprint paper, and sea containers.

Founders of Hobbs Trucking (left to right), Charles W. Hobbs, Orlo M. Hobbs, and Miles P. Nesbitt, with two of the company's twenty-five Peterbuilt truck-tractors used in hauling trailer loads of crops and goods in Southern California.

In the 1940s Pappy was joined in the business by his son, Charles "Chuck" W. Hobbs, and his son-in-law, Miles "Lani" P. Nesbitt, both experienced truckers and World War II veterans. In 1948 the three formally organized Hobbs Trucking Company, Inc., using land located at the family residence on Tustin Avenue in the city of Orange as the newly formed venture's first truck terminal

An early 1950s view of Hobbs Trucking Company equipment parked at a citrus packinghouse in Orange.

facility.

The ensuing growth and prosperity of Hobbs Trucking has paralleled that of Orange County, and each has contributed to the development of the other. As Hobbs hauled building materials, including structural steel and rebar; concrete drainage, irrigation, and sewer pipe; and food items such as fruit, vegetables, milk, whole grains, and flour to supply some of the county's basic needs, Orange County's ever-expanding consumer population increasingly demanded more and different transportation services.

In 1962, in order to keep pace with such demands, Hobbs Trucking relocated to expanded facilities at 501 East Julianna Street in Anaheim. In 1964 the firm acquired the W. Harold Finley Trucking Company of Tustin, followed two years later by the Merrifield Transportation Company of Anaheim.

In 1965 A. Lee Hobbs, Pappy's grandson, joined the business and now serves as the Anaheim terminal manager. Further expansion was evidenced by the 1978 purchase of Jensen Trucking Service, also long rooted in the agricultural economy of Southern California, and that purchase enabled Hobbs Trucking Company, Inc., to transport an even wider assortment of crops, goods, and materials within the state.

ALUMINUM PRECISION PRODUCTS, INC.

The word "forging" can be defined as a process of forming hot metal by a mechanical or hydraulic press using a set of dies. A die is a tool for imparting a desired shape, form, or finish to metal by means of impact or pressure. Traditional forging processes produce parts that resemble the required configuration but require costly machine operations to meet all blueprint dimensional requirements.

In the early 1960s the need to reduce these costly machine operations was recognized by two engineer/machinists, Philip S. Keeler and Philip D. Spencer, who gradually developed a new method of forging called "precision" forging. Innovative tool and die designs as well as controlled amounts of pressure, heat, and lubricants, skillfully applied to appropriate metals, were some of the basic elements used by Keeler and Spencer in their new process. Their

precision forging enabled them to accurately shape metal component parts according to the exact and specific dimensions required by aerospace customers, while still retaining strength, reliability, and weight requirements in the finished product.

In 1965 Keeler and Spencer founded Aluminum Precision Products, Inc. (APP), as a means of fully implementing the new precision forging process. During APP's first year of operation it employed approximately ten people and had a monthly payroll near $5,000. In 1986 there were 350 employees at APP, and a monthly payroll of $600,000. Initially, one building at 3210 West Central in Santa Ana housed the firm's manufacturing facilities; today six buildings, containing more than 120,000 square feet on a five-acre site at 2621 South Susan Street, Santa Ana, provide ample corporate headquarters for all administrative, research, production, forging, machining, engineering, and quality-control staffs, thereby eliminating reliance on subcontractors.

These complex precision forgings, typical of current aircraft construction, demonstrate some of the high-technology products possible through innovative use of space-age materials, manufacturing processes, and management resources.

Over the past twenty years APP has acquired three affiliated companies in Newport Beach, Anaheim, and in France, which have greatly contributed to the corporation's annual sales of twenty-five million dollars. APP sells its precision-forged parts to both civilian and military accounts in the United States, Canada, Japan, China, France, England, Scotland, Ireland, Italy, and West Germany. Such parts include tail rotors, support frames, bulkheads, and hydraulic systems, and are common components in various fixed-wing and hover craft, and space shuttle aircraft.

In 1976 Aluminum Precision Products, Inc., began a special research program for the precision forging of titanium alloys and other high-strength, space-age materials of interest to aircraft manufacturers. Other ongoing research and development programs assist it in meeting the complex, ever-increasing needs of the firm's domestic and foreign markets worldwide.

Typical precision forgings, manufactured on one of eleven hydraulic presses at Aluminum Precision Products' Santa Ana facility.

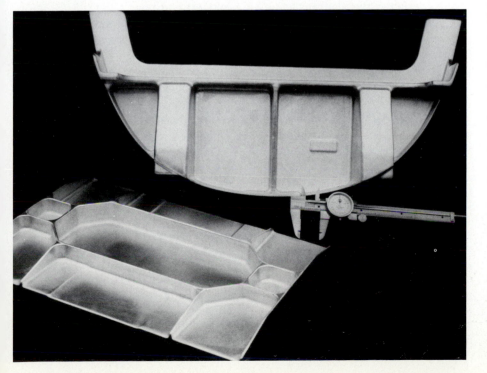

McMAHAN DESK, INC.

The history of McMahan Desk, Inc., began in 1967 when Jay McMahan and two employees opened a budget and used office furniture store in Anaheim at 1830 South Anaheim Boulevard, one block north of the firm's present headquarters at 1960 South Anaheim Boulevard. Originally, McMahan supplied economy-priced metal desks, desk chairs, and filing cabinets to local businesses that were then primarily concerned with strictly functional items. Gradually, as the demand grew, all-new, higher-quality items were added, including executive furniture, open-space systems, custom computer furniture, and ergomatic seating. A space planning and design department and a service department were also established.

Four generations of the McMahan family have worked at the original and present stores, where current employees number thirty. Over the past eighteen years McMahan's staff has accumulated the expertise and knowledge necessary to provide a more sophisticated line of products and services to an increasing number of commercial, industrial, and high-

technology firms, as well as to county and city governments in Orange County. Therefore, as Orange County has evolved from primarily an agriculture-based economy to one of the country's major business centers, McMahan has recognized the need to provide businesses with an overall design system concept featuring integrated, well-planned work spaces, furnishings, and environments.

McMahan's design system includes the use of natural and simulated woods instead of, or in addition to, metal; color-coordinated upholstery, carpeting, drapes, lamps, and other accessories; adequate lighting; custom-designed work stations; and work-flow planning as some of the means by which employee production and efficiency may be increased and by which a favorable corporate image may be projected to potential clients.

Experience and research have shown that office design and environment directly affect the performance, behavior, and morale of a company's employees. McMahan's recognition of such research has led his firm to embrace ergomatics, in

Looking east, this aerial view shows McMahan's present corporate headquarters, showrooms, and warehouse at 1960 South Anaheim Boulevard, Anaheim.

which scientifically designed seating provides maximum lumbar and leg support and body weight distribution, proper posture, and fatigue prevention, all based on anatomical principles.

McMahan's design system concept also includes furniture that is designed and manufactured to accommodate both personal and office computers, word processors, and software. Heavy-duty casters for mobility, locks for security, and select wood veneers for beauty are some of the special features of the firm's computer desks, shelves, racks, work stations, and tables.

Both contemporary and traditional designs, in which aesthetics and utility are combined, will continue to be displayed in the company's 30,000-square-foot showroom and warehouse as McMahan Desk, Inc., grows and progresses along with Orange County businesses.

CANON BUSINESS MACHINES, INC.

In late 1973 Canon, Inc., the Japanese company famous for its fine cameras and business machines, started a manufacturing capability in the United States. This subsidiary was called Canon Business Machines, Inc., and was formally incorporated as a California corporation in March 1974. The following September the new company moved to its ten-acre site in the Irvine Industrial Complex in Costa Mesa.

The firm's initial facility was opened by a nucleus of key personnel drawn from selected American industries; from Canon, Inc., the parent corporation located in Japan; and from Canon U.S.A., Inc., a subsidiary of the parent company, for the purpose of providing electronic calculators and copy machine supplies and components to Canon U.S.A.

Spearheading Canon's new operation were Michihiko Senoh, G. Douglas Michie, Hideo Yamamoto, and Hiroshi Ohwada. Under them, a work force of local employees began assembling electronic calculators and began operating a pilot plant for blending liquid copy machine toner.

In 1975 Canon's second building was ready for the large-scale blending and packaging of the then-common liquid toner as well as for the resurfacing of photo-sensitive copy machine drums. The following year saw the addition of a warehouse to the firm's business complex to facilitate expanded calculator design and production. Continued corporate growth mandated additional construction in July 1980 to house the manufacture of seamless photo-sensitive drums.

Canon Business Machines, Inc., phased out production of electronic calculators in mid-1984, when it retrained existing employees to manually assemble ribbon cassettes for Canon electronic typewriters. In mid-1985, in conjunction with such manual assembly, a fully automated assembly line also produced the cassettes.

Employees totaled about 300 in 1984, when Canon began to reduce its work roster to 150 as a result of more automated production and a shift in emphasis to less labor-intensive products. At the time of this publication, then, the company was engaged in the manufacture of copy machine drums, liquid and dry toners for the copy machines, and typewriter ribbon cassettes.

Canon Business Machines' desire to be a good corporate neighbor in the community is reflected in its participation in various civic and business organizations and activities, including the United Way, Red Cross blood drives, the World Trade Center Association of Orange County, the California Chamber of Commerce, and the Industrial League of Orange County.

Aerial view of Canon's ten-acre corporate facility, located at 3191 Red Hill Avenue in Costa Mesa.

DONNELLEY MARKETING
A COMPANY OF THE DUN & BRADSTREET CORPORATION

Donnelley Marketing is an organization in the business of delivering direct mail advertising messages to prospective buyers in seventy-three million American households. Donnelley's extensive market research, based on the demography of U.S. population groups, enables it to determine the extent and location of specific consumers to be targeted as recipients of advertising from many major American businesses.

Demography has been defined as "the statistical study of human populations, especially with reference to size and density, distribution, and vital statistics." From such statistical studies and other research sources, Donnelley has made available to its commercial clients a comprehensive data base from which diverse potential consumers can be matched to the products and services of its clients. Information in the data base includes names and addresses, automobile descriptions, phone numbers, geographic data, income levels, education completed, age, sex, home values,

and ownership.

Donnelley Marketing originated in 1919 as a regional two-man enterprise in Nevada, Iowa, where it was known as M&F Mailing Systems. In 1922 the Reuben H. Donnelley Corporation of Chicago purchased the Iowa operation in an expansion move and gradually became a major direct mail marketing organization employing more than 3,500 on a nationwide scale. In 1961 the rapidly growing business merged with The Dun & Bradstreet Corporation. In 1976 Donnelley Marketing became a separate operating company of The Dun & Bradstreet Corporation.

Also occurring in 1961 was the first installation of corporate computers in Nevada, Iowa, which has become the data center for Donnelley's entire Marketing Division. Before computerization, all address labels of prospective consumers were typed by hand in more than 600 Nevada, Iowa, homes; today laser printers generate more than 400,000 address labels per hour. The data center

Donnelley Marketing, a company of The Dun & Bradstreet Corporation, has two Orange County locations, one in Anaheim and this facility at 2337 West Commonwealth Avenue, Fullerton.

stores, updates, and maintains all of Donnelley's special consumer lists, which provide access to approximately 90 percent of all American households. Strict security precaution safeguard the privacy of the consumer mailing lists, which are stored on magnetic tape.

Donnelley Marketing opened its Western Region offices in Los Angeles in 1929. In 1968 the firm consolidated its Los Angeles and San Francisco production facilities to Orange County, where David A. Marotta, vice-president and general manager/ Western Region, has his executive offices located at 2401 East Katella Boulevard in Anaheim, one of the two Orange County locations. The other offices and plant are at 2337 West Commonwealth Avenue, where general operations manager

Harold G. Sellin directs the processing of all orders for the entire western part of the United States. The two facilities contain approximately 72,000 square feet of work space. There, 175 to 275 employees (some on a seasonal basis) reflect a current annual payroll of eight figures, as compared with ten to twenty employees and a five-figure payroll in the original Los Angeles office.

The Fullerton plant contains computer tie-ins to the Iowa data center as well as specially designed production, labeling, and shipping equipment and devices that are capable of handling a wide range of customized mailings. Those mailings may contain money-saving coupons, sales catalogs, product samples, mail-order merchandise, and other advertising items.

One of the special features of the Fullerton operation is its immense mail distribution warehouse where U.S. Postal Service personnel daily load dozens of presorted, zip-coded mailbags directly into waiting Postal Service semitrailers for swift shipment and delivery to thousands of consumers throughout the Southwest and other regions of the country.

Rapid increases in the past twenty years in both the residential and business populations in Southern California, and Orange County in particular, have mandated plans for enlarging Donnelley's Fullerton facilities in the near future. The means of providing an even wider range of strategic marketing programs to all segments of the county's growing population will be implemented by the many dedicated and loyal Donnelley employees whose goal is that of their employer—a 100-percent delivery rate of advertising materials to consumers from commercial clients of Donnelley Marketing.

In recognition of the long-term service of numerous employees who make such a goal possible, Donnelley Marketing awards its workers certificates of service and gifts of merchandise at company-sponsored banquets that are held biennially to honor all recipients.

All marketing orders for the entire western part of the United States are processed from the Fullerton plant, which contains computer tie-ins with Donnelley's Iowa data center. The facility is equipped to handle a wide range of customized mailings.

ALEX FOODS, INC.

The original concept of retailing Mexican-style foods to the public was pioneered by Alex Morales, Sr., and his wife, Della, in 1907, when Alex began delivering by horse and buggy homemade tamales, hand-wrapped in corn husks, which Della had prepared in the couple's kitchen using family recipes. This relatively simple operation of a young husband-wife team was the forerunner of a multimillion-dollar corporation now known as Alex Foods, Inc., employer of 1,000 people who produce a wide variety of fresh prepared food.

The couple's homemade tamales were so well received in Anaheim that Alex and Della rented a light-manufacturing-type building near their residence, and concentrated on the large-scale production of several Mexican-style food items. Today a diversity of products includes Mexican food, prepared salads, snack foods, desserts, and entrées, all sold under various corporate and generic labels to wholesale and retail food outlets.

Over the next forty years Alex

Alex Morales, Sr., began delivering homemade tamales by horse and buggy in 1907. As the firm grew so did its fleet of delivery vehicles. Shown here is an Alex Foods truck of the 1950s.

Foods grew to be a national company with sales in each of the fifty states as well as Canada and the Far East.

Parallel with the couple's expanding business was its growing family, which in time numbered ten children—one daughter and nine sons—all born at home at 415 North Olive in Anaheim. Ultimately, eight brothers served concurrently in the U.S. Army and Navy during World War II, and, once discharged from service, four joined their parents in the operation and development of their business. The eldest, Alex Jr., has served as chairman since the firm's incorporation in 1951 and has guided Alex Foods through a series of acquisitions. Throughout this growth the Morales brothers have continued to maintain residences in Anaheim, close to their parents' original factory.

The Morales brothers have worked hard in building Alex Foods, but on a lighter side, the family has shown the same intensity in becoming one of the premier race car owners in the nation. Alex Morales, Jr., heads up a racing team that operates both Indianapolis cars as well as dirt and sprint cars. The team has been in the top five almost every year since 1975 at the "Indy 500"; however, victory has eluded them. Alex is still looking for the "ultimate success" in racing—an Indy 500 victory.

Currently, Alex Foods' headquarters is located in Anaheim, only a few miles from the original house where Alex Morales and his wife started the business over seventy-five years ago. Overall, the company operates more than 450,000 square feet of manufacturing facilities, producing almost 200 million pounds of product each year.

This 1964 photograph shows the original building that housed Alex Foods, Inc., located behind the Morales family residence at 415 North Olive in Anaheim.

WILLIAMSON AND SCHMID

Williamson and Schmid Civil Engineers was established in January 1962 with five employees. Bob Williamson, a native of McCloud, California, and a graduate of the University of Southern California, resigned from the Orange County Road Department in June 1959 to begin a one-man consulting business. Dick Schmid, a native of Orange County and a graduate of the California Institute of Technology, left the Orange County Flood Control District in October 1961 to join Bob in forming the dynamic consulting firm that exists today. Jerry Oldenburg permanently joined the firm in 1962 and became a major stockholder in charge of mapping and surveying.

A converted single-family residence at 1523 East First Street, Santa Ana, was the firm's first office. The business expanded each year and in 1964, with a space need for twenty employees, constructed a 3,400-square-foot office building at 1535 East First Street. In 1975, with continuing growth, the firm relocated to its present location at 17782 Sky Park Boulevard, Irvine. Williamson and Schmid currently occupies a modern 13,000-square-foot, two-story

The firm's present location at 17782 Sky Park Boulevard, Irvine.

office building with additional space leased to provide for its 135 employees. The firm also maintains a major office in Ontario, California.

Included within the current staff are seventeen registered civil engineers and five licensed land surveyors. Office equipment has expanded from one mechanical calculator to a high-speed digital computer with forty work stations; additional CADD systems are presently on order. Surveying equipment has evolved from one transit and level to multiple electronic, automatic recording/measuring devices.

Williamson and Schmid has contributed significant expertise in the continuing industrial, commercial, and residential growth of Orange County and the rest of Southern California. The company has prepared plans and specifications and performed surveys for the construction of public and private improvements, including industrial, commercial, and residential development; arterial highways; bridges; storm drains; and airport improvements. Williamson and Schmid has completed its preparation of hydrology manuals for Orange and San Bernardino counties. The firm's greatest contributions still lie ahead.

Williamson and Schmid's first office was located at 1523 East First Street in Santa Ana.

ASSOCIATED CONCRETE PRODUCTS, INC.

A part of Orange County, originally swampland and later used to produce crops of farm vegetables, now forms a sprawling forty-acre industrial site for a multimillion-dollar manufacturing corporation whose annual "crop" consists of thousands of precast concrete products. The firm is Associated Concrete Products, Inc., and its industrial site is in Santa Ana at 4301 West MacArthur Boulevard. Some of ACP's concrete "crops" cannot be fully utilized until such items have been "planted" underground.

One of ACP's earliest products for underground use was a precast concrete sewer manhole unit developed by Walter G. Barnes, the company's founder. This manhole unit was highly regarded by engineers and sanitation district officials for its strength, easy cleaning, accessibility, and safety, and was first manufactured by Barnes at 1680 Superior Avenue in Costa Mesa, where he originally organized ACP in 1948. Barnes' brother, Raymond, supervised the firm's early manufacturing, and Loren E. Blakely acted as consulting engineer and sales manager.

Following incorporation in 1953 ACP relocated to five acres at its present address, where Walter Barnes served as president until his retirement in 1958. The City of Santa Ana was the first purchaser of Barnes' unique manhole units and has used them consistently since 1950.

Jack Dorris succeeded Barnes as president and general manager of ACP and served from 1958 to 1974, during which time the number of employees expanded to more than 250 (from only twenty in 1969), and the number of acres in use increased to forty. During that same period of growth, Walter B. Hahne was vice-president and took an active role in production and product design.

Over the years ACP has manufac-

The original plant location at 1680 Superior Avenue in Costa Mesa and a 1952 delivery truck.

tured many different precast items that are superior to standard poured-in-place concrete construction because of lower costs, reduced excavation and installation time, minimal traffic interruption when placed in city streets, and fewer safety hazards to workers and the general public. The firm manufactures the majority of its products specifically for public utility companies to house equipment and valves for the electric, telephone, gas, and water agencies.

The vault-like structures that the public utilities purchase are steel-reinforced concrete, in various sizes, the largest of which is eight feet wide, thirty-six feet long, and nine feet high. Originally developed by

Dorris and Ted Bowles, ACP's current vice-president of sales and marketing, the underground vaults provide protected enclosures for transformers and other equipment, as well as for various cables, lines, and utilities distribution systems.

Since the company's beginning in 1948, and as Southern California and Orange County attracted a great diversity of commercial, industrial, and recreational enterprises, ACP responded with numerous innovative products to supply the many needs of

The current forty-acre plant site at 4301 West MacArthur Boulevard in Santa Ana and a boom truck.

such markets. Some of its products include bank vaults weighing 60,000 to 100,000 pounds, foam-filled marina pontoons and docks for pleasure vessels, tilt-up construction panels for buildings and fences, retaining walls, planters, business park signs, freeway median dividers, auto-racing crash barriers, various components for water treatment plants, decorative panels, meter boxes, enclosures for fiber-optic telecommunications systems used between Northern and Southern California during the 1984 Olympic Games, drainage systems for the Alaska Pipeline, and burial vaults.

In 1974 Hahne became ACP's president and chief executive officer and has provided the leadership and imagination that developed many of the aforementioned innovative concrete products. The firm's current work force of 420 men and women has contributed to ACP's nationwide reputation as a pioneer in the manufacture of precast products.

Associated Concrete Products, Inc., now has satellite offices and plants in San Diego, Santa Paula, Livermore, Orland, and Tulare, California, in addition to its corporate headquarters and manufacturing facilities in Santa Ana.

For the past twenty-one years ACP has honored its employees and their families with an annual Christmas party, providing photos with Santa, clowns, and pony rides for the children, as well as refreshments for all family members.

399

MANUFACTURING AND CONSULTING SERVICES

When Dr. Patrick Hanratty speaks to computer industry groups, he is often introduced as the father of CADD/CAM (computer-aided design and drafting and computer-aided manufacturing). He has received that industry's most prestigious awards, and it is estimated that between 70 and 90 percent of all commercially available CADD/CAM software is based on early concepts developed by Hanratty and his Orange County co-workers at Manufacturing and Consulting Services (MCS) in Irvine.

Hanratty's accomplishments in the CADD/CAM field, embodied in long strings of computer code, might seem arcane to most, but one of his inventions has touched the lives of everyone: While working for General Electric in the late 1950s, Hanratty designed the machine-readable characters printed across the bottom of bank and payroll checks.

In point of fact, CADD/CAM is an integral part of modern life. When you buy a good camera, the lens is sharper, lighter, more compact, and less expensive because CADD software lets designers test their ideas on a computer, eliminating the need to build expensive prototypes to check each little variation the designer might want to try. When you buy a car, you're getting a vehicle that was assembled and painted mostly by robots controlled by CAM software. Such examples can be multiplied almost indefinitely.

Hanratty entered the computer industry in 1955, when he was hired as a programmer by the Convair Division of General Dynamics. At that time he was a junior in college, and he was not to receive his bachelor's degree in math from Arizona State University until 1960.

Two years prior to his graduation, Hanratty was working for General Electric and beginning to experiment with computer graphics, using an oscilloscope for a terminal. Those ex-

Dr. Patrick Hanratty with some of the artwork in his collection.

periments began to pay off in the early 1960s. In 1961 Hanratty went to work for General Motors Research Laboratories, where he eventually became part of the DAC (Design Augmented by Computer) Project.

Turning numbers in a computer into lines on an oscilloscope was one thing, but DAC was quite another. It became the first true CADD/CAM system to employ interactive graphics. That meant designers could immediately see what happened when they moved a line on a drawing because they could talk to the computer, not in terms of computer language, but in terms of the lines, points, and curves that comprise a drawing.

In 1967 Hanratty moved to Southern California. He worked at McDonnell Douglas for three years, developing two important CADD/CAM programs. He then left to form his own company, ICS. It lasted just

one year, in part because its software could only run on a single brand of computer, one that proved unpopular with users.

When Hanratty founded MCS in 1971, he vowed not to repeat that mistake. He did not want to see MCS's products become obsolete because they were tied to a particular computer. His goal was to create CADD/CAM software that would run on virtually any computer.

The first MCS software package, called ADAM, was released in 1972.

The MCS headquarters reflects founder Patrick Hanratty's desire for a building that is attractive as well as functional.

It computerized mechanical drafting and numerical-control tape generation, and was the only such system commercially available at that time. MCS soon received licensing requests from a dozen companies, and ADAM is still at the heart of many of their products.

ADAM was designed for sixteen-bit computers. (A bit is the basic unit of computer data; a sixteen-bit computer has a "word" that is six-

On September 2, 1983, MCS principals (from left) Cathryn Ettelson, vice-president of administration; Patrick Hanratty, founder and president, with his German shepherd, Duchess; and Brian Hanratty, CADD/CAM scientist; broke ground for the company's headquarters in Irvine.

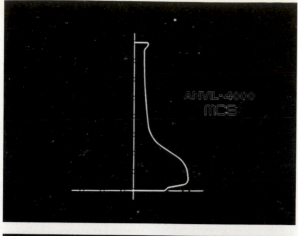

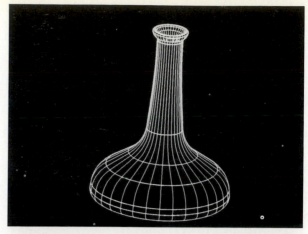

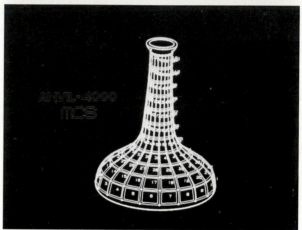

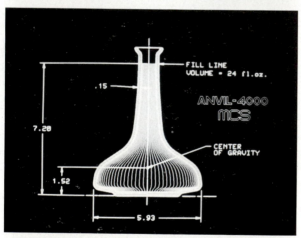

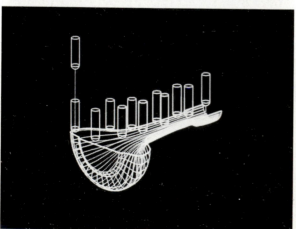

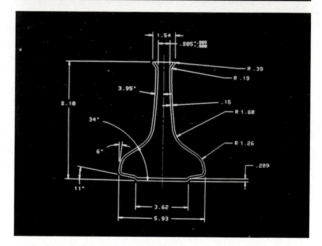

Designing a bottle provides a simple explanation of what engineers can do with MCS's *ANVIL-4000 CADD/CAM system.* The process begins with an outline of the bottle (top left), the initial definition of the bottle's geometry (top right), and an image of what the final bottle will look like (second from top left). A process known as finite element mesh generation allows the design to be interfaced with an analysis program (second from top right). The software can also calculate the bottle's volume and its center of gravity (above left). The dimensions are then automatically added (above). ANVIL-4000 generates the tool paths needed to create the manufacturing molds for the final bottle (left).

teen bits long.) As the years passed more powerful computers using larger words began to appear, and MCS adapted its software to run on them, too. ADAM's successor, AD-2000, appeared in 1974. The ANVIL software family, embodying significant improvements, was introduced in 1981 and continues to be expanded.

Hanratty's interests range far beyond the world of CADD/CAM, and that attitude is reflected in the way MCS does business and the way it relates to the growing community around it. In his youth Hanratty spent eight years training to be an opera singer, turning to mathematics only after suffering lung burns during the Korean War, in which he served as a gunner on B-29 bombers.

"I don't have any logical explanation for it, but I'm convinced there's a relationship between music and computer programming," Hanratty says. "Maybe it has something to do with establishing a sense of order and keeping things moving at the proper pace. What I can say is that about 90 percent of the best programmers I know have had some musical training."

Hanratty is also an avid art collector, and his concern with aesthetics is reflected in the design of the MCS building. When you enter MCS headquarters, the first things you see are mural-size reproductions of the famed prehistoric cave paintings in Spain and France, and the furnishings throughout the building reflect Hanratty's belief that the workplace should be attractive as well as functional.

This concern with art is part of a larger concern: the relationship between what is done at MCS and what happens outside the company's walls. Hanratty has devoted considerable time to nurturing the ties between MCS, the surrounding community, and its educational institutions, particularly the Irvine campus

of the University of California, where he earned his doctorate in information and computer sciences.

"I think the biggest change I've seen since MCS was founded has been in the area of community-industry relations. Ten years ago people just wanted money. But now, when people solicit the industrial world's help with projects, they're asking for real participation. The City of Irvine has asked MCS to help bring in industry, to help create the right kind of growth. And we've also been asked to take part in community affairs like the annual Harvest Festival," states Hanratty.

But the bulk of Hanratty's personal efforts has been devoted to building ties between Orange County's industrial community and UC Irvine as a member of UCI's Chancellor's Club. He also has actively supported the computer program at Arizona State University, where he received his bachelor's degree.

"I think the CADD/CAM industry as a whole can benefit greatly by combining the practical experience gained in the design shop or on the factory floor with the academic's approach to solving problems. I've tried to build that kind of balance here at MCS.

"One of the things that makes Orange County an attractive place to do business is its colleges. The community colleges are an extremely important resource, more important than many businessmen realize. Saddleback College in Mission Viejo is a good example of how a school can improve its educational program by working with industry. It's been our pleasure to work with Saddleback in training programmers and CADD/CAM operators, and it's been a mutually beneficial relationship.

"Cal State Fullerton adds a second layer of expertise, while UC Irvine provides yet another, particularly in its graduate programs. UCI doesn't

provide us with programmers, but that's not what we look to it for. We look to it for help with long-term research and development efforts," says Hanratty.

When Hanratty founded MCS in 1971, south Orange County was just beginning to catch up to the growth the northern half of the county had experienced in the 1950s and 1960s. He had moved to Orange County in 1967 and built MCS there because, "Quite simply, that's where I wanted to live."

Although the county has made great strides in its industrial and educational growth, Hanratty believes it still has a long way to go in other areas.

"The high cost of living has caused MCS some recruiting problems, and the county is still lacking in cultural growth. Like a lot of people, I dislike always having to drive into Los Angeles to see a Broadway show. But that situation should change when the Performing Arts Center opens in Costa Mesa," he says.

Overall, though, Hanratty believes MCS gains much more than it loses by being in Orange County. "Right now, I think Orange County is a focal point for new developments in the CADD/CAM industry, and in three years or so everybody in the industry is going to recognize that fact," he states.

It can easily be argued that the industry already has. In 1982 the Numerical Control Society gave Hanratty its prestigious Joseph Marie Jacquard Award for his achievements in interactive graphics for computer-aided design and manufacturing. Two years later the National Computer Graphics Association followed suit, granting Hanratty its highest honor, the Caby C. Smith Award for his "pioneering efforts and creativity in the development of effective systems which led to the phenomenal growth of the computer graphics industry."

LEE AND ASSOCIATES
COMMERCIAL REAL ESTATE SERVICES

Lee and Associates is a California-based real estate firm concentrating its efforts on the sale, purchase, lease, and exchange of commercial and industrial real property throughout the United States. This successful brokerage firm is comprised of independent partnerships, all sharing the unique and innovative management philosophy of Bill Lee, the firm's founder.

When Lee opened his first Orange County office at 23622 Rockfield in El Toro in September 1979, he was motivated by the goal of establishing and maintaining mutually beneficial business relationships among his professional associates. Accordingly, ideals of cooperation, shared information, camaraderie, and ethical principles became common practices in their business transactions.

Lee's spirit of entrepreneurship and cooperation for the common good of all provided the incentive for the original El Toro operation to expand rapidly to its present sales staff of twenty-two agents and partners, with Lawrence O'Brien as managing part-ner. Original founding partners O'Brien, John Matus, John Sullivan, Al Fabiano, and John Vogt joined Lee in 1979 and assisted him in fostering Lee's unusual management style, which includes sharing profits and awarding bonuses to those men and women who achieve a consistent earning level.

In May 1983 Lee and Associates expanded its brokerage services in Orange County by opening an office at 2200 West Orangewood in the City of Orange, where managing partner Vogt directs the activities of twenty-four agents, ten of whom are partners in the firm. Further growth and development is reflected in the 1984 opening of a third office at 18401 Von Karman in Irvine, where twenty-four agents and partners operate under managing partner Don Pokorni. All offices maintain their own computer systems that contain current commercial and industrial listings and analyses of investment opportunities, and all offer management services through a Property Management Division.

Unlike some real estate firms that warehouse their agents and brokers in one crowded, nonprivate work space, at the company's offices in Orange County integrated design systems provide both professional and support staffs with an attractive work environment that is conducive to greater productivity and comfort. Private offices, conference rooms, reception area, and other work stations are efficiently planned and well designed, and all areas contain color-coordinated furniture, carpeting, drapes, and accessories.

The future plans of Lee and Associates include the opening of offices in every key market area in the United States, maintaining in each the same management structure and philosophy that has already proven so profitable to the firm's clients and staff.

In 1983 Lee and Associates Commercial Real Estate Services opened its second office in Orange County at 2200 West Orangewood Avenue, Orange.

GREATER SANTA ANA CHAMBER OF COMMERCE

The directors of the Orange County Chamber of Commerce, as it was then known, meet in 1897. The name was changed in 1898 to Santa Ana Chamber of Commerce to reflect the area it was representing.

Membership in the Greater Santa Ana Chamber of Commerce has been an investment in Santa Ana itself for over ninety-two years. Today, as it was nearly a century ago, the chamber is a nonprofit, action-oriented membership organization serving as the leading spokesman for, and representative of, business in Santa Ana. The chamber has built a reputation as an organization that gets things done.

The group's official birthdate was March 13, 1893. At that time it was decided to name the organization the Orange County Chamber of Commerce. It was felt that this name would unite the interests of the newly created county in one program. Five years later the advisability of making it strictly a Santa Ana institution became apparent and the name was changed to the Santa Ana Chamber of Commerce.

The first officers of the chamber, chosen on the night of March 16, 1893, were John McFadden, named as president; J.W. Ballard, vice-president; W.S. Taylor, secretary; and L. Ball, treasurer.

Since those early days the chamber has grown right along with Santa Ana—from the participation of a few concerned citizens to an organization with a membership of over 1,000 businesses representing 20,000 employees.

The year 1985 was one of dramatic accomplishment for the chamber under the theme, "Growing Together in Excellence." The board of directors, with input from the membership, public officials, and community representatives, adopted a ten-point plan of action for that year. Along with a new and larger headquarters and a brand-new logo, programs were developed to serve the needs of a growing membership.

Among the ideas explored to promote Santa Ana as a place to live, work, shop, or play, was the establishment of plans for a Visitors and Convention Bureau with a first-class convention center for meetings, sporting events, and entertainment. The chamber is also supporting the private development of a high-rise hotel and office complex in the downtown area that will attract business and visitors. In addition, a major marketing plan was adopted with the goal of creating a city magazine and a media campaign, all designed to promote Santa Ana.

Chamber councils are active participants in business, city, and community issues. From business retention and development programs to downtown promotion strategies and community events such as Golden City Days, Adopt-A-School, and the annual Christmas Parade, chamber volunteers give their time for Santa Ana's future.

As the Greater Santa Ana Chamber of Commerce strives for excellence in 1986, it upholds the credo set down in the bylaws back in 1893: "A body of business and professional citizens of all classes, voluntarily banded together to do all the good they can for the community in which they have made their homes."

The Greater Santa Ana Chamber of Commerce's directors meet on the issues of today.

KNOTT'S BERRY FARM

No history of Orange County could possibly be complete without the inclusion of Walter and Cordelia Knott and their family, whose immediate ancestors came west driving covered wagons through rugged wilderness beset with perils at every turn of the trail—a true-life saga that later would provide the inspiration for Knott's Old West Ghost Town.

The year 1920 was bright with promise. The "war to end all wars" had been fought and won, and California was beginning to move again. It was then that Walter Knott and his wife, Cordelia, came south to Orange County after years in the Mojave Desert as homesteaders, and later, in a more successful stint, sharecropping in San Luis Obispo. The hardy pioneer Knott family was inured to hardship and united in a search for their own personal Eldorado. Although not aware of it at the time, they were about to discover it in the most unlikely of places, the dusty berry fields of Buena Park.

When the Knotts embarked on their trek in a battered old Model T Ford, they brought with them their entire life savings of $2,500, gathered as a result of long hours of toil in the fields of San Luis Obispo, supplemented by Cordelia's profits from making homemade candy for sale in the village. With their savings, unquenchable optimism, and a willingness to work long hard hours, they rented ten acres of land at Beach and La Palma and set out to make the American Dream come true.

Soon folks from throughout the county were stopping off at Knott's tiny wooden berry stand set by the side of a dirt road to purchase boxes of berries from Walter, Cordelia, their son, Russell, and daughters Virginia, Toni, and Marion. The Knott family soon became known as the outstanding berry farmers of the county, and after years of labor, Walter was able to purchase his beloved land.

Walter Knott, developer of the boysenberry, and son, Russell, in their early Buena Park berry fields.

In an ironic twist of fate, he had barely succeeded in acquiring title when the Great Depression hit the nation. Knott's heavily mortgaged acreage was soon producing berries that were unable to be marketed profitably—even in the berry stand in which the whole family worked.

But adversity can often be the great propellant to success, if one does not give up in despair, and the Knott family had never been quitters. In the best American tradition, they tightened their belts, dug in their heels, and worked even harder. Walter Knott was able to turn Rudolf Boysen's dream to reality by successfully cultivating the new boysenberry. And while her husband was tending the farm, Cordelia was using this delicious new berry in her homemade jams, jellies, and pies. But that was still not enough to thwart the disaster of the Depression. Soon Cordelia was cooking up home-style chicken dinners and serving them to guests on the family wedding china. The first day they had eight customers and grossed five dollars.

By 1940 the tide had turned, and hundreds of people waited in line for hours all along Grand Avenue for a chance to taste Mrs. Knott's delectable dishes. Walter decided to entertain them while they waited. He brought the Gold Trails Hotel, built in 1886, from Prescott, Arizona, and created a cyclorama inside, showing the trek westward of his ancestors in the wagon trains. That was the start of Ghost Town, and the beginning of what is now the world's oldest themed amusement park and, except for Disney's parks, the nation's most-attended.

Walter Knott's original Ghost Town, reinvigorated and brought to life in 1985 with many delightful Old West arts and crafts, new shows, and interesting new street characters, was joined over the years by the Fiesta Village, Roaring Twenties, and Knott's Airfield themed areas. The year 1983 saw the birth of Camp Snoopy, Knott's newest themed area alive with the verdant beauty of California's High Sierra, including a rich bounty of trees, shrubs, and rushing white waters. It is also home to America's beloved beagle, Snoopy.

Walter and Cordelia believed in getting their children involved in running the farm. Their daughter Virginia started her business on a card table in the lobby of her mother's early Chicken Dinner Restaurant, and that venture has prospered into one of America's largest and most renowned gift shops. Toni and

President Ronald Reagan, then governor of California, and actor John Wayne were among the dignitaries at Knott's Berry Farm on June 19, 1971, to help Walter and Cordelia Knott celebrate their sixtieth wedding anniversary.

Ken Knott, Darrel Anderson, and Mike Reafsnyder.

Although Walter and Cordelia have passed away, the Knott family, with creative and imaginative five-year plans, have Knott's Berry Farm firmly headed toward future improvement and enlargement. Orange County can be assured that the "Golden Promise" will still be alive and well at Knott's when the twenty-first century dawns.

Marion's interests lay in the world of fashion, and they opened Marion & Toni's Fashions. Marion later spearheaded the expansion of the park, creating three new themed areas. Toni's husband, Ken Oliphant, and later their son, Don, built Knott's food products business into a global success story, and Russell Knott spearheaded the financial and administrative side of the business. All played their parts in turning Knott's Berry Farm into one of the world's most famous amusement parks.

Knott's is still owned and operated by Walter and Cordelia's children and grandchildren, and to this day they continue the tradition begun by Walter of holding family meetings to discuss the major operating decisions of their park. Grandchildren who attend the meetings and who, at one time or another played important roles in the park's management, also include Don Oliphant and his sister, Jana Oliphant Hackett, Steve and

Colorful costumed characters populate Knott's Old West Ghost Town, where guests can ride an authentic narrow-gauge train powered by an original 1881 locomotive.

LEIGHTON AND ASSOCIATES, INC.

F. Beach Leighton, company founder, chairman, and chief executive officer.

Leighton and Associates, Inc., is a geotechnical consulting firm with its corporate headquarters in Irvine and eight regional offices in Southern California: San Diego, Irvine, Riverside, Walnut, Palm Desert, Westlake, Valencia, and Carlsbad. The company celebrated its twenty-fifth year in 1986.

The firm's entire professional and support staff numbered seven in 1961. Today the full-time staff count has risen to more than 230, including over 100 engineering geologists, hydrogeologists, geophysicists, soil

Leighton and Associates board members (left to right, seated): Richard Lung, vice-president and principal engineering geologist; Dr. Bruce R. Clark, president and chief operating officer; Iraj Poormand, executive vice-president and principal geotechnical engineer; and (standing) Dr. F. Beach Leighton, chairman and chief executive officer; and Lawrence R. Cann, executive vice-president and principal engineering geologist.

and material engineers, and other professional and technical people. The technical staff is supported by a complete administrative staff, full technical and nontechnical computer capabilities, and an extensive working library and library information specialists.

Leighton and Associates' consulting services are sought by developers, public agencies, insurance companies, architects, design and structural engineers, building contractors, lending institutions, and other private and public entities. Technical emphasis is placed on detecting, evaluating, and mitigating geotechnical constraints in advance of development and correcting the consequences of geotechnical damages once they occur. In recent years, divisions of hazardous waste, groundwater, geophysics, and materials testing and inspection have grown within the company.

In Orange County, notable geo-

technical projects have included those for The Irvine Company, the Mission Viejo Company, the William Lyon Company, the Lusk Company, Coto de Caza Development Company, and many agencies within the County of Orange. Seismic safety studies and geotechnical studies have been performed for a number of Orange County cities including Huntington Beach, Laguna Beach, Newport Beach, Irvine, and La Habra.

Landslide and earthquake fault maps of Orange County and its cities have been prepared by the firm. The agencies listed above have requested consulting services on many notable landslide disasters, including the Bluebird Canyon Landslide of 1978 in Laguna Beach and the Vista Verde Landslide of 1983 in San Clemente. Leighton and Associates' geotechnical role included studies of temporary and long-term repair for the respective cities and included geotechnical reconstruction of building pads for the twenty-five homes lost in the Laguna Beach slide.

The firm provides consultation for utility companies on public works projects and on groundwater problems. Oil companies and public agencies have sought its services for treatment of hazardous waste products and mitigation of existing and potential contamination of the county's land and water supplies.

THE FIELDSTONE COMPANY

The Fieldstone Company was founded in May 1981 by Peter M. Ochs. In five years it has become one of the major home builders in Southern California. Ochs, who is president and chairman of the board, is assisted by executive vice-president and San Diego County manager Keith A. Johnson, senior vice-president and Orange County Division manager David R. Langlois, and a staff of over eighty dedicated employees.

In its first year of operation The Fieldstone Company constructed eighty-one single-family, detached homes for a sales total of $10.4 million. In 1985 total sales were $150 million with nearly 1,000 homes built.

Fieldstone attributes its rapid development and success in part to the fact that it stresses traditional values that include integrity and excellence. One of its goals is to construct quality homes at affordable prices, keeping

in mind knowledge of market conditions and consumer tastes. Within a well-defined organizational structure, dedicated and experienced personnel give careful attention to detail, providing assurance that the standards that have been set are kept.

Realizing the impact made on the community by a home builder and resolving to act as a responsible community citizen, the company established The Fieldstone Foundation in 1983, a nonprofit organization that would facilitate distribution of charitable funds in four areas: community, cultural, humanitarian, and educational. All employees are encouraged to suggest charities for the company's support. To date the recipients of its substantial charitable donations include the City of Hope Medical Center in Los Angeles, The Globe Theatre in San Diego, the San Diego Museum of Art, Orangewood (Orange County shelter for abused children), Children's Hospital of Orange County, the Laguna Art Museum, the Orange County Performing Arts Center, and South Coast Repertory. Ochs served as president of the

The Fieldstone Company executives include (left to right) Peter M. Ochs, president; Keith A. Johnson, executive vice-president; and David R. Langlois, senior vice-president.

South Coast Repertory board of trustees during the 1984-1985 season. In 1980 he was named Man of the Year for Orange County by the City of Hope Medical Center.

In 1985 Fieldstone made a conscious decision to develop a collection of artwork with a historical perspective—paintings that depict the region of Southern California as it was. The Fieldstone Collection now has over fifty paintings, which span the fifty-year period from 1900 to 1950. The paintings, primarily by California Impressionist artists, provide a beautiful record of the unique geographical area that is Southern California. The collection is displayed in the Fieldstone offices in Newport Beach and in San Diego. In 1985 the Orange County Business Committee for the Arts gave special recognition to The Fieldstone Company for its commitment to the visual and performing arts.

It is clear to see that The Fieldstone Company has in only a few years established itself as a leader in the Southern California business community.

One of the foremost builders in Southern California, Fieldstone's belief in quality homes is evidenced in this Harbor Point model in Newport Beach.

MDB SYSTEMS, INC.

In 1970 the entire product line of MDB Systems, Inc., could be carried in the briefcase of its founder/owner, Amos R.L. Deacon, Jr. Today, due to the initiative, energy, imagination, and pioneering spirit of this entrepreneur, more than 250 computer-related products are designed, manufactured, and quality tested by Deacon's company and sold throughout the world.

Even before 1970 Deacon had studied the computer industry and had foreseen the need for electronic devices that would facilitate and permit independent, diverse computer systems (originating from different brand-name manufacturers) to interact and communicate with each other in a compatible manner. Such devices also needed to be designed to enhance the individual capabilities of each computer system.

In 1970, as a result of his foresight, Deacon, with only two employees and a small, 1,200-square-foot plant, set out to supply these needed electronic devices as well as other innovative computer products. Today MDB Systems, headquartered

Today the firm is headquartered in this 100,000-square-foot-plus facility at 1995 North Batavia Street, Orange.

The original home of MDB Systems, Inc., in 1970.

at 1995 North Batavia Street in Orange, employs 200 people and utilizes more than 100,000 square feet of office and manufacturing space for the production of printed circuit boards, super-micro and minicomputer interfaces and logic modules, and other hardware and equipment required by users and manufacturers of computer systems.

With an emphasis on initiative and innovation, Deacon has expanded MDB Systems into nineteen regional sales offices throughout the United States, and has also established a California subsidiary: Orange Precision Circuits. MDB now maintains manufacturing plants in Ireland, Mexico, and Puerto Rico; international sales offices in Switzerland, England, Australia, and Germany; and distributors in Canada, Japan, Israel, Australia, and several other overseas locations.

Such widespread corporate growth and development is based on Deacon's business philosophy in which

initiative and "completed staff work" are the keys to success. Deacon's dedication to accomplishment, based on personal initiative, is illustrated in an essay, much-favored by him, that was written on February 22, 1899, by Elbert Green Hubbard, an American novelist, editor, and printer.

In the essay entitled "A Message to Garcia," Hubbard describes the qualities of dedication to duty and personal initiative as successfully practiced by U.S. Army Lieutenant Andrew S. Rowan during the Spanish-American War in response to a command by President William McKinley. Hubbard's essay recounts how Rowan, in 1898, personally delivered a written request for military cooperation to General Garcia, a leader of Cuban insurgents. Rowan's initiative led him to Garcia after three weeks of solitary foot travel through hostile Cuban jungles, preceded by a four-day, open-boat trip and a nighttime landing off the Cuban coast. This example of personal initiative serves as an inspiration for all MDB employees and Deacon as he guides MDB Systems, Inc., toward a future sure to include additional growth and expansion.

A&C PROPERTIES, INC.

"Success and achievement are the results of cause and effect. Things just don't happen; someone must make them happen," states Kathryn G. Thompson, who is not only one of the top real estate developers in Orange County, but is also one of the county's most effective philanthropists—and does she ever have a knack for making things happen.

As founder, president, and chief executive officer of A&C Properties, Inc., and Gore Development Corporation, Kathryn is responsible for making residential and commercial developments happen in ten states.

Kathryn's interest in real estate stretches back to age eight when she tried to sell her parents' Dallas home to a neighborhood boy. This childhood interest became strong-willed determination when she moved to California and sold a diamond ring for $500 to tide her over before she made her first sale with Walker & Lee. Through intense study and fourteen-hour workdays, Kathryn ended her first year with one million dollars in sales on $18,000 homes.

But the hard work didn't stop there. Two years later, in 1966, Kathryn founded A&C Properties, and began buying apartment complexes so she could refurbish and sell them for a profit. Never above rolling up her sleeves and doing the work herself, Kathryn obtained a general contractor's license and did repair work on her own projects, including carpentry, drywalling, and plumbing.

In 1970 Kent Child became Kathryn's partner in A&C Properties and shifted the emphasis of the firm to commercial ventures. At this time A&C did the complete packaging of more than one hundred 7-11 convenience markets, complete packaging or development of over thirty Color Tile stores, and packaging for twenty-eight Stop N' Go markets.

A&C then became involved in condominium conversions. To date

Kathryn G. Thompson, president of A&C Properties, Inc.

the firm has converted over 2,000 apartment units to condominiums in Los Angeles, Orange, and San Diego counties. A&C has also built residential projects from the ground up, such as South Coast Springs, a unique 153-unit water-oriented condominium community in the heart of the South Coast metro area of Santa Ana.

A&C's most recent project is The Terraces, a luxury town home community nestled in the rural hills of Laguna Beach. The unusual aspect of this 152-unit development is its unique design, which makes maximum use of the scenic rolling countryside through terraced units plotted in circular configurations.

Kathryn exhibits the same exuberance in her work with charities and community organizations as she does in her business dealings. Her involvement in this area includes serving as leadership chairman and member of the board of directors of Orangewood, a home for dependent children; member of the board of directors of South Coast Repertory, United Way, the Boy Scouts of America, and the Young Presidents' Organization; trustee of the board of directors for the College of Medicine at the University of California, Irvine; chairman of the March of Dimes Gourmet Gala for 1986; and current member of the Bowers Museum, Santa Ana Country Club, the Pacific Club, and the University of California, Irvine, Chancellor's Club.

With Kathryn Thompson's passion and ability for "making things happen," only the future will tell what lies in store for Orange County.

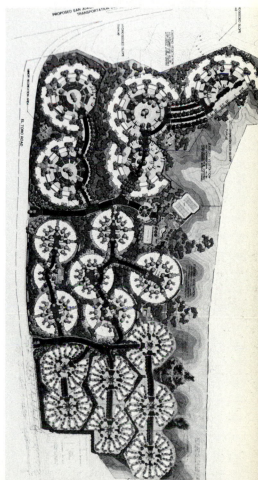

The Terraces, an A&C project, is a luxury town home community nestled in the rural hills of Laguna Beach.

BELL PIPE & SUPPLY CO.

Frank M. Bell, a native Californian, is an entrepreneur whose foresight in the potential growth and development of Orange County motivated him in 1956 to lease one acre of land at 215 East Ball Road in Anaheim. He viewed this location as an ideal site to establish his new industrial wholesale business. Thus, in May 1956 he incorporated Bell Pipe & Supply Co. for the purpose of providing the immediate piping requirements for new industrial and manufacturing facilities within the area.

Bell Pipe & Supply Co. is an authorized stocking distributor of industrial supplies serving the Southern California marketplace with a complete line of valves, pipe, fittings, pumps, hose products, and pneumatic and hydraulic controls.

Parallel to the growth of Orange County during the past thirty years is the growth of Bell Pipe, as reflected by the number of employees needed to service its many customers during that time span—two in 1956, twenty-five in 1975, and thirty-eight in 1985. The firm's development is further shown by the number of square feet of space being utilized—5,000 in 1956, 9,000 in 1975, and 30,000 in 1985, including a two-story, 20,000-square-foot warehouse added in 1983. A total of 2.5 acres is now owned by Bell Pipe at its original location in Anaheim.

Under the leadership of Frank Bell, a staff of thirty-eight dedicated employees—including eleven exceeding fifteen years' service—contribute to the success of Bell Pipe & Supply Co. The employees with at least fifteen years' service include Lewis S. Hofmann, 1956, manager; George J. Ledger, 1959, sales man-

ager; Arthur A. Crane, 1959, inside sales; Jo-Ann M. Rahe, 1961, controller; Mike Fedorchek, 1962, warehouse superintendent; Larry O'Rourke, 1962, semi-retired; Clarence Ratterman, 1964, inventory control; Carmine Cangero, 1966, counter sales; Jack E. Nelsen, 1968, marketing manager; Russell L. Burdg, 1968, purchasing agent; and Allan L. Ratliff, 1970, inside sales.

Today Bell Pipe & Supply Co. is recognized as one of the leaders in the industry. In turn, the firm's customers have come to rely on professional knowledge, complete inventory, and prompt service to fulfill their product requirements.

The original building on Ball Road in Anaheim presently provides offices and warehouse space accompanied by a new two-story, 20,000-square-foot warehouse.

HOWARD F. THOMPSON & ASSOCIATES, INC.

Since founding his architectural and land-planning firm, architect Howard F. Thompson has established a reputation as an innovative leader in the practice of "business architecture," the designing of office buildings, industrial/business parks, and shopping centers. Photo by Elson-Alexandre, Los Angeles

Since its founding in 1967 Howard F. Thompson & Associates, Inc. (HFTA), has been in the business of providing professional architectural and land-planning services to business entities throughout Southern California and in Arizona, Texas, Florida, Washington, Colorado, and Hawaii. Such services include preliminary investigations and feasibility studies of proposed design projects; land-use and space planning; structural, civil, and electrical engineering; and landscape design and irrigation.

Howard F. Thompson, AIA, a registered architect in California since 1962 and president of HFTA, recognized early in his career that his firm's designs must be cost-efficient, well planned, competitive, and innovative in order to appeal to land owners, developers, builders, and investors. He also recognized that aesthetically pleasing as well as functionally practical work environments benefit employee production and morale.

As a result, Thompson carefully acquired a team of design and planning experts made up of individuals who possessed a wide range of education and experience, and who collectively could implement the goals of Thompson's new corporation. One such expert is Karl C. Danyi, who joined HFTA in 1969 and currently serves as corporate vice-president and managing partner in charge of production, quality control, and contract administration. Joan A. Thompson, corporate secretary and office and financial manager; John S. Delacy, AIA; Ruben Burrola, AIA; Sohrab Charna; Leonard Malmquist, AIA; Daniela Bogdan; and Robert Johnston are associate members of the firm.

Century City was the site of Thompson's first office. However, upon observing, in 1971, the present and potential development of Orange County and the need for his firm's services there, Thompson relocated first to Orange and then to Santa Ana in 1975 as larger corporate facilities be-

Kierulff Electronics, Warland Business Center, Cypress.

came necessary to accommodate his rapidly growing business. In 1979 Thompson designed his own 5,000-square-foot office building at Aston Street in the Irvine Business Center. The new facility includes ample and attractive work space for his professional and support staffs, which number more than thirty employees.

Since 1967 Howard F. Thompson & Associates, Inc., has designed over 500 commercial and industrial structures, including research and development facilities, office buildings, shopping centers, financial institutions, and industrial/business parks. It has also developed numerous land-use plans involving mixed-use business complexes ranging in size from 20 acres to 1,300 acres. Eight of the projects have received regional and national architectural design awards, including the 1984 Grand National Award from *Builder* magazine for the best research and development facility in the United States. Located in the city of Cypress in Orange County, this award-winning concrete and glass structure contains 127,000 square feet of flexible high-tech space.

SIXPENCE INNS OF AMERICA, INC.

Tustin, in Orange County, is the site of the third motel to be opened in the Sixpence chain. The 176-room inn displays signs advertising Sixpence budget rates prevailing in 1973.

Shelter and sleep are two of the basic physical necessities of life that must be satisfied in order for human beings to survive. Sixpence Inns of America, Inc., is in the business of supplying such basic needs to the traveling public by means of conveniently located motel accommodations offered at reasonable prices.

Sixpence Inns was incorporated in 1970 by Donald Sodaro, who now serves as the firm's president and chief stockholder. Joining Sodaro in the formulation of corporate strategy are several family members. Sodaro's brother-in-law, William Caine, Jr., serves as executive vice-president; his function is to oversee the internal systems development of Sixpence

Inns and to be responsible for the chain's overall operations. Mrs. Donald Sodaro supervises and conducts quality-control inspections in individual motels throughout the chain. Her father, William Caine, Sr., is on the corporation's board of directors.

Sodaro's background as a Certified Public Accountant, corporate financial manager, and partner in another budget motel chain has amply provided him with the expertise with which to fulfill his goal of developing and operating a chain of high-quality, moderately priced motel lodgings throughout California and other states. In 1972, with this goal in mind, Sodaro opened his firm's first motel in Anaheim; it had sixty-five rooms. He chose Orange County as the site of three other motels that the company established in Tustin, Orange, and Westminster.

By the end of 1985 Sodaro was operating a total of thirty-three Six-

pence Inns containing a total of 3,718 rooms throughout California, Arizona, Colorado, Connecticut, and Illinois, with a 90- to 100-percent average annual occupancy rate. In the

Sixpence Inns of America's original corporate headquarters in Fullerton in 1970. The 600-square-foot building is in marked contrast to the present spacious facilities in Santa Ana.

Donald E. Sodaro (left), president of Sixpence Inns, and William A. Caine, executive vice-president, in their Orange County corporate headquarters in Santa Ana.

first half of 1986, seven new motels, containing 100 to 174 rooms each, were completed, and additions were made on two existing structures. Such expansion and progress have been directed by Sodaro from corporate headquarters located, since 1980, at 1751 East Garry in Santa Ana.

In the process of developing his budget motel chain, Sodaro has combined several basic business concepts that enable him to offer the public maximum room value at a minimum of cost. His experience and ongoing financial analysis have shown him that the location of each motel is of prime importance in ensuring above-normal occupancy levels. Sodaro personally visits and investigates each potential motel site, where he looks for nearby facilities that will attract to Sixpence the maximum number of customers on a continuing basis. Some of the features sought include easy freeway access, tourist and recreational attractions, convention/exposition centers, airports, shopping malls, universities, business/industrial complexes, government installations, and other points of local interest near which guests may wish to temporarily house themselves and their families.

Once a site is selected, construction of slightly smaller rooms, omission of large lobbies and meeting rooms, and elimination of room service are some proven methods used by the firm to lower building and operating costs and to reduce room rates. Another business concept basic to the successful operation of Sixpence involves careful selection and training of husband-and-wife teams to manage and staff each motel.

As a matter of corporate policy, the firm does not provide within motel premises food and beverage services for its customers because it chooses not to be in the business of operating restaurants. However, the importance of these services to guests is recognized by Sodaro, and he accordingly selects each motel site near independently owned and operated, moderately priced restaurants that

This view of the Sixpence Inn in Riverside shows the Old English Tudor style of architecture commonly used throughout the chain, making each inn easily recognizable.

maintain standards compatible with those of Sixpence.

Extensive soundproofing, quality mattresses and bedding, appropriate maintenance, consistent cleanliness, and guest laundry facilities are some basic services offered by the company that provide comfort and convenience to guests and encourage them to repeat their stays at Sixpence Inns in the future.

Continued controlled growth over the next eight to ten years, at a projected rate of seven to ten new motels per year, is one of Sodaro's corporate goals for the future. Maintaining a 90- to 100-percent occupancy rate throughout the firm's existing motels is another goal, as is the establishment of that same high-occupancy level in future additions to the Sixpence chain.

Assuming a relatively stable money market, with a reasonable level of interest rates, Sodaro anticipates that Sixpence Inns of America, Inc., will continue to expand while maintaining its policy of providing the general public with the basic necessities of shelter and sleep at affordable rates in a modern, pleasant surrounding.

CONNECTOR TECHNOLOGY, INC.

George Dobelis, co-founder and president.

Robert C. Bianchi, co-founder and vice-president.

Connector Technology, Inc., is considered one of the fastest-growing and most successful companies in Orange County, according to the November 1984 issue of *Business to Business* magazine. Only privately held businesses in existence on or before 1981 with minimum annual gross sales between $100,000 and $25 million were considered during the selection process that singled out CTI and forty-nine other Orange County firms for special recognition.

According to the magazine, certain significant traits distinguish CTI and its peers from their slower-growing competitors. Those traits include a focused leadership style, creative financing approaches, limited formal controls, and business strategies emphasizing market "nichemanship." To these may be added an energetic entrepreneurial spirit that thrives on the risk-taking prevalent in founding a new business.

George Dobelis and Robert C. Bianchi, founders of CTI, are two such risk-takers who left established corporate management positions to form their own company in January 1978. Both men had worked together in the same firm for about ten years, when their entrepreneurial spirits, coupled with a distaste for intracorporate politics, motivated them to combine their sales, administrative, and engineering skills and experience in order to manufacture and market computer hardware. Their goal was to produce and sell standardized and custom-designed components for business computers, telecommunications equipment, medical electronics, and testing equipment. Dobelis and Bianchi opened their new business in Los Angeles County, with approximately 500 square feet of office and manufacturing space and two employees.

By 1980 CTI had grown to such an extent that it became necessary to move to Orange County where centrally located industrial sites, an ample labor pool, numerous support services, and other high-tech manufacturers could provide the firm with an environment conducive to future expansion and development, as well as provide for its immediate needs.

There, in CTI's new 24,000-square-foot corporate headquarters at 2850 Via Marten in Anaheim, Dobelis as president and Bianchi as vice-president direct the operations of the firm and its three subsidiary/support companies in Anaheim and Placentia as they produce solderless backplane interconnect systems and other computer-related products.

One factor contributing to the rapid growth of Connector Technology, Inc., is its corporate philosophy, which emphasizes that service to clients is of primary importance. Professional engineering, state-of-the-art designs, reliable quality-tested products, competitive pricing, and timely delivery are standard operating procedures at CTI. Also a major part of CTI's management policy is its consideration of the needs of its 121 employees. Such regard has fostered an esprit de corps throughout employee ranks where morale is exceptionally high and turnover is less than one percent annually.

FRANCO MANUFACTURING, INC.

Franco Manufacturing, Inc., was founded in June 1977 by Eduardo Franco for the purpose of manufacturing and marketing waterbed furniture, which included headboards, bed frames, and drawer storage pedestals, as well as matching nightstands, hutches, chests, and dressers. Originally, Franco was in the business of building kitchen cabinets, and any waterbed furniture that he created was solely for his personal use. It wasn't long, however, until his entrepreneurial spirit prompted him to open a 500-square-foot facility with his brother, Jaime, in order to build and distribute their own designs to furniture retailers throughout the country. The brothers incorporated their business in 1982.

According to the November 1985 issue of *Waterbed* magazine, the waterbed industry was begun in the early

1960s as a cottage-type industry by a small group of businessmen on the West Coast. Initially this new industry was totally experimental in the manufacturing and marketing of its products. However, as technology, manufacturing facilities, distribution systems, and consumer acceptance gradually improved and developed, these new flotation sleep devices matured enough to become a permanent part of the home furniture industry. *Waterbed* magazine also states that in 1984 nearly one out of every five beds sold was a waterbed.

Franco Manufacturing, located in Santa Ana, began modestly with an annual payroll of $11,000 and used just twelve furniture designs. Today it employs 250 in two shifts and uses 87,000 square feet of work space to complete its production quotas of 25,000 units per month. A second 13,500-square-foot manufacturing plant in Anaheim contributes to total annual sales of twelve to fourteen million dollars.

Currently, Franco Manufacturing consumes two million board feet of pine lumber per month in order to

produce its fifty different furniture designs. Names of major American cities and states have been chosen to identify each design/model. Wood finishes of cherry, walnut, or honey walnut, as well as solid brass or antique fittings and fixtures, are some of the features incorporated in the firm's designs.

Corporate management strategies require the regular use of computers to track and update information vital to healthy business operations including payroll, inventories, invoicing, scheduling, production, sales, pricing, and deliveries. Keeping abreast of financial trends, identities of competitors, technological and social changes, consumer demands, and new markets is also part of the corporation's management policies. Consistent-quality products, responsive customer service, workable lead times, employee teamwork, and on-time deliveries have resulted from such forward-thinking corporate policies. As a result, Franco Manufacturing, Inc., has been able to develop and prosper in a still-maturing and highly competitive industry.

One of Franco Manufacturing's most popular models of waterbed furniture is the "New Hampshire," which features a mirror in the headboard frame and a captain's pedestal storage cabinet.

M.K. PRODUCTS, INC.

Donald L. Martin, M.K. Products' president, in front of the company's facility in the Irvine Industrial Park. The 72,000-square-foot building houses the research, engineering, manufacturing, sales, and administrative functions of the company.

Milo Milford Kensrue is a native Californian who was raised and educated in Southern California. His entire business career as a sales engineer, process welding engineer, and welding firm partner was centered in Los Angeles County until 1966. That year Kensrue's entrepreneurial spirit motivated him to choose Santa Ana as the ideal location for an industrial plant of his own. Orange County, he believed, represented the best location for him to manufacture welding equipment that he invented and patented himself. Kensrue was convinced his product was superior in quality and design to the equipment then available from competing manufacturers.

Kensrue had originally become interested in welding as a result of his fascination with aviation; he believed that learning the skill of welding would help him to build his own aircraft. In acquiring that ability, Kensrue came to realize that the inadequacies of the welding equipment then in use could be best remedied by producing his own patented inventions. Thus, he incorporated M.K. Products, Inc. (MK), in 1966 for just that purpose. Subsequent business demands have prevented him from building his own aircraft, but he has been the owner of many, and currently owns a helicopter.

MK's first small manufacturing plant at Warner and Grand avenues in Santa Ana contained 2,400 square feet of floor space and employed approximately ten people. In just a few years the firm had expanded into seven separate structures, and it became necessary to relocate, in 1974, to a larger facility at 16882 Armstrong Avenue in the Irvine Industrial Park. There all manufacturing operations were consolidated into one modern, 72,000-square-foot facility. Today that facility houses MK's corporate headquarters and a professional and support staff of 100 people.

Early on, Kensrue acknowledged the value of a strong sales and management team. Accordingly, he invited Paul E. Miller to join MK in 1970; Miller is now senior vice-president in charge of sales and worldwide distribution of the firm's products.

Kensrue also was able to recognize that electronics would play an integral part in both MK's future and the welding equipment it produced. Thus, in 1972 Kensrue recruited Donald L. Martin, another native Californian whose professional education was at Stanford and whose business experience had been obtained in Southern California. Martin possessed a substantial background in electrical engineering and management and was a patentee in his field. He became president of MK in 1977 after serving as chief engineer for five years.

Electric arc welding is replacing other processes, such as riveting, for joining metal parts, because of its economic advantages and compatibility with automation.

Twenty years later the modern solid-state-controlled, electrically driven welding torch still looks very much like the original handmade air-driven model.

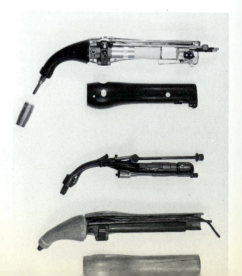

Milo M. Kensrue, founder, chairman, and majority owner of M.K. Products, Inc., with his Hughes 500c helicopter.

In the 1960s and early 1970s, industry began to use welding robots to improve product output and quality, especially in the manufacture of automobiles, home appliances, and other goods that depend upon strong, consistent welds. During that time Kensrue foresaw the need for an interface device by which the firm's welding equipment could be adapted for compatible incorporation into existing welding robots. Consequently, an interface control unit was designed for that purpose, thereby making the MK welding system all the more versatile and marketable as it kept pace with robot-related technology.

Whether hand held or programmed and manipulated by robots, the automated welding system of M.K. Products, Inc., is frequently reviewed by its engineers to discover new applications and to develop additional products that will better serve the welding equipment needs of present and future customers in Orange County and worldwide.

Traditionally, welding operations have been performed manually by a welder using a consumable rod electrode. An arc melts a portion of the pieces to be joined and filler metal is provided as the rod melts off. A flux coating on the electrode is actuated by heat of the arc to protect the molten metal from atmospheric contamination. This method is very dependent on the skill of the welder to achieve high-quality welds, and is not well suited to automation.

Semiautomatic welding torches use continuously fed electrode wire from a supply spool and utilize shielding gas to protect the weld. The quality of the resulting weld is highly dependent on the uniformity of feed rate of the electrode wire.

Kensrue and his designers have developed sophisticated, automated welding torches, filler-wire feeders, power sources, and self-propelled, travel-carriage devices that, in combination with each other and with additional MK products, constitute a complete automated welding system.

In using the firm's automated system, time is saved, production is increased, and accuracy is improved. In addition, strong precision welds can be made in a variety of steel, aluminum, copper, and nickel base applications, all at reduced costs. Furthermore, the human welder is freed to perform more intricate welding tasks while experiencing less fatigue and danger from hazardous applications.

Paul E. Miller, senior vice-president/sales, with the Cobramatic wire feeder and the newest product developed by the company, a powerful (300 ampere) transistorized welding power source with an exceptional range of digital control capability.

TRAVELAND U.S.A.

It's been said that dreams are something precious, something to be cherished and nurtured at all costs. Ed Pope, a native Southern Californian and owner of Traveland U.S.A. in Irvine, certainly believes this is so.

When Pope purchased Traveland in late 1974, it was more like a dream gone sour than a profitable business. The original developer had envisioned a one-stop shopping center for the display of recreational vehicles—or RVs as they are more commonly called. His goal was a location where people could browse in pleasant surroundings, ask questions freely, and just explore all the exciting possibilities available in RVs.

Unfortunately, the Arab oil embargo almost squashed this dream just as construction was being completed on the 35-acre site. As gas prices soared and shortages loomed, the entire RV industry took a beating. Dealers and manufacturers who were approached to lease sales space at Traveland were understandably hesitant, given the dismal economic conditions.

Yet Pope was convinced that Traveland had a lot going for it: a prime location in south Orange County, just off Interstate 5; lush

This sign welcomes you to Traveland U.S.A., just off Interstate 5 in south Orange County.

Lush landscaping and three lakes create a garden-like setting and spaces for the products of some fifty dealers and manufacturers.

landscaping and three lakes that created a garden-like setting; and spaces for the products of some fifty dealers and manufacturers. Other pluses included a complete RV service center and a general store that offered a wide range of RV parts and accessories. In addition, Traveland was the only shopping center of its kind in the nation—if not the world. The dream, Pope decided, certainly deserved a second chance.

Pope's first objective as new owner was to fill the sales spaces at Traveland; the second was to attract customers. Pope achieved the first by becoming a dealer at Traveland himself. In fact, he soon became the largest RV dealer in the state of California. This success helped convince dealers and manufacturers that moving to Traveland was a good idea.

Attracting potential customers was even easier, considering all Traveland had to offer. Pope immediately planned a series of special events that were widely publicized. In 1974, and again in 1975, dealers decorated several dozen RVs with Christmas finery and set out on a "Parade of Lights on Wheels" through the

Traveland is the only shopping center of its kind in the nation for recreational vehicles and RV parts and accessories.

streets of several south Orange County cities. Timed to coincide with the annual Parade of Lights in Newport Harbor, this event was warmly received by the community.

Also popular were the carnival attractions that appeared at Traveland each weekend in mid-1975. During this time, visitors to Traveland were entertained by trained elephants, exciting high-wire performers, and daredevil motorcyclists.

The following year Pope inaugurated Traveland's annual Fuel Economy and Performance Run. The aim of this grueling three-day, 700-mile road performance test was to put various recreational vehicles through travel conditions typical of different parts of the United States. The event also encouraged manufacturers of RVs and RV component parts to keep pace with new requirements for more fuel-efficient motor homes and travel trailers by allowing them to test their products under actual recreational conditions.

Thanks to improved economic conditions and the efforts of industry leaders such as Ed Pope, the entire RV industry experienced an upsurge

in 1976. In fact, the next two years were some of the best ever for the RV industry. The times were good for Traveland, too; by 1979 the center was virtually 100-percent occupied and annual sales reached $75 million.

Unfortunately, 1979 brought another crisis, which hit both the RV industry and Traveland. Higher gasoline prices, President Jimmy Carter's gas allocation program, and rising interest rates combined to frighten away many would-be buyers of recreational vehicles. Within six months scores of RV manufacturers and dealers went out of business and half the sales lots at Traveland stood vacant.

Yet Traveland weathered this crisis, too. The cooperative nature of the center, which allowed operating expenses to be shared by a group of like-minded business people, proved to be one of its major strengths. As a result, Traveland was poised to take advantage of the RV industry's recovery in 1981. Soon all the sales lots were once again occupied.

This period of recovery also brought a major shift in RV sales from Los Angeles County to Orange County. Although the sales in these neighboring counties remained constant, RV sales in Orange County showed the greatest percentage of in-

crease. Today Orange County dealers sell some 16 percent of all RVs sold in California—and nearly 50 percent of all the RV dealers in Orange County maintain sales sites at Traveland. In 1985 annual sales at Traveland reached $140 million.

What does the future hold for Traveland? Nearly twelve years after acquiring this unique shopping center, Ed Pope is still dreaming and planning. One current project is an RV Education and Training Center, which would offer seminars on the various aspects of owning and using an RV. Also in the works is a Special Events Center that would be available for use by local RV clubs. And, who knows, Traveland II may soon be appearing to serve the needs of RV customers elsewhere. Pope is now considering possible sites for such a development.

On a personal level, Pope recently has served as president of the Southern California Recreation Vehicle Dealers' Association. He has also served on the board of directors of the California Recreation Vehicle Dealers' Association. Clearly, Ed Pope is the sort of hard-working dreamer who helped make Orange County what it is today: one of the fastest-growing, most prosperous regions in the United States.

MAXWELL'S BY THE SEA

Maxwell's By The Sea, at 317 Pacific Coast Highway in Huntington Beach, is an oceanfront restaurant with a nine-year history of serving quality cuisine and beverages. However, the structure in which this popular dining-out facility is housed has a past that dates back to 1938, when a Federal Works Progress Administration (WPA) project resulted in the construction of the building for use as a railroad station. At that time passengers traveling between Los Angeles and Newport Beach detrained at the station for visits to Huntington Beach's pier and seashore.

The structure was next used as a dance hall called the Pavalon, and touring bands including those of Stan Kenton, Harry James, and

The 317 Pacific Coast Highway location of Maxwell's By The Sea has undergone a complete metamorphosis. Originally constructed by the WPA in 1938 as a railroad station, it became the Pavalon dance hall during the 1940s and featured big-name bands such as Stan Kenton, Harry James, and Tommy Dorsey— all prior to its emergence as a restaurant. Courtesy, The Public Information Office of the City of Huntington Beach

Tommy Dorsey performed there in the early 1940s. The Pavalon was then converted for use as a roller-skating rink. Later, when the facility was being used as a dance hall for teenagers, extensive fire damage to the interior of the structure resulted in its transformation into an eatery known as The Fisherman restaurant.

In 1977 Maxwell's By The Sea became the occupant of the historic premises as a full-service eatery, serving breakfast, lunch, and dinner 365 days a year. Maxwell's is owned by Paul Wimmer and William Schroeder. Wimmer functions as the restaurant's day-to-day manager and creator of its bill of fare. His thirty-seven years of experience in the food-service business, chiefly with the Marriott Hotel chain in the eastern United States, more than prepared him for the challenge of establishing Maxwell's as an upgraded, stylish restaurant at a prime seaside location, in conjunction with the City of Huntington Beach's revitalization of its main business district. Under Wimmer's skilled management, annual receipts have increased from $1.4 million to

Today patrons are attracted to Maxwell's By The Sea for its gourmet food, well-trained staff, and the spectacular seascapes and sunsets.

$4 million since Maxwell's began operating as a seafood specialty restaurant.

It was Wimmer's imagination and careful planning that enabled Maxwell's to present its first annual Seafood Spectacular in November 1985. That month he arranged to import by air numerous unique fresh fish from waters around the globe— Africa, Australia, Europe, Hawaii, India, Japan, New Zealand, and South America—to be featured daily on lunch and dinner menus.

Personal attention by Wimmer to all facets of the restaurant's operation has created an ambience that continues to attract patrons who wish to reexperience Maxwell's By The Sea's gourmet-type foods, consistently prepared with talent and flair. Adding to its attractiveness is its efficient service by a well-trained staff, thoroughly familiar with its extensive menus; its spectacular seascapes and sunsets; and its live music and dancing, all amid an art deco motif.

PATRONS

The following individuals, companies, and organizations have made a valuable commitment to the quality of this publication. Windsor Publications, Inc., and the Bowers Museum gratefully acknowledge their participation in *The Golden Promise: An Illustrated History of Orange County.*

A&C Properties, Inc.*
AirCal*
Alex Foods, Inc.*
Aluminum Precision Products, Inc.*
American Association of University Women:
    San Clemente/Capistrano Bay Branch
Anaheim Memorial Hospital*
Associated Concrete Products, Inc.*
Bank of America NT&SA*
David Belardes
Bell Pipe & Supply Co.*
Birtcher*
Bob Black Oldsmobile*
Robert Borders and Associates*
Buena Park Lumber and Hardware*
California Computer Products, Inc. (CalComp)
Camino Real Savings Bank*
Canon Business Machines, Inc.*
Case-Swayne Company, Inc.*
Century American Corporation*
Cherry Division of Textron, Inc.*
Coldwell Banker*
Connector Technology, Inc.*
Covington Technologies*
Trammell Crow Company*
Datapower Inc.*
Deloitte Haskins & Sells*
Disneyland*
Disneyland Hotel*
Donnelley Marketing
    A Company of The Dun & Bradstreet Corporation*
Ducummun Electronics Group Div. Ducummun,
    Incorporated
Dynamic Air Engineering, Inc.*
FHP, Inc.*
The Fieldstone Company*
First American Title Insurance Company*
Fleet Services
Fluidmaster, Inc.*
Forsum/Summers & Partners*
Founders K Corporation*
Franco Manufacturing, Inc.*
Great American First Savings Bank*
Greater Santa Ana Chamber of Commerce*
Hoag Memorial Hospital Presbyterian*
Hobbs Trucking Company, Inc.*

Huntington Beach Company*
The Irvine Company*
Irvine Ranch Farmer's Markets*
Carl Karcher Enterprises, Inc.*
Kelly-Wright Hardwoods Inc.
Knott's Berry Farm*
Kraft, Inc.*
Leason Pomeroy Associates, Inc.*
Lee and Associates Commercial Real Estate Services*
Leighton and Associates, Inc.*
Martin Luther Hospital Medical Center*
M.K. Products, Inc.*
McLean Cadillac*
McMahan Desk, Inc.*
Manufacturing and Consulting Services*
Maxwell's By The Sea*
MDB Systems, Inc.*
Near-Cal Corporation*
Northrop Corporation*
Orange County Historical Society
Osterkamp Trucking Inc.*
Pacific Bell
The Pacific Mutual Life Insurance Company*
Pacific Scientific Co.
Betty J. Prizio
Rancho Mission Viejo*
Richardson Nagy Martin Architecture/Planning*
Rutan & Tucker*
Saddleback Area Historical Society
St. John Knits*
St. Joseph Hospital*
St. Jude Hospital*
Santa Ana Nissan/Datsun*
C.J. Segerstrom & Sons*
Merel E. and Geraldine M. Sexton
Signal Landmark Properties, Inc.*
Sixpence Inns of America, Inc.*
Smith International, Inc.*
Southern California Edison
Steffy Buick Co.*
Steinbrugge, Thomas & Bloom, Inc.*
Elizabeth Swanson
Marie Patterson Swanson
Taylor Bus Service*
Howard F. Thompson & Associates, Inc.*
Barbara H. Towne, M.D.
Traveland U.S.A.*
TRW Information Services Division
Western Medical Center/Santa Ana*
Williamson and Schmid*
World Travel*

*Partners in Progress of *The Golden Promise: An Illustrated History of Orange County.* The histories of these companies and organizations appear in Chapter 13, beginning on page 305.

BIBLIOGRAPHY

BOOKS

Anonymous. *Focus on Orange County, An Economic Study of the Anaheim, Santa Ana, Garden Grove Metropolitan Area.* Bank of America National Trust and Savings Association, l965.

Armor, Samuel, ed. *History of Orange County, California.* Los Angeles: Historic Record Co., 1911 and 1921.

Associated Chambers of Commerce of Orange County. *The Majestic Eyes of Orange County.* Orange County Board of Supervisors, Santa Ana: l953.

Ball, C.D. *Orange County Medical History.* Santa Ana: Flagg, 1926.

Bancroft, Hubert Howe. *California Pastoral, 1796-1848.* San Francisco: A.L. Bancroft, 1888.

_____. *History of California.* 7 vols. San Francisco: A.L. Bancroft, 1884-90.

Banks, Homer. *The Story of San Clemente.* San Clemente: El Heraldo de San Clemente, 1930.

Bell, Horace. *Reminiscences of Ranger or Early Times in Southern California.* Santa Barbara: Wallace Hubbard, 1927.

Booth, Louise. *Villa Park—Then and Now.* Villa Park Historical Society, Santa Ana: Friis Pioneer Press, 1976.

Boscana, Geronimo. *Chinigchinich.* Santa Ana: Fine Arts Press, 1933.

Bowers, Stephen. *Orange County, California: History, Soil, Climate, Resources, Advantages.* Board of Trade of Santa Ana, Los Angeles: Los Angeles Printing Company, l891.

Butz, Mareh. *Yorba Linda: Its Hisory.* Santa Ana: Pioneer Press, 1970.

Camp, C.W. "Bob." *La Mirada: From Rancho to City.* Fullerton: Sultana Press, 1970.

Carpenter, Virginia. *A Child's History of Placentia.* Placentia: Courier Press, 1969.

_____. *Placentia, A Pleasant Place.* Santa Ana: Friis Pioneer Press, 1977.

_____. *The Ranchos of Don Pacifico Ontiveros.* Santa Ana: Friis Pioneer Press, l982.

Carrillo, Leo (with Ed Ainsworth). *The California I Love.* Englewood Cliffs: Prentice-Hall, 1961.

Century I Historians. *Santa Ana's 100 Years: Prelude to Progress.* Santa Ana: Aladdin Litho and Art, 1969.

Chapman, Charles E. *A History of California: The Spanish Period.* New York: McMillan and Co., 1921.

Cleland, Robert Glass. *From Wilderness to Empire: A History of California, 1542-1900.* New York: Knopf, 1944.

_____. *The Cattle on a Thousand Hills: Southern California, 1850-1880.* San Marino: Huntington Library, 1941.

_____. *The Irvine Ranch of Orange County, 1910-1950.* San Marino: Huntington Library, 1952.

Corney, Peter. *Early Voyages in the North Pacific, 1813-1818.* Washington: Ye Galleon Press, 1965.

Costanso, Miguel. *The Portola Expedition of 1769-1770.* Ed. Frederick J. Teggert. Berkeley: University of California Press, 1941.

County of Orange. *Bienvenidos al Canon de Santa Ana: A History of the Santa Ana Canyon.* Environmental Management Agency, Interpretive Series #5, 1976.

_____. *Historical Guide to Carbon Canyon Regional Park.* Environmental Management Agency, Interpretive Series #3, 1975.

Cramer, Esther R. *La Habra: The Pass Through the Hills.* Fullerton: Sultana Press, 1969.

Cunningham, Captain William. *The Log of the Courier, 1826-1828.* Early California Travel Series, Los Angeles: Glen Dawson, 1958.

Dana, Richard Henry. *Two Years Before the Mast.* New York: Dutton, 1912.

Davis, William Heath. *Seventy-Five Years in California.* San Francisco: John Howell, 1929.

Dimmit, Richard Bertrand. *The Spurgeon Story.* Orange: Orange County Public Library, 1971.

Doig, Leroy L. *Newhope Days.* Santa Ana: Pioneer Press, 1971.

_____. *The Town of Garden Grove.* Santa Ana: Pioneer Press, 1966.

_____. *The Village of Garden Grove.* Santa Ana: Pioneer Press, l962.

Dominguez, Arnold. *Jose Antonio Yorba I.* Santa Ana: Orange County Historical Society, 1967.

Dumke, Glen S. *The Boom of the Eighties in Southern California.* San Marino: Huntington Library, 1944.

Edwards, Dixie. *Anaheim and So It Was.* Santa Ana: Friis Pioneer Press, 1976.

Engelhardt, Zephyrin. *San Gabriel Mission.* Chicago: Mission Herald Press, 1927.

_____. *San Juan Capistrano Mission.* Los Angeles: Standard Printing Co., 1922.

Federal Writers Project. *California: A Guide to the Golden State.* New York: Hastings House, 1939.

Forbes, Mrs. A.S.C. *Mission Tales in the Days of the Dons.* Chicago: A.C. McClary, 1909.

Fox, Clara Mason. *A History of El Toro.* Santa Ana: Public Steno Shop, 1939.

Friis, Leo. *At the Bar.* Santa Ana: Friis Pioneer Press, 1980.

_____. *The Charles W. Bowers Memorial Museum and Its Treasures.* Santa Ana: Pioneer Press, l967.

_____. *Orange County Through Four Centuries.* Santa Ana: Pioneer Press, 1965.

_____. *When Anaheim Was 21.* Santa Ana: Pioneer Press, 1968.

Garrison, Myrtle. *Romance and History of the California Ranchos.* San Francisco: Wagner, 1935.

Gibson, Wayne Dell. *Tomas Yorba's Santa Ana Viejo, 1769-1847.* Santa Ana: Santa Ana College Foundation Press, 1976.

_____. *The Olive Mill, Orange County's Pioneer Industry.* Santa Ana: Orange County Historical Society, 1975.

Guinn, James Miller. *Historical and Biographical Record of Southern California.* Chicago: Chapman Publishing Co., 1902.

_____. *History of California and Extended Histories of Its Southern Coast Counties.* 2 vols. Los Angeles: Historic Record Co., 1907.

_____. *Southern California: Its History and Its People.* 2 vols. Los Angeles: Historic Record Co., 1907.

Hallan, Pamela. *Dos Cientos Anos en San Juan Capistrano.* Irvine: Walker Color Graphics, 1975.

Hallan-Gibson, Pamela. *Ghosts and Legends of San Juan Capistrano.* San Juan Capistrano: Coastline Printers, 1983.

Harding, Purl. *The History of Brea, California: From Early Oilfield Days to 1950.* Brea: Brea Progress Publishers, 1950.

Hardy, John. *Tustin Tintypes: A Pictorial History of Old Tustin.* Laguna Beach: Hardy House Publishing Co., 1974.

Hart, Don. *A History of Orange County.* Santa Ana: Miles M. Sharon, Santa Ana High School, 1939.

Hill, Merton E. *One Hundred Years of Public Education in Orange County.*

Santa Ana: Orange County Schools Office, 1957.

James, George Wharton. *In and Out of the Old Missions.* Boston: Little, Brown and Co., 1906.

Janssens, Augustin. *Life and Adventures in California of Don Augustin Janssens.* Ed. William H. Ellison and Francis Price. San Marino: Huntington Library, 1953.

Kenneally, Finbar, ed. *The Writings of Fermin Francisco de Lasuen.* 2 vols. Washington: Academy of American Franciscan History, 1965.

Knowlton, Charles S. *Post Offices of Orange County, California, Past and Present.* Placentia, 1947.

Kroeber, Alfred Louis. *Handbook of Indians of California.* Washington: Bureau of American Ethnology, Bulletin 78, 1925.

Lavender, David. *California: A Bicentennial History.* New York: W.W. Norton and Co., 1976.

Lee, Ellen K. *Newport Bay: A Pioneer History.* Fullerton: Sultana Press, 1973.

Lindley, Walter and J.P. Widney. *California of the South—Its Physical Geography, Climate, Resources, Routes of Travel and Health Records.* New York: D. Appleton and Co., 1888.

Lund, William S. *Orange County: Its Economic Growth 1940-1980.* Stanford Research Institute, Southern California Laboratories, 1959.

MacArthur, Mildred Yorba. *Anaheim: The Mother Colony.* Los Angeles: Ward Ritchie Press, 1959.

McDannald, D.W. *Orange County, California—Spring Eternal—A Pleasing Story Interestingly Told of One of the Richest Sections of the Universe.* Orange County Board of Supervisors, Santa Ana: 1915.

McFadden, Michael. *Only in Laguna.* South Laguna: John Hardy, Publisher, 1972.

Meadows, Don. *Historic Place Names in Orange County.* Balboa Island: Paisano Press, 1966.

_____. *Orange County Under Spain, Mexico and the United States.* Los Angeles: Dawson's Book Shop, 1966.

Meyer, Samuel A. *Fifty Golden Years: A History of the City of Newport Beach, 1906-1956.* Newport Beach: The Newport Harbor Publishing Co., 1957.

Miller, Edrick J. *A Slice of Orange: The History of Costa Mesa.* Irvine: Hendricks Printing Co., 1976.

_____. *The Hayburners of Orange County.* Costa Mesa Historical Society, 1978.

_____. *The SAAAB Story, (Santa Ana Army Air Base).* Santa Ana: Tri-Level Inc. Lithographers, 1981.

Modjeska, Helena. *Memories and Impressions of Helena Modjeska, An Autobiography.* New York: McMillan Co., 1910.

Morison, Samuel Eliot and Henry Steele Commager. *Growth of the American Republic.* 5th ed., 2 vols. London: Oxford University Press, 1962.

Newmark, Harris. *Sixty Years in Southern California, 1853-1913.* New York: Knickerbocker Press, 1916.

Oral History Program, California State University, Fullerton. *Community History Project: San Juan Capistrano.* Fullerton, 1976, 2 vols.

Orange County Genealogical Society. *Saddleback Ancestors, Rancho Families of Orange County.* Santa Ana: Aladdin Litho and Art, 1969.

Orange County Historical Commission. *Yesterdays in Orange County.* County of Orange, 1977.

Orange County Historical Society. *Orange Countiana.* Vol III. Fullerton: Christian Printing Service, 1982.

_____. *Orange County History Series.* Vol I. Santa Ana: Santa Ana High School and Junior College Press, 1931.

_____. *Orange County History Series.* Vol. II. Santa Ana: Santa Ana High School and Junior College Press, 1932.

_____. *Orange County History Series.* Vol. III. Santa Ana: Santa Ana High School and Junior College Press, 1939.

Osterman, Joe. *Fifty Years in Old El Toro.* Fullerton: Sultana Press, 1982.

Palou, Francisco. *Historical Memoirs of New California.* 4 vols. Ed. Herbert Bolton. Berkeley: University of California Press, 1926.

_____. *Life and Apostolic Labors of Venerable Father Junipero Serra.* Trans. C. Scott Williams. Pasadena: G.W. James, 1913.

Parker, Charles Edward. *A Manual of Orange County History.* Santa Ana: Orange County Title Company, 1964.

Parker, Charles Edward and Marilyn. *Orange County: Indians to Industry.* Santa Ana: Orange County Title Co., 1963.

Payne, Theodore. *Life on the Modjeska Ranch in the Gay '90s.* Los Angeles: Kruckenberg Press, 1962.

Pico, Pio. *Historical Narrative.* Trans. Arthur P. Botello. Glendale: Arthur P. Clark Co., 1973.

Pitt, Leonard. *Decline of the Californios.* Berkeley and Los Angeles: University of California Press, 1970.

Pleasants, Adelina (Brown). *History of Orange County, California.* Los Angeles: J.R. Finnell and Sons, 1931.

Quill Pen Club. *Rawhide and Orange Blossoms: Stories and Sketches of Early Orange County.* Santa Ana: Pioneer Press, 1967.

Ramsey, Mabel and Merle. *Pioneer Days of Laguna Beach.* Laguna Beach: Hastie Printers, 1967.

_____. *This Was Mission Country, Orange County, Ca.* Laguna Beach: Mission Printing Co., 1973.

Rambo, Ralph. *Tiburcio Vasquez.* San Jose: Rosicrucian Press, 1968.

Roberts, C.E. *Adobes of Orange County.* U.S. Works Projects Administration, California, Orange County Series, WPA Research Project No. 3105, Santa Ana, 1936-37.

Robinson, Alfred. *Life in California.* Oakland: Biobooks, 1947.

Robinson, W.W. *Land in California: The Story of Mission Lands, Ranchos, Squatters, Mining Claims, R.R. Grants, Landings, Homesteads.* Berkeley and Los Angeles: University of California Press, 1948.

_____. *Old Spanish and Mexican Ranchos of Orange County.* Los Angeles: Title Insurance and Trust Co., 1950.

Santa Ana Chamber of Commerce. *Orange County and the Santa Ana Valley of Southern California.* Undated, unattributed, University of California, Irvine, special collections.

Santa Ana Register. Legacy: The Orange County Story. Santa Ana Register Supplement, 1979.

Santa Ana Valley Immigration Association. *Santa Ana Valley of Southern California—Its Resources, Climate, Growth, Future.* Los Angeles: Burton-Taney Steam Printing House, 1885.

Sleeper, Jim. *A Boy's Book of Bear Stories: A Grizzly Introduction to the Santa Ana Mountains.* Trabuco Canyon: California Classics, 1976.

_____. *Great Movies Shot in Orange County.* Trabuco Canyon: California Classics, 1980.

_____. *Orange County Almanac of Historical Oddities.* 3 vols. Santa Ana: Ocusa Press, 1971, 1974, 1983.

_____. *Turn the Rascals Out: The Life and Times of Orange County's Fighting Editor Dan M. Bak-*

er. Trabuco Canyon: California Classics, 1973.

Smith, Vi. *From Jennies to Jets: The Aviation History of Orange County.* Fullerton: Sultana Press, 1974.

Stephenson, Shirley. *John J. Baumgartner Jr.: Reflections of a Scion of the Rancho Santa Margarita.* Oral History Program, California State University, Fullerton, Community History Project, San Juan Capistrano, OH 1657, 1982.

Stephenson, Terry Elmo. *Caminos Viejos.* Santa Ana: Santa Ana High School and Junior College Press, 1930.

_____. *Shadows of Old Saddleback.* Santa Ana: Fine Arts Press, 1931.

Swanner, Charles Douglas. *Fifty Years a Barrister in Orange County.* Claremont: Fraser Press, 1965.

_____. *Santa Ana: A Narrative of Yesterday.* Claremont: Saunders Press, 1953.

_____. *The Story of Company L, Santa Ana's Own.* Claremont: Fraser Press, 1958.

_____. *Those Were the Days: Recollections of Charles D. Swanner.* Elsinore: Mayhall Print Shop, 1971.

Talbert, Thomas. *My Sixty Years in California.* Huntington Beach: Huntington Beach News Press, 1952.

_____. *The Historical Volume and Reference Works: Orange County, California.* 3 vols. Whittier: Historical Publishers, 1963.

Walker, Doris. *Dana Point Harbor/Capistrano Bay: Home Port For Romance.* Dana Point: To-the-Point Press, 1981.

Warner, J.J., Judge Benjamin Hayes, and J.P. Widney. *An Historical Sketch of Los Angeles County.* Los Angeles: O.W. Smith, 1876.

Webb, Edith Buckland. *Indian Life at the Old Missions.* Los Angeles: Warren F. Lewis, 1952.

Wieman, William Wallace. *The Separation and Organization of Orange County.* Publisher unknown, 1938.

Wilson, John Albert. *Reproduction of Thompson and West's History of Los Angeles County, California.* Berkeley: Howell-North, 1959.

Wolcott, Marjorie Tisdale. *Pioneer Notes from the Diaries of Judge Benjamin Hayes, 1849-1875.* Los Angeles: McBride Printing, 1929.

ARTICLES

Alleman, R. "Riviera in our own Backyard." *Vogue* 167(October 1977):210.

Baker, Charles C. "Mexican Land Grants in California." *Historical Society of Southern California Annual Publication,* IX(No. 3):236-43.

Barrows, Henry D. "Abel Stearns." *Historical Society of Southern California Annual Publication,* IV(No. 3):197-99.

Bowman, J.N. "The Resident Neophytes (Existentes) of the California Missions." *Historical Society of Southern California Quarterly,* XL(No. 2): 138-48.

Champlin, Charles. "Musings on Masterful Irvine Plan." *Los Angeles Times,* May 28, 1983.

Garr, Daniel. "Planning, Politics, Plunder: The Mission and Indian Pueblos of Hispanic California." *Historical Society of Southern California Quarterly,* LIV, Winter 1972.

Geiger, Maynard. "New Data on Mission San Juan Capistrano." *Southern California Historical Society Quarterly,* XLIX, March 1967.

Getlin, Josh, and David Reyes. "Dreams Gone Sour—The Newest Slums Out in Suburbia." *Los Angeles Times,* October 2, 1983.

Goodhue, T. "Orange County Isn't What It Used to Be." *New Republic,* 159(October 12, 1968):17-18.

_____. "Report on the Two Cultures." *New Republic,* 162(June 20, 1970):12-13.

Haas, Jane Glenn. "Santa Margarita: Betting the Ranch." *The Register,* February 3, 1985.

Holt, Raymond. "The Fruits of Viticulture in Orange County." *Historical Society of Southern California Quarterly,* XXVIII, Part 1, March 1946.

"Imported Water: Protection to Ground Water Supplies." *American City,* 75(April 1960):117-18.

Killingsworth, James C., pub. *Orange County Illustrated.* Irvine: 1962-69.

La Jeunesse, Anne. "Ghosts, A Frightening Account of the Ghostly Phenomenon that Haunt Orange County." *Orange Coast Magazine,* October 1980.

"Little Piece of America." *Newsweek,* 68(November 14, 1966):32.

Mabbutt, F.R. "Greening of Orange County." *Nation,* 218(March 23, 1974):367-70.

"More Than a Suburb, Less Than a City." *Business Week,* (September 5, 1977):76-77.

Morgan, J. and N. "Orange, A Most California County." *National Geographic,* 160(December 1981):750-79.

O'Dell, John. "Early Railroad Kings Ran

the State But Not Irvine." *The Register,* August 14, 1978.

Parker, Charles Edward. "Ranchos of Mission San Juan Capistrano." *Orange County Newsmagazine,* IX, February 2, 1965.

Savage, Thomas. "Interview with Don Juan Forster." *Historical Society of Southern California Quarterly,* September 1970.

Seelye, Howard, and Don Smith. "A Century of Politics in Orange County." *Los Angeles Times,* May 21, 1976.

Sleeper, Jim, ed. *Rancho San Joaquin Gazette.* All vols. Irvine Co., 1968.

Walker, Ruth. "County May Reach No. 3 in High Tech Field." *Christian Science Monitor,* Western Edition, September 14, 1984.

_____. "Few are Gung Ho About John Wayne Airport." *Christian Science Monitor,* Western Edition, September 14, 1984.

_____. "Irvine Ranch: Master-Planned Living." *Christian Science Monitor,* Western Edition, September 14, 1984.

_____. "Lack of Affordable Housing Threatens Industrial Base." *Christian Science Monitor,* Western Edition, September 14, 1984.

_____. "New Political Coalition Fights Traffic Congestion." *Christian Science Monitor,* Western Edition, September 14, 1984.

_____. "Tomorrowland in the World's 30th Largest Economy." *Christian Science Monitor,* Western Edition, September 14, 1984.

_____. "45,000 Newcomers Yearly Hail From Everywhere for Jobs." *Christian Science Monitor,* Western Edition, September 14, 1984.

Zalaznick, S. "Double Life of Orange County." *Fortune,* 78(October 1968): 138-41.

DOCUMENTS

Mission San Juan Capistrano, Baptismal, Marriage and Death Records, 1776-1886.

Orange County Annual Survey, Mark Baldassare, Director, University of California, Irvine, 1982, 1983, 1984.

Padron of Los Angeles, 1836, Los Angeles City Archives.

Padron of Los Angeles, 1844, Los Angeles City Archives.

Seventh Census of the United States, 1850, Los Angeles County, California.

INDEX

PARTNERS IN PROGRESS INDEX

A&C Properties, Inc., 411
AirCal, 360-361
Alex Foods, Inc., 396
Aluminum Precision Products, Inc., 391
Anaheim Memorial Hospital, 336-337
Associated Concrete Products, Inc., 398-399
Bank of America NT&SA, 370-371
Bell Pipe & Supply Co., 412
Birtcher, 312-313
Black Oldsmobile, Bob, 343
Borders and Associates, Robert, 374
Bowers Museum, 308
Buena Park Lumber and Hardware, 386
Camino Real Savings Bank, 362-363
Canon Business Machines, Inc., 393
Case-Swayne Company, Inc., 340-341
Century American Corporation, 389
Cherry Division of Textron, Inc., 348-349
Coldwell Banker, 383
Connector Technology, Inc., 416
Covington Technologies, 378
Crow Company, Trammell, 354
Datapower Inc., 342
Deloitte Haskins & Sells, 315
Disneyland, 310-311
Disneyland Hotel, 314
Donnelley Marketing
   A Company of The Dun & Bradstreet
   Corporation, 394-395
Dynamic Air Engineering, Inc., 379
FHP, Inc., 373
Fieldstone Company, The, 409
First American Title Insurance Company, 338-339
Fluidmaster, Inc., 268-269
Forsum/Summers & Partners, 384
Founders K Corporation, 358-359
Franco Manufacturing, Inc., 417
Great American First Savings Bank, 367
Greater Santa Ana Chamber of Commerce, 405
Hoag Memorial Hospital Presbyterian, 328-329
Hobbs Trucking Company, Inc., 390
Huntington Beach Company, 356-357
Irvine Company, The, 345
Irvine Ranch Farmer's Markets, 376-377
Karcher Enterprises, Inc., Carl, 309
Knott's Berry Farm, 406-407
Kraft, Inc., 365
Leason Pomeroy Associates, Inc., 366
Lee and Associates Commercial Real Estate Services,
   404
Leighton and Associates, Inc., 408
Luther Hospital Medical Center, Martin, 352-353
M.K. Products, Inc., 418-419
McLean Cadillac, 322-323
McMahan Desk, Inc., 392
Manufacturing and Consulting Services, 400-403
Maxwell's By The Sea, 422
MDB Systems, Inc., 410
Near-Cal Corporation, 385
Northrop Corporation, 387
Osterkamp Trucking Inc., 382
Pacific Mutual Life Insurance Company, The,
   334-335
Rancho Mission Viejo, 316-319
Richardson Nagy Martin Architecture/Planning, 372
Rutan & Tucker, 330-331
St. John Knits, 380-381
St. Joseph Hospital, 324-325
St. Jude Hospital, 332-333
Santa Ana Nissan/Datsun, 355
Segerstrom & Sons, C.J., 320-321
Signal Landmark Properties, Inc., 350-351
Sixpence Inns of America, Inc., 414-415
Smith International, Inc., 326-327
Steffy Buick Co., 344
Steinbrugge, Thomas & Bloom, Inc., 388
Taylor Bus Service, 375
Thompson & Associates, Inc., Howard F., 413
Traveland U.S.A., 420-421
Western Medical Center/Santa Ana, 346-347
Williamson and Schmid, 397
World Travel, 364

GENERAL INDEX

Italicized numbers indicate illustrations.

A
Abbott, William, 78, 80
Agriculture, 27, 30, 37, 70, 78, 84, 86, 99, 100, 105,
   108, 112, 113, 124, *143,* 148, 149, *150-151,* 154,
   156, *164,* 174, 183, 194, 205, 227, 236, 237, 240,
   243, 256-259, *267,* 269, 274, 276
Aguilár, Isídro, 23
Air California, *252, 253,* 256
Alamitos Bay, 64, 186
Alemany, Joseph Sadoc, 55
Aliso Beach, 122
Aliso City, 116
Aliso Creek, 24
Allen, Gabriel, *69*
Alvarado, Juan Bautista, 34, 41
American High Speed Rail Corporation, 272. *See
   also* Bullet Train
American Institute of Architects, Orange County
   Chapter, 261
Amerige, Annette J., *ll9, 120*
Amerige, Edward, 114, 116, *119, 130, 170*
Amerige, George, 114, 116, *118, 120, 170*
Amtrak, 271
Amúrrio, Gregório, 19
Anaheim, 35, 58, 62, 64, 65, *66,* 67, 69-70, 83, 84,
   88, 98, 99, 103, 114, 124, 134, 135, 149, 183,
   206, 227, 231, 240, 241, 249, 261, 276, 280, *297;*
   early pumping station of, *79;* 1894 picnic, *87;*
   founding of, 58, 59, 62, 64; penny carnival of, *296;*
   population of, 1915, 231
Anaheim Baseball Team, *254*
Anaheim City Park, *208;* 1927 Old Timers' picnic at,
   208
Anaheim Civic Center, *273*
Anaheim Colony, 64, 68, 99, 103
Anaheim Convention Center, *272, 303*
Anaheim First Presbyterian Church, *89*
Anaheim Hills, *270-271*
Anaheim Landing, 64, 65, 70
Anaheim Lighter Company, 65
Anaheim's State Guard Company G, *88*
Anaheim Stadium, 253, *255,* 261, 273
Anaheim Union Water Company, 86; flume Number
   8, *86-87*
Anaheim Water Company, 64, 84, 86
Apricot production, *81,* 84, 149, 154, 186, 205
Arch Beach, 186
Arguello, Santiago, 26, 35
Armor, Samuel, 135
Army Air Force Personnel Distribution Command,
   228
Army Corps of Engineers, 212
Arrillaga, José Joaquín, 23
Associated Chambers of Commerce, 236
Atherton family, Edward, *162*
Atwood, 122
Automobiles, 194, *196, 197, 199,* 201, *211*
Avery, Alice O'Neill, 269
Ávila, Juan (Don), 35, 147; adobe of, *38*
Ávila, Modesta, 136, 139
Avocado production, 173, 205; Fuerte variety, 173
Ayuntamiento (provincial council), 31

B
Baker, Dan, 126
Balboa Island, 163
Balboa Pavilion, *234,* 250
Balboa Peninsula, *234*
Balboa Pier, *234, 300*
Banana production, 84
Bandini, Arcadia, 33
Bandini, Juan (Don), 32, 40
Bandits' Rendezvous Tree, *51*
Bank of America, 265
Barber City, 241
Barton, James, 51, 54
Bastanchury, Domingo, 70, 160
Bastanchury family, *71*
Bastanchury Ranch, *56*
Battin, Robert, 260
Battle of Los Angeles, 225
Battle of San Pasqual, 46
Bay City, 162, 186. *See also* Seal Beach
Bay Island, 101
Bayshore-King's Road. *See* Pacific Coast Highway
Bayside Land Company, 162
Bear Flag Republic, 45
Beckman Instruments, 260
Bennett, James, 232
Benton, Thomas Hart, 47
Berry, C.E., 231
Best, S.C.: bus of, *197*
"Big Four," 112
Birch Oil, 158
Birch Society, John, 244
Bishop, A.D., 84
Bixby, Jotham, 70
Bixby, Llewelyn, 70
Bixby Land Company, 149
Black Star Canyon, 52
Boca de la Playa, 35
Boege family, T.J.F., *131*
Bolsa, 183
Bonanza Airlines, 254
Boomer Canyon, 258
Booth, Edwin, 100
Boscana, Geronimo, 24, 25
Bowers Memorial Museum, Charles W., *247, 250,*
   273
Boyd, J.P., 101
Boyd, Rosa, 101
Boysen Park, *297*
Bradford, Ward, 76
Brea, 35, 156, 162, 169, 173, 232. *See also* Randolph
Brea Cañon Oil Company, 158
Brea Canyon, 156, 160
Brea Canyon oil field, *307*
Brown, Edmund G., Jr., 271
Browning Winery, Ernest: workers of, *63*
"Brunner's basement," 136, 139
Bryant, Sturgis, and Company, 31
Bucareli, Antonio Maria, 29
Buena Park, 34, 83, 116, 183, 240, 241, 249
Buena Park Fire Department, 232
Buena Park Volunteers, 232
Bullet Train, 273-274
Burnett, Peter, 50
Burrows, Albert, *122*
Burrows, Mrs. Albert, *122*
Burruel Point, 116

C
Cabrillo, Juan Rodriguez, *16*
Cajón Irrigation Company, 86
Cajón Water District, 84
California Angels, 253, 273
California Division of Forestry, 211
California Hotel, *171*
California of the South, 125
California Peace Officers Association, 136
California Sheriffs' Association, 137
California Southern Railroad, 116. *See also* Santa Fe
   Railroad
California State Assembly, 244
California Supreme Court, 243
Camp Pendleton, 261
Capistrano Beach, 35, 192
Capistrano Nights, 146, 147
Carbon Canyon, 122, 126
Carbon Canyon Regional Park, 125, 126
Carlton, 116
Carpenter, Virginia, 84
Carpenter Adobe, *53*

Carrillo, Carlos Antonio, 41
Carrillo, José Antonio, 40
Carrillo, Ramón, 46
Caspers, Ron, 260
Caspers Regional Park, 126
Castro, José, 40, 41, 46
Catalina Island, 183, 224
Catalina-on-the-Main, 112
Catholics, 31. See also Roman Catholic Church
Cattle industry, 28, 45, 47, 48, 50, 52, 58, 67, 68, 70
Cayucos, 224
Celery production, 148, 163, 183
Cella, Louis, 260
Central Oil, 160
Central Pacific Railroad, 112, 113
Chapman, Albert, 70, 76
Chapman, Charles C., 191, 192
Chapman Building, 193
Chapman College, 194
Chapman Ditch, 76
Chapman No. 1 (oil well), 192
Chico, Mariano, 32, 40
Chinese laborers, 84, 148, 149, 179
Chino, 149, 158
Chlapowski, Count Karol Bozenta, 98, 99, 100
Citrus Growers, Inc., 228
Citrus industry, 83, 84, 149, 151, 154, 205, 227, 228, 236, 258, 294; 1930s citrus queen, 207; orange pickers at Rimpau Grove, 82; sausage tents of, 225
Civilian Conservation Corps, 206, 211
Civil War, 68, 70
Clark, J. Ross, 113
Clark, W.A., 113
Clark, William A., 149
Cleland, Robert Glass, 70
Cleveland National Forest, 34, 35, 212, 237
Coast Royale, 191
Coffee, Robert, 42
Collins, Sam L., 244
Collins, William S., 125, 163
Collins Radio Company, 257
Columbia Oil Company, 158
Confidence Fire Company No. 1 (Anaheim), 231
Congdon, Joel, 83
Cook, Alonzo G., 83
Cook, Gardner, and Victor, 116
Corney, Peter, 26
Corn production, 84, 156
Corona del Mar, 34, 237, 254
Cortese, Ross W., 243
Cory, Ken, 260
Costa Mesa, 30, 125, 135, 186, 194, 228, 232, 238, 240, 241, 256, 257, 259, 271, 273; Mesa del Mar housing tract, 256
Costanso, Miguel, 16
Cotton, H.H., 191, 192
Cottontail Switch, 111
Cox, John B., 136, 204
Coy, Maggie, 169
Coyote Creek, 46, 134
Coyote Hills, 160
Cranston, E.J., 117
Crespi, Juan, 17
Crestline, 122
Cristianitos Canyon, 12, 17
Crocker, Charles, 112
Crystal Cathedral, 265, 302
Curtis, E.A., 148
Cypress, 34, 166, 183, 233, 241. See also Waterville

D
Daguerre Ranch, 258
Dairyland, 240. See also La Palma
Dana, Richard Henry, 31; statue of, 264
Dana Point, 146, 147, 189, 191, 201, 273
Dana Point Harbor, 253
Daniel, Pancho, 51, 52
Daniels, Bebe, 136, 204
Dannemeyer, William, 260
de los Reyes, Alvina, 278. See also Pink Lady
Dillin Flour Mill, 108-109
Dillon, Thomas, 116
Disney, Walt, 249

Disneyland, 244, 245, 246, 249, 250, 279
Doheny, Edward L., Jr., 192
Doheny, Edward L., Sr., 158, 192
Doheny Park, 192. See also Capistrano Beach
Drainage Act of 1881, 148
Dreyfus, Benjamin, 98, 103
Dreyfus Winery, 102; wine pump of, 102
Droughts, 67-68, 70, 84, 103; of 1876-1877, 88
Duflot de Mofras, Eugene, 27
Dumke, Glen, 116
Dunbar, Wiggin, and Stevens Real Estate: office of, 121
Dunlap, Jonathan, 96
Dunlap Blue Light Mine, 96, 98
Dunnells, Samuel, 78, 80
Dyer Company, E.H., 149

E
East Newport, 163
East Newport Town Company, 163
Echeandía, José María, 39, 40
Edinger, 220
Education, 55, 64, 99, 124, 179, 253; Orange County school bus, 92
Edwards, E.E., 134, 135
Earl Fruit Company, 148
Earlham, 122. See also El Modena
Earthquake of 1812, 23
Earthquake of 1933, 137, 205, 206
Eastman, Frank, 115, 142; Rural Free Delivery mail carrier of, 142
Egan, Richard, 101
Elliott, Jesse, 137
El Modena, 30, 183
Elsinore, 33
El Toro, 35, 116, 149, 183, 186, 243, 256, 274. See also Aliso City
El Toro Marine Corps Air Station, 232, 274
El Toro School, 151, 154
El Viaje de Portolá, 273
Engelhardt, Zephyrin, 146
Environmental Impact Report, 274
Equal Rights Amendment, 266
Erickson, O.S., 232
Escondido, 46
Estancia Adobe, 68-69
Estudillo, José Antonio, 32
Eureka, 224
Eureka Stables, 95
Exclusionary Order, 227

F
Facio, 32
Fairview, 83, 122, 135, 186, 220. See also Costa Mesa
Fairview Hot Springs, 125
Fashion Island, 237, 259
Festival of Arts, 211-212. See also Pageant of the Masters
Figueroa, José, 40
First National Bank building (Santa Ana), 104
First National Bank of Tustin, 117
First Presbyterian Church of Fullerton, 92
Flint, Benjamin, 70
Flint, Thomas, 70
Flood, James, 125, 269
Flood of 1938, 137, 212, 213
Floods, 67, 70, 84
Flores, José María, 46
Flores, Juan, 51, 52, 54
Fluor Corporation, 261
Foothill-Eastern Corridor, 271
Ford, Herbert Alvin, 131
Ford family, 130
Ford Motor Company (Aeronautics Division), 257
Forster, Adam, 231
Forster, Francisco Pío, 32
Forster, John (Juan), 32, 33, 35, 41, 46, 51, 52, 55, 125; spurs of, 53
Forster, John Fernando, 32
Forster, Marco Antonio, 32
Forster, Marcos Enrique (Don), 54
Forster, Ysabel, 42, 178

Forster family, 178
Foster, George E., 135
Foster, Stephen C., 50
Fountain Valley, 34, 183, 232, 241
Frantz, Billy, 15
Freedom Train, 261
Frémont, John C., 46, 47
French's Opera House, 101
Frohling, Amelia Hammes, 61
Frohling, John, 58, 59
Fruitland, 122
Fullerton, 35, 114, 136, 156, 162, 169, 173, 183, 205, 231, 232, 240, 241, 244; archway of, 241; irrigation ditch lines of, 144; ostrich farm in, 114; pool hall in, 172
Fullerton, George Hubert, 116, 122
Fullerton Consolidated, 158
Fullerton Elementary and Union High School: students and teachers of, 91
Fullerton Four Corners, 170
Fullerton Grammar School: students of (1889), 95
Fullerton Grocery, 132
Fullerton Land and Trust Company, 116
Fullerton Oil Company, 158
Fullerton Post Office, 94
Fullerton Racket Store: advertisement of, 165
Fullerton Train Station, 110, 112
Fullerton Tribune, 168
Fustér, Vicente, 23

G
Gallum, George, 137
Garcia, Anastacio (Three-Fingered Jack), 50
Garden Grove, 34, 83, 166, 183, 194, 206, 228, 232, 241, 261, 266, 280; Buena Clinton apartment complex in, 266; population of, 1956, 241; 1965, 241
Garden Grove Home Builders, 194
Gardiner, Jim, 95
Gates, Brad, 137
German prisoners of war, 228
German residents, 58, 59, 99, 191, 225
Gilman, Richard H., 84
Glassell, Andrew, 70, 76
Glassell, William, 78
Gold Rush, 13, 76, 146, 147
Goleta, 224
Gómez, Francisco, 17
Goodman & Rimpau store, 66
Goodwin, Almon: home of, 107
Gospel Swamp, 78
Grape production, 58, 59, 62, 64, 83, 98, 103, 108; Pierce's Disease and, 103; production of wine brandy, 103
Great Depression, 136, 137, 192, 206, 211, 233, 276
Greater Gem Pharmacy, 130
Great Stone Church, 23, 278
Greeley, John P., 135
Grijalva, Juan Pablo, 30
Guinn, James Miller, 67
Gutiérrez, Nicolás, 40, 41
Gwin, William M., 47

H
Hale, W.L., 71, 85; home of, 62
Hale family, 62
Hanna, Richard T., 260
Hansen, George, 58, 59, 62
Hanson, Charles, 163
Hanson, Ole, 192
Harber, Fred, 260
Hardin, W.N., 84
Harding Canyon, 100
Hardison, Wallace, 160
Harper, 186
Harper Reservoir, 185
Harriman, E.H., 169
Harris, R.T., 135
Harris, Richard J., 136
Harrison, Kenneth J., 212
Harrison, Paul T., 232
Hiatt, Robert C., 169
Higuera, José, 50

Hiltbrunner, Joseph H., 136, 139
Hinde, George, 96
Holabird, William, 113
Hole, W.J., 169
Holiday Stage stock company, *237*
Holly Sugar Beet Factory, *149*
Holly Sugar Factory, *251*
Holmes, Larry, 233
Home Oil, 160
Hopkins, Mark, 112
Hughes Aircraft Company, 259
Huntington, Collis P., 112
Huntington, Henry, 162, 163, 169, 174
Huntington Beach, 34, 149, 163, 166, 183, 194, 227, 232, 244, 261
Huntington Beach Company, 162

I
Immigrant and Refugee Planning Center, 261
Indians, 16, 17, 19, 20, 23, 24-25, 27, 30, 37, 39, 41, 47, 50, 52, 59, 68, 125, 126, 147, 274; life-style of, 24-25; maze stone of, *18*
Indochinese community, 261
Irrigation, *74,* 76, 83, 84, *85,* 86, 124, 143, 148; results of, *86*
Irvine, 34, 186, 220, 228, 233, 258, 259, 269
Irvine, James, Jr., *98,* 113, 203
Irvine, James, Sr., 70, 98, 113, 179, 181
Irvine Company, 257, 258, 269
Irvine Industrial Complex, 258-259, *304*
Irvine Park, 220, *299*
Irvine Ranch, 113, 186, 205, 237, 257

J
Jackson, Calvin E., 136
Jackson, George Logan, 136, 137
Janss, Peter, 173
Janssens, Augustín, 41
Janss Investment Company, 173
Japanese residents, 225, 227; relocation of, 227
Jernigan, Sam, 136
John of Capistrano, Saint, 19
Johnson, Hiram, 112
Johnson, James, 32
Judah, Theodore, 112

K
Kearny, Stephen W., 46
Kiesig, Howard, 126
Kinsler, Charles, 232
Knight, Goodwin, 249
Knott, Cordelia, *247,* 249
Knott, Walter, *247,* 249
Knott's Berry Farm, 249, 250, 280
Koenig Vineyard, *103*
Kohler, Charles, 58, 59
Koll, Frederick, 70
Kraemer, Daniel, 65
Kraemer, Samuel, 192
Kraemer Zone (oil well), 194
Kraszewski, Michael (Miguel), 51, *125,* 126

L
Lacy, Theo, Sr., 136
Laguna Beach, *7,* 34, *128, 177,* 186, 201, *209, 210,* 211, 227, 232, 250, *292, 293;* founding of, 211
Laguna Beach Hotel, *210*
Laguna Beach Museum of Art, 273
Laguna Canyon, 54
Laguna Hills, 35, 243, 267, 269
Laguna Hotel, *209*
Laguna Niguel, 35
La Habra, 35, 83, 149, 158, 160, 162, 169, 173, 183, 194, 228, 232
La Habra Heights, 194
La Habra Valley, 70
Lake Forest, 35
La Llorona ("the crier"), 278
Land Act of 1851, 47, 68
Langenberger, Augustus, 58, 64, 65; adobe of, *61;* residence of, *60*
Langenberger, Clementine Zimmerman Schmidt, *60*
Laon Junction, 173

La Palma, 34, 233, 240
Las Flores, 41
Lasuén, Fermín Francisco de, 19
La Vida Bottle Works Company, 126
La Vida Hot Springs, 125, 126
La Vida Lemon and Lime, 126
La Vida Mineral Springs Corporation, 126
Lawson, H.C., 232
Leandry, Juan Bautista, 47
Lee, Ralph, 232
Leffingwell Ranch, 160
Leisure World, 243, 244; residents of, *242, 243*
Lemon Heights, *226*
Lemon production, 83, 84, 205
Liberty Amendment, 244
Liberty Bonds, 186
Lido Island, 163
Lido Marina Village, *266, 290*
Limestone Canyon, 65
Lincoln, Abraham, 55
Lineberger, William, *117*
Littlefield, Sheldon, 135
Long Beach, 201, 206, 220, 232
Lopez, Maximo, 147
Los Alamitos, 34, 113, 149, 183, 220, 233, 241, 243
Los Angeles, 23, 32, 33, 46, 51, 54, 55, 69, 76, 111, 116, 134, 135, 143, 162, 166, 183, 224, 259, 273, 274
Los Angeles and San Bernardino Land Company, 80
Los Angeles and Santa Ana Land Bureau, 114
Los Angeles City Council, 33
Los Angeles County, 13, 34, 50, 54, 55, 103, 124, 126, 134, 239, 269
Los Angeles County Jail, 136
Los Angeles International Airport, 256, 274
Los Angeles Rams, 273
Los Angeles Star, 50, 54
Los Angeles Times, 126, 238, 244
Los Angeles to Phoenix Road Race (1913), *166*
Los Angeles Vineyard Society, 59, 64
Los Nietos, 169
Los Piños Peak, 32
Lucas Canyon, 147
Luxembourger, John, 231

M
McDonnell-Douglas Corporation, 259
McFadden, James, 70, 78, 80, 113, 134
McFadden, Robert, 78, 80, 113, 166
McFadden family, *163,* 166, 181
McFadden's Landing, 113
McFadden's Wharf, 113
McKelvey, William, 136, 139
McKinley, James, 32, 41
McPherson, 116, 183
Marine Science Institute, 273
Marquez, Manuel, 51, 52
Martin, Eddie, *185*
Martin, Glenn, 181, *182,* 183; airplane of, *183*
Martina, Chola, 52
Martin Brothers Airport, 254, 256
Martinez, Celestino, *43*
Meadows, Don, 147
Menges Oil, 158
Merry Troupers, The, *195*
Mesa (Indian saint carver), *43*
Metropolitan Water District, 206
Mexican-American War, 32, 46, 147
Mexican Independence movement, 27; aftermath of, 32
Mexican Republic, 31
Mexican Revolution, 31
Micheltorena, Manuel, 41
Midway City, 241
Miller, Edrick, 220, 228
Miller, S.T., *176*
Miller, William Newton, 126
Mills, Ira D., 135
Missionaries, 13, 17, 19, 20, *22,* 23, 30, 31, 125
Mission Revival Railroad Station, *263*
Missions and mission system, 13, 16, 17, 19, 20, 23, 27, 29, 30, 31, 41, 55, 125, 146, 147, 274. See *also* individual missions

Mission Viejo, 35, 266-267
Mission Viejo Company, 267
Mission Viejo Ranch, 237
Modjeska, Madame Helena, 98, 99, *100,* 101, *286;* Arden (home), 101; theatrical trunk of, *101*
Modjeska, Rudolphe, 99, 100
Modjeska Park, *300*
Modjeska Ranch, 136, 139
Moiso, Tony, 269
Monterey, 19, 46, 50
Monterey Bay, 16, 17
Morales, Stanislado, *43*
Morillo, Maria Rafaela Romero de: document of, *67*
Mosserman, Francesca, *208*
Moulton, Lewis, *201*
Moulton, Nellie Gail, *201*
Moulton Ranch, 237, *258*
Mugártegui, Pablo, 19
Murieta, Joaquín, 51, 52
Murphy Oil, 160
Musick, James, 137

N
National Guard, Company I (Orange), 224; Company K (Anaheim), 224; Company L (Santa Ana), *174-175,* 186, 224
National Industrial Recovery Act, 211
Naval Air Station (Tustin), *220, 221*
Naval Ammunition and Net Depot, 220
Navarro, Rafael, *85*
Newport, 80
Newport Bay, 78, 113, 253, 257, 258, *266, 291;* Gospel Swamp of, 78
Newport Bay Investment Company, 163
Newport Beach, 30, 34, 101, 113, 122, 125, 163, 166, *176-177,* 183, *232, 234, 249,* 250, 256, 274
Newport Beach Company, 163
Newport Beach Municipal Pier, 163
Newport Center, *237, 259, 301*
Newport Environmental Preserve, *290*
Newport Harbor, 137, 211, *289*
Newport Harbor Art Museum, 273
Nichols, Joe C., 136
Nieto, Josefa Cota de, 34
Nieto, Juan José, 34
Nieto, Manuel Pérez, 29, 30, 34; land grant of, 34
Night Fruit Patrol, 137
Nixon, Richard M., 260
Norris, Frank, 112
Northrop Corporation, 259
Number 21 Streetcar Stables, *142-143*
Nyboe, Rudolph, 231

O
Oak Canyon Nature Center, *288*
Oceanside, 147
Oil, 156, *158,* 160, 162, *192,* 194, 240, 243, 276
Oldfield Tires, *198*
Olinda, 158, 183
Olinda Oil Company, 158, 160
Olive, 30, 116, 183
Olive Heights, 116
Olvera, Augustín, 32, 35
Olympic Games (Twenty-third Olympiad, Los Angeles, 1984), 274, *303*
Olympic Torch Run, 274, *276-277*
O'Neill, Richard, 125, 269
O'Neill, Richard O., 260, 269
Ontario Airport, 274
Ontiveros, Juan Pacífico, 35, 47, *48,* 58, 65; adobe of, 65
Ontiveros, Martina, *48*
Ontiveros, Petra, *59*
Orange, 30, 76, 78, 103, 114, 116, 135, 143, 183, 231, 232, 241
Orange Coast College, 219, 228
Orange County: population of, 1900, 183; 1910, 183; 1940, 212; 1950, 237; 1960, 237; 1964, 259
Orange County Airport, 220, 253, 254, 256, 258, 274, *303*
Orange County Board of Supervisors, 135, 136, 191, 206, 233, 244, 260, 269, 274
Orange County Courthouse, 141, 143

Orange County Fairgrounds, 219, 228
Orange County Fire Department, 233
Orange County Fireman's Association, 232
Orange County Hall of Records, 122
Orange County High School, *194*
Orange County Historical Society: members of, *210*
Orange County Illustrated, 250, 256
Orange County (Irvine) Park, 191
Orange County Jail, 136, *137;* 1890 facility, 136, 139
Orange County Mutual Air Compact, 137
Orange County Peace Officers Association, 136
Orange County Performing Arts Center, 273
Orange County Sheriffs' Department, 137
Orange County Sheriffs' Reserves, 137
Orange County Survey, 266, 271
Orange County Transportation Commission, 271
Orange Drive-In Theatre, *250*
Orange Dummy (trolley), 143, 173
Orange Growers' Protective Union, 154
Orange Plaza, *9;* fountain of, *9*
Orange production, 83, 84, 124, 134, 154, 205, 212, 236, 249, 254, 256, *287;* crate label art, *222, 223, 282, 284, 285;* Tahitian variety, 84; Valencia variety, 84
Orange Ranger Unit of the State Division of Forestry, 233
Orangethorpe, 83
Orange Volunteer Fireman's Mutual Association, 232
Ortega, Francisco, 19
Overell, Beulah, 137
Overell, Beulah Louise, 137
Overell, Walter, 137
Owens, Tom, 136

P

Pacific City, 162-163. *See also* Huntington Beach
Pacific Coast Highway, *239, 259*
Pacific Electric Land Company, 166
Pacific Electric Railway Company, 162, 163, 166, 169, 201, 205; Santa Ana, Garden Grove, and Artesia line of, *161;* Triangle Trolley Trip of, 166
Pacific Land and Improvement Company, 114, 116
Pacific Railroad Bill, 112
Pageant of the Masters, 212, 250
Palóu, Francisco, l9
Paprocki, Lucian, 99, 100
Parker, E.T., 232
Paularino, 186
Pellegrin, Pansy, *64*
Peralta, Juan Pablo, 30
Peralta family, 70
Pereira and Associates, William, 257, 258
Petrolia, 158, 160
Pflugardt, George, 51, 52
Phillip Morris Incorporated, 267
Phillips, William J., 254
Pico, Andrés, 32, 46, 52, 57
Pico, Pío, 32, *39,* 40, 41, 45-46
Pico, Saloman, 51
Pico, Ysidora, 32
Pico family, 51, 55
Pilgrim, 31
Pillsbury, 169
Pink Lady, 278
Placentia, 35, 83, 84, 96, 162, 183, 192, 194, 233, 243
Plano Trabuco, 146
Planters Hotel, 231
Pleasants, J.E., 100, 101; ranch of, 100, 101
Pleasants, Mrs. J.E., 100, 101; ranch of, 100, 101
Pleasants, Joseph, 65
Portolá, Gaspar de, 16, 17, 273; expedition of, 16
Poston Relocation Center, 227
Potrero El Cariso, 32, 35
Potrero La Cíenega, 32, 35
Powers, Jack, 51, 52
Prado Dam, 212
Prohibition, 126, 136
Project 21, 256
Pryor y Avila de Landell, Soledad, *43*
Puente Oil Company, 158

Q

Quaker settlers, 173

R

Railroads, 69, 80, 108, 111, 112, 113, 125, 162, 166. *See also* individual railroads
Raisin production, 84, 183
Rambo, Ralph, 50
Rancheros, 31, 33, 37, 39, 46-48, 50, 52, 55, 57, 67, 68, 70, 75; bandits and, 50; copper powder flask of, *46;* life-style of, 37, 39, 46-47, 52; map of ranchos in Orange County, *44;* Mexican lariat of, *46;* Mexican saddle of, *36;* problems with squatters, 47-48
Rancho Bolsa Chica, 35, 58
Rancho Cañada de los Alisos, 35, 57
Rancho Cañon de Santa, 34
Rancho Ciénega de las Ranas, 34, 35
Rancho Jurupa, 33
Rancho La Brea, 51
Rancho La Habra, 35, 52, 57-58
Rancho La Laguna, 33
Rancho La Puente, 35
Rancho Las Bolsas, 33, 34, 58
Rancho Lomas de Santiago, 34, 57, 70, 113
Rancho Los Alamitos, 33, 34, 58, 70
Rancho Los Cerritos, 34, 70
Rancho Los Coyotes, 33, 34, 37, 58
Rancho Los Coyotes Adobe, *58*
Rancho Los Desechos, 32
Rancho Mission Viejo, 269
Rancho Mission Viejo (Rancho La Paz), 32, 35, 146, 280
Rancho Niguel, 35
Rancho Palos Verdes, 70
Rancho Potrero Los Piños, 32, 35
Rancho San Antonio, 33
Rancho San Joaquín (La Bolsa de San Joaquín), 34, 35, 52, 70, 78, 80, 98, l13, 136
Rancho San Juan Cajón de Santa Ana, 33, 35, 47, 58
Rancho Santa Gertrudes, 34
Rancho Santa Margarita, 55, 269
Rancho Santiago de Santa Ana, 30, 33, 34, 58, 70, 76, 78
Rancho Temescal, 33
Rancho Trabuco, 35
Randolph, 173
Randolph School District, 169
Ray, B.C., 232
Recession of 1875, 88
Reconstruction Finance Corporation, 206
Recreational activities, 179, 211-212, *236, 249,* 257, *268, 294, 295*
Red Cars, *160, 161,* 162, 163, 166, 169, 174, 201, 241
Red Cross, 186
Redondo, 224
Redondo, Tomás (Procopio), 50
Reese, Michael, 33
Reeves Ranch, 237
Religion, 16, 19-20, 31, 124
Rice, James, 101
Rice, Mrs. James, 101
Richfield, 122. *See also* Atwood
Richland, 78
Rimpau, Fred, 231
Rimpau Grove, *82*
Rincon de la Brea, 35
Rios, Gregorio, 51
Rios, Santiago, 35
Rios Adobe, 51, 278, 280
Rios family, 51
Riverside, 33
Riverside County, 32, 169, 212, 269
Roberts Commission Report, 225
Robinson, Alfred, 24, 39, 80
Robinson Trust, 33
Rockwell International Corporation, 260
Roldan, Mariano R., 35
Roman Catholic Church, 27, 55
Roosevelt, Franklin Delano, 244
Roosevelt Coast Highway, 201
Ropp, Roy M., 211-212

Ross, Jacob, Jr., 135
Ross, Jacob, Sr., 70
Rossmoor, 242
Rowan, Alexander Hamilton, 125
Ruby's Cafe, *300*
Ruddock, Charles E., 136
Ruiz, Catarina, 34
Ruiz, Joaquín, 35

S

St. Anne's Inn, *202*
St. Clair, Norman, 211
St. George Hotel, *170*
St. George's Episcopal Church of El Toro, *184*
St. James, 116
Salazar, Abelardo, 50-51; family of, 50
San Antonio Chapel, 48-49
San Bernardino, 69
San Bernardino and San Diego Railroad, 113
San Bernardino County, 33, 126
San Clemente, 17, 32, 35, 41, 192, 201, 232, 241, 256, 271; train station of, *190*
San Diego, 16, 17, 19, 23, 32, 46, 50, 69, 76, 113, 273
San Diego County, 13, 32, 55
San Diego Freeway, *257*
San Francisco, 47, 59, 70, 84, 99, 100, 134, 231
San Francisco Bay, 19
San Gabriel, Mission, 19, 20, 24, 30
San Gabriel River, 30, 40, 65, 134
San Joaquín Hills Corridor, 271
San Joaquín Slough (New Port), 78
San Juan, 147, 278
San-Juan-by-the-Sea, 101, 122
San Juan Capistrano, 19, *21,* 35, 41, 51, 52, 54, 55, 70, 83, 101, 122, 125, 136, 137, 139, 183, 233, 241, 256, 261, 278, 280
San Juan Capistrano, Mission, *14,* 17, 19, *20, 21,* 23, 24, *26,* 27, 30, 32, 35, *40,* 41, *42-43, 54, 55,* 68, 125, 146, 231, 250, 278; postcard of, *14;* statue of St. Anthony Padua, *20*
San Juan Capistrano Cemetery, 280
San Juan Capistrano Depot, *262*
San Juan Creek, 20
San Juan Hot Springs, 125, 126, *127. See also* Caspers Regional Park
San Juan Point Association, 191
San Luis Obispo, 58, 224
San Onofre, 227
San Pedro, 32, 113, 166
San Quentin (prison), 50, 51, 52, 136, 139
Sansinena, José, 160
Santa Ana, 30, 51, 54, 76, 88, 101, *104,* 112, 113, 114, 125, 126, *134,* 135, 136, 139, *140,* 141, 143, 147, 149, *157,* 166, 181, 183, *205,* 206, 217, 219, 220, 228, 231, 241, 250, 254, *263,* 271; milk bottling plant of, *224;* 1905 parade in, *173;* 1918 "Welcome Home Parade," *186-187*
Santa Ana and Newport Railroad, 163
Santa Ana Army Air Base, *218, 219,* 228, *230;* Service Club of, *221;* servicemen of, *216*
Santa Ana Army Airdrome, 220
Santa Ana Board of Trade, 139
Santa Ana Breakfast Club, *180*
Santa Ana Canyon, 116, 280
Santa Ana Chamber of Commerce, 143, 179, 191
Santa Ana Cooperative Sugar Company, 136
Santa Ana Freeway, 238
Santa Ana Gas Company, 23l
Santa Ana High School: 1908 girls' basketball team, *153*
Santa Ana Mercantile Company, *83*
Santa Ana Mountains, 100, 146, 147
Santa Ana Naval Air Station (LTA), 220
Santa Ana-Newport Railroad, 113
Santa Ana River, 17, 30, 59, 62, 67, 76, 78, 80, 84, 122, 148, 212, 231
Santa Ana Standard, 125, 126
Santa Ana Valley, 52, 80, 105, 111, 114, 116, 124, 134
Santa Ana Valley Immigration Association, 105, 106
Santa Ana Valley Irrigation Company, 84; irrigation stock certificate of, *144*

Santa Barbara, 23, 51, 68
Santa Clara County, 51
Santa Fe Railroad, 108, 111, 113, 116, 139, 147, 158, 163; Anaheim station, 109; Fullerton Train Station, 110
Santa Monica Harbor, 113
Santa Monica Mountains, 54, 96, 103, 212
Santiago, Juan Norberto de, 23
Santiago Canyon, 65, 98, 100, 179
Santiago Orange Growers Association, 152; workers of, 152
Santora Building, 298
Savage, Thomas, 32
Savanna, 83
Schaefer's candy shop, C.H., 90
Scherman, Joe, 233
Schlesinger, Louis, 96
Schorn, Louis, 116
Schuller, Arvella, 248
Schuller, Robert, 248
Scott, J.R., 47
Scully, Thomas J., 55
Seal Beach, 34, 64, 162, 220, 232, 243
Seal Beach Cafe, 136
Seal Beach Volunteer Fire Department, 232
Secularization Act of 1833, 27, 31
Seelye, Howard, 238
Segerstrom family, C.J., 259, 273
Segerstrom Ranch, 257
Semi-Tropic Water Company, 76, 84, 86
Sepúlveda, José Andrés (Don), 34, 35, 37, 52, 70
Sepúlveda, Vicenta, 39
Serra, Junipero, 16, 19, 20, 29, 41
Serra Chapel, 23, 55, 265
Serrano, José, 35, 57
Shaffer-Wakeman Block, 134
Sheep industry, 70, 88
Shell Oil, 158
Shiffer family, 206
Shrewsbury, Sam, 65
Sienkiewicz, Henryk, 98, 99, 100
Sievers Adobe, 38
Silverado, 98, 280
Silverado Blue Light Mine, 97
Simi Pass, 54
Skinner, Otis, 100
Sleeper, Jim, 134
Sloat, John, 46
Smallpox epidemic (1862), 68
Smeltzer, 113, 183
Smeltzer, D.E., 148
Smith, A. Guy, 135
Smith, Don, 238
Smith, George Washington, 147
Smith, S.W., 93
Smith and Tuthill Mortuary: forerunner of, 93
Smythe, Fred C., 135
Societas Fraternia (Placentia Grass Eaters), 96
Sonoma, 45, 46
Soto, Juan, 50
South Coast Plaza, 259; construction of, 260
Southern California Bible College, 228
Southern California Fruit Exchange (later Sunkist), 154
Southern Pacific Railroad, 88, 108, 111, 112, 113, 166, 169; Engine No. 2215, 148
Spangler's and Johnson's blacksmith shop, 159
Spurgeon, William, 75, 76, 134, 135, 136, 139; store and building of, 76, 77
Spurgeon Building, 140
Stafford, Nelson, 76
Standard Oil, 160, 192, 194
Stanford, Leland, 112
Stanton, 34, 166, 183, 232, 241. See also Benedict
Stanton, Phillip A., 162
Starbuck, Raymond, 124
Starbuck, William, 124, 130
Starbuck family: windmill of, 84
Starr Ranch, 237
State Agricultural Extension Service, 228
State/County Cooperative Agreement, 233
Stearns, Abel, 31, 32-33, 40, 52, 58, 65, 70, 80; El Palacio (home), 33; water company of, 86

Stearns Ranchos, 80, 84
Stern, 169
Stern & Goodman (store), 132; advertisement of, 133
Stern & Goodman Warehouse Number 5, 112
Stewart, Lyman, 160
Stock market crash of 1929, 206
Stockton, Robert, 46
Stovall, A.O., 179
Strange, Charles L., 143
Strawberry production, 81
Strodhoff, Adele, 65
Strodhoff, Dietrich: residence of, 65
Sugar Beet production, 149, 150
Sunset Beach, 35, 186
Sutter's Mill, 47
Swanner, D.W., 116
Swing-Johnson Bill, 206
Sypniewski, Jules, 99, 100

T
Talbert, 183, 241. See also Fountain Valley
Terken, J.R., 264
TeWinkle, Charles, 240
Thirty-second Fair Association, 141
Tobacco industry, 84
Tobias, E.J., 232
Toler Ranch, 160
Tonner Canyon, 156, 158
Torres, Francisco, 136, 139
Towner, James W., 135, 139
Trabuco Adobe, 49
Trabuco Creek, 23, 278
Treaty of Guadalupe Hidalgo, 46, 47
Tuffree Reservoir, 74
Tuholski, Josephine, 100
Tustin, 30, 76, 101, 113, 114, 129, 183, 233, 244
Tustin, Columbus, 70, 76
Tustin school bus, 198

U
Union Oil, 160
Union Pacific Railroad, 112
United States Air Corps Replacement Training Center, 219
United States Bicentennial, 261
United States Land Commission, 47, 55, 58; hearings of, 33
United States Marine Corps Air Station (El Toro), 220
United States Naval Air Station, 220
United States Soil Erosion Service, 211
United States Supreme Court, 47
United Way, 261, 273
University of California, Irvine, 253, 256, 257, 258, 266, 275
University of California Regents, 257
Utt, James B., 244

V
Valencia Orange Show: 1922, 283
Valles, Juan, 43
Vasquez, Tiburcio, 50-51, 52
Vejar, Emigdio, 35
Ventura, 41
Verdugo Adobe, 146
Vickers, William, 232
Victoria, Manuel, 32, 39-40
Vietnam War, 259, 261
Villa Park, 30, 116, 233, 241; farming in, 123
Von Strobel, Max, 124

W
Walker, Simeon O., 166
Wall, William B., 135, 155; orange packinghouse of, 155
Walnut industry, 80-81, 83, 138, 156, 205; Chapman's Brand of 156; Placentia Perfection variety, 96
Warner, Willis, 244
War Relocation Authority, 227
Waterman, Robert, 134
Waterville, 166

Watts, 166
Wave Street House (Laguna Beach), 200
Wayne, John, 256
Webber, Lemuel P., 80, 83
West Anaheim Volunteers, 232
West Coast Army Air Corps Training Command Headquarters, 220
West Coast Land and Water Company, 162
West Coyote Hills, 160
West Los Angeles Filter Center of the Fourth Fighter Command, 220
Westminster, 34, 80, 136, 148, 183, 232, 241, 261
Wheedon, John T., 173
Whitaker, James A., 116
White, Stanford, 101
White Lady, 278
Whiting, Dwight, 116
Whittier Fields, 160
Wickham, R.Q., 135
Williams Ranch, 160
Wilshire, H. Gaylord, 114, 116
Wilson, Albert, 68
Wintersburg, 183
Wolfskill, William, 52, 57, 70
Wolfskill Ranch, 65
Wood, Samuel O., 135
Woodmen of the World: Anaheim Chapter of, 158
Woodruff, S.H., 191
Wool industry, 70, 84
Works Progress Administration, 211
World War I, 136, 186, 191, 211, 217, 276, 280; armistice of, 191; local servicemen of, 188
World War II, 137, 217, 220, 224, 227, 228, 229, 235, 254, 276; rationing during, 227

Y
Yoch, Joseph, 101
Yoch, Mrs. Joseph, 101
Yorba, 122, 183
Yorba, Bernardo, 34, 37, 52, 54, 55; adobe of, 35, 36, 37, 52, 54
Yorba, José Antonio I, 30, 34
Yorba, José Antonio II, 30, 34
Yorba, Lucrezia (Dona), 43
Yorba, Teodocio, 34, 54, 57, 70
Yorba, Tomás, 34, 37, 39
Yorba Cemetery, 278, 280
Yorba family, 34, 70
Yorba Linda, 34, 169, 173, 233, 243, 260
Yriarte Ranch, 160

Z
Zalvidea, José María, 27, 146
Zamorano, Augustín, 40